PINK F... ...RON

BHP '91 to '95

DAVID GAMAGE

Earthisland
publishing

First published in Great Britain 1991 by BHP

Reprinted in full collection 2019 by Earth Island Publishing, 22 Church Road, Tunbridge Wells, Kent TN1 1JP

wwww.earthisland.co.uk

© Copyright Earth Island Publishing Ltd

ISBN 978-1-9997581-2-7

Earth Island Publishing always endeavours to use materials and processes from sustainable sources. The paper for this book is X-per White from Fedrigoni, which is FSC certified, 100% recyclable and made to ISO 14001 environmental standards.

Printed and bound in Great Britain by Longridge

To my two beautiful sons, Carl and Jake, who make everything worthwhile, and my absolutely wonderful wife, Louise, without whom I would be a far lesser mortal. May you always find things to inspire you!

CONTENTS

BHP 6, Girl's face and skater, pages 163 – 186.

Articles on AIDS, mercury in dentistry and writing songs the Bad Religion way.
Interviews with Rancid (US), All (US), Mr T Experience (US), Shelter (US) and Daniel
Clowes (Eightball comics).

Also live reviews including Bob Tilton, Supersuckers, Girls Against Boys, Ironside, Spirit of
Youth, Understand, Lagwagon, Conflict, Scalplock, Holy Rollers and Credit to the Nation.

Loads of reviews including the Crazy Ace's amusing take on Xerox Girls and The
Ceramic Hobbs.

BHP 7, Hi Time cola walrus, pages 187 – 214.

Articles on bad art, animals in circuses, a Croatian underground scene report, a Portland
scene report, how to stop animal cruelty, reviews and a main focus on a comical German
tour report with a pop-punk band in a tour van that had already done 350,000 miles.

BHP 8, Dad's taking me to the lab, pages 215 – 238.

Articles on the ecological crisis, cannabis, all fashion no substance, veal crates, Green
Day news.

Interviews with Jawbreaker (US), Down By Law (US) and Couch Potatoes (UK).
NB. Around this time bands start signing to major labels in the independent DIY hardcore
scene. Also cassettes have mainly been replaced by vinyl and CD releases now.

BHP 9, Punk Fiction Tigger, pages 239 – 278.

Articles on Quentin Tarantino & Roger Avary, Brat Pack movies, the fairly humourous BHP
readers' poll, Garbage (band), drink driving, self publishing, logos, and playing a gig in
a squat in Germany.

Interviews with Pennywise (US), Civ (US), Riverdales (US), Annalies (UK), No Empathy
(US), Dawson (UK) and Schema (UK).

FOREWORD

"There wasn't always a place to go, but there was always an urgent need to belong."
Rancid – Journey to the end of the East Bay

My journey towards and through the UK hardcore and punk scene in the 1990s was typical, in that, for all its idiosyncrasies, it was based on a search for meaning and belonging. The world of my parents and peers as I encountered it when I emerged, blinking and confused, into adolescent consciousness, didn't make a lot of sense. A lot of things seemed manifestly unjust, a lot of social trends seemed exclusionary and judgemental. I needed to find my own tribe, people I could be myself with, and I needed a sound as an outlet for my frustration.

I'm a bit younger than Dave, but the scene documented in BHP is the one I wandered into in the late 1990s. My journey started, as it did for most people my age, with Nirvana, closely followed by Green Day and The Offspring. Those bands opened a small crack for me, through which I was able to glimpse harder, more intense stuff, like Black Flag and Negative Approach. Only about one in a hundred fans of that pop punk explosion made the journey deeper into the murk of hardcore punk rock, but sooner or later, we found each other.

In the easily glorified days before the internet, that process of location was infinitely harder than it is now, but ultimately perhaps more rewarding. Personally, I found out that Agnostic Front were playing at the Garage in Highbury, North London, and they were listed as a hardcore band, so even though I didn't know their music, I went down, on a rainy night in December 1997. Standing in the queue, I watched in fascination as, one by one, a strange group of like-minded people emerged from the darkness to gather for their communion. Inside the show, the music blew my mind, but so did the sense of camaraderie. I encountered my first distro, run by Lil from Household Name Records, and picked up some DIY compilation CDs. I was hooked.

Over the next few years, underground DIY hardcore was my life. I went to shows, and played a few myself, in a band called Kneejerk. I bought records, and released a couple too, burning off CDRs and hand printing and folding the covers. I went to as many shows as I could, mostly in London but also in Winchester and Southampton, and even put on a couple here and there (with varying levels of success!). I even did one issue of a zine myself, called "Paper Cuts", which has thankfully been forgotten by history.

Zines were a huge and integral part of the scene, in a way that's quite hard to explain to people who have come of age in our more connected, immediate digital world. Nostalgia can be overly facile, and there is a lot to be said for the immediate, democratic access to information that we can all now enjoy. Nevertheless, there was a romance in the hunt for culture that zines represented and facilitated. Chasing the latest issue of Fracture, Subbaculture, Synthesis, Cometbus, Maximum Rock'n'Roll, or any of the countless other, shorter-lived titles, was a passion in itself. I read those inky pages like manuals or manifestos, and much of my knowledge of music and view of the world is still influenced by those words.

More than anything else, hardcore and the zine culture around it was exciting because it was a supremely bold act of youthful self-creation. DIY meant literally that – do it yourself. There was a real sense that we didn't need to wait for the world to catch up with us and what we had to say, we had to make our own culture and art, there was no time to waste. Some of it seems naïve to the point of awkwardness now, in retrospect, but I wouldn't change a thing. Hardcore and punk taught me to put my best foot forward, to take the plunge and see what happened, to seek out my own people and connections. It showed me that you just have to throw your heart over the fence, and the rest would follow.

Frank Turner.

London, 2019.

60 MINUTES OF COUCHCORE

COUCH POTATOES

EXCESS ALL AREAS OUT NOW!

£1.50 ppd from:
GOTHAM TAPES,
1 CHANDOS ROAD,
TUNBRIDGE WELLS,
KENT, TN1 2NY.

COUCH POTATOES

GENUINE KENTIFORNIAN COUCHCORE

S'RIGHT.

BE THERE, OR EAT PLUTONIUM DEATH !

GREEN DAY

COUCH POTATOES

JAILCELL RECIPES

GENUINE

RUMBLE CLUB
The PANTILES
TUNBRIDGE WELLS

X'MAS SPECIAL
WED 18th
DEC. £4.

Convert to PURE GEN...

8.26 '96

GREEN DAY

POPCORE GODS FROM the USA!!

+ JOEY FAT

+ THE STROOKAS

THE FORUM

THE PURPOSE-BUILT VENUE
ON T.W. COMMON OPPOSITE THE PANTILES

TUNBRIDGE WELLS

MONDAY
3 rd of MAY
8 pm

CELL RECIPES

COUCH POTATOES

PUNK FACTION
BHP '91 to '95

Fanzine

noun.

a fanzine (blend of fan and magazine or 'zine') is a non-professional and non-official publication produced inexpensively by enthusiasts of a particular cultural phenomenon (such as a literary or musical genre) for the pleasure of others who share their interest.

Punk

noun.

1. a loud, fast moving, and aggressive form of rock music, popular in the late 1970s.
2. a worthless person (often used as a general term of abuse).

adjective.

1. relating to punk rock and its associated subculture.
2. in poor condition.

verb.

trick or deceive

Faction

noun.

a faction is an organised group of people within a larger group, which opposes some of the ideas of the larger group and fights for its own ideas.

INTRODUCTION

BHP was a fanzine.

From 1991 to 1995 British Hardcore Press was an insight into the punk rock bands and hardcore scene of the day. Packed to bursting with alternative articles, band interviews and reviews, it was trying to spread news to its readers and foster a common goal in the days before the internet.

BHP was always enthusiastic, so although often frustrated, the editorial of the zine spoke with bands about their message as much as their music.

Encouraging the personal to be political, a kind of 'think globally but act locally' rationale took hold and the undeniably angry undercurrent was tempered by a positive creative energy and a thick slavering of humour.

This positive attitude was combined with a real openness and honesty, so opinions were shared and trust was freely given. There are many direct contacts, telephone numbers, home addresses and the like published throughout. Ideas and music are shared and traded, as were cassettes, then vinyl and CDs. All this of course was long before the internet brought streaming and downloads, and the sit on your arse, get involved at a distance, consumer culture. (And even further before today's ineffectual GDPR and privacy legislation).

It was all about belonging really. The heart and soul of it was just about being a part of something, a group, a scene, a gathering of likeminded individuals. Whether straight edge or cider punk, skater or skinhead, these teens and twenties brought energy, devotion and dedication. Gigs and events, books and records seemed much more important before the worldwide web brought the modern form of social media. For now, this was it! And if you wanted something to happen you had to get up, go out and do it yourself. In fact that whole DIY ethic became a hugely important part of the underground hardcore punk scene of which BHP and the bands and writers were a part.

To belong to a scene, to really be an active part of it, even if just to sing along with one of your favourite bands surrounded by all your friends in a small sweaty club – that was the stuff BHP and the alternative underground was made of. Put on a gig, join a band, write a zine. Don't just be an idle consumer but create and produce something worthwhile. It was fun, but it was also something much more. It stirred something inside that wanted action and needed change. This change though would take effort, tenacity and energy, and the frustrations caused inevitably led to some anger and clashes.

BHP didn't really encourage outright revolution or rebellion on the streets, but it certainly didn't go in for comfortable acceptance of the status quo either. Heavily influenced by politics, animal welfare, human rights and environmental concerns as well as the music we so loved, it was certainly trying to spread those influences as far as possible. There was a heartfelt need to share the 'message in the music' and 'do the right thing' that was never self-censored or stifled by any political correctness.

Beyond that, BHP fanzine would speak with and write about all the artists and contributors pretty much equally. Any well known touring US band on a larger record label would get the same space and treatment, or sometimes less, than an unheard of new UK band that was totally independent. They were all there on their own merit and many of the UK and European bands were just as good, if not better! Apart from being the fair and right way to do things, this also added to the feeling of discovering new acts and spreading the word about them. The message again was all about creativity and ability. Paradoxically this could lead to some pretty harsh reviews and strong opinions too. But then again how else could you find out about new art? And how strongly could it inspire you? The questions constantly being asked were 'is art any good despite it being relatively unknown?', and 'did an artist, author or musician really need to sell thousands of copies to have value?' BHP had made up its own mind.

To put things in context at the time of writing I was just nineteen years old, already playing in a punk rock band and interested in doing things very differently to most people I'd been at school with. Over the following years I'd change jobs, girlfriends, and even bands several times, so change, music and my close friends seemed my only constants.

I was known as Dave Potato (amongst other things) when editing the zine, as the main band I played in at this time was Couch Potatoes, a pop-punk skatecore band heavily influenced by US hardcore acts such The Descendents, Samiam, Big Drill Car, MTX and Green Day. Later there was Joeyfat too, (we were influenced more by the likes of Alice Donut, Shudder to Think and Fugazi) and then the new version of Couch Potatoes, (an emocore prototype for Rydell and Come the Spring) as well as various others, for which I stood in on guitar, shouted a bit and generally made a racket.

I also put on shows at several local clubs, one of which was the Winchester or Rumble club, the pre-cursor to Tunbridge Wells, well known and often lauded venue, The Forum, where as well as booking some of the bands I also worked both on the door and behind the bar at various times. We toured quite a lot but made sure we played all the local venues too. The Shelley Arms in Nutley was a huge favourite and as soon as I had a car I could be found there most weekends for at least one evening with a real motley crew of punk rockers and heavy metallers diving off the bar to various noisy bands.

There were many memorable evenings out in Brighton at The Basement, Richmond, Freebutt and Albert, also The Joiners in Southampton, Cardinals Cap, Expose and Penny Theatre in Canterbury, Red Lion in Gravesend, Crypt in Hastings, 101 Club in East Grinstead, Quigleys in Maidstone, Angel Centre in Tonbridge, Rumours in Eastbourne, Flappers in Worthing, Railway Inn in Winchester, and further out to play The Lord Nelson in Clacton, Zaks in Southend, Cavern in Exeter, TJ's in Newport, Square in Harlow, Boat Race in Cambridge, Charlotte in Leicester, Duchess of York in Leeds, 1 in 12 Club in Bradford, and then back to the great London rock venues where we argued with the soundmen and poured out our energy, sweating into the spit and sawdust and tripping over guitar leads on the sticky stages at The Camden Underworld, Islington Powerhaus, Finsbury Park Robey, Tufnell Park Dome, Camden Falcon, Hampstead White Horse, Greenwich Playpen, Bethnal Green Stick

O Rock, St Johns Archway, George IV Brixton, Fulham Kings Head, Camden Dublin Castle, LSE, City Poly, Kingston Gravity and between the record racks at Shake Some Action in Croydon too. Finally arriving back home to play more local shows for the Tunbridge Wells' crew at Watson Hall, Victoria Hall, Rumble Club, Forum, various house parties and even the Pagoda youth club. And all these road trips were just warm ups for the European tours we were about to embark upon. I'd really gotten the bug for music and travel, and these shows allowed me to meet many great bands and speak with them on a personal level. This made the interviews for the zine pretty easy, if not always rapturously interesting, and there were always plenty of compelling leaflets at these punk rock shows too to inspire any articles. As well as compiling the zine and playing shows around this time I also started a tape label, Gotham Tapes, mainly to trade live shows of what I thought was good music, and then onto vinyl and CDs, through various iterations with Scene Police and then Ignition, I would later start the Engineer Records' label too.

BHP started way after the first wave of punk was long dead and buried, its mohicans had been flattened by oily new wave, ponderous prog rock and flabby pop. This was the second wave – for me far more believable and hardcore. Led by urgent bands who to me, whilst individual, all had a certain unity – Minor Threat, Black Flag, Dead Kennedys, 7 Seconds, The Descendents, Dag Nasty, OP IV, Youth of Today and Gorilla Biscuits, then Fugazi, Green Day, Jawbreaker, All, Samiam, Down By Law, SNFU, No FX, Rancid, Quicksand, Lifetime and many of the bands featured in the zine. God I love them!

The zine ran from just '91 to '95 and towards the end of this period there were big changes in the hardcore scene with it evolving from chiefly an underground thing to become widespread and see several of its better known bands signing to major labels and going mainstream with varying success. This caused much consternation in the predominantly independent and DIY based genre. The bands themselves wanted their music and message to be heard by as many people as possible, so I for one can't really blame them, but inevitably it was mainly watered down by the media and big business so lost its impact and energy.

On a positive note, this did later lead to post hardcore and emo with loads of great music that I love even now, including, and chronologically to suit my OCD, for the next five years, Hot Water Music's Finding the Rhythms on No Idea and Split Lip's Fates Got a Driver on Doghouse in '95, The Promise Ring's 30 Degrees Everywhere on Jade Tree in '96, The Get Up Kids Woodson on Doghouse and Mineral's Power of Failing on Crank in '97, Braid's Frame and Canvas on Polyvinyl in '98, Jimmy Eat World's Clarity on Capitol in '99, Appleseed Cast's Mare Vitalis on Deep Elm in 2000, and so on. There's always something good that carves its way through!

Although the zine focused mainly on the music it did also have some articles that I was proud to share back then and that still seem to be an important focus of the media and news today. Remaining unresolved even now, such as the environment and the continuation of various 'isms'. Let's hope for all our sakes people come to their senses, and soon! There's also a few not so great parts of course, and some that seem a little naive now, but you just have to forgive that and put it down to youthful exuberance.

The inspiration I gained from back then is still with me now. I still play in a hardcore rock band (Come The Spring), run a record label (Engineer Records), and put on the occasional show. I also write and publish articles. I still share pretty much the same opinions and social political views that I formulated back then too. And I still try to 'think globally but act locally' and 'do the right thing'.

So that's my introduction to this collection. I'm just trying to put it all into some context. Take from it what you will. Although not perfect by a long way, BHP, and certainly the bands it reported on and the scene it was based in, really did inspire me and many of my friends at the time, and still does. Looking back now it seems a window into that era, maybe even an interesting argument waiting to happen for social historians. I still feel and hope that BHP is a good representation of what was an important and rarely covered part of the UK hardcore punk scene. I hope you enjoy it!

If you were there. Thank you.
If you weren't, you missed some good times!

David Gamage
(aka Dave Potato)

Tunbridge Wells, 2019.

LIVE AT THE SHELLEY (Compilation)

GOTHAM TAPES

GOT 003

GOTHAM TAPES

ANGUS BAGPIPE
1. MONKEY MAGIC
2. CRIME SQUAD
3. YOU'RE NOT A PUNK
4. PRISONERS
5. BETTER THAN YOU

BEANFEAST
6. FIGHT BACK
7. BEANFEAST
8. COVER UP
9. NOBODY WINS
10. BORDERS

HEADWAY
11. REFLECTIONS
12. BELIEFS
13. CHANGE FOR THE BETTER
14. PROVING A POINT
15. ...

COUCH POTATOES
16. LUNCHBOX
17. WHY
18. NEWUN
19. TIRED
20. HEY HEY

B.B.M.F's
21. FRASER T.F.R.
22. E.R. PINKUS
23. NO SLEEP 'TIL (THAT BLOKE)
24. SUPERFLY HEDGEHOG
25. UNBELIEVABLE #

GOTHAM TAPES
1 CHANDOS RD
TUN WELLS
KENT
TN1 2NY

J.P. LEMARCHAND
ROUTE DE CLARES
...
FRANCE

GOTHAM · TAPES
BT 009·1992

WELCOME TO OUR BAND
GUTLESS
DOWN
YOU'RE RIGHT
SOFTCORE
LAWN
THIS IS BIG
FREEBIRD
WANT

SEE THRU SKIN
DRIVEN
FINE DAY
EQUALIZED
SHIELD YOUR EYES

GOTHAM TAPES
1 CHANDOS RD
TUN WELLS
KENT
TN1 2NY

Thanks to the band and to Nox
Jawbreaker has no address for the
moment and they haven't reply to
our last letter. Sorry!

COUCH POTATOES

8 SONGS THAT SUCK!

RECORDED AT HILBURY RD STUDIOS ...
ADDITIONAL TAPES, SINGLE, ETC (0892) 279651

EIGHT SONGS THAT SUCK!!!

1. NO MORE 2. SABD
3. TIRED! 4. THE
SOUND 5. I DON'T
THINK SO 6. NEW
ONE 7. GET STRAIGHT
8. COLD CAN PT. II

BASS: ADAM
GUITAR: DAVE
DRUMS: JIM
VOCALS: YAN

THANKS + HELLO'S: OPEN (NIK
PAUL NIK) RICH KEV ALEX
STEVE RIORDAN CHARLIE
ROB CLIVE TONE + VIQUE JOHN
DUMPTANK BBMF's ACTIVE
RESPONSE HEADWAY STRATING
VFL'S JOHN D + ALL IN BRIGH-
TON WARREN + ALL AT SHEL-
LEY YAN'S GRANDMA & +
HIS FAMILY DAVES MUM
JIM'S FAMILY ADAM'S FAMILY
NIK (FINLAND) VAL + MIKE
DUNCAN TRUDY THE PIKE
PAULA LOUISE DONATELLA
WINKEY CHARLOTTE CALVIN +
HOBBES ANNE GREGG CHRIS
AT HILBURY RD & ALL REAL
HARDCORE, ALL

+ ANYONE WE FORGOT.

DEDICATED TO
ANT. SUTCLIFFE

KXC

GOTHAM TAPES

TEE-HEE! (COMPILATION)

TEE-HEE!

SIDE 1 - BBMF's - SUPERFLY HEDGEHOG (MARK
0742 81 3105) BIG POP TROTSKY - FORK (JASON
0892 30822) COUCH POTATOES - BAD HABIT
(DAVE 0892 279651) SLEEP - IF ONLY (ROB
0273 607034) ACTIVE RESPONSE - HANG UP (ROB
0242 327346) ELECTRIC SEX CIRCUS - ORANGE
ALBERT (MARCK 081 304 1912) SIDE 2 HEAD-
WAY - OPINIONS VOICED (SIMON 0273 400390)
EXISTANDO - AMNESIA (304 0892 31418) THE
EUROPEANS - GREM (0892 665833) M.T.A - GANG MY
STR (DM 0702 211334) JUSTICE (DAVE 0892 27969.)

GOTHAM
TAPES
c/o DAVE
1 CHANDOS RD
TUN. WELLS
KENT TN1 2NY

RUMBLE
CLUB
MUSIC VENUE
EVERY FRI + SAT
PANTILES
TUN. WELL

GOTHAM TAPES - SOUP

GOT 010

JOEY FAT - SOUP

1 CHANDOS RD TUN. WELLS KENT TN1 2NY

AT WORK SIDE: 13·3·92
WINDSCREEN
TEAR
PEOPLE come into your house
Amusement
PIECEMEAL
SPOILT
SUGARHEAD
SIMMER DOWN,

at play SIDE: 17·1·92 LIVE
WINDSCREEN
SPOILT
TEAR
Amusement
MR. SMUGFELLOW
PASS THE SPROUTS
SIMMER DOWN

Gotham Tapes

B.H.P. #1

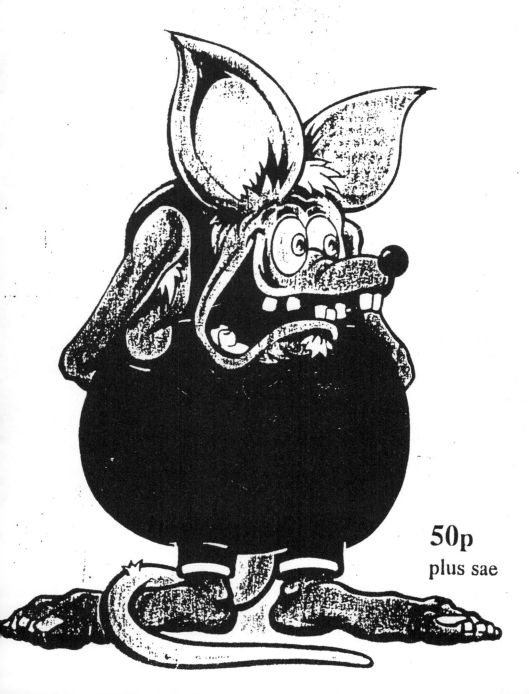

50p
plus sae

BIGGEST SPUD IN THE WORLD

Your piz or your li

TWO armed robb
spurned cash and gra
three large pizzas
stead.

The peckish ban
masked and armed w
rifle and a pistol, held
21-year-old pizza deli
man in Hastings. Su

They threw away
wallet still containin
takings and fled w
the grub. Police wer
their scent last night.

> "Your true nationality is the human race."
> H.G. Wells.

Hello and Welcome to the first issue of BIIP. A lot of effort has been put into producing this fanzine, so we hope you read it, think about it and enjoy it. Hopefully, this will be the first of many issues, but we need your help and support. Any relevant contributions (articles, adverts, interviews, reviews, artwork...) will be greatly appreciated. You can write to us (we might even start a 'letters' page) at - BIIP, 1 Chandos Road, Tunbridge Wells, Kent, TN1 2NY. We look forward to hearing what you think. Thanx and take care.

Dave & Steve.

There was to have been a 'Robbie Reids Skate Column' in this issue, but it didn't arrive in time, so it'll start in the next one, OK.

We've got some space to fill here, so I'll relay a few rumours. Big Pop Trotsky, Tunbridge Wells' infamous indie unit, may have split up. So have Drive and Brighton's Sleep. However, there are rumours that Tunbridge Wells' Anti-Nowhere League are reforming to play a gig at the Astoria on February 2nd with the Lurkers, Peter and the Test Tube Babies and, possibly, JoeyFat. SNFU may also have reformed, and although the Quicksand tour was cancelled, good ones coming up are Samiam + Mr. T Experience, Libido Boyz, Pegboy, Fugazi, Jawbox, Poison Idea, Born Against, and All.

Special Thanx to : Jase 'the face' Dormon, Jase(LTB), Kris(Pseudo Hippies), Rob(Protest), Richard(AWA), Robbie & Jailcell Recipes, GreenDay, Goober Patrol, Angus Bagpipe, Understand, Hard-Ons, Ian Carvell, Steve Geer, Garbled Tales, Eat Shit, Warren, All our advertsisers, and most of all...All our friends for being cool.

R. McGRATH PSYCHIATRIST

Pssst... remember you're a Womble

GONOKO

The Hard-Ons are Australia's best export, well, better than neighbours anyway. They don't nee any introduction for this interview that Ray answered on 26th November 1991.

BHP : What are you up to at the moment, apart from answering this?

Ray : We are in the process of touring Australia and New Zealand. We also want to record something (an E.P.) in December and an album in April or May.

BHP : How is the "Dull E.P." doing and are you pleased with it?

Ray : We are quite happy with the "Dull E.P." because we like the songs and the sound quality. We don't know how it is doing and moreover we couldn't give a fuck. Who cares how many record Hard-Ons sell in England. More importantly, who cares about England.

BHP : What was the last U.K. tour like? Did you have any favourite gigs?

Ray : We had a good time at the shows but none of us like England because of the depressing atmosphere and the weather. The people, especially in the North, are very friendly. On the whole, England is a horrible place to play because of primitive P.A.'s and the way bands get treated by organisers. I especially despise the fickle way music fans in England latch on to fads like "Grindcore" or "Manchester". It's more fashion than music over there it seems. The best band in England, "Snuff", broke up, I'm sad to say.

BHP : Is it really hard work in a three piece band, or do you like it that way?

Ray : It isn't hard work because we obviously prefer the three piece set up. It's a unique situation with the drummer singing. We have a good rapport amongst ourselves.

BHP : Are you mellowing out your songs on purpose, or is this just a natural progression?

Ray : Because we are not playing total thrash songs anymore people see this as "mellowing". Well, say what you like.

BHP : Are there age limits at shows in Australia, like in the U.S.A.? If so, how do you cope with the problem?

Ray : We have a situation in Australia which is similar to that in the U.S.A., where underage shows have to be organised independently, away from publicans. We do it as often as we can becaus we think a 14 year old Hard-Ons fan is just as valid as someone older than 18. We played some underage shows with such bands in Australia as "Meanies" and "Cosmic Psychos".

BHP : You seem to play a lot of skate gigs. Do any of you skate and have you had any really bad slams?

Ray : We have may be played one skate gig in the last three years. We used to skate regularly but now we tour so much more, it is stupid to risk a broken finger.

BHP : Who does your excellent artwork?

Ray : Me.

BHP : Do you actually live on a beach?

Ray : We don't, but we spend a lot of time there. Australia is very warm most of the year, even down South where we live and the beaches here are great.

BHP : Why are you all holding tools on the inside cover of "Love is..."?

Ray : We found those tools on the beach while we were looking for coins etc. with our metal detector, so we got a friend with a camera to take a photo of us with our find.

BHP : How did the 12" with Rollins come about?

Ray : Rollins tours Australia because Timmy, our manager, brings him out to Australia so we relished the opportunity to work with a powerful voice.

BHP : What are your future plans?

Ray : We plan on getting mega-rich like Senseless Things or Mega City Four.

BHP : Anything to add?

Ray : Hello to all our friends in England, Scotland and Wales, especially Bomb Everything, Snuff guys, Abs, Senseless Things, MC4, Sink, Stevie Snax and Kalv.

VENUE REPORT

In each issue of BHP we will try to review a different venue so that people know where good entertainment can be found and when it is available, so bands will be able to book a gig with greater ease and know something of the venue's capabilities beforehand.

The first venue report is for a club I help out - THE RUMBLE CLUB in Tunbridge Wells.

THE RUMBLE CLUB is Tunbridge Wells' alternative music nightclub. It is run by local musicians and hosts gigs every Friday and Saturday night. (Possibly Thursdays too, in the future.) It has been running for three years, one and a half of those at it's latest home in the Pantiles. Admittance is from eight o'clock onwards and costs £3.00, but for this you get live music until eleven thirty and a disco playing Alternative Hardcore Dance music until one in the morning. Also, there are cheap bar prices, not club prices, and it is only £1.00 per pint until nine thirty. The Rumble Club only holds up to 150 people so there is always a good crowd and the bands are paid well; even the support acts are paid a minimum of 'petrol money'. The sound at the club is excellent; it has it's own 1k P.A. with a 12 channel desk, various effects and a 350 watt monitor system. It also has a full lighting rig with pinspots, scanners and strobes.

The Rumble Club has become an important date on many band's tours, and has hosted gigs for : Jailcell Recipes, Couch Potatoes, Angus Bagpipe, Drive, Goober Patrol, Understand, Pseudo Hippies, Milk, Electric Sex Circus, Skydogs, Thrilled Skinny, Sons of Ishmael, Slunk, Spitfire, The Keatons, Rescue, Midway Still, Strookas, Surfin' Lungs, Badgeman, The Price, Boo Radleys, Wat Tyler, Bollweevils, Heavenly, Nature Things, Shelley's Children, Love Kittens, Brilliant Corners, 2000 A.D., Big Pop Trotsky, Bassinger, The Becketts, Some Have Fins, Earwig, Silver Chapter, Dr. Phibes, Spin, Popguns, Jasmine Minks, Chesterfields, Dumptank, GreenDay, JoeyFat, Forheads in a Fishtank, God Machine...

Any bands wishing to appear at the club can write, sending a demo if possible, to this 'zine, or to either :

Jason,
4 Ashbourne Court,
Bretland Road,
Rusthall,
Tunbridge Wells,
Kent,
TN4 8PF.

The Rumble Club,
(Winchester Club),
The Pantiles,
Neville Street,
Tunbridge Wells,
Kent.

PLANET EARTH IS 4,600 MILLION YEARS OLD.

If we condense this inconceivable time-span into an understandable concept, we can liken Earth to a person of 46 years of age.

Nothing is known about the first 7 years of this person's life, and whilst only scattered information exists about the middle span, we know that only at age 42 did the earth begin to flower.

Dinosaurs and the great reptiles did not appear until one year ago, when the planet was 45. Mammals arrived only 8 months ago; in the middle of last week man-like apes evolved into ape-like men, and at the weekend the last ice age enveloped the Earth.

Modern man has been around for 4 hours. During the last hour man discovered agriculture. The industrial revolution began a minute ago.

During those 60 seconds of biological time, modern man has made a rubbish tip of Paradise.

He has multiplied his numbers to plague proportions, caused the extinction of 500 species of animals, ransacked the planet for fuels and now stands like a brutish infant, gloating over this meteoric rise to ascendancy, on the brink of the final mass extinction and of effectively destroying this oasis of life in the solar system.

The above is an excerpt from a Greenpeace leaflet.

KIDS!! EARLY START THE GIFT THAT KEEPS
SKATEBOARDS.
ON GIVING. HAVE A
PARN GOOD DAY.

THE THIRD WORLD DEBT

MANY PEOPLE IN WESTERN COUNTRIES OFTEN CONTRIBUTE TO VARIOUS CHARITIES TO 'HELP' THE POOR PEOPLE IN THE THIRD WORLD (AND TO RELIEVE THEIR OWN GUILT).IN FACT THE COMMON PERCEPTION IS THAT 'SOMETHING IS BEING DONE' TO HELP PEOPLE SUFFERING IN THE THIRD WORLD.YET THE HUNGER CONTINUES.WHY ? HALF A MILLION CHILDREN ARE DYING EVERY YEAR AS A RESULT OF THE THIRD WORLD DEBT;HUGE AREAS OF FORESTS ARE BEING RIPPED DOWN TO HELP REPAY THESE DEBTS.FOR EVERY £1 WE GIVE TO THE THIRD WORLD,£3 IS TAKEN BACK IN DEBT PAYMENTS.THE FOLLOWING ARTICLE TRYS TO EXPLAIN THE COMPLEXITY OF THE SITUATION AND WHAT CAN BE DONE TO HELP RESOLVE THE MATTER...

To give a better understanding of the situation,it is necessary to briefly mention the reasons for the debt and to show why many high-street banks originally lent millions to the third world.
During the early 70's,many oil producing countries increased their prices by massive amounts.Much of these profits were invested in western banks.
Due to these price rises,many third world countries were encouraged by Western governments to borrow money to meet these price rises.
Whole armies of loan salesmen from Western banks were sent to developing countries - international banks were anxious not to miss out on the large profits to be made.
By the early 80's,the majority of international banks had lent money to developing countries - however the economy worldwide was on a downfall,resulting with loan interest rates gradually increasing. Eventually,many countries simply could'nt afford to continue their loan repayments.Many banks had left themselves to be massively overexposed.The Midland bank for instance had lent more than twice it's capital to developing countries.Needless to say,all further lending was stopped.
The International Monetary Fund (IMF) then stepped in to counteract the banks fears of a world banking collapse.The IMF basicly agreed to collect the banks debts and to take their payments from the developing countries themselves by 'structural adjustment measures.' In real terms this ment huge cuts in the individual goverments spending programmes;which led to high unemployment,falls in wages (up to 50%),massive increases in inflation (causing much higher food prices,higher cost of living etc),and led to falling standards of health and education.As a result,cases of malnutririon and preventable diseases rapidly increased.These were basicly all knock-on-effects.

THE ENVIROMENT

Many people have been suprised that many countries were able to make debt repayments at all.However many developing countries have rich material resources which were grossly overdeveloped in a bid to repay part of the loans.Countries such as Brazil,Indonesia and the Philippines have been strongly critised for their destrucion of their rainforests,in a bid to produce cheep products for export to Western countries.

Several UK banks have lent money to very questionable projects; for instance several nuclear reactors were to be built in earthquake zones (fortunatly never built).

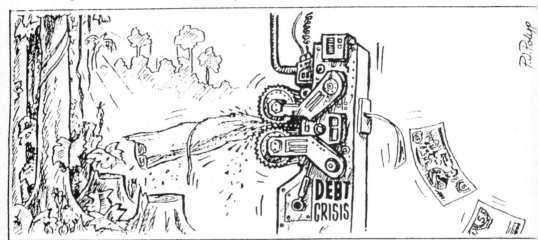

HUMAN LIFE

As I've previously mentioned,the cutbacks in developing countries economy leads to decreasing standards of health.Alone,UNICEF estimate 1300 children have starved to death today due to the policies of the IMF (who are incidently dominated politically by the U.S.goverment),and Western banks.

Currently the banks are making huge profits.At the end of 1982, the nineteen most effected countries owed $328 billion to the banks. By 1989,the money given to the banks has actually been exeeded by interest rates.The amount had actually raised to $356 billion. Currently this has since increased further.Altogether,the third world currently has a debt of $1,300,000,000,000 to International banks.

Do you care, and if so, why?

THE SOLUTION

The simple solution to the problem would be for the banks to write-off the debt. Increasing amounts of pressure is being put on the banks to do this. Ironically writing off the debts would actually cost the banks very little. Provisions have been made against the eventuality of this happening - the UK goverment have given them huge tax releifs to cover the amount owed to the UK banks.

WHAT YOU CAN DO

The main four banks in the UK that are involved in the third world debt are the MIDLAND, NATWEST, BARCLAYS and LLOYDS. If you have an account with one of these banks you are involved in the debt. Switching to a Building Society account (they have no part in the debt) doesn't take much effort. Therefore if you are concerned with the situation, however slight, I'd encourage you to switch accounts. Banks are starting to take notice...

For further info please send a SAE to

THE WORLD DEVELOPMENT MOVEMENT
25 BEEHIVE PLACE,
LONDON. SW9 7QR.
U.K.

If you wanna write to me, please feel free:
RICHARD.6 ENNERDALE ROAD, BRADFORD, WEST YORKS.BD2 4JE.UK

Thanks.

WHILE WE WAGE OUR WAR OF WORDS WE ARE NEGLECTING TO REALIZE THE FATE OF FUTURE GENERATIONS

under stand

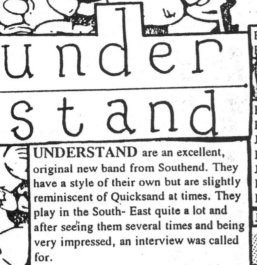

UNDERSTAND are an excellent, original new band from Southend. They have a style of their own but are slightly reminiscent of Quicksand at times. They play in the South- East quite a lot and after seeing them several times and being very impressed, an interview was called for.

This interview was conducted on 8th November 1991 at The Rumble Club in Tunbridge Wells, after they had supported Bassinger. Jon and Rob, the guitarists were present...

BHP	Give us a brief band history and line up.
Jon	We've been together for a while, but with the present line-up, about a year. We started at school as a cheesy Rock 'n' Roll band, doing Youth Clubs and stuff.
Rob	Doing JFA covers.
Jon	Then we became funky, funk metal which was worse. Then, for about a year, we've been Understand and Rob joined.
Rob	Yeah, I was pushed by peer pressure into this band called "Crafty Cats", a Rock 'n' Roll band, then I moved on to "DDD" who are Death Metal - "Doom Death Destruction". They had the "No Excuse" guitarist, playing drums. Then I was in "Cynical Smile", a crossover band, with Hallam Standoff. Then I joined "54 Funk" with Jon and played funky songs about Peewee Herman and whose had a yap. Then we changed our name, stopped drinking and edged out.
BHP	What's the current Understand line-up?
Jon	Dom Stand - Vocals and general positiveness, Stu Q - Bass, and me on guitar.
Rob	And me on guitar, six positive strings, and Andy veggie beats - the vegetarian drummer.
BHP	Is Andy the only vegetarian?
Rob	No,3/5 veggies, 4/5 straight edged, the non- straight edged member does play a lot of sports and doesn't take drugs or smoke, so he's fairly straight.
BHP	So are you a straight edged band?
Rob	No.
Jon	We're a Hardcore band.
Rob	We're not particularly hardcore.
Jon	We're Emo-core.
Rob	Guitar and toad rock really.
BHP	What was your first gig like?
Jon	At the Esplanade, we were 'Under'. It was in a pub on the Southend seafront supporting a band who completely ripp us off.
Rob	So I wrote "Grab" the next day.
BHP	So who writes the lyrics then?
Rob	Me and Jon.
Jon	We do some songs combined.
Rob	And the band fills it out.
BHP	How many gigs have you played, and you still get nervous?
Rob	No, not really.
Jon	For the first time tonight I didn't reall feel nervous.
Rob	I was nervous last night. All those starchy people with pool cues. My col clenched.

SUNDAY NOVEMBER

HARMONY AS ONE
M. T .A
Understand

NE
KI
SU

Jon	We've done 14 gigs, or 4.
BHP	You've got two really good demos ou so do you prefer a studio sound to live
Jon	It sounds shit when we play.
Rob	We'd be better if we practiced, but we end up beating Dom.
BHP	So what bands influence you?
Rob	Verbal Assault, Once and for all.
Jon	Quicksand, that comes out, and we're well into Hip Hop, some of our lyrics are Rap orientated.
Rob	Urban Dance Squad and Fishbone.

on — Also we're well down with all the new straight edge stuff.

Rob — Billingsgate.

on — We play "Bodycount", and Ice T's mad, Public Enemy.

BHP — Any local bands?

Rob — "Standoff" - they really rock.

on — The scene round our way, as far as hardcore and even indie goes, is really shit. We have a psychobilly band called "Vulture Squadron" and a cheesy punk band called "Nuclear Anarchy" who are quite amusing. That's it.

BHP — Do you like any U.K. bands?

on — Jailcells, Couch Potatoes.

Rob — Strength Alone, Angus Bagpipe, Pseudo Hippies.

BHP — Have you had any label interest?

on — We sent off to First Strike and haven't heard anything.

Rob — Meantime blew us out.

BHP — What do you think of 'zines?

Rob — I think 'zines are really good.

on — This is our first interview.

BHP — Do you liken yourselves to any other bands?

on — All the bands we sound like I don't really like. I heard Token Entry's new album and I don't really like it.

b — There's a bit of a "Shelter" rip-off, but we're not krishnas.

P — So what's your view on the straight edge / crusty argument? You have songs about that.

— All our songs about that are not to be taken seriously. It's just people at London shows scrounge money and then go inside and drink expensive pints.

b — Not that we're against drinking, but I've got a job and I can't afford to drink all night at the Boston Arms. It's a joke! If they said "can I have some money to get off my face" then at least that's honest. We joke about crusties, but we're not serious.

b — The "Visions of Change" drummer's shirt smells, after 5 washes. He's in your face.

P — Apart from swap shirts, what's the most punk thing that you have done?

b — Oh, spat at someone. (laughter) I had a tattoo of a spider. (more laughter)

Jon — We haven't done anything out of order.

Rob — We're not really a punk band.

BHP — You've got an anti-racism song. Is that a subject you feel strongly about?

Jon — It is and it isn't.

Rob — Basically, it just goes out straight to Ian Stewart and Skrewdriver, who hassle me. They think they're so special. When the three minute warning goes off and all the VIP's go down to their cellar there will be no Chinese, no blacks, and Skrewdriver aren't gonna be there either. They will just fry with everyone they hate.

BHP — OK, What's the best gig you've been to?

Jon — It depends. Gigs here (Tunbridge Wells) are so mad. Seeing the Jailcells was so good. Urban Dance Squad and Fishbone were good, but too big. Seeing Nirvana at Reading was mad, but I prefer smaller gigs.

Rob — Majority of One was good, and Go!

Jon — Gorilla Biscuits and Quicksand. But it's cool to come here and know everyone and just hang out. This is about as good as it gets.

BHP — Do you think if the really good, melodic hardcore acts got airplay, they would be a commercial success?

Rob — People would like it if they were exposed to it.

Jon — Jailcells could, Smiles and classic stuff. Drive.

BHP — What is the best thing about being in a band?

Jon — Just hanging out and meeting new people. We've made so many friends.

BHP — And what's the advantage of two guitarists?

Jon — It's two songwriters in the band.

Rob — Two contrasting creative influences.

Jon — We don't get too technical though.

BHP — If you had a cheesy question, no, if you had 3 wishes?

Jon — Peace and Harmony.

Rob — Being on a caribbean island with Nadine Garner.

Jon — And Julia from Press Gang.

Rob — And Elaine Smith.

Jon — Rob's got an Elaine Smith vegetarian cooking video.

Rob — Everyone liking Understand.

Jon	Gorilla Biscuits to be straight edged again or stop.
BHP	There always seems to be lots of girls at your gigs. What do you think of sexism within hardcore?
Rob	They all fancy Dom.
Jon	My sister brings her friends, it's just friends.
Rob	It would be better if girls were in there, but it's sexist to ask why not. If someones in the pit they are just a person.
BHP	While we're being sexist and asking about girls in the scene, can you think of any cool female bands?
Rob	"Babes inToyland", "Calamity Jane".
Jon	"Lunachicks", "Bangles" - I love them.
Rob	"Voice of the Beehive". James did a great dive when we saw them.

BHP	Do any of you skate?
Jon	Yeah, but I'm really shit. It's cool to crap.
Rob	I used to skate, Andy's good and Joh...
Jon	We know Lewis Child, and we gave a demo to Tony Hawk.
BHP	OK, so what are your future plans for "Understand"?
Rob	Try to get a record deal, write new songs, play cool gigs.
Jon	Just keep going.
BHP	Anything to add?
Jon	The address for the demo is: Dom (Understand), 3 Woodend, Hockley, Essex, SS5 4QL.
Rob	It's free, but if you could send a blank tape, we will put a cover on it. Thank...

COUNCIL IN FILTHY FILMS

The entire Tunbridge Wells Council were arrested last Thursday following a raid by police earlier in the day on the offices of Filthy Films plc.

The raid on Filthy Films premises in Mount Pleasant rewarded the police with their biggest haul of filthy books, films, magazines and farm animals since the smashing in 1985 of the notorious 'Rubber Ring' circle at their HQ in Langton's 'red light' district.

It is still not known what the exact link is of the Council and Filthy Films, but a police sargeant told waiting newsmen 'unofficially' that all Council members are "thought to be partners in Filthy Films" adding that "Police suspicions were aroused by the regular movement of sheep into the Town Hall on a Thursday evening, and the loud bleating that followed".

The new batch of arrests pushes the Tory controlled Council into turmoil just as it was starting to recover from last years 'Sex for Sale' scandal which was rumoured to have involved many local councillors right up to MP level.

A spokesman for the minority Labour group on the council said: "None of our members were involved in this vile and depraved occurance... unfortunately".

"Disgusted; Tunbridge Wells"

We've had to put up with that condescending view of Tunbridge Wells for too long, yet now in the light of recent events it does seem to be coming true. The whole town is shocked, horrified and above all disgusted at the way our elected Councillors willingly become involved in acts of sexual perversion. It is a disgrace, does being elected to council office suddenly turn all these men and women into sexual deviants, obviously yes. The whole rotten lot should be removed from office immediately Only Labour members it seems were not involved, although this was because they were not invited, rather than not wanting to take part.

OPPORTUNITY FOR OPINION

In life, opportunities arise seldom to alter the status quo. I do not mean from a personal matter; I mean for a community or a society of sorts.

When such an opportunity occurs, it is up to every thinking man or woman from whatever walk of life to act. To act either individually or lay your faith behind people who care. People who care, people who are active should be entrusted.

Imagine a scenario : A country has a regime that has ruled over it ever since its creation. Without opposition they have been able to create their own rules, their own domain (we're getting over the top now aren't we?). An opportunity arises for the people to change this.

If this scenario were anywhere else in the world, our normal conservative (with a small 'c') would rise in support of the population of the oppressed nation.

Figure this out of people in my fair town. The Borough Council (those people who set your poll tax) have always had a conservative party in control.

1992, the year for change in Europe, can mark a year for change in Tunbridge Wells.

The majority in the council is only 2 seats. For the first time in the history of Tunbridge Wells there could no longer be this majority. Whatever your political persuasion, the responsible thing to do in May 1992 is to vote for a new beginning.

OH GOD! WHY CAN'T MY BOYFRIEND SKATE?!

HOT POTATO:

HUNT SABOTEURS

HUNT SABOTEURS

Each year in Britian over 200 foxhunts kill 20,000 foxes, while a further 130 hunts kill hare,deer,otter and mink all in the name of sport,in addition over half a million shoot wild animals and birds and an estimated 3 million go fishing. At present over a thousand people sabotage the activities of between 50 and 60 hunts by using such methods as false scents, false cries,hunting horns and anything else which helps the animal to escape.Hunt sabotuers use non-violent direct action tactics which are harmless to animals and humans. HE hunt claim the foxes enjoy being chased which really shows the mental capability of these murderers. Most sabbing is done on saturday though also in mid-week. those who cannot be active are always needed to leaflet, raise money,find out information and in many other ways. Your help is desperatly needed and if you contact the resse below they will put you in contact with your nearest group

It's in your hands –
you can stop bloodsports

**HUNT SABOTEURS
ASSOCIATION**
PO Box 1, Carlton,
Nottingham NG4 2JY

Tel: 0602 590357

ROB (PROTEST).

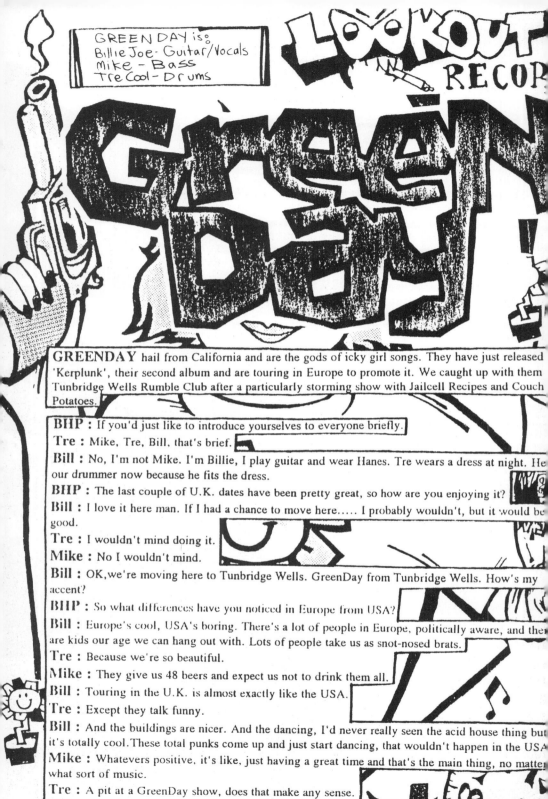

GREEN DAY is:
Billie Joe - Guitar/Vocals
Mike - Bass
Tre Cool - Drums

LOOKOUT RECOR

GREENDAY hail from California and are the gods of icky girl songs. They have just released 'Kerplunk', their second album and are touring in Europe to promote it. We caught up with them Tunbridge Wells Rumble Club after a particularly storming show with Jailcell Recipes and Couch Potatoes.

BHP : If you'd just like to introduce yourselves to everyone briefly.

Tre : Mike, Tre, Bill, that's brief.

Bill : No, I'm not Mike. I'm Billie, I play guitar and wear Hanes. Tre wears a dress at night. He our drummer now because he fits the dress.

BHP : The last couple of U.K. dates have been pretty great, so how are you enjoying it?

Bill : I love it here man. If I had a chance to move here..... I probably wouldn't, but it would be good.

Tre : I wouldn't mind doing it.

Mike : No I wouldn't mind.

Bill : OK, we're moving here to Tunbridge Wells. GreenDay from Tunbridge Wells. How's my accent?

BHP : So what differences have you noticed in Europe from USA?

Bill : Europe's cool, USA's boring. There's a lot of people in Europe, politically aware, and there are kids our age we can hang out with. Lots of people take us as snot-nosed brats.

Tre : Because we're so beautiful.

Mike : They give us 48 beers and expect us not to drink them all.

Bill : Touring in the U.K. is almost exactly like the USA.

Tre : Except they talk funny.

Bill : And the buildings are nicer. And the dancing, I'd never really seen the acid house thing but it's totally cool. These total punks come up and just start dancing, that wouldn't happen in the USA

Mike : Whatevers positive, it's like, just having a great time and that's the main thing, no matter what sort of music.

Tre : A pit at a GreenDay show, does that make any sense.

Bill : Thatcher on Acid came out, and it was 'what's all this running in circles', it was really strange.

BHP : OK, Kerplunk, the new album, do you have a favourite song to play, and are you pleased with it?

Tre : I wish you had written a song on it.

BHP : So do I!

Mike : I'm real happy with it, we worked hard.

Bill : There's more stories and places and people, like Christie Road, Welcome to Paradise. People re still gonna take it as GreenDay love songs, that's cool, we like love songs but there is other stuff.

BHP : Where did the name 'GreenDay' come from?

Tre : Trees, agriculture, seeds, crystals, irrigation, navigation, fertilizing, organic, environmental..

BHP : Why do you wear a dress, Tre?

Tre : Ridiculousness.

Bill : You should watch a band as well as listen to them, so it don't get boring.

Tre : You should wear a dress to the pub.

Bill : You gotta watch Homophobic Assholes.

Mike : It's better here in the U.K.

Bill : In Tampa, Florida, me and Tre kissed. It went totally silent, in Disappearing Boy, 450 people st standing there.

HP : How long has the tour been going?

ill : This is our eighth week.

Mike : We're leaving on 10th January. We've been in the U.K. for one and a half weeks.

re : We're coming back soon, so get ready.

Mike : We're touring the USA again soon.

Bill : I've not been home for summer in two years, so I'm staying home to learn how to surf.

Mike : We're gonna live on the beach.

Tre : I know where two surfboards are in Berkeley, that never get used. We're stealing them when e get home. We're all 19 by the way.

ill : Tre turned 19 at our first show in England.

HP : How did you arrange this tour?

re : Christie Colcord, the head stooge.

ill : Aiden, and Julia in Germany, Hose Antonio in Spain.

At this point, Yan from Couch Potatoes turned up and drew an Allroy to prove that he is an artist)

Mike : Everyone who says they're an artist is just lazy.

re : Come on in. So that's Yan. Good accent.

HP : I heard you may be doing a video?

re : We're doing a tribal video, maybe.

HP : Anymore vinyl?

ill : We're on a compilation with the Libido Boyz and Scherzo.

HP : I guess that's it. Anything to add?

ll : Hello. Goodbye. (Sung in unison)

Mike : Pal Gume. (Get out?)

he new album is brilliant, so get it if you can. You can write to:

GreenDay,
c/o Lookout Records,
P.O. Box 11374,
Berkeley,
CA.94701,

PROTEST
PROTEST

ROWS OF CHILDREN LINE THE HOSPITAL WARD, LIKE CATTLE IN TRUCKS

AWAITING THE SLAUGHTERHOUSE. NO MORE SAFE HAVEN INSIDE YOUR MOTHERS

WOMB. INSTEAD YOU GROW UP WITH LIES, TRADITION AND

MURDER, BE DADS LITTLE

SOLDIER, THE ARMY'S PIECE OF MEAT TO EXPLOIT.

YOUR COUNTRY NEEDS YOU TO KILL THE ENEMY WHICH

AUTHORITY CREATED. THE GRAVEYARD, A PLACE TO CALL HOME.

YOUR OBSESSIONS ARE THE WEAPONS OF WAR. THE BLOODSUCKING GOVERNMENT

HAVE NO GUILT IN THEIR EYES, NO BLOOD ON THEIR HANDS, THEY TREAT I

AS A JOB EVEN IF IT MEANS THEIR EMPLOYEES LOSING AN ARM OR A LEG

THE NEWSPAPERS GLORIFY OUR BOYS AS THE BRAVE YOUNG LADS BUT

NOT THE

STENCH OF THE ROTTING CORPSE, NOT THE INNOCENT IN THE KILLING FIELD

THE MILLIONS WASTED FOR PROFIT TO LINE THE POCKETS OF THE

WEALTHY. THE ONES WHO WOULDN'T DARE TO FIGHT, TO THEM IT MEANS PRIDE.

A GAME OF SOLDIERS EXCEPT THE SOLDIERS HAVE FLESH, BLOOD AND BONES

FROM THE CHRISTIANING TO THE CEMETARY, THE INCUBATOR TO

THE INCENERATOR WERE TOLD THAT FIGHTING IS WRONG

BUT LEGALISED MURDER IS FINE, AND IN THE SLAUGHTERHOUSE

THE ANIMALS STILL DIE

refuse their murder.

ROB.

refuse their murder.

ANGUS BAGPIPE

THE WINCHESTER CLUB

DRAG CITY

ANDROMEDA

ANGUS BAGPIPE

ANGUS BAGPIPE are the latest mega-band to spring up in the Tunbridge Wells area. They play great, thrashy, melodic hardcore with a truck load of catchy hooks. One of the most entertaining bands I have seen live, their stage presence will blow you away.

We interviewed Nik, Dunc, and Paul.

Nik - Vocals
Ire - Drums
Dunc - Guitar
Paul - Bass

BHP Ok, why form Angus Bagpipe instead of leading a normal life?
AB Because its fun!
BHP So what was the first gig like?
AB Scary; it was Paul's birthday gig, it must have attracted him to the band.
BHP What bands inspire you and do you like any local bands?
AB All hardcore bands inspire us and locally Couch Potatoes, Understand and BBMF's.
BHP Who would be your ideal band to support?
AB Gorilla Biscuits, or Jailcell Recipes, or GreenDay.
BHP Have you done any previous interviews, and what do you think of 'zines?
D No, never.
N Kerrang, Metal Hammer.
D Thats not funny Nik.
P There aren't many good 'zines, but this will be. I agree with fanzines, it lets the people know there's a scene out there, somewhere.

BHP You've only recorded one track for a compilation. When are you doing a demo?
P In about 2 weeks, for definate, no bulls**t.
BHP You were successful in a local band competition, weren't you?
P Yes, we were joint first and got loads of money for it. The woman who introduced us fancied me and it was judged by the bassist of OMD.
BHP How did you get your wacky name?
D We all tried to think of a good name and it sprang into Nik's head - Angus Bagpipe. Why not!
BHP You've got some varied songs, so who writes what?
P Duncans the musician.
N I write some of the lyrics, I've written a couple of songs.
P And I changed the bass line to one of them.
BHP Is there a cover you would like to be able to play?
N No, don't say Dagnasty.
P Revolution of values, by Token Entry.
D My favourite would be a Couchies song.
N A Treponem Pal song, they stayed in a van outside my house.
BHP So what is Hardcore, music or lifestyle?
D Depends on how its interpreted by the individual.
P But it should be fun.

SLOW MOVING PEDESTRIANS
KEEP RIGHT

SIGH! ALL THAT PRANCING ABOUT EXHAUSTING

ANGUS BAGPIPE

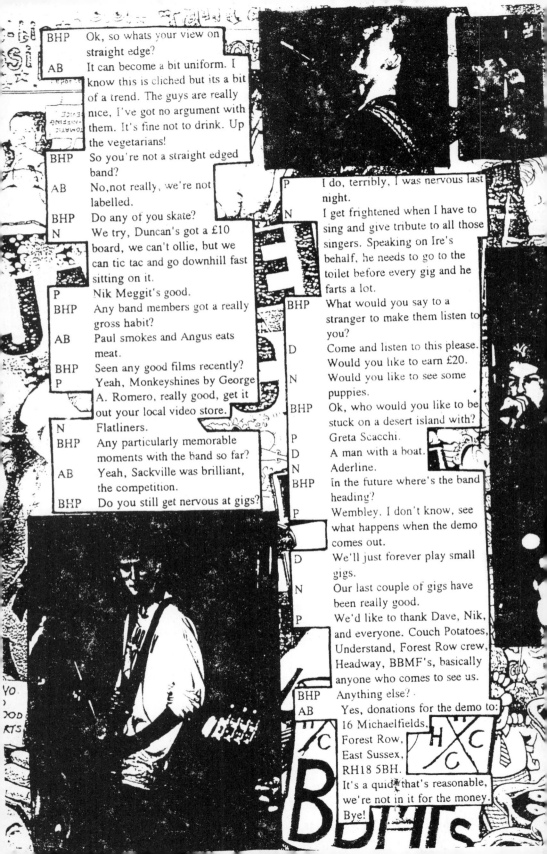

BHP Ok, so whats your view on straight edge?

AB It can become a bit uniform. I know this is cliched but its a bit of a trend. The guys are really nice, I've got no argument with them. It's fine not to drink. Up the vegetarians!

BHP So you're not a straight edged band?

AB No, not really, we're not labelled.

BHP Do any of you skate?

N We try, Duncan's got a £10 board, we can't ollie, but we can tic tac and go downhill fast sitting on it.

P Nik Meggit's good.

BHP Any band members got a really gross habit?

AB Paul smokes and Angus eats meat.

BHP Seen any good films recently?

P Yeah, Monkeyshines by George A. Romero, really good, get it out your local video store.

N Flatliners.

BHP Any particularly memorable moments with the band so far?

AB Yeah, Sackville was brilliant, the competition.

BHP Do you still get nervous at gigs?

P I do, terribly, I was nervous last night.

N I get frightened when I have to sing and give tribute to all those singers. Speaking on Ire's behalf, he needs to go to the toilet before every gig and he farts a lot.

BHP What would you say to a stranger to make them listen to you?

D Come and listen to this please. Would you like to earn £20.

N Would you like to see some puppies.

BHP Ok, who would you like to be stuck on a desert island with?

P Greta Scacchi.

D A man with a boat.

N Aderline.

BHP In the future where's the band heading?

P Wembley. I don't know, see what happens when the demo comes out.

D We'll just forever play small gigs.

N Our last couple of gigs have been really good.

P We'd like to thank Dave, Nik, and everyone. Couch Potatoes, Understand, Forest Row crew, Headway, BBMF's, basically anyone who comes to see us.

BHP Anything else?

AB Yes, donations for the demo to: 16 Michaelfields, Forest Row, East Sussex, RH18 5BH. It's a quid that's reasonable, we're not in it for the money. Bye!

SEX, LIES AND CENSORSHIP

From politicians to the media to schools, all tell us sex is something bad for our health and not to be enjoyed".

Who's Responsible?

They're right in many ways, as for a lot of us sex is the most traumatic negative experience imaginable. But the question to ask is – who's responsible for this? One example is so-called sex education in schools. This has more to do with trying to make sure we end up in, "happy, married families" with no other form of relationship being acceptable. Sex is shown to be about reproduction and sexual diseases, rather than something to gain pleasure out of.
The media also play their part,

portraying men and women in roles unimaginable in real life (only 26% of the population live in conventional nuclear families). Women bear the brunt of this sexual stereotyping, constantly being shown as sexual objects available to be used and abused by men. In short, sex in the media fosters exploitative relationships rather than equal pleasurable ones.

Guilt

As for the church, sex has always been a dirty word, with the whole emphasis towards encouraging guilt, confusion and suppression around sexuality. Their idea of healthy sex is making babies under the consent of marriage. It's easy to say "who listens to these religious bigots?" but they

do still have a hold on people's lives.

But at the end of the day, people do cut through the bullshit they try to feed us, with sex being central to many of us as a means for pleasure and comfort.

This isn't ignoring the misery and frustrations it causes: sexual abuse, rape and impotency to name but a few, but these are all a product of how our sexuality is repressed and manipulated by those in power. Lots of us are rejecting the constraints and bigotry being fostered around us, making sex what it should be – something to mutually share and enjoy with whoever and however we please.

Sex can be magic when we start to break free!

REPEATER - SOCIETYS LUST.

Born to be direction less.

Solitude of heart, whose soul was a window to greater wonders ?
I kicked the toys, i broke emotion, manacled it to dust
Solitude is mind, its mind that governs fear
You were born, i saw to that, to be direction less
Stole your dreams before this cerebral love blossomed
Caged you lovely, impressed myself, and laughed arrogantly
Weeping in summers rain, brought to a visionary eye
Solitude of heart, this is needless, warmth is hope
I kicked my heels, i ran amok, i had been shown no fear
No inclination for deep warmth never existed, i just existed
I stole from others the emotion, that i had been deprived
Exploited but shunned, bedeviled and listless, i was alone
Trembles, i do so, fight, i will so, alone, just god knows
Solitude of heart, whose soul was a window to greater wonders ?

Desperate in a quiet town, lonely in a mesh of technology
Faces crawl in automation, black bags slide in twilight rush
They kick their toys, they silently explode, did they ever exist
Solitude is a cruel but luckless child, spurned to haunted corners
So direction is none, its tracks gleefully ripped to ragged edges
For the love of hope, leave me shame, we will escape in summers rain
Fists in air raised like cranes, toys of destruction whirring on
I know i imagined that colour exists, i remember from past lives
I stole from people passion, hate, love and anger, cheap refuse
No solitude is required in this heart, its direction is clear as love
Mazes of ices, a society whose arteries run cold, comfort is broken
Trembles, i do so, fight, i will so, alone, just god knows
Solitude of heart, i open windows and doors of light expand in rage
I am a torrent of released pressure, an icicle born to boil

anger.

P GEER. 91

FINIS by W.S.LANDOR.

I strove with none, for none was worth my strife.
Nature I loved, and next to nature, art,
I warmed both hands before the fire of life.
It sinks, and I am ready to depart.

INSIDE.

I am inside of you, delivering the mortal blow
Entwined in flesh, grasping, pulling, creating a rift
Shot, speed, this flush of arrogance, appealing
Remove your tainted lies, away from my silent gaze
I am inside of you, shaping and reforming, producing
The production line of life, rattles its liquid cage
Shot, speed, high emotion, travelling heads
You become three, four, five, infinity love ten
Conquers, derives pleasure, fills and vacates
I am inside, you are inside, outside, no romance
Entwined in flesh, grasping, pulling, creating a rift
Suction, tunnels, races sensations, travelling heads
The production line of life, rattles its liquid cage
We respire, and perspire, rolled in rumbled sighs
To obtain a higher moment, to vision two to three
I am inside, you are inside, outside, lies a dream
Mortal blow is loving, sensation feel so sweet
Romance and its whisper, the pulsating gift called life

S P GEER. 91

"The idea of nudity doesn't worry me"

BROKEN TAPES
J P LEMARCHAND/ROUTE DE CLERES
78570 LIMESY, FRANCE

JAILCELL RECIPES

Jailcell Recipes are, in our opinion, the best band in the country, but they have been quiet for a while so we thought that we should write to find out what is going on at the moment.

BHP : OK, I know you've been having some 'drummer' trouble recently. Can you explain what happened and what the situation is?

Rob : Well Ian, our old drummer, wanted to go to Europe travelling around for six months so he had to leave, as obviously we couldn't wait around for him to come back. So we got a guy called Carl. He's a raging drummer, picks up real quick and willing to gig. He was also filling in for Drive, but they seemed to have split, so he's all ours now.

BHP : If you're gigging again, what's lined up for the near future?

Rob : GreenDay is next. We play four gigs on the tour and hopefully go to Ireland in January with Decline. Other than that, just play as many gigs as possible in England.

BHP : Do you have a favourite venue?

Rob : I personally have a few; The Shelley Arms at Nutley, The Rumble Club at Tunbridge Wells, The Den in Wigan, and Planet X in the 'pool, but any with a good crowd reaction and good sound both on and off stage.

BHP : Is '2 years...' still selling and are you pleased with it?

Rob : I think it's still selling. You'd have to ask Mr Woods!! But we have plans to record a new one in Spring. I know most or the CD's have sold. I don't even have an LP or CD, so if any ones got a spare one, ha!

BHP : How did you persuade Karl Alvarez to do the artwork.

Rob : We just asked him when we played with All. He said yes straight away so we gave him a pen and a pad. He didn't even want any credit for doing it, not even a thank you.

BHP : Are you influenced more by U.S. or U.K. hardcore, and what bands?

Rob : We are not really influenced by any country. I couldn't really say who we sound like. I'll leave that up to others. As far as music goes, I'll just list the bands I'm listening to at the moment: Farside, No FX, Superchunk, Didjits, Pegboy, Burn, Shudder to think, Mr T Experience, Asexuals, New Decline EP.

BHP : Do you get a lot of radio airplay?

Rob : No, not really. Peel has played us a few times. Also a few local stations, but other than that no. Who listens to the radio anyway!

BHP : How did you manage to arrange your Euro- tour?

Rob : Mr Woods arranged it for us, just through people he knew in Europe.

BHP : Will we ever hear 'Deep down inside' live again, and if not, why not?

Rob : Nope, no, nada, none, zip, zilch, zero, jack, squat. Because we hate it, Carl can't play it, and is not going to learn it.

BHP : Skate wise, what are your favourite set-up and tricks?

Rob : My fave set was the first Chris Miller that came out on Schmitt after he left G&S. It had Indy 159's and Hosa rockets on it. It was ace. I got it cheap off a kid called Pinhead; he'd cut the nose down and covered it in caution stickers, but it was smart. I learned a lot of tricks on that board. At the moment I've got a Smallroom 'nine', Indy's (of course), Spitfires. As for tricks, well I wouldn't know of any faves 'cause I can't do any!!

BHP : Is Jamie a 'Guitar God' yet?

Rob : Jamie can't even play guitar 'cause I broke his fingers with a brick for playing too many solos and too many David Bowie and Sex Pistols covers.

BHP : Anything to add?

Rob : Cheers to Dave Potato for the interview. If he doesn't send me a copy of the 'zine I'll turn him into chips!! A big cheers to Kate for doing all my mail! Hello to Val Leuman, Peter Pinne, Peppino, Dave Smalley, Billy and his zimmer.

Guy with Descendents T shirt, 180 ollie grab.

REVIEWS

BASINGER :
Something/scared.

WEST RECORDS

Basinger - who have long been championed by the Becketts as the second best guitar band in the South West (after themselves no doubt!) came up with a deout 7" of two very contrasting sides.

"Something" is the slow moody track, while "Scared" is the poppier track(more in the keeping with Basingers' main mans past-he was the lynch pin of the Chesterfields) however, it is essential to know that the Basinger that play on this record are not the Basinger of today. A few line-up changes, including the addition of a second base have racially altered the sound of the band. They are now altogether more noisey and benefit immensely from this. It is worth scouring the old record shops for a copy, although I think you'll be lucky to get one. See'em live(there always on sale there), and decide for yourself.

FIGFACE :
Welcome to Mexico

This has its moments, but not enough. It starts with 11 minutes of intro. that is little more than feedback and screaming but unfortunately it continues in much the same way. The recognisable songs off the GUB LF are O.K. and Skinny Puppies T.F.W.O is well covered, but on the whole it's a bit sad really.

LOVE and RESPECT :
Record.

This is a wonderful noisy sub pop, along the same lines as the COWS/THROWN UPS but for more acessible/musiacal??? + Steve Turner (Mudhoney) plays loads of cool slide guitar on this short, but very entertaining disc. Definatly one to hear.

BABYLAND :
1991 7"

Prodigy meets Ministry head on,(Industrial Acid?) Metal percussion, spiteful vocals and plenty of bleeping! I can't wait to hear what they do this year.

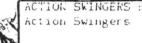

ZINE

ACTION SWINGERS :
Action Swingers

I am going to have a hard time persuading you to get this. Its grungy guitar stuff with distorted vocals, the best way to describe it, is with 3 simple words; ROCK, FUCK and KILL.

HILT :

Call an ambulance before I hurt myself. Various mixtures of styles make this interesting but, not all of it works. The industrial stuff does but, some of the indie pop experiments sound awful. For Skinny Puppy fans that don't mind taking risks it's O.K. but the rest of you should avoid it

Directions for use:

Positioning:

Left-side position: Lie on left side with knee bent. arms at rest

Knee-chest position: Kneel, then lower head and chest forward until left side of face is resting on surface. Position arm comfortably.

Administering enema:

Remove protective shield from rectal tip before using:

Hold bottle upright, grasping grooved bottle cap with fingers. Grasp protective shield with other hand, pull gently to remove. (See illustration.)

With steady pressure. gently insert enema with tip pointing toward navel Squeeze bottle until nearly all liquid is expelled. Remove tip from rectum. Discontinue use if resistance is encountered. Forcing the enema can result in injury.

Note: It is not necessary to empty unit completely. Bottle contains more than the amount of liquid needed for effective use. A small amount of liquid will remain in bottle after squeezing. Maintain position until urge to evacuate is strong (usually 2 to 5 minutes).

Method of action: Promotes evacuation of the bowel by increasing bulk volume and water content of stool.

Effectiveness: Usually produces evacuation within 2 to 5 minutes. Effectively relieves constipation and cleanses lower bowel.

DECEDENCE WITHIN

PAY-OFF TIME

DECEDENCE WITHIN

Pay-Off Time

3 new songs recorded at White House Studios. Strictly Limited Edition of 1,000, all numbered. Initial copies on clear vinyl.

Postpaid rates (airmail!)

UK	EUR	USA	OTHER
£2.50	£3	$5	£4

USA must send cash – others cash or IMO. In the USA try ordering from Blacklist

FIRST STRIKE RECORDS
The label of Distinction
Since 1988

39-41 HALLGATE ♥ WIGAN
LANCASHIRE ♥ WN1 1LR ♥ ENGLAND
Tel: 0942 826598 ♥ Fax: 0942 821469
All orders shipped same day!

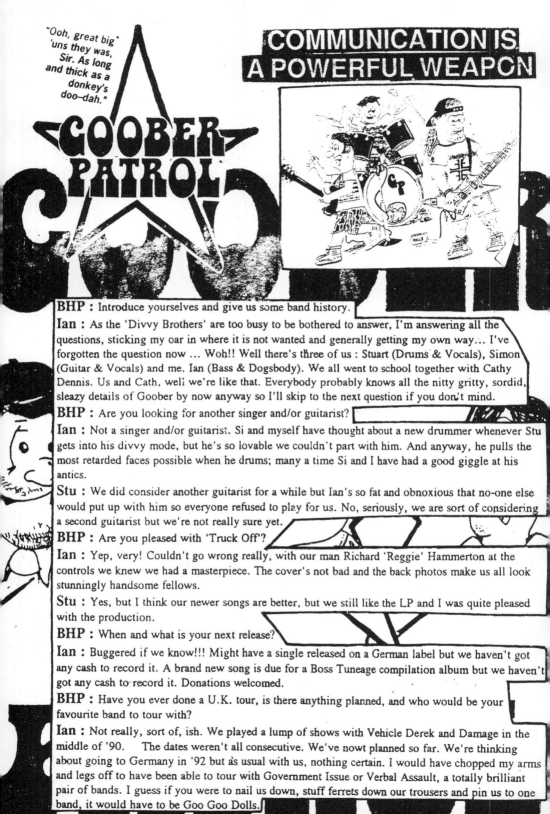

"Ooh, great big 'uns they was, Sir. As long and thick as a donkey's doo–dah."

GOOBER PATROL

COMMUNICATION IS A POWERFUL WEAPON

BHP : Introduce yourselves and give us some band history.

Ian : As the 'Divvy Brothers' are too busy to be bothered to answer, I'm answering all the questions, sticking my oar in where it is not wanted and generally getting my own way... I've forgotten the question now ... Woh!! Well there's three of us : Stuart (Drums & Vocals), Simon (Guitar & Vocals) and me, Ian (Bass & Dogsbody). We all went to school together with Cathy Dennis. Us and Cath, well we're like that. Everybody probably knows all the nitty gritty, sordid, sleazy details of Goober by now anyway so I'll skip to the next question if you don't mind.

BHP : Are you looking for another singer and/or guitarist?

Ian : Not a singer and/or guitarist. Si and myself have thought about a new drummer whenever Stu gets into his divvy mode, but he's so lovable we couldn't part with him. And anyway, he pulls the most retarded faces possible when he drums; many a time Si and I have had a good giggle at his antics.

Stu : We did consider another guitarist for a while but Ian's so fat and obnoxious that no-one else would put up with him so everyone refused to play for us. No, seriously, we are sort of considering a second guitarist but we're not really sure yet.

BHP : Are you pleased with 'Truck Off'?

Ian : Yep, very! Couldn't go wrong really, with our man Richard 'Reggie' Hammerton at the controls we knew we had a masterpiece. The cover's not bad and the back photos make us all look stunningly handsome fellows.

Stu : Yes, but I think our newer songs are better, but we still like the LP and I was quite pleased with the production.

BHP : When and what is your next release?

Ian : Buggered if we know!!! Might have a single released on a German label but we haven't got any cash to record it. A brand new song is due for a Boss Tuneage compilation album but we haven't got any cash to record it. Donations welcomed.

BHP : Have you ever done a U.K. tour, is there anything planned, and who would be your favourite band to tour with?

Ian : Not really, sort of, ish. We played a lump of shows with Vehicle Derek and Damage in the middle of '90.   The dates weren't all consecutive. We've nowt planned so far. We're thinking about going to Germany in '92 but as usual with us, nothing certain. I would have chopped my arms and legs off to have been able to tour with Government Issue or Verbal Assault, a totally brilliant pair of bands. I guess if you were to nail us down, stuff ferrets down our trousers and pin us to one band, it would have to be Goo Goo Dolls.

Stu : If I could pick a band to tour with it would probably be Samiam or maybe even someone famous like Nirvana 'cos then we could swear at a wider audience. No, only joking, it would have to be Samiam if it were up to me.

BHP : Are there any other U.K. bands you listen to?

Ian : Nope!

Stu : Personally, I don't listen to many U.K. bands but there are some really good ones that I do listen to such as Visions of Change, Snuff, Vehicle Derek, and of course the Couch Potatoes.

BHP : You don't seem to have any really political songs. Do you have any strong views on this?

Ian : Not to write songs about. We'd rather sing about the necessary things in life like... love, chips, beer, sex, and more beer.

Stu : Not really. I don't think that they would turn out very inspiring, as our lyrics are normally pretty made up on the spot jobs.

BHP : We've heard that you are all vegetarians, and don't drink, so what's your view on Straight Edge?

Ian : Both the 'Divvy Brothers' are veggies and little old me's a vegan. That rumour about Straight Edge isn't strictly true, though I have to admit that I don't drink... in my sleep. I kept choking and I don't take to being called a 'beer waster'. We all drink. There was a time a while back when Si and Stu didn't drink but we were never a straight edge band as I used to guzzle the brew. I've no strong views either way, for or against, straight edge. Each to his/her own.

Stu : I agree with fat Ian on this one. I got no strong views for or against, although I used to not drink a couple of years ago.

BHP : What's the scene like in Norfolk, and do you get many gigs?

Ian : There's not really a scene. Unless we play the Norwich Arts Centre supporting the likes of Lemonheads, Tad, MC4, so all the students turn out. The few shows we play or are organised are poorly attended. We prefer playing away from Norwich anyway. There's nothing like going to a different town or city and finding a super-duper chip shop.

BHP : What's your favourite shop?

Ian : Well Stuart has a tendency to hang around the ladies underwear department in Marks & Spencers. The amount of times he's been thrown out of there. As you can tell from my stunning dress sense, the clothes shop is a taboo subject and by looking at Si, you can tell the barber's not a rich man from Si's visits. If we opened a shop it would definately be a chip/beer shop.

Stu : If I opened a shop it would be a chip/beer/record shop.

BHP : Any words of wisdom to give to the masses?

Ian : Look both ways before you cross the road, always wash your hands before a meal, never go out without telling a grown up where you're going, always check your change after making a purchase of chips/beer as some shops do make mistakes, always unplug all electrical appliances before retiring to bed, try to have the correct fare when travelling on public transport, never walk into the Wharf Public House in Huddersfield wearing a badge "I'm not sexist, but if she's offering, I'd give her one", it may offend the female bar staff (didn't it Aston). Always buy a large portion of chips, never say bugger in front of your mum, always be kind and helpful to those less fortunate than yourself, buy our piggin' album, never buy a bible on a Sunday, it's illegal to do so, always take necessary precautions when travelling in a motor vehicle driven by Tim 'Lee Majors Fall Guy' Snelson, if the chance should arise buy a member of Goober Patrol a beer or several, always get a grown up to help if you are using sharp instruments, never fake an orgasm, always live within your financial limits, on no account whatsoever should you drink and drive, never stick your hand in a pot of boiling water, always check strangers identity cards before allowing them into your home, never use a stiff wire brush to scratch your bum........... Thanks a lot for the interview. I doubt I've inspired anyone to write but I'm sure you'll have our address plonked somewhere. Don't forget to buy our album... please. It is good isn't it Dave?!

Stu : Thanks for the interview. If you come to see us ever, then ignore Ian 'cos he's so obnoxious. Thanks and God bless and sleep tight.

GOOBER PATROL

GOOBER'S STRAWS

Makes 20; calories per portion 116

6 oz./175g plain flour
2 oz./50g American roasted peanuts, finely ground
1 teasp. mustard powder
1-½ teasp. cayenne pepper
4 oz./100g butter
4 oz./100g grated Cheddar
1 egg, size 3

Set oven to Gas 6, 400°F, 200°C. Place flour, peanuts, mustard and cayenne in bowl. Rub in butter, stir in cheese then mix to a dough with egg and 2-3 tablespoons water. Roll out to ¼ in./6mm thick. Cut into strips 2½ in./5.5cm long × ¼ in./6mm wide. Place on greased baking sheets and bake for 10-15 mins. Cool on a rack.

You can write to the Goobs for more recipes, waffle, or a recipe for waffles, at 49 Exmouth Road, Norfolk, NR30 3DP. Gt. Yarmouth,

JAWBREAKER

9 out of 10 Fabulous babes PREFER skateboarders!

Stop skate harassment. Open a world-wide chain of 24-hour donut shops.

USE A SKATE GO TO PRISON

I think your magazine is cool. I can't wait to see your new issue come out. I have a couple of issues, but mostly I read them in the stores.

...y is the product of a bad upbringing ... small Wiltshire town. His father, who ...iolent and alcoholic, died when he was ...Jay soon joined the thriving drink and ...s scene in the town, did some petty ...ing and got caught. He came to Bath ...years ago, when he was 20, and has ...indulging his twin passion for cider ...punk rock music ever since. He lives ...£1 a week dole, and has no intention ...et working. "I'm lazy," he explains.

...obody here owns a dog on a string, ...egs. To the neighbours, they are still ...sty buggers" who make a lot of noise ...regularly splatter the street in vomit, ...as far as the household is concerned, ...are not Crusties but Cider Punks.

O.K. here is a list of distro-services, all doing their bit on different levels, all are worth sending an S.A.E. and a nice letter to, if you have something to sell or just want to get your hands on a few goodies.

Mediocre Distro-29 Kylemore Pk,Belfast,BT1465A,N Ireland

A.K. Distribution-3 Balmoral Place,Stirling,Scotland,FK82RD

Simon Dell 0/2 95 Logan Street,Glasgow,G50HP,Scotland

The Motivator-7 Staniforth Court,548 Aftercliffe Road,East Fand,Sheffield 9,South Yorkshire,England

Cellar Distribution c/o Clifton Hotel,Nairn IV124HW,Scotland

Wetspots,22 Meadow View,Southwell,NO250EQ

Sick"n"Tired-43 Warner Rd,London N87BB

Polamic-28 Bellaville Drive,Oadby,Leicester LE24NA

4th Dimension-7 Wentworth Gdns,Bullockstone,Hearne Bay,CT67TT

Looney Tunes,Top Flat,23 The Esplanade,Scarborough,N Yorks

Full Circle-12 Bell St,Newsome,Huddersfield,W Yorks

Dole Drums-17 Percy Rd,Renfrew,PA48AZ

Hardcore Pumpkin-21 Gibson St,Hillhead,Glasgow,G128NU

Inward Collapse-2 Somerton Place,Newport,Gwent,NP92DE

Warzone-P.O.Box 148,Belfast,BT1

1 in 12 Club,21-23 Albion St,Bradford

BBP-90 Grange Rd,Swindon,Wilts,SN34LD

Acid Stings-P.O.Box 282,Hitchen,SG40HA

Reaching Out-12 Chestnut Ave,Clacton-on-Sea,CO152BG

NUFFZANUFF-12 Thompson St,Darwen,Lancs,BB32EY

No Life-54 Carleton Rd,Pontefract,W Yorks,WF83NF,England

If you run a distro of any sort send us a copy of your latest list for inclusion in the list of distro services.

Is this tolerable?
Is this tolerable?
Is this tolerable?
Is this tolerable?
Is this tolerable?
Is this tolerable?

NO TRESPASSING

L.T.B.
F.A.N.Z.I.N.E
Less Than Brainless

A.D.V.E.R.T.I.S.E.M.E.N.T

Featuring
JAILCELL RECIPES
FUDGE TUNNEL
COWBOY KILLERS
EXIT CONDITION
COUCH POTATOES
CITIZEN FISH
THRILLED SKINNY
SINK
M.T.A.
& Loads More !

ARTICLES
REVIEWS
ARTWORK

A5,60 pages.

40p & S.A.E.

From
26 SUMMERDOWN ROAD
EASTBOURNE
SUSSEX ('PK)
BN20 8DR

Our lives are controlled by peer pressure. We are moulded by our parents, school, work, TV. Everything anyone else does, even our best friends, affects us and we even feel we have to look good to fit in so you're never happy for long enough to recognise whats made you happy. OK, you smile when someone falls over in the street but thats not happiness. We worry about far too much. Worrying is no good unless you do something active about it, then its OK to worry about foxhunting, famine etc. etc., the list is endless. But don't be sad if your convictions 'aint that strong - just admit you're not as "nice" as you'd like to be. There's nothing wrong with honesty, especially when you're owning up to yourself. You need to know who you are and not care who others are and what they do. I've said "Be yourself" before but its so true, you can't buy friendship, and remember, acts of kindness are just that - don't expect someone to do for you what you've done for them. If ever you think someones taking advantage of you ask yourself why you did the favour and if it was important enough an act for you to feel ill of someone thats doing what they want. You should be doing what you want and not be generous expecting returns. Generosity can only gain respect if its honest - most people can recognise creeps, some can smell them.

So who are the happy? Maybe they're the ones that don't think "Do labotomies make you smile?" I know people that are racist, sexist, liers etc. - all manner of nasty things and they don't give a monkeys. Perhaps they don't know. Recognising the problem is half the solution. No-one wants to lose friends so no-one is gonna tell you, but if you think I'm talking about you then you're paranoid like me or there's something I've said thats hit a nerve which is good 'coz thats what I was trying to do. But what is racist behaviour? Now obviously shouting at them at football matches is, but you might not do anything extreme, in fact you might be shocked to find you're racist and sexist. I can deal with both subjects together 'coz the whole problem in the first place is treating people differently. We are all equal. You shouldn't treat anybody differently. Bowing to authority is worse of all, just 'coz they have some posh job, more money, a title, so called "power." It still shouldn't make you feel inferior. Judges in court sit high up, behind large benches, they're in control and very smug - but you shouldn't respect them anymore than the homeless in tube stations or your mum or dad.

Think about it, think about everything. Are you sexist? Are there subjects you freely talk about with your own sex - but wouldn't dream of talking about in front of a member of the opposite gender. if there is then you're sexist or trapped by conditioning. Years of school, parents telling you to open doors for girls etc. - its all fuck, and I'm pissed off now, be yourself FOREVER.

WORK - Just a quick word about your job; Don't take it so seriously!

REVIEWS

reporter Frank Sidebottom

Husker Du-Flip your wig L.P

The best album by far from The legendary Dü.If you're into Dinosaur Jr sounding indie/hard driven hardcore you'll love this.The L.P contains some utter gems such as the unrivalled classic 'Makes no sense at all','Hate Paper Doll','Wig' and 'Divide and Conquer'.If it wasn't for Husker there'd be no Lemonheads,Dino Jr,MC4,Senseless Things,M.B.V or even Nirvana and the indie/ alternative rock scene would not be like it is today.Figures made for this new fuzz-pop generation.One of the most emotional,frenetic, all out fuzzed guitar records of the 80's. Buy it,Steal it,Tape it-Get it.A must for your collection.

The Misfits-Bullet E.P(1980)

A classic single by the best band in the world,ever! A monolithic sentinel which stands tall for all to imitate.If any of you havn't heard it then you'd be a total fool not to check it out-or any other of their stuff.4 slabs of psyco horror-sci fi core in the form of 'Bullet','Attitude'(the song GnR are gonna slaughter on their punk e.p),'We are 138' and 'Hollywood Babylon'.i know it's been said before but you have to own this record if you class yourself as sane.

Ramones-Locolive L.P

12 years since their last live L.P and they're still the same 3-chord surf punk;except Joey's voice has finally fucked up something chronic-he sounds like Lemmy!Oh yeah,and they're 5 times as fast.32 tracks crammed on to two sides of vinyl. Classics include 'Lobotomy','Rockaway Beach','Bop' and 'Judy'&'Sheena' plus some great newish stuff like 'Wart Hog' and 'Bonzo goes to Bitberg'.Worth buying just for a laugh!

Buzzcocks-An other music in a different kitchen L.P

Yes i know this album is ancient but i only just bought it recently and what can i say?Amazing 70's melodic punk oozes from the grooves as the turn-table churns out 'Fast Cars','Love Battery','I NEED' and 'No Reply'.This is as good as their final L.P. A vital piece of history.Not to be overlooked!

Ramones & Damned-Brixton Academy.8th Dec'91

Missing the Joney Theives i jostled my way to the front of a packed Academy,just in time to see the Damned take the stage.The crowd greeted them like long lost brothers as they crashed into 'New Rose'. The 1000 man moshpit go into pogo hyperdrive.Period. Captain Sensible was pissed as a newt.He tells the crowd they're ugly cunts;they call him a fat bastard; he says it's their fault for buying his records then he strips totally naked-the bloke's a total nutter! Anyway ,they played "Neat,Neat,Neat","Help","Born to kill","How can i be happy today" and "Smash it up" and loads more stuff.The band were so good live even if they are getting on a bit.(What is this,their 10th reformation??)They were so energetic and tight and the crowd loved 'em-Great stuff!
Onto the Ramones-I'd never seen them before but i'd heard they were a touch monotonous,well whoever said that was spot on.They aped the Loco Live album exactly-even down to between song raps.Johnny and Joey didn't seem to move for two hours as they looked bored silly. Jesus!Could you imagine playing 'Lobotomy' for 16 years? Dee.Jay got into it though;he reminded me of those fans who played R'n'R Swindle with the Pistols-you know,a young fan in awe invited to perform.He must feel well chuffed he's filling Dee Dee's converse.And he does inject alot of life into the otherwise mediocre show. If you wanna know the songs and the order,just take a look at their Loco Live album(Although the 2nd night they encored with "I Wanna Be Well","Havanna Affair", "Listen To My Heart" and "Gonna Kill That Girl") Yeah they were good but they could have been much better by just simply getting into it!

Gang Green-King of Bands L.P

The name says it all.This is a 'farewell' comp L.P. Don't know who chose the songs but they could have chosen better ones.2 new ones-'Thunder' and 'Rub it in your face'-typical Gang Green.Plus other stand outs-'ALCOHOL','Ballad','Wasted Night','We'll give it to you' and 'Bartender'.A great party-punk me(n)tal band that will be sadly missed,well,by Tom anyway.Advice-Buy the live album.

Nirvana-Nevermind L.P

Jesus Christ!Have you ever brought an album home, played it and was totally bowled over on first listen?Well this is THE album of the last couple of years!An utter classic of grunge fuelled garage rock 'n' roll!This undoubtedly will be considered to be one of the most significant rock albums of the 90's-mark my words.Classics include'Teen Spirit' 'Territorial Pissings' and 'Breed'.Miss this at your peril!

Ned's Atomic Dustbin-Trust 12"

3 slices of great indie/punk from one of the best U.K bands around at the mo.The B-Sides 'Faceless' and 'Titch' outclass the A Side but then so do all their B-sides!A more metallic(a) sounding Ned's this time round but still the same abstract lyrics that 50,000 students somehow relate to and running basslines.Get it at your next visit to the record

The Fiendz-L.P

Great bubble gum-surf-pop-punk from this newish American band.Clichéd 3 chord Ramones/Descendants/ Hardons sort of thing yet still amazingly endearing. Can't remember the names of the songs but they're all utterly catchy like a bubonic form of crabs. Quite hard to find in the shops so if you come across it,buy it.If you don't like it I'll buy it off of you 'cos i've only got a copy!

Senseless Things-First of too many L.P

After buying and loving their debut 'Postcard C.V' album and the two 'major label' singles'Everybody's Gone' and 'Delmar',I musy say i was quite disapointed with the much hyped album.A lot of the songs just don't hit it off.Sure there's the singles but the rest are just mediocre to above average fillers. Gone are the 2 minute thrash bubble gum pop songs and in are the 'mature' intricately woven long winded numbers.Best bet-tape it off a mate-though they kick it live!

Green Day-Kerplunk! L.P

Green Day's second L.P and a mighty fine one at that. I really wanna love this L.P as much as their older shit but I have to admit-Ican't.It's excellent melodic hardcore but it somehow lacks the urgency of their previous stuff(they seem to have mellowed in their old age.-wot? they're only 20??)Don't get me wrong,it's a bloody good album and for another band it would be excellent but knowing how good their old stuff is, this record falls just short of the mark.My advice; It's good...but not that good-No seriously,it's a good album and worthy of your purchase and if you get the chance to see them live-do!They're excellent. Stand outs are;"2000 light years","Razorbacks" and "Welcome to Paradise".

The Hard-ons-Dull 12"

The latest vinyl offering from the best Oz band around. Recorded again,these versions of "Dull" and "Sri Lanka" are far superior to the original ones and with better production(loud crunchy guitars,up in the mix vocals) to boot.Two new songs in the guise of the excellent "Just being with you" a sort of Transvision Vamp meets The Ramones and a more slower progressive track called "Growing Old"(irony intended?).Anyway for 3 quid you can't go much wrong as it's a bloody good record. Happy;fun;danceable;air guitarable.....Oh! Bugger! get the picture??

RETCH RECORDS PRESENTS

Forthcoming Attractions

SELF DESTRUCT SELF DESTRUCT 12" LP
(Featuring Ex Skitzo members and features a
splendid rendition of Blitz's I DON'T NEED YOU)

COMPILATION L.P.
Get Yourself a Crash Helmet and a bit of Tax - you can
go anywhere you like in the daytime.
*(Featuring Blitzkrieg, The Insane, Paradox U.K.,
Parasites, Juice, Self Destruct, Couch Potatoes and
many more)*

COUCH POTATOES 12" (Mini L.P.)
*(Title not yet known, latest signing for the Retch
Emporium. Musically in a Descendents Vein)*

THE INSANE - LIVE AT THE LYCEUM L.P.
*(This classic 1982 performance features the El
Salvador Line-up.)*

ALSO AVAILABLE

PARADOX U.K. 'Charmed Existence' E.P.
PARADOX U.K. 'Disenchanted Land' (12")
PARADOX U.K. 'Mere Dead Men / Split' L.P.
BLITZ - 'All Out Attack' (12")
JUICE - 'Fundamental' (12")

*7" Singles £1.75 LP's £4.50, 12" £3.50, all prices include postage and packing FOREIGN
ORDERS 7" EP's £6, LP's £25, 12" £5, these also include post & pack.*

*All cheques P.O's payable to Retch Records, 49 Rose Crescent, Woodvale,
Southport Merseyside England PR8 3RZ*

For Blitzkreig T-Shirts write to:

PLASTIC HEAD MUSIC
Alalanta House, Old London Road
Benson, Wallingford
Oxon. OX10 6PL England
Tel: 0491 25029 Fax: 0491 25121

Pixies-Trompe Le Monde L.P

Well,the first L.P for the Pixies now that they've
broken bigtime.A more metallic affair than 'Bossanova'
and 'Doo Little' and not bad too i must say.There's
some really catchy shit on side one.Can't really
remember much of side two and i can't be bothered to
give it another listen(Woah!Punk rock eh?)but i do
remember the first song sounded like Ride on athetamines
and "Planet of Sound" is a gem.Oh and "Sad Punk" is a
sort of industrial/hardcore sort of thing and pretty
groovey too.They also cover a Mary Chain song called
'Head On' which sounds like Birdland meets the Pistols,
and is also...hem..what's that word?.....nice.
Well yeah,if you havn't heard any of their stuff then
i'd recommend this and hurry before they become TOO
big and therefore to 'commercial' for you to be caught
listening to.

Understand-Demo

Understand hail from sunny Southend and are one of
the best new bands in the country.I first saw them
supporting the Pseudo Hippies in London and for being
so young,they're so tight and progressive it's
frightening!The music is in a hardcore/industrial/
groove vein,leaning towards bands live Fugazi and the
like and their seven song demo is utter brilliance!
Commencing with the excellent hardcore/rap of "Shove
the Dove" it's obvious you're onto a winner.The next
up is the best on the demo-"Auto Parts" a frantic
S.N.F.U affair with it's humourous 'Rebo Man' film
effects at the begining.The others that follow come
in the forms of "Net wot i C","Open Arms"with its
Chemical People's 'My Tatoo' opening riff,"Brand X",
"I Want" and "Ponny *".I think they're releasing a
split single in a couple of months-but in the meantime get hold of this,one of the best hardcore demos
of 1991. contact Dom-0702 201334.

Wurm-Feast L.P

Featuring Chuck Dukowski and Dez Cadena on SST,cor!This
has got to be good,right?-Wrong.This is utter shite!
Maiden sounding metal for morons.Sounds like German bar
rock Eurovision Song Contest entries!They do a song call
'padded cell' which is not the Black Flag song but some
Halloween sounding drivel.Avoid this at all costs.
Nuff said.

Dinosaur Jr-Whatever's cool with me.12"

At last a song to rival "Freak Scene" and the "Wagon".
All the ingredients are present.A lazy,meandering,
floating melody;Fuzzed Husker chord progressions and
the mandatory ear screeching acidic solo;Classic Mascis.
"Sideways" however is a different affair.A stretched out
tapestry of acoustic arpeggios lazily stitched together
when J. feels like singing.Does this guy hurt when he sings?
It seems that every syllable he utters twists his body in
pain(I'm getting a touch pretentious here.I'm moving into
Melody Maker lingo....help!)
Oh well,(sigh)side two features two live versions of "Thumb"
and the great "Keep the glove"(No,not sniff!).The first
not being the best song on his Green Mind L.P to say
the least-it don't arf drag on and on and on and on and on
and-comprendez?The second,being a drag through a Dahli
dreamscape;"Hey babe where d'you go?Left it sitting in the
road.You can trape it all over the room,Sit back an' let it
shower you...Keep the glove."What's this guy on??Sedatives
that's for sure.If he got anymore subdued he'd be singing
in his sleep!
Needless to say it's fab,pucker(oh please not that word)and
all things complimentary.Enter new guitar god.

Green Day & The Couch Potatoes-Tunbridge Wells.18th Dec '91

A full house at Tunbridge Wells excellent Rumble Club was
a potent of things to come.The Couchies(or Potties??)took
the stage(albeit a 2" one)first and gave us an excellent
set.Three new ones,"Kill it","Three" and " Morning"-up beat
melancholic tunes-very progressive compared to their older
stuff and they then moved onto familiar territory with the
cool "Why","Tired" and the superb"No More".
Some drunk accompanied them for "Six Pack" and "Warriors
of Ghengis Khan" which was amusing and then that was it.
The crowd loved them and all were satisfied,merry,hunky
dora etc etc.
On to Green Day-what a band!They were brilliant.Just like
their records only louder,carasmatic,lively,amusing,frenetic,
entertaining and just plain amazing.They played all their old
stuff bar "Rest" and the best stuff from the new L.P.
(They were even better the next night in Euston although the
venue was'nt as cool)Overall,an excellent gig;great bands;
a blinding night out!!

SOUNDS RECORDS - Is a fairly new record, tape and CD shop that opened at the end of October 1991 at The Botany in Tonbridge (just off the high street). It is run by Mark and Simon, who will be able to help you find many bargains and collectable records. It's open from Monday to Saturday, 10 to 5, and any new or secondhand records can be bought, sold or exchanged. Go down and check it out.

CHALICE - Is possibly the mellowest place I've been in my life! It is one of Tunbridge Wells' newest shops, opening back in December 1991, and worth a visit just for the sounds and smells. Chalice is a 'New Age', or 'Mind, Body and Spirit' shop and has stocks of books, tapes, crystals, oils, candles, jewellery, cards and various other interesting items. They may also be doing therapies soon. Pop down and see Barbara at 48 Mount Ephraim Road; you'll be welcome to go in and browse.

> If you are never scared,
> or embarrassed,
> or hurt,
> It means you never take chances.
>
> Julia Soul

COUCH POTATOES

8 SONGS THAT SUCK!

DEMO TAPE
£1.50 PPD

GOTHAM TAPES
1 CHANDOS RD
TUN WELLS
KENT
TN1 2NY

the PSEUDO HIPPIES

The PSEUDO HIPPIES are a bunch of drunks we know. It was either interview them or fight - unfortunately, we chose the mental scars.

BHP Predictably, what's the bands line-up and history?

D Denny 'sticks' Morrison; I've been playing drums for about one and a half years.

K Kris with a K, and a red face.

T Tom, the bassman.

BHP So how long have you been a band?

K We formed at a GangGreen gig about two years ago, but we couldn't play.

BHP I heard that your first song was 'My little Louisa'. Who's that about?

K It was a love song about a girl who fancied me.

D No, you fancied her.

K That turned into 'Real mixed emotions'.

BHP How many gigs have you done now?

D Seven.

K My favourite was the first Tunbridge Wells gig.

T My favourite was the one in my room.

BHP Are gigs easier to get coming from London?

K The problem is there's so many bands, unless you're big no one's interested.

BHP Are there any problems caused by being a three piece band?

D Yeah, Kris can't sing.

K I used to be awful, now I'm mediocre.

D And we don't have to split the money so many ways.

BHP I thought your first demo was pretty good. Were you pleased with it?

K At the time we were, but we've dropped half of them.

BHP Didn't you take a lot of hassle for the lyrics?

T Our lyrics are pro-feminist in disguise.

K They are just jokes, not serious.

BHP Is there going to be a new demo soon?

K Yeah, in January - We'll send it to everyone.

BHP Who came up with your name?

D Tom, he was pissed at a Wolfsbane gig. (At this point the interview stopped as an attractive young lady walked by - lots of whooping followed.)

BHP Do you have a favourite own song?

T Another wasted night, or Alcohol.

K Our own, you fool.

T Oh, we haven't got any good ones.

K My favourite is Weirdo, or Pretty Gi

T I turned into a martian.

K That's not our own either.

D Pretty Girl.

BHP You seem to drink copious amounts o beer. Are none of you straight edgers.

D The music's good but the lyrics suck.

K Understand are good, thier demo's gr The Couch Potatoes are the best Engl band at the moment.

T You said last year that was Iron Maid

BHP So, what are your influences?

T GangGreen, Led Zeppelin, Black Sabbath.

K Ramones, Hard-Ons, Misfits, Dead Kennedys, Black Flag.

T Couch Potatoes, Understand.

BHP Do you prefer CD's or vinyl.

PH Vinyl!

D And I prefer marrows to aubergines.

BHP Kris, I've been told that you spy on a girl you live near.

K You bastards! It's true, she wrote to n though.

BHP Anything to add?

K Our new demo will be out in January will be free, from :
Pseudo Hippies,
5 Henryson Road,
Brockley,
London, SE4 1HL.
It mat be called "A different kind of sl on a different kind of tape" or "Volum 4" or "Suck 'n' Swallow".

T Thanks to Dave and Steve.

K And the Couch Potatoes for support. Thanks to Understand for being cool, and the baby eating bishop of Bath and Wells for the kinky, leather session.

T And the Bruno fight was a pantomime.

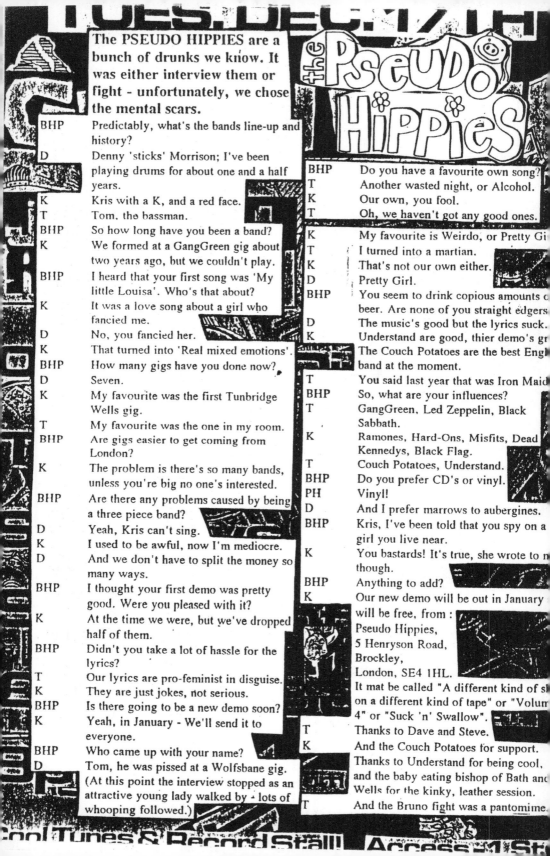

JB's MUSIC STORE
41 ALBION RD
T/W 522141

GUITAR SALE!

ELECTRIC ACOUSTIC GUITARS AT UP TO 30 % DISCOUNT

OPEN MON-SAT 10am-6pm

VISA, ACCESS H.P-P/EX

FACTORY FARMING

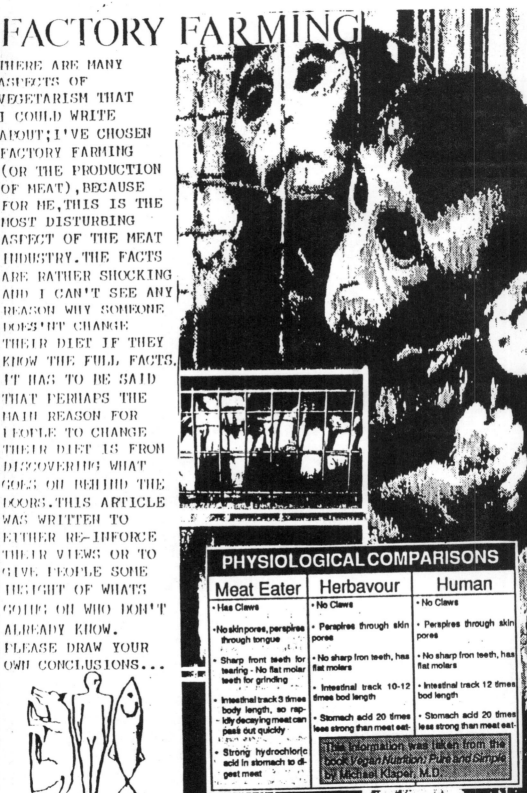

THERE ARE MANY
ASPECTS OF
VEGETARISM THAT
I COULD WRITE
ABOUT; I'VE CHOSEN
FACTORY FARMING
(OR THE PRODUCTION
OF MEAT), BECAUSE
FOR ME, THIS IS THE
MOST DISTURBING
ASPECT OF THE MEAT
INDUSTRY. THE FACTS
ARE RATHER SHOCKING
AND I CAN'T SEE ANY
REASON WHY SOMEONE
DOES'NT CHANGE
THEIR DIET IF THEY
KNOW THE FULL FACTS.
IT HAS TO BE SAID
THAT PERHAPS THE
MAIN REASON FOR
PEOPLE TO CHANGE
THEIR DIET IS FROM
DISCOVERING WHAT
GOES ON BEHIND THE
DOORS. THIS ARTICLE
WAS WRITTEN TO
EITHER RE-INFORCE
THEIR VIEWS OR TO
GIVE PEOPLE SOME
INSIGHT OF WHATS
GOING ON WHO DON'T
ALREADY KNOW.
PLEASE DRAW YOUR
OWN CONCLUSIONS...

PHYSIOLOGICAL COMPARISONS

Meat Eater	Herbavour	Human
· Has Claws	· No Claws	· No Claws
· No skin pores, perspires through tongue	· Perspires through skin pores	· Perspires through skin pores
· Sharp front teeth for tearing - No flat molar teeth for grinding	· No sharp fron teeth, has flat molars	· No sharp fron teeth, has flat molars
· Intestinal track 3 times body length, so rapidly decaying meat can pass out quickly	· Intestinal track 10-12 times bod length	· Intestinal track 12 times bod length
· Strong hydrochloric acid in stomach to digest meat	· Stomach acid 20 times less strong than meat eat-	· Stomach acid 20 times less strong than meat eat-

This information was taken from the book Vegan Nutrition: Pure and Simple by Michael Klaper, M.D.

Up to 50% of pigs are kept in sow stalls. Each stall is 2 feet wide with metal bars. They cannot turn around, take more than a step either way and many are chained to the floor-permanantly. The pigs spend 16½ weeks in the cages whilst pregnant. After the birth, they are then artifically inseminated again to start the process once again.

Soon after birth, the piglets receive injections, have their teeth removed by pliers and have their tails cut off (without anaesthetic). The male pigs are castrated (again with no anaesthetic).

Once strong enough, they are removed to fattening pens, kept in dark conditions until they reach the required weight for slaughter.

Most bull calves are castrated in their first week of life by placing a rubber band around the scrotum to cut off the blood supply. This can legally be done (without anaesthetic), by any person ie. no qualifications or experience nessary.

Calves have their horns removed by means of chemicals or use of a hot iron. Again no qualifications, experience or anaesthetic nessary.

The calves are then fattened up by means of foods including silage, fishmeal, turkey, poultry manure and remnants of diseased sheep (the cause of BSE or mad cow disease). After the fattening up process, they are then usually slaughtered between 10 months and 2 years depending on the system used.

Many cows are bred by artificial breeding procedures. Calves usually having to be born by caesarian section as being too large to be born.

t is hard to grasp the immense waste caused by a meat-based diet:

Less than 10% of agricultural land in Britain is used to grow food for people — most of it is used to grow livestock feed.

We import food for the same purpose . . .

The EC is the largest buyer of animal feed in the world. 60% of the grain imported by the EC comes from Third World countries.

94% of the protein fed to beef cattle is lost.
88% of protein fed to pigs is lost.
83% of protein fed to poultry is lost.
. . . most of it as dung.

Every year 15 million children die from starvation or from diseases related to undernourishment.

Meanwhile, the world's cattle alone consume a quantity of food equal to the calorific needs of 8.7 billion people — nearly double the human population of the planet.

The land space needed to feed these animals is vast, 10 acres of land (or 5 football pitches) will support . . .

. . . 61 people on a diet of soya beans
. . . 24 people on a diet of wheat
. . . 10 people on a diet of maize
. . . 2 people on a diet of cattle meat.

Worldwide, this has meant that four-fifths of all agricultural land is now used to feed farm animals.

Dairy cows are exploited to produce as much milk as possible, plus another calf every year. The calf is taken away from it's mother within 12-24 hours, and after having had their first feed, either go for slaughter straight away to be used for pies and the stomachs used for rennet in the production of cheeses, or alternatively, used for veal which is considered a "luxary" meat. This is because of the unaturally soft, white flesh created by confining the animal to a small wooden crate to restrict movement (to prevent the growth of muscles).

Dairy cows have short lives, often slaughtered when they have an infection or if milk production is low. They are preferably slaughtered whilst pregnant as this means more profit for the farmer as the unborn animals meat is particularly tendor. Most old "milk machines" end up in processed foods eg burgers, sausages etc.

Poultrey is a very popular meat and is considered healthier than red meat. Chickens are reared in huge windowless sheds housing up to 10,000 birds in 1 shed. Between 20 - 30 million birds die before they ever reach slaughter per year due to the conditions they are forced to live in. Workers collecting dead chickens often find that due to the heat and conditions,"When you pick up a dead bird, it is quite common that they are putrid - they are just bags of bone and fluid". Infection is so high, 90% - 100% of the birds are infected with salmonella.

THE MYTH OF "HUMANE SLAUGHTER"

There are around 900 slaughter houses in the U.K. Most being privately owned. All animals are required by law to be stunned prior to death - apart from religious communities.

The captive bolt methord is used for cattle, some calves and some sheep. A 3 inch bolt is propelled by compressed air into the animals brain. This is a very effective methord, apart from if incorrectly placed or if the animal's head moves, which frequantly happens.

Electrical stunning is used for pigs,sheep and some calves. An electrical current is passed through the head by metal tongs. A shock for 3 - 4 seconds is sufficient to make the animal immobilised for around 20 seconds.The time taken to have the throats of the animals cut after being stunned is between 5 - 82 seconds.This means many thousands of animals are killed each year whilst still fully conscious.90% of Danish pigs and some British pigs are stunned by carbon dioxide gas but pigs often struggle violently and usually go into convalsions.

Bulls and horses are simply killed by bullet.

When the arteries in the cattles throat are cut,the blood is then drained.Brain failure follows.Until recently,the animal was often kept alive to achive a "good bleed" out with the heart still pumping.

Birds are usually stunned by their heads being immersed into an electrical water bath then taken by conveyor belt to an automatic knife cutter.This process often fails as the bird can lift it's head above the bath avoiding stunning.It is then cut alive at the throat,although different sized birds are cut in different places.Therefore the bird can still be alive when reaching the feather plucking machine.

Every year 40 million,one day old chicks,are slaughtered. They are males which are genetically unsuitable for meat production.They are usless to the industry and therefore have no profit;Although recently experiments have been made to change the animals sex which may "solve" their problem.

Various methords are used in killing the chicks. Carbon dioxide can be used;Sometimes suffocation is used by using sacks or containers;Some are drowned in cages or by using nets; Boiling water is also used frequently;Finally,they can also be fed into a mechanical mill to be crushed to death.

SOURCES : VEGETARIAN SOCIETY
          THE VEGETARIAN IN YOU by BILLY RAY BOYD

FOR MORE INFORMATION CONTACT - ANIMAL AID
                              7 CASTLE STREET,
                              TONBRIDGE,
                              KENT TN9 1BH

Printed with the permission of
          'Armed with Anger' fanzine.

By the way,If anyones interested in knowing where their local slaughterhouse is,poultry farm, etc,then check out your Yellow Pages.You might be surprised.

THE FISH PAGE

> *"All is the total extent and the utmost possible when nothing else remains."*
>
> **Bill Stevenson**

sturgeon

CUSTOMERS at the Robot Music Store in Minneapolis have begun buying compact discs from a giant yellow mechanical arm in what its owners claim is the world's first fully automated shop.

The shop resembles a huge vending machine with CDs on shelves on the inside walls of a transparent room. Using keypads, customers are able to listen to music through directional speakers. The robot checks its inventory, takes orders from a user-friendly touch screen, accepts payment by cash or credit card, hands over the goods and returns change and receipts.

WHAT INFLUENCES YOU? I get stok on the UPS (United Parcel Services) ma The UPS man is happening. He's alwa bringing me stuff, he's real cool. He kno me. I would be stoked if I could cru around with him in his truck for a little whi That would be hot.

Everybody likes him. Nobody knows him a person but everybody gets stoked on h for bringing stuff all the time.

goby

BUY UNDERGROUND

gudgeon

cyprinid

Little fat boys take the cake

FOUR tubby 10-year-ol boys were revealed yester day as the Plum Cake Gan of Sicily.

They were caught trundl ing £500-worth of stole cake through Trapani in pram. The leader, calle Fattie, confessed to 150 cake shop break-ins.

Police found tuck wort £5,000 in their bedrooms.

A FEW years ago, when I was a Sunday-school teacher for three- and four-year-olds, we were discussing how Jesus is always with us, even though we can't see him. One little boy agreed. "I know he is," he said. "He's the one who opens the doors at the supermarket."

SEARCHING through the frozen turkeys at the supermarket, a friend couldn't find one large enough. Pointing to the turkeys, she asked an assistant, "Do they get any bigger?"

"No, madam," he replied. "They're dead."

zander

AN CHEEK is a twat. Your so-called reporter, who Scott Reynolds can't sing, must be deaf as w unbelievably f**king stupid. All are the best band the ever be. Please sack this utter knob-end.
THE COUCH POTATOES, Tonbridge
PS: You can stick all that Manchester stuff up you ar
PPS: Ian Cheek is a twat.

In Their Own Words

Henry Miller.

WE ARE ACCUSTOMED to think of our-selves as an emancipated people; we say that we are democratic, liberty loving, free of prejudices and hatred. This is the melting pot, the seat of a great human experiment. Beautiful words full of noble, idealistic sentiment. Actually we are a vulgar, pushing mob whose passions are easily mobilised by demagogues, newspaper men, religous quacks, agitators and such like. To call this a society of free-peoples is blasphemous. What have we to offer the world besides the superabandant loot which we plunder from the earth under the manacal delusion that this insane activity represents progress or enlightenment? The land of oppurtunity has become the land of senseless sweat and struggle. The goal of all our striving has long since been forgotten. We nolonger wish to succour the oppressed and homeless; there is no room in this great empty land for those who, like our forefathers before us now seek a place of refuge. Millions of men and women are or were until very recently, on relief, condemned like guinea-pigs to a life of forced idleness. The world, meanwhile looks to us with desperation such as it has never known before. Where is the democratic spirit? Where are the leaders?

To conduct a great human experiment we must first of all have men. Behind the conception MAN there must be grandeur. No political party is capable of ushering in the kingdom of man. The workers of the world may one day ..if they stop listening to their bigoted leaders, organise a brotherhood of man. But men cannot be brothers unless they first become peers, that is, equals in a kingly sense. What prevents men from uniting as brothers is their own base inadequacies. Slaves cannot unite, cowards cannot unite, the ignorant cannot unite. It is only by obeying our highest impulses that we can unite. The urge to surpass ourselves has to be instinctive, not theoretical or believable merely. Unless we make the effort to realise the truths which are in us we will fail again and again. As Democrats, Republicans, Fascists, Communists we are all on one level. That is why we wage war so beautifully. we defend with our lives the petty principles which divide us. The common principle which is the establishment of the empire of man of earth, we never lift a finger to defend. We are frightened of any urge that lifts us out of the muck. We fight only for the status quo, our particular status quo. We battle with heads down and eyes closed. Actually there is no status quo, except in the minds of political imbeciles. All is false. Those who are on the defensive are fighting phantoms.

"IDEALS
BUY
MORE
THAN
MONEY"

BYE!

LOVE MUSIC . HATE FASCISM

· rumble club ·

THE PANTILES, TUNBRIDGE WELLS

ALTERNATIVE LIVE MUSIC
EVERY
FRIDAY & SATURDAY

Jan 17th ANGUS BAGPIPE + PROTEST
+ JOEY FAT + PSEUDO HIPPIES.

Jan 18th HYBRAZIL + CRYSTAL HEIGHTS.

Jan 24th EVEN AS WE SPEAK + HED DOKTERS.

Jan 25th OUT OF MIND + PUMP.

Jan 31st STROOKAS + ASW.

Feb 1st UNDERSTAND + 4 x FOR.

Feb 7th PLAYGROUND + GUINEAPIGS.

Feb 8th DR. TILT.

COMING SOON

GOOBER PATROL, SLUNK, 2000AD, CODE...

£1.00 a Pint 'til 9.30pm

ENTRANCE £3.00
8pm - 1am.

BHP

#2

50p
+ sae

It's summertime, the temperature's rising, hormone levels are rising, bands are gigging, exams are over... and you're reading BHP #2! Ask yourself why - I hope it's late at night and you just can't sleep. But anyway, seeing as you are showing an interest, lets get on. We know there are less interviews in this issue (although the Joeyfat one is very 'interesting' and the U.A. one is 'funny') but that's because there are more general articles to read and a letters section to help encourage your further correspondence. We hope you enjoy it anyway, and if you don't...
You can write to us at :

> BHP,
> 1 Chandos Road,
> Tunbridge Wells,
> Kent, TN1 2NY.

Thanks to everyone who helps and supports us.

> BHP

OK, time for a few bits and pieces. On the 27th June there is a festival type gig at Rusthall playing fields, featuring Joeyfat and lots of 'not so good' bands. Also, on 9th July, Joeyfat are at the Victoria Hall. (Angus Bagpipe were playing there too but it looks like they've broken up now - that sucks!) The Mr T Experience will be at the Robey, in London, on 7th July promoting their new album 'Milk, Milk, Lemonade' with Alloy (Ex-Dagnasty), That's it (Ex-Youth Brigade) and Goober Patrol. Also, Tunbridge Wells' superb hardcore heroes Couch Potatoes have a new LP/CD available in July, called 'Excess All Areas'. It contains 14 great new tracks and is available (£5/LP - £9/CD Postpaid) from Vice Records, 95 Hexham Avenue, Hebburn, Tyne & Wear, NE31 2DL. If you're wise you'll send for it now.

The next 'Gotham' release is a live Jawbreaker tape. Quicksand, Jawbreaker and several other hardcore acts have now signed to majors. Hopefully, 'wunjer' aren't playing soon, but 'code' played at the Rumble club recently and were utter slash. Canterbury's 'Playground' have a new CD out called 'Resilience' - and there are far too many crummy local R'n'B bands around at the moment to shake a shitty stick at. I'm getting bored so I'm stopping here.

"Beauty is Nature's coin...
and the good thereof consists in mutual and partaken bliss."
"Paradise Lost", Milton.

If the Earth were only a few feet in diameter, floating a few feet above a field somewhere, people would come from everywhere to marvel at it. People would walk around it, marvelling at its big pools of water, its little pools and the water flowing between the pools. People would marvel at the bumps on it, and the holes in it, and they would marvel at the very thin layer of gas surrounding it and the water suspended in the gas. The people would marvel at all the creatures walking around the surface of the ball, and at the creatures in the water. The people would declare it precious because it was the only one, and they would protect it so that it would not be hurt. The ball would be the greatest wonder known, and people would come to behold it, to be healed, to gain knowledge, to know beauty and to wonder how it could be. People would love it, and defend it with their lives, because they would somehow know that their lives, their own roundness, could be nothing without it. If the Earth were only a few feet in diameter.

RAMONES

From Blitzkrieg Bop to the 88 bus stop outside the Kensington Hilton. And after eight years I finally get to meet the Ramones. Back in 1976 the Ramones were about the only thing in the USA that *wasn't* boring. They played in London and fulfilled all the hysterical promise of 'Ramones' (an LP). Seeing them live was like driving a car into a wall at 100mph — continuously! After two years of striving and starving in NYC they crossed the sea and found a (spiritual) home. Their impact was phenomenal.

Joey Ramone remembers: "That was the beginning, it was great, historic. Playing the Roundhouse and Dingwalls and selling out. Having all those kids coming to our soundcheck. A lot were to become the Clash and the Sex Pistols and all the groups that followed. It was great. Wild.

"Punk rock changed the world. I feel we revolutionised rock and roll. It was something that just happened. I guess in the same way the Beatles didn't know what was going to happen, or Elvis Presley didn't know what was going to happen. Things were getting pretty dull then and it's getting like that again now. All that synthesiser stuff to me isn't rock and roll, it's elevator music or something. I hear better music in my elevator.

"I guess the groups I liked best were the Buzzcocks, the Undertones and the bands of that era. When they all disbanded I was sorta ... hurt. I thought they were great, even Sham 69."

Last Christmas I heard 'Too Tough To Die' and something in me went WOOSH! Suddenly the Ramones were sounding as fresh and exciting and as gutsy and energetic and as necessary and as *without seat belts* as they were over their first three albums.

Yet 'Too Tough' isn't a throwback or even a mere return to form. Regardless of pedigree it is a vital 1985 record. It has a real *politic* (some thing significantly overlooked by reviews in both The Guardian and Time Out) that explodes in big chunks all over the listener. It is vital in a realist sense. Something that the early 'cartoon' Ramones could never have been.

Joey Ramone opened the hotel room door and bent down to shake my hand. These days the Ramones are very, very real.

Joey: "Whenever I'd read that we were a cartoon it really upset me. I remember doing an interview on the phone with a guy who said 'you're like cartoon characters'. I got really pissed off and said 'what d'ya mean by that?' He said that we had very definite, distinguished personalities. So I didn't mind. *If* that's what it meant."

Dee Dee: "I guess our image paid homage to juvenile delinquency and everybody took us for a bunch of juvenile delinquents."

Joey: "Most bands have no personality. There's millions of synth bands and millions of metal bands all spiked up like David Lee Roth. They usually have one song which is really catchy. To me it's a joke that these guys are stars. These guys are horrible but they make it in America cos America's horrible."

Once upon a time it seemed the Ramones all lived in Manhatten lofts, ate junkfood, watched TV and went to Rockaway Beach in summer.

Joey: "Well, in the beginning I used to share a loft and eat junkfood. I remember the early days when we were all broke with nothing. I used to hang out at CBGB's because it was across the street, just to get warm. I'd rather drink a couple of beers, I guess it's nutritious — I couldn't afford to eat so I figured I'd go across the street and have a couple of beers for dinner. Things have picked up now ..."

In the British press it was Joey the giraffe and Dee Dee the dumb.

Dee Dee: "Yeah, and I don't know why they did that, to me but ... I don't think I'm dumb. I think I'm a very sensitive, deep thinking person. I have a lot of knowledge about life. I've led a very deep and experienced life and I've a lot of knowledge that an older man probably wouldn't have."

Joey: "Just by reading his lyrics how could you think he was dumb? I think he's real articulate. There were things that came out in the press that I wasn't too thrilled about. In fact, at one time I didn't wanna do another interview with the British press ... it was sick. They'd start ripping apart your household, your mother. It was crazy."

Maybe the early Ramones were just too good to be true and no one (in Britain) could believe they really existed! But between 'Rocket To Russia' and the present LP they endured a trough: various so-so producers and a tiresome search for the hit single that would establish them as a mainstream band in the USA. Fortunately (sez I) they never found it despite record company ploys and coloured vinyl (Joey: "'Road to Ruin' came out on *disgusting* yellow vinyl. I think I'm the only person who got a red copy.")

Like a kid defending an ugly pet everybody else wants to stamp on, Joey still claims those mid-period records were good even if, he admits, nobody else likes them.

But now in America hardcore has struck and the Ramones are its natural Godfathers. 'Too Tough' is essential Ramones and essential hardcore. The sound is tough, the vision is bleak.

Dee Dee: "We wanted to make a real Ramones record and recapture us. America is a pretty bleak place, there's no hope really. When we started out singing about politics and stuff all of a sudden it was 'hey, the Ramones preaching left-wing propaganda'. But that's how we felt. We wanted to show we had feelings. We've gotten serious with this album."

Joey: "These lyrics represent us whereas most bands just don't care anymore. There aren't that many that you can really respect. In the 60s I looked up to Pete Townshend and John Lennon, even people that fooled me a bit. I thought they might be more real than they were ... like Alice Cooper. When I first got into him in '72 I thought 'this guy is really sick'! Then I found out he was straight and I was real disgusted and upset. I thought the guy was a real sick necrophiliac and that was great HA! HA! There really aren't many people you can really believe in, they're either dead or don't exist anymore or else they've gotten commercial.

"I feel our product, even though we might have got a little side tracked, is now back on course! It's the perfect album. Very diverse and yet very intense. I think it just reflects the state of the world right now. A lot of tracks touch on the political side like 'Planet Earth 1988' — that song, hey Dee Dee remember when you played it to me on that piano thing? I thought it was great. Every word perfectly stated."

Dee Dee: "It's very flattering to be the top hardcore band in the world but we're not a trend. We're the perfect band for hardcore kids to dance to but they make fun of the old rock and roll of the 50s and 60s whereas we have allegiances to that rock. We really like Buddy Holly."

Joey: "If you take all that old stuff and '76 punk rock there is so much similarity. For a while back then I wanted to do 'Peggy Sue'. I think it's great. I can hear John's guitar in there. Er, John's our guitar player."

Dee Dee: "And everybody copied his style."

Joey: "But that early stuff is great. Purity, the real thing. That's rock music simple, basic and exciting."

Dee Dee: "People have created images of what we're supposed to be like, never give our personalities a chance. Everyone thinks that the Ramones go on stage smashed out of their heads but we don't even get high before we go on."

Joey: "I don't mind them thinking we're out of our minds but we're real, we're us. We're gen-u-ine."

Dee Dee: "We could never be phoneys. The only thing we have to maintain is our dignity. In the future I'd like to write for other people and stuff but I don't want to put pressure on myself. I've already done everything now and I have to live the rest of my years as easy as I can. I hope I never have to get a job!"

The best group in the world. Again.

Learn the secrets of sleeping well

Choose the right kind of mattress

IF YOU were to make a list of your most important possessions, where would your mattress fit in? Probably at the bottom of the list.

Yet this is a big mistake. Most of us spend around one third of our lives in bed – even more than many spend at our jobs. So why do we pay so little regard to our mattresses?

One reason may be that, by the time we get to them, we feel too tired to give the matter any attention. But, by six o'clock next morning, we may feel differently. We may be stiff. Achey. Slow to rise – much less shine.

All night long, according to one doctor, your muscles are working overtime to align your spine. It's no coincidence that many people wake up in the morning with backache, as they haven't given those muscles any time off to rest.

So how can you tell what degree of firmness and which type of mattress is right for you?

Only by experimenting, and letting comfort be your guide. There isn't a bed or a mattress made, that is perfect for everybody – which is why all manufacturers give us a choice. We are all built differently, and have different needs.

But there are two general rules of thumb:

★ An ideal mattress should hold the spine as close as possible to a position you would assume while standing with good posture.

★ This position should be held in a way that distributes body weight evenly, with no one part of the body being pressured more than another.

Before making your mind up, give a mattress a good ten-minute test lie-down in the store. And when the salesman begins to talk about the 'number of coils', don't just shut off. Coils do count, in terms of durability and performance.

A bed board is not a good idea particularly if you've got a sensitive back.

Water beds, however, *are* a good idea. and next to a hard mattress, are the best choice for anybody with back trouble.

Pillows are important too

A good pillow is also important for a restful night's sleep, as you may have noticed if you've ever had to spend a night or two on a couch. But what is the best kind of pillow?

This really depends on what kind of sleeper you are. Those who sleep on their backs should use a pillow that is thin and soft, but not *too* thin and soft, as this can force you to scrunch up your neck and shoulders to keep the pillow in place. This 'work' obviously doesn't relax neck and shoulder muscles.

Anyone who sleeps on their side should also use a thin pillow, but the correct width partly depends on shoulder width. A side sleeper with narrow shoulders would be best off with a really thin pillow, whereas a broader-shouldered individual should choose a thicker type.

The 'best' pillow, generally speaking, is one that discourages you from sleeping on your stomach. This sleeping posture puts pressure on your jaw and irritates neck muscles. It should also eliminate the need to put your arm or hand under the pillow. Sleeping this way can cause pinched nerves in the elbow or wrist.

ARE YOU PREJUDICE... AT ALL?

Prejudism has always been a malignant disease of our society. Deep seated racism and sexism have been a recurrent problem, we have all been confronted by the brick wall of agism, not to mention the political extremities such as facism,which even causes wars. Right now there is a prejudice that is virulently infesting our modern world. It is as bad as agism. It is as bad as racism. It is as bad as sexism. That prejudice is 'Weightism!'

Only a small and ignorant minority of the population still harbour deep racist or sexist views a these prejudices are commonlyseen as unfair and ungrounded; yet weightism is rife, generally being accepted as normal by the public and the media. However, these people are not the same people who are being subjected to hurtful comments every day of their lives. Until you have been on the receiving end of such mindless abuse, you cannot possibly realise what pain and sadness it can cause. Those emotional injuries take far longer to heal than mere physical injuries. Everyone has a personal characteristic that sets them aside from the crowd, but not everyone suffers abuse because of it.

If you are prejudice, then you are a victim of society, narrow-minded, and ignorant. Why can' you wake up and realise that you cannot despise or even criticise a person because of their buil any more than you can criticise them because of their sex or the colour of their skin. What righ have you to dictate how much a person should weigh or how a person should look? None! How would you like to be told what clothes to wear, what music to listen to or what food to eat?

Every single person is a unique individual and as such they must be allowed to be whatever the desire. You should respect a person for what they are; not put them down because they are not what your narrow mind considers to be perfect. Unfortunate people whose minds are so shallo that they will only judge a person by their outward appearance should be pitied as they are depriving themselves of the opportunity of meeting many deeper individuals and thereby broadening their own personality.

The next time that you boast proudly to your friends that you are not prejudice, think carefull about what that statement entails. I hope that your boast is the truth. Prejudism of all sorts must be eliminated from our society before we can all live in harmony!

MAKE 'EM PAY

ROBIN HOOD BANK MANAGER HARTMUT HUETTIG, FROM WEST GERMANY, GAVE OUT OVER £25,000 TO SOME OF HIS POOR CUSTOMERS!

And the best bit, is that ALL the money came from the bank accounts of his RICH clients!

Hartmut, 38, doled out the dosh for almost FIVE years, plundering the lolly from those who would never miss it, he said "why should the rich have everything in this world, its about time we started having an equal share"

Quite right mate, and by the way have you thought about getting a job over here?

RAGE DEDANS (Raging Inside) are "The most new athletic pop band!" Take your distance, we pack a punch. On stage sound machine like an Olympic marathon man. Influenced by Dead Kennedys, Ramones, Stupids and other Bad Brains, we shaped you up all over France and are coming to England soon. This kind of music shoots dead punk dash crackers and middle of the road, semi-retired teenagers. Sensible minds be careful. It hurts

Dr. Sprunghel
Graduated of Parisian Fun Philosophic University

Write to : Brasselet Frederic,
        9 Rue Dauphin,
        94800 Villejuif,
        France.

STROOKAS are a great band, in the Husker Du style, from the Maidstone area. Formed back in April '86, they have a couple of EP's under their belts and have just got around to recording an LP 'Deaf for Dawn' for Vice Records. (Guitar Gangsters, Guttersnipes, Couch Potatoes, Surf City Rockers...). The album is very good and well worth getting hold of. Also check them out live, as they're great... like Kelloggs Frosties.

Write to : Dave Bloomfield,
        70 Rede Wood Road,
        Barming,
        Maidstone,
        Kent, ME16 9HR.

FREEDOM is a plant which grows only from knowledge. It must be watered by faith. It will come to leaf and fruit and flower only in the benevolent sunlight of peace.

—Adlai Stevenson in *The Hutchinson Book of Essays* (Hutchinson)

ANTI SOCIAL BEHAVIOUR

Sweet-Talk

A CHOCOLATE bar has been developed to save lives in sub-zero temperatures. The Canadian Cold Buster bar maximizes heat energy generated when eating it by enhancing use of the body's fat reserves. Students at Canada's University of Alberta tested it by spending three to six hours at between eight and ten degrees C wearing T-shirts and shorts. Those who ate a Canadian Cold Buster were shown to have a 50-per-cent greater tolerance of the cold. Somebody lost or stranded would have at least twice as much time to seek help or shelter.

—*The Times*

FEW things concentrate the mind more efficiently than the necessity of saying what you mean. It brings you face to face with what you are talking about, what you are actually proposing. It gets you away from clichés that not merely substitute for thought but preclude it.

—Edwin Newman in *Across the Board*

A CHILD is not spoiled by giving him what he wants nearly so much as by giving substitutes for what he really wants—attention, interest and understanding.

—Sydney Harris

IF YOU are willing to admit you are all wrong when you are all wrong, you are all right.

—Los Angeles Times Syndicate

DYLAN THOMAS: "Poetry is what in a poem makes you laugh, cry, twist your toes, twinkle, prickle, be silent, know you are alone and not alone in an unknown world."

Buoy Wonder

A WARNING system could save thousands of dolphins each year from death in fishing nets.

A team from Cambridge, Loughborough and Aberdeen universities has been testing a type of "cat's-eye" reflector, detectable by dolphins' sonar. The reflectors are placed on a barrier like a fishing net which stretches 220 yards out to sea across a known dolphin path. Underwater microphones pick up the animals' sonar as they approach. An increase in sonar activity marks the point at which the animals detect the reflectors and alter their course to avoid the barrier.

Early results are encouraging and the next step is the development of a design which can be easily fixed to fishing nets.

—Tom Morton in *The Scotsman*

BEING nice to people who are rude to you is being like a fox.

Unexpected—and undeserved—civility throws people off balance and allows you to take the advantage. "Turn the other cheek" isn't an endorsement of wimps—it is sound advice.

MAN has two ears and one mouth, since he should listen more than he speaks.

—Danish proverb

GAIN all you can, save all you can, give all you can.

—John Wesley

Vicar hit me with a plank

... MORE EXPLOITATION!

Jose Palazo is a man with a passion for conservation. His job as Head Ranger in the Taieen sanctuary, a wetland wilderness of coastal lagoons in the Rio Grande de Sol region of Southern Brazil, means that he must risk his life every day to stop the illegal fur and animal trade in Brazil and protect the large concentrations of ecologically important wildlife that live there.

One of the creatures whose existence in the Taieen sanctuary is threatened by poachers is the Nutria. The Nutria is a small rodent that survives in the wetlands and breeds prolifically all year round, but they are heavily hunted for their beautiful furs. Whilst just over the border in Uruguay it is legal to hunt Nutria, Jose must eradicate the poachers who hunt within the confines of the sanctuary.

Jose and his helpers patrol the sanctuary in all-terrain vehicles, confiscating traps laid by poachers around Nutria nests. These cruel traps initially catch one Nutria in a vice-like grip around its leg, but its cries of pain and anguish soon attract other unsuspecting Nutria who also become ensnared in the hunters' evil iron teeth. Their paws crushed by the traps, bleeding and screaming in pain, the Nutria suffer for between eight and ten hours before the hunter arrives to club them to a final, brutal death, provided that the unfortunate creatures haven't already drowned. The hunters then skin the Nutria and dry their pelts, leaving their corpses to fester in the sun, before selling the furs to factories at a price of £4 for each Nutria skin. The furriers in Montevideo, who are often in league with the government, then export the Nutria fur coats to Europe, North America and Japan, where they are popular status symbols. It takes 24 Nutria skins to make one fur coat, which would then be sold for $1,100. The furriers are not concerned where the Nutria skins come from and the government supports the export of fur coats from Uruguay as a profitable means of obtaining foreign currency.

Jose and his fellow conservationists decided that it was time to put an end to these cruel and needless deaths and smash the contraband in Nutria skins. In order to do this, they needed to catch the middle men who paid the hunters. His friend, Paolo, an undercover agent, disguised himself as a buyer and contacted an infamous dealer to arrange a meeting. Armed enforcement agents then lay in wait for the dealer and his sub-machine gun toting minders to arrive. Fortunately, this time, the dealer and his cronies fell for the trap and were all arrested. Four bags of Nutria skins and one bag of traps were recovered by the Federal Police during this raid. The sting had worked and this ring was broken. The dealer, who will remain anonymous, goes on trial in two months time and if found guilty he will face up to five years in jail. This term may seem a lenient punishment, but as one officer commented : "Brazilian jails are pure hell!".

Even today, thousands of Nutria are killed for the Uruguayan fur trade, despite the courageous efforts of conservationists such as Jose Palazo, and this is only one of many examples of defenceless animals being slaughtered for their coats. It is a fact that all living creatures have a right to exist on this planet, whether they are useful to mankind or not.

So, you might be thinking : "What can I do about this?" Well, it is also a fact that there are still many ignorant, ostentacious people in this country who wear fur coats. You could buy some chewing gum to stick on the next idiot you see wearing a fur coat in the street, or you could try writing to your MP, or the Uruguayan Government, to express your feelings on this matter. Best of all, you could support movements such as 'LYNX' who are doing all they can to ban the fur trade.

Uruguayan Ambassador's Residence,	'LYNX'
1 Camden Hill Road,	P.O.Box 300,
London,	Nottingham,
SE19.	NG1 5HN.
Tel. no. (071) 7276557.	Tel. no. (0602) 413052.

"It takes up to 40 dumb animals to make a fur coat, but only one to wear it!"

JOEYFAT Interview

Joeyfat are a great new band from Tunbridge Wells. We interviewed Matt, the vocalist...

BHP: Joeyfat are a fairly new band, but seem to be causing quite a stir already. Have you played many gigs and what is the 'live' reaction?

Matt: Joeyfat have made a few steps in the right direction, I suppose the showbiz euphemism is 'a handful' of performances so far. I hope that we have bemused people in the audience enough for them to either instinctively revile us or hold a special place for us in their shoddy hearts. Either way they seem to be making the right shapes with their limbs and forcing the right sounds from their hands and mouths. We are a success.

BHP: Your songs seem to be a little out of the ordinary (Cushion Fed, Pass the sprouts, The day I realised I was God...). What are they about and why do you write like this?

Matt: Whatever the opposite of epic is, that's the way to describe the words to the songs. Songwriters always seem to be desparately trying to attach some grand mystery to their subject matter. "I am not a cowboy, a street fighting man or a bluey tinged cloud floating on a sea of damson jam, I'm just this collection of skin, blood and hair". What's so great about that? Well, I'll tell you. Hormones, hunger, getting bits of scum out from under your fingernails; There's so much to discover just about your own personal environment. There's nothing mundane about life and if I want to write a song, a book, a musical about... well, soap for instance, why shouldn't I? I want to cover the component parts of everything, chop them up, stick them back together again and have a righteous belly laugh in the process. Clear? It's all one word you know, but I digress... If I could write one word about each song, it would be the title and if some of the titles have more than one word...

BHP: Has the demo provoked any label interest yet and is there any vinyl on the way? What's your view on the vinyl verses CD argument?

Matt: Yes, the demo has provoked furious head-scratching in some quarters, some glee in others and rumbling apathy in yet another. That's only three quarters as yet. I'm not going to talk about offers we've had because talk is all I'd do. We do have interested labels, it's up to them to garner our interest. When they do a vinyl product (Yum! Marketing, storyboards, make-up, extras...) will be forthcoming. This will probably be a regular, old-fashioned single with two or three tracks on it, if I may state the probably quite obvious. As far as the great pressing debate, I would have to say this: Vinyl is sensual; slipping it from it's sleeve, caressing it with a needle and adoring it's imperfections. CD's are cheeky and cute, but rather unsatisfying aesthetically. I do not care how much it takes for Mr Bloke to update his Buddy Holly collection; I do care if increasing expense takes innovative snippets out of the reach of the discerning public, be they producers or receivers.

BHP: Joeyfat have a very original sound. Does the band have any influences, or set out to create a certain sound? Who do you listen to?

Matt: About influences, I can only talk personally. In musical terms I love anything melodramatic or just plain witty; po-faced posing is not for me. I would name some names, but I know from my own appalling musical snobbery that this would merely lead anyone reading this to have dreadful preconceptions as to what we at Joeyfat are doing. We are creating a certain sound.

BHP: Is being a 'Tunbridge Wells band' good or bad? What's the 'scene' like. in your opinion?

Matt: Being based in Tunbridge Wells is both good and bad, or neither. Young people here are stuck in the same terrifying ruts as everywhere else, but they are united by common features. Most suffer from a middle-class lethargy, from which their only release is an irritating tendency to bring everything down to one sentence - "Nothing ever happens here!" I suggest the death penalty for utterance of this phrase. However, I also believe that the contrast of something as agile, intelligent and internally violent as Joeyfat coming from a town known only for it's self-righteous disgust and revolting shopping arcades will bring down the very walls of... well, the music industry anyway. Small but important victories.

BHP: What would be your ideal day?

Matt: A day free from snivelling irritants but full of coriander and cumin.

BHP: Do you enjoy working in the studio? Are you happy with what you have done so far?

Matt: The studio is a necessary evil, as far as I'm concerned. Parts of it are exhilarating, when something that you hadn't expected rears it's head from the mix, but mostly it's just a time piece exercise, getting a representation of what the band does to a neat format. Jason is probably the man to speak to about this because he understands the technicalities of it all better than I do; what he doesn't know about gates and compression buts worth knowing. As far as being happy with what we've recorded so far, yes, I'm extraordinarily happy with the songs and the way they come across and I know that they are much, much better than anything else I'm hearing at the moment, but there is so much more Joeyfat can do. Frightening!

BHP: What do you think of TV? Do you have a favourite programme?

Matt: TV is astonishing isn't it. If you stared out of the window for five hours a day, people would certify you (and probably quite rightly), which means that TV is supposed to be more spiritually and intellectually challenging than staring out of the window, a pastime, a hobby. I hate it because I watch it, I would be glad if I was rationed to say two hours a week, then you'd really have to be choosy about your viewing. The only programme I can remember having a burning need to watch was Twin Peaks, but I dare say that's suffering a giant backlash at the moment so I shouldn't say it. Even then, much as I loved watching it, I can honestly say that if I'd never seen it my life would be much the same. So that's TV in a cocked-hat matey.

BHP: How would you label Joeyfat - Hardcore, grunge, jazz, pop or what?

Matt: I'm looking forward to a time quite soon when the music press will be making up a new label just for Joeyfat; how about Sprout-tending or Slugblubbery? We are what we are, the only way I could describe us would be to tell you what sort of people won't like us, because there are many I'm afraid that just will not be able to cope.

BHP: What are the bands' main aims? What do you hope to acheive musically, lyrically and personally?

Matt: Joeyfat's aims are to please ourselves and keep on being selfish in front of as many people as possible. We know the shortcuts, they are just as unappealing as their results. As for the three 'llys', I just want to explore everything as far as I can in the time available.

BHP: What are Joeyfat's future plans, say over the next 12 months?

Matt: As soon as we've signed the right package we will throw our first release into the pit of expectation. We will then be confronting people, as many as possible, in person. I can't tell you what to expect, only that it will be extreme.

BHP: Closing comments?

Matt: Only this - It's all one word!

Joeyfat can be contacted at 1 Chandos Road, Tunbridge Wells, Kent, TN1 2NY. Get in touch!

Are you a positive person?

Most of us are aware that we can make ourselves ill with excessive worry, fear or sorrow. But did you know that we can also stay healthy – or become healthy – by adopting positive attitudes and behaviour?

We tend to think that, though we may make ourselves ill, in order to become well again, we must consult a doctor. But your state of mind can have a far more profound effect on your health than all the pills and treatments in the world. If your attitudes can work to make you disease-prone, they can also operate the other way, to make you health-prone.

DON'T GET CAUGHT!

Pissed off from Tunbridge Wells..............
10 things that really get up my nose.

1. Taxi drivers.They think they know everything about everything and they're the most arrogant, cocky loud-mouthed gits to ever walk this earth. Wankers!
2. The way pakies train their little kids to spy on you while you're in their corner shops-just incase you nick something.Cunts!
3. Total nob ends who punch and kick in a mosh pit thinking they're well 'ard.Fucking shits!
4. Cocks who walk around in Nirvana t-shirts thinking they're so weird and alternative. Sad bastards!
5. Indie fans who wear beads in their hair and long tassely purple dresses and think they're different and original when they're just the same as a million other dipsticks and talk a load of bollocks about the environment and other pretentious shit like "society" and "oppression".6th form tossers!
I shit on you!
6. Total utter plebs who work in guitar shops and treat you like a thick shit,patronising you silly.Go anally consume a Charvel you annoying toss pots!
7. Fucking dickheads in utter shite cheesy bands who huff and puff if you ask them if you can borrow a plectrum for you to support them. Why don't these ageing rockers get real and give up or better still-kill themselves. Frigging wankheads!
8. When BMW 5 series do 40 mph in the middle lane of the motorway.If you fucking brought a 2000 cc fuel injected car-fucking use it you cunts!!
9. How many times have you bought a drink in a club or gig and have had more water in it than alcohol? Stingy gits!The next time i'm served a watered down pint i'm gonna drink it whole and puke it over the barman! Shit heads! I paid for a pint of strong bow not strong H2o.Cunts!
10. And finally,the way the shower always goes ice cold the split second you're lavered in shower gel.There's some one up there who does'nt like me.The cunt!

The Relentlessness of Nature

The wind blows across the valley
the blue mirror is no longer still,
reliable as the tickings of a grandfather clock
it laps against it's rocky surround
in perfect time with each beat of my heart,
tumultuous and undulating,
it's movements will remain long after I am gone,
relentlessly eroding mans rocky dam
it will once again be free.
You cannot contain the forces of nature
they are stronger than those of man
and will exist long after we have departed.

Steve Gamage '92.

'Dad'.

The greatest man that ever lived,
Noble, considerate, honest and kind,
The only man that gained my respect,
And justified my unique admiration,
His love created and cultured me,
Now to bloom as his rightful heir,
Caring and trusting, he never failed me,
Securing my happiness and safeguarding my future,
The cornerstone of my youthful years,
Who educated my mind and stimulated my conscience,
So that I might truly appreciate the finer things in life,
Above all that was petty, his unquestionable loyalty,
Conjuring joy from the bleakest of times,
He congratulated me on my acheivements,
And guided me through my darkest problems,
He imparted his wisdom to broaden my character,
Through him I grew into a man,
Forever my closest ally, my truest friend,
Trustworthy and dependable as a grandfather clock,
My raft in a swirling sea of torment,
My gun in a room of hooded gangsters,
Perfect in every way, my priviledge to bear his noble name,
Worthy of the highest praise and still more before surfeit is re
Nature's flowers cannot compare to his beauty,
Firelight dwindles in comparison to his aura of shining stars,
My lovers came and passed, like fleeting showers in spring,
But his love for me remained each day as the sun in my sky,
They declared 'true love' but I know now,
That I have only once felt that emotion,
This love goes deeper than my human heart,
This indestructible bond everlasting,
Unbroken by time, or the grim intrusion of death,
Unjust premature demise, wrenching him from my arms,
Our bodies no longer entwined, our souls will always be togeth
The comfort of a soft, warm bed on a cold, wet night,
Replaced by the cold harsh rock of reality,
Being mortal, I am powerless,
So unfair, and yet I am helpless,
Immortal, he will live with me for all eternity,
His memories will always live within me,
His glorious name survives by my life,
I miss him with all of my heart,
I would give all that I own and more,
To hold him and hear his voice once again,
Mutual pride and mutual love,
Exclusive emotions of father and son.

Steve Gamage '92.

LETTERS

Dear Dave & Steve,

I am writing to congratulate you on your brilliant first issue of BHP. I enjoyed the Green Day interview, although I would question Tre's subconscious sexuality, and I thought that the Jailcell Recipes live photos were excellent. Also, I agree with Understand; i've been to several Couch Potatoes, Angus Bagpipe and Joeyfat gigs in Tunbridge Wells and they were all great.

It's good to read a fanzine that is not pretentious and politically orientated, but is just good fun. Talking of good fun, I noticed a few references to skateboarding in your fanzine and look forward to reading a whole skate page in the next issue, as I'm trying to learn to skateboard at the moment but I'm not very good. By the way, who is Robbie Reid? Also, who writes your reviews? - He doesn't pull any punches does he! Keep up the excellent work.

Cheers
Jon

Ed. Glad you liked issue one Jon. Robbie is, or was, Jailcell Recipes' vocalist and is also a rad skater, but it doesn't look like his stuff made this issue either, sorry. Most of our obnoxious reviews are written by a demented little creature called Kris and I'm afraid he's probably made more enemies this issue. But to all brave bands - send in stuff for a review, we'll tell him to be kind.

Dear BHP,

I know this is a case for many arguments to start but don't you find religion interesting in some way? There is so much of the stuff about, ranging from the nerdy Bible bashing Evangelist - don't talk about sex, less of the dirty talk, _ sort of people to the secretive brain washing moonies. There are so many questions raised about the meaning of life : why us humans actually exist. Have we got a meaning in life, or are we just here to fulfil our own needs? These 'religions' try to find the answer to these questions and more, but do they succeed?
All religions around the world are based on a supreme being, something that is beyond our understanding. I think all tribes and cultural human beings have a sense to worship. Like people worshipped the sun which was way beyond our time. But as God isn't visible it's more of a mystery. All people need to base their life on something, eg, music, drugs, money, or whatever. I'm sure everyone should believe in something. I believe in God and Christianity!
I think people need to decide whether they believe in God or not. If you are agnostic you must be a really doubtful and confused person.
Atheism has no moral power; it doesn't change lives, like people can just turn round a new man/woman. To be this kind of person must feel as if life has no purpose. I think religion has a purpose; people feel that they are not quite complete as a person and they have a desire to search for something.
Our conversation shows our values as away that we've done wrong, condemning dishonesty, greed, selfishness along with mugging and rape. Why should we care about these values? If we are all here to eventually die, why care about standards and values? But no society lives like this. It's come from a wise moral mind - God.
That is all I have to say for now.

C.L.

Ed. Make up your own minds!

Dear BHP,

My friend bought a copy of the first issue of BHP whilst shopping in *That Shop* and passed it to me to read after she had read it, saying that it was the best 50p that she had spent all day. I thoroughly enjoyed reading your magazine but I thought I should make a few suggestions.

Firstly, whilst I totally agree with your views on subjects such as 'factory farming' and support all the animal rights campaigns, I think that the problem could be addressed with a little more tact, in order to acheive better results. Whilst exposing the true horrors of factory farming is necessary, the author almost scares the reader and makes them feel sick rather than prompting them into action, and this article was, in my view, excessive and out of place in your otherwise light-hearted and well written magazine.

Secondly, perhaps you should review films currently showing at local cinemas and newly released videos, as well as local concerts of all types of music, as your magazine comes across as a local 'whats-on' magazine. I like reading about local bands and events as they are more relevent to our lives than internationally acclaimed bands. Please can we have an interview with the Couch Potatoes - they're great!

Thirdly, I feel that BHP would be the ideal vehicle to express views on really important local topics and I would strongly urge you to look closely at local goings on as they will provoke the most interest.

In closing, I would like to say good luck with BHP and I will certainly buy my own copy of the next issue, especially if my letter is printed.

Yours sincerely,

Su Kitard

Ed. Thanks Su. That can't be your real name! Firstly, about the 'Factory Farming' article; we weren't being scary or sick, we were simply stating facts, trying to be informative. The truth often sucks! Secondly, about reviews; BHP is an 'open fanzine' that welcomes any contribution from anyone. Maybe you could write us some reviews and send them in. Also, if anything interesting happens locally we'll try to cover it, if we don't die of shock first!
PS. There was to have been a Couch Potatoes interview in this issue, but they're so lazy they haven't given it to us yet!

Dear Sirs,

What can I say, I am impressed. Never before have I read a musically orientated fanzine that has stirred me so much that I feel compelled to write. BHP is the most professional and intelligent fanzine ever published and if you manage to maintain this high standard of thought provoking articles I am sure that your local efforts will be rewarded with a nationwide readership. Your contributors seem to be able to capture the essence of the more important things in life and put their views across with such conviction that it really puts all trivial matters into perspective. I thought the article about 'being yourself' was great and I would love to meet the author. The pensive quotations from H. G. Wells and Julia Soul added an intellectual touch to your 'zine and I strongly suggest further Henry Miller excerpts - the man is a genius. The Editor of BHP must be a genius too.

A fellow intellectual.

Ed. Cheers Magnus!

Dear Editor, & sports fans,

What is music and why do we like it ?

Having lived for two and a half years in Northern Scandinavia, Finland to be exact, I have really come to the conclusion that music in England is an 'excuse'. An excuse for what? you may ask. Well, whatever you want - for good or bad. Having read your first edition, I agree with Ray from the Hard-Ons (Music is more about fashion in England). It works from the Plastic Pop music you see on Top of the Pops to the so called metalheads, hip-hoppers, Indie and assorted Punk music. Each has their own purpose for liking any particular style of music.

Let's look at why we like music; is it because of the screaming lead guitar solos?, is it because you fancy the lead singer?, maybe because all your mates are into it?, clothes?, stage diving?, you name it - what is the reason? I find nothing more funny than watching teenagers, aged 17 to 19, with an attitude problem. Silly little middle class kids into hardcore, like nothing else matters. You can guarantee that in 3 or 4 years time they will denounce what they were into and say 'Oh what a laugh that was', when at the time it was their way of life. 'Bullshit'. Nothing worse than seeing someone selling his old record collection and saying how could I have liked that. Surely what you like at the precise moment you will say in a few years time is crap. So stop and look at why we like music. Music should be a personal thing. Ok, you like a band and it suddenly becomes a success and all of a sudden people who you thought idiots are listening to the same music as you. Virtually everyone I know would say that I don't like them anymore. The band hasn't changed, they play the same music. Of course there is commercial music; 99% of chart music is, but just because a band becomes successful it doesn't mean it has sold out. Think am I liking this because 'Oh we think we are being different' or do we really love the music for what it is. Music should not be a fashionable thing, or something that is only liked because you think you're being different. I personally would listen to nearly everything, apart from Rap as they have nothing to say. Racism does work both ways you know Public Enemy. Anyway, if you agree or disagree, or don't understand nevermind. Long live good music!

Nik
An old buddy of Steve & Dave's.

PS: Long live Couchies! Good Chinese food (Mei Mei House). Saying somebody is good looking is not sexist. Opening doors for women is purely polite, not sexist. I like a good steak, but I don't strangle chickens. Finnish beer is great - try it. Manchester United will win the first division. Old friends are the best friends. People living on mumsy & dadsy's money suck - get a job. Vote Labour. The world doesn't hate you, so remove the chip. I like my Mum & Dad, So should you!

<u>Ed.</u> Well, Nik's letter has raised some controversial points, which is the sort of letter I like. However, I can't agree with his comments on Rap. I feel it is the most important music genre of the '90's, with plenty to say about most important subjects. Check out Ice-T.

NECROSANCT (EXITERNITY DEMO) - Hideous raw buzz! This is just a few songs off the next LP, so wait 'til that comes out and then don't buy that either. One of the songs is called "Undeath Dead Dying" which made me laugh, but alas I fear the band weren't joking! Avoid at all costs.

Dear BHP,

Ray from the Hard Ons sucks!

?

<u>Ed.</u> Sucks what?

MEGA CITY 4 - STOP 7"

A nice mellow indie/fuzz pop offering from the Megas.Watered down guitars and rich harmonies blend to make this a very radio friendly song. It has a sort of catchy laid back feeling to it,similar to the vibe you get offof Dinosaur Jr(it's as if he sung this sitting under a tree in a field one sunny day).I prefer their harder tracks myself,but this is a fine single and worth buying if you dig this stuff.Other trax include "Desert song","Back to Zero" and "Overlap".On red vinyl everywhere!

"Mum", said her adolescent son, "What is Capitalism?" "I heard some bloke talking about it on the bus today."

"Well," said the mother, surprised at her son's question "Capitalism was a system and a system is what a society lives in, like Socialism, or Apartheid, or Facism, but we live in a system who believe in Anarchism."

"Yeah, but the man on the bus said there was a lot of trouble when there was Capitalism!" said the boy quizically.

"Oh there was." replied the mother.

"What kind of trouble was there? I don't understand." he said.

"Like I said, Capitalism was a system that society lived in," she said, "But very different from how we live today. Firstly, the biggest trouble with Capitalism was that to eat, live, have anything or even go anywhere you would have to have worked long hours for money which you exchanged for food, clothing and shelter, and worst of all health, because you had to pay for treatment in hospitals or at the dentist. People believed that the more money you had, the more superior a person you were, which in turn caused a lot of trouble. Obviously not everyone agreed with Capitalism and fought back, so the leaders of the society employed people to enforce their rules and laws, hence their name of the 'Police Force'. You're Grandad could tell you a few stories about the police force; he still remembers the last years of Capitalism."

"But Mum" said the boy, "If everyone didn't break the law, then there would be no more trouble."

"It wasn't that simple my dear. Laws weren't invented and enforced to benefit poor lower class people, as the system named us all, because say for example if someone steals food or clothing or money to get the bare essentials because they couldn't find work to purchase such goods, if caught they were locked in a prison, which was a place you would have been locked up in until the people who enforce the ruler's wishes say you should be allowed to be free again. Sometimes people were even killed for breaking the law or going against the State or Government."

"So why don't people steal food and all that now?" asked the boy.

"Because now everything is free and we all work together to produce our needs and to share our skills and knowledge, and anyone can have whatever they need, as all production is shared equally.

"The man on the bus said we could have had been in Anarchy sooner, but we were fighting each other." said the kid.

His mother had to think hard about this one as she didn't understand why people wanted to fight all the time, and not direct their anger on the real problem.

"Well darling, as I understand it, Capitalism breeds violence and hatred into peoples' minds through television and newspapers known as the media."

"But how could the media make people fight?" interupted the son.

"Not all people were equal; some considered themselves better because of their position in society and of course having loads of money helped them to get whatever they wanted. This made people angry so they fought back, but they were struggling for freedom. But for a long time a lot of peoplr fought each other over the colour of their skin, or even which football team they supported. This hindered any chance of freedom because it divided the people. Instead they could have worked together to beat the rulers, which inevitably happened but only when all the people got together to fight together..."

"And people realised that all we have to do is stand together and we can achieve anything." the kid said, continuing his mother's sentence.

The mother gave her son a big hug and said "Things really were strange in those days. I'm just glad to be able to say that the human race didn't tolerate a world run by violent, greedy people and watch the destruction of their planet. I mean we are an intelligent species. We can think for ourselves and understand that if we are all equal and work together WE PROSPER TOGETHER!

REVIEWS

DAG NASTY - FOUR ON THE FLOOR L.P.

Shit!Shit!Shit!This is a MONSTER!!
I thought DN were a spent force after the pathetic
Field Day L.P. So did i,but this is just poptastically
brilly nicey!(And their best record ever to boot!)
A titanic album packed with emotion,power,melody,riffs
that make you shit your pants and punchy hooks that
leave every song a sparkling gem.So here goes the run-
down.Opener "Still Waiting" is the best song ALL never
wrote."Going Down" is an adrenaline rush of pure pop
H/C."Turn it Around" is a mellower sumery affair with
a beautiful ending that would make the most hardened
philistine weep with utter appreciation for musical
aesthetics(What the F!!!!-Ed)."Million Days" is so
summery it oozes pollen,it brings a tear to my eye.
An amazingly uplifting song which has such a positive
vibe that runs thru it.The first side closes with
"Roger" a 2 minute hardcore stomp.Ripping!!
Side 2 opens with the poptasmically spiffing "S.P.3".
Some of the best lyrics i've readia stroke of genius.
"We went wrong" is a melancholic love song but is so
rousing(coer!) i end up getting a sore throat shouting
the words (not that you'd care though)."Down Time" is
probably the weakest song on the album but is still
slipping nice though!"Lie Down and Die" is a U.K Subs
cover sung by bassist Roger and is excellent and last
up is the humungus "Mango".A true classic if ever there
was one.That a song!
This is THE album to drive to with the windows down and
the sun roof open on a summers afternoon.Total utter
classic.Buy it or..buy it!?

SPERMBIRDS - EATING GLASS L.P.

Their latest L.P offering and a fine one at that
mein führer.'Eating Glass' is a real grower and
there are some hot cuts (man!) such as the title
track and the blinding 'You're only as good as
your last war' which deals with the jingo-istic
post Gulf fever that swept the U.S.
Things follow in the same vein as 'Common Thread'
although the music has a slight 'chugga-chugga'
American thrash touch to it and Hollis's vocals
sound alot like Nuclear Assault,although this is
by no means a thrash album!!But a more groove H/C
with a punk edge.Live the 'birds were awsome,
Hollis is such a brilliant frontman/singer-he blew
me away.Anyway,if you're a fan then you've probably
got it already,if you're not then tape it off a mate.
It's good but they're better records around to spend
your money on like...um...well...Green Day...Samiam..
Dag Nasty...Fugazi...Nirva(STOP IT-Ed!)..um...who else?
...Mr T Experience...Couch Potatoes...get the picture??

BUZZCOCKS - covers comp L.P.

Buzzcocks covers compilation time.Um...interesting.
Best cuts are the Dough Boys "Girl from the chain
store" fucking utter classic!The Fluid's "Ch Shit"
is real good(sounds like the actual original)end
Big Drill Car's "I don't mind" is a peach.Oh,and
Alice Donut's "E.S.P" is both original and exellent.
Okay cuts are Naked Raygun's "Love Battery" and
Coffin Break's "What do i get?".Electric Love Hog's
"Boredom" is not bad,oh before i forget-stick Porn
Orchard's "Why can't i touch it?" in the 'best cuts'
section of this review cos it's....er..good.
Pretty shit ones are Dead Spot's "Orgasm Addict"
which is the worst bastardization of a good song i've
ever heard(along with the Almighty's cover of 'Bodies')
The Accused "Lipstick" is donkey shit and the Lunachick's
"Noise Annoys/Promises" is surprisingly crap.All in all
an interesting album but really for fans only.Unless
you've got loads of wonga to dosh around.

DICKIES - Live in London 1990 (at the Dome) L.P

A pissing hot live album by the Dickies(woops,typing error!)
America's answer to the Damned and punk legends to boot.
Listen to this and you're in for a treat:Hi-energy
modified party punk trax(with touches of Hanoi Rocks
+ Ramones) fall over themselves to grab you by the
nasty scrotum till you cum with delight.There are truck
loads of cool songs on this album including loads of covers
such as the brilliant "Eve of Destruction",Sabbath's "Paranoid"
the Zep's "Comuni Breakdown" plus a weird version of
"Bana Splits" which just about sums up the attitude of this
zaney group.If you're into '77 punk-get this or be damned.

COUCH POTATOES + PSEUDO HIPPIES (live)

The Pseudo's took to the stage at 9.30 to a busy Rumble
Club and opened with their superb "Hey You!" a sort of
mega fast 'Last Caress' and 'Blitzkreig Bop' hybrid.
Cool stuff.A new one "A.P.L.S" rushed by (very Hardons)
before the 50 second 3 chord mosher "Bubble gum"
erupted from the marshalls.A brief interuption followed
re-erecting the mic stands due to the stage diving,
before they plunged into their other 3 chord monsters.
A couple of covers ended the night,i think they were
'Territorial Pissings','Wasted' and 'Sniff some glue'.
And it was all over.The Pseudo Hippies are a very young
3 piece and have improved over their months of gigging.
Their brand of 3 chord fuzz pop follows in the same line
as the Buzzcocks,Ramones,Identity,Hardons and the
Senseless Things and if you like popcore you'll love them.
Good stuff!!
The Tun. Wells H/C heroes the Couch Potatoes return for
the first home gig since the Green Day christmas bash.
Fresh from the studio recording their debut album they
launch into the groove instrumental of "Lunchbox" then
onto the scorcher "Why",oh and incase the Couchies are
new to you they play a blend of Californian style riffy
popcore similar to groups like All,Samiam,Dag Nasty,
Green Day,Big Drill Car,Descendents etc..Very happy and
very good!
They play tons off their album-to-be such as the awesom
"Three" and the Big Drill Car-ish "Hole".Then onto a few
covers,"Six Pack","Yuppies Suck" and "I like food" which
go down brilliantly.By now the crowd is well an' truely
cream crackered,the walls are dripping sweat but the
Couchies and various members of Understand,Angus Bagpipe
and the audience dive into a cover of the Pseudo Hippies
blistering "Hey You!".Cripes!Excellent!
Anyway,the gig was a total stormer.All went away feeling
totally satisfied,wet(coer!),knackered,pissed,ears ringing
and panting for more.Till the next time......

Tun.Wells.Rumble Club. 24th APRIL 1992

DEMOS-DEMOS-DEMOS

Demo section.Right i'll keep it fairly brief coz
i don't know how much space i've got left.Well
here is a collection of the demo's from the best
bands that play in the Tun.Wells area.Check 'em
out quick before they get big-then you'll have
something to boast to your friends about.

Demo no.1 JOEY PAL.
What a mixed bag we have here.I honestly can't
say what style of music this excellent band play.
There are bits that remind me of Meds,then
Fugazi then All then Danzig then (old) Nirvana-
oh shit! well,look,if you're into guitar based
rock then you will love this lot.A superb demo.
8 songs-all of them killers.Played with real
conviction.Excellent production-better than most
of my records i've got!!

Demo no.2 UNDERSTAND-rung.
This Southend quintets 3rd demo to date and
record companies have started sniffing.I feel
sorry for them-the Undies stink!!
Anyway,we have 6 fucking immense songs in the
funk/groove H/C vein similar to Quicksand
Fugazi and Shelter but with a lot of originality.
There are some awesom songs on this,like "Downer"
and "Which Direction".Seriously,if you're into
any guitar bands then get your dirty paws on this
gem NOW!!!!

Demo no.3 The PSEUDO HIPPIES-okki-tokki-unga.
The Pseudo Hippies first 'proper' demo to date
and a real corker too!The Pseudos play simple
3 chord popcore that'll have you bouncing off
the monitors in no time!From the Buzzcockonian
'Pretty Girl' through to the Hardonesque
'Bubble Gum' you can't go much wrong.Stand out
track is the awesom 'Hey You!' a classic in the
making.I've got it on good authority that their
next tape will be a ripper!and probably secure
them a deal!Can't wait.See ya down the front.

Demo no.4 ANGUS BAGPIPE.
I've seen this band live more times than i can
remember an' i tell you,they fucking kill!
But this demo was a bit of a disapointment.
Sure it's their first but the production could
be a lot better.The vocals are too loud,
guitars too soft and everything is muffled.Well,
that aside the actual music is top notch.Great
groove H/C like the Spermbirds but with a rap
edge vocal delivery.Although the lyrics suck
in places ("eat meat then you advocate death??")
I know they can do better but we've gotta wait
till the next tape.Stand outs are "Killing Fields"
"Crime Squad" and "Violence Free".A real good demo.
Get it.But please see 'em live-they're the best!!!

To obtain any of these demos contact the fanzine
address.Cheers!!!!

SENSELESS THINGS - HOLD IT DOWN 7"

Yet another coloured vinyl 99p single from those
Twickenham noisters.'Hold it down' boasts a fine
melody (albeit a Nirvana one) that oozes maturity.
Gone is the heads down 3 chord Ramones stuff and in
is the spagetti western intros and eerie harmonics.
Still fugging cool though.And it charted too!

Hard-ons - WHERE THE WILD THINGS ARE - DOUBLE 7"

The latest Hardons 7" comes with an extra single by
another Oz band 'the Celibate Rifles' who guess what?
Are'nt much cop.Though the Hardons are and their two
songs-"Sorry" and "Lose it" are superb."Sorry"(for
those who care)is a 2 minute grunge/pop feast with
ch so familiar 3 chord melodic chorus."Lose it" is
a stonker of a balled,similar to "Jaye's song" but
borrows heavily from Sabbath,building towards the end.
Different but safe!Can't wait for the album.This
limited double 7" retails for a fiver.Beware.

MEGA CITY FOUR - SHIVERING SAND 7" (big life)

A brilliant summer single from the Mega's.Mellow,warm,
melodious,happy,sunny-oh shit-i can feel my hay fever
coming on.'Shivering Sands' sounds like a laid back
Identity and makes me feel like running thru corn
fields naked(What?-Ed)The two new B-sides are also
groovy.'Everybody loves you' is a more pacey affair
and the short burst of 'Disturbed' reminds me alot
of Green Day.By the time you read this it's probably
already charted.Worth buying just for the cover.

PARASITES - EN HOMAGE AUX BEATLES 7"(shredder)

No 942 of a pressing of 1,966.Shipped all the way from
New Jersey via Rough Trade,London.Ha!Three songs,two
of which are Beatles' covers.The first original is the
super-duper popcore of 'Love me too'-what the Ramones
would have sounded like in the 60's.'I feel fine' is
identical to the fab 4's version and 'Paperback Writer'
is cool too,although i can't compare it as i hav'nt
heard the original.A bloody good record,but not worth
£4.My advice,get hold of 'Parasitmania' it's a corker!

YOUTH FED UP - ...rising sun

French Canadians hey? Jesus Christ!The French are
bad enough,but Canadian aswell!!The music's shit-
boring,uninspiring drivel and the 'singer' sounds
like the police man from 'Allo Allo'.Take a load
of these lyrics-"If you see someone all diform,
you should not laugh from him cos imagine that
this thing succeed to you,ofcourse you won't find
funny,so never smile.So here they come,walking all
quaver.They don't look truley pity.They're not able
to express themselves a lamentable cry,it's all you
ear!'And they get worse (or better if you like a
laugh).AVOID.

BUZZCOCKS - The Grand · 31-1-92.

Me and Tom made our way round the corner to the
'Grand' in Clapham(S.London) after getting pissed
in McDonalds.9,40 and the Buzzcocks greeted this
new Actoria type venue with the riotous 'I don't
know what to do with my life'-Ace!
But,Jesus,are they old!And seeing them sing '..My
Life' at about 35 years old,did make me cringe a
bit.But it's entertainment right?An' tonite they
sure did entertain!
They played 'Get on your own' and 'I don't mind'
which were pure refined estasy.Then onto a couple
of new ones which were excellent on first listens
(and even better on the 2nd night) plus their last
single 'Last to know' which was fugging great!
Next up was another classic (an over used word i
know,but when youre dealing with this band,no other
word suffices) 'Harmony in my head' and the much
covered 'Everybody's Happy Nowadays'.
 A few more rushed by,till they finished with the
utter gems of 'What do i get?' and 'Ever fallen in
Love'.Iwet myself.Full stop!
 Off they hobbled for the customary break till the
crowd chanted them on again.The dual buzz bombs
'Orgasm Addict' and 'Boredom' blasted the set to
an end.The bouncers gave up,as a stage invasion
brought 'Boredom' to a rousing finale.(On the 2nd
night they came on again and played the punk classic
'Fast Cars')
I died and went to heaven with an angel sucking my
fat one!Nuff said.

MORAL CRUX - Live radio broadcast '89

Moral Crux.The latest Gotham Tape release.The crux
live are reminiscent of the Ramones/Descendents and
White Flag.This was recorded in the U.S of A in 198
and is good quality,catchy-definatly a grower.Keeps
in the 'Gotham' tradition. i.e. cool.

SUSPECT DEVICE - shouting Music Vol.4

In conjunction with Suspect Device fanzine.A fairly
decent tape.Stand outs include-Flame On,Couch Potat
and Goober Patrol.Rejects include-Herb Garden & Wall
for effect.The rest?Mediocre.Period.S.D. have got
their hearts in the right place but maybe next time
better bands will get in touch with them.

BEHIND THE MASK - comp

McDonald's benefit tape.And not bad again.Fairly ave
shit,apart from two gems from the Couchies;'New One
'I don't think so'.Again not bad.But when will i
hear a comp tape that will blow me away? Answer-
When the Pseudo's,Understand,Angus Bagpipe and the
Couchies are on it-that's when.

GIVE ME HOMEBREW OR GIVE ME DEATH - com

Right!I'm gonna review this while i'm listening to
it-so here goes.
HayWire? Boring H/C.
Raging Kipper? 'Bangs Drums' Stone Roses cover.Amusi
Stormed?Reggae!!Yeah!
Couchies? 'No More'-classic!
Shock Treatment? Endearing H/C
Nick Toczek? Some hippy poet.Fuck off!
Bear Beast? It's that road drill again!
V.S.S? Early sounding Cure with woman singing.
Raging Kipper? What a name!
HayWire? See above.
Nick Toczek?Fuck off again you sad,sad turd.
Second side,same as the first,judy is a punk,her mot
...-Kris,don't get carried away!

DINOSAUR Jr - GREEN MIND L·P

Right!Time to educate all you H/C freaks!
Total guitar overkill.Fuzz,arpeggios,power chords,
grunge,wild solos-Mascis.Period.
'The Wagon' kicks of affairs-and what a song.Total ut
classic."I ring the door bell in your mind,but it's
locked from the outside."Yeah...right mate.
The whole first side is a blast through dreamland,flo
on the husky(dü) meandering melodies and surfing on
those fuzzed out geetars.Fucking ace!(oh,can i swear
these reviews Dave?).Side 2 is a mellower affair read
orgasm with the excellent title track.Dinsaurs best
album by far and their first on a major(WEA).
A supremely triumphant record.

LEATHER FACE - Not superstitious 12"

First single from their 'Mush' album and what a
corker too!Actually i expected them to be in a more
H/C vein but musically this is very reminiscent of
Mudhoney's jangly shit.I suppose they're the U.K's
biggest H/C band now that Snuff have split and
they've probably got the biggest crusty following
this side of Ozric Tentacles-don't know why cos this
stuff is really melodic-not that crusties don't like
melody,but...you know.Anyway the single is pretty
excellent and worth all of its £1.50 cos it's backed
with "Message in a bottle" and "Trench foot" giving
the poor crusties their value for (begged) money.

Mudhoney - Every Good Boy Deserves Fudge LP

Mudhoney.Good name that.Sums this album up perfectly
There's grunge oozing here and there like nobody's
business.'..Fudge' is a natural progression from
their 'Mudhoney' opus and definetly better too.
There are some pretty amazing songs on this record.
You know,the ones that whatever you're doing you jum
up and pretend you're in the band.Jumping around you
bedroom with your teeth clenched,shouting the choru
Deja-vu anyone?"Thorn","Let it slide","Into the drin
and "Shoot the moon" are prime examples.
Mudhoney did say they were gonna split up after 3 ye
but now the record companies have seen how much mone
can be made from this genre,they've lured Mudhoney in
a big bucks contract-typical hey?Oh well,await comme
album.
Verdict:Good music to slam to when you're pissed.

PUNK 'N' DISORDERLY - '91 VOL.I

Listening to this tape i realise 'punk' has died and gone to hell(twice!).This is the worst tape i have ever had the misfortune to hear.I'm thinking of sueing them for wasting 30 minutes of my life! Some of the 'bands' included are 'Nation of Bigots' 'Active Malfunctions' and 'Distorted Noise'(apt moniker)All the music sounds like a road drill with a cement mixer full of glass going ape in the background.Get the picture?I'd rather be mounted by a randy camel than listen to this again!

Senseless Things - easy to smile 7"

So the 99p pink vinyl gimmick worked! They've got their first hit single.Well,number 45 anyway.And not a touch more commercial than their other stuff.Typical melodic fuzz pop that's played in every 'indie' disco from John Agrotes to Lands End;and that's fine by me.Cool shit.

GREEN DAY - skene 7" E.P (re-issue)

I felt quite excited finding this in Rough Trade. Wow!Some old Green Day stuff-Can't wait to get it home..Well...um...you know what i'm gonna say next. Not so hot.It's got the same G.D. sound but the songs just don't hold up.This came out in the summer of 1990,before their debut album,so they must have been like 17!And this is no mean feat! Anyway,songs include-'Sweet Children','Best Thing In Town','Strange Land' and the Who's 'My Generation' This 7" is included on the CD of their new 33⅓ 'Kerrplunk',which is a total killer.But don't buy the CD cos they're shite-and the Government wants you to, so if you want,buy this 7" instead.

MIDWAY STILL - wish 7"

Their 2nd single and first since Melody Maker has been wanking all over them.They cum from just down the road from me (Bexley) and this mellower single is heavily influenced by the mighty Husker and Dino Jr.Though not as catchy as their brilliant debut 7", this is still a good grower and is worth your money if you like this distorted guitar pop.

BUZZCOCKS - Last to know 7"

Well this is their first single in what,11 years? I was expecting a totally different sounding Buzzcocks but I'm glad to say they havn't changed a bit.Really catchy guitar pop with all their customary hooks & melodies.A great comeback 7" and definetly a must if you see it around.

WHITE FLAG - Beyond Hurt 7"

A newish single from these American pop punkers(?) and they've changed a lot.They used to be fast catchy Ramones clones but now they're more jangly Husker,Birdland types.Which is no bad thing,cos this single is really excellent melodic jangly guitar pop on puce yellow vinyl-euch!Oh well, can't win 'em all.

NIRVANA - sliver 7"

A oldish single from way back in 1990 when they were "the 'other' band on Sub Pop".Now record shops are pushing the price up on this 7", exploiting their new mega-band status.Thank God i got this before they broke big.Anyway this single is a total gem.A-Side 'Sliver' is a hyper catchy journey into country/thrash pop land,while B-Side 'Dive' is a contrasting grunge feast,blissed out and totally awesom.A potent of things that came. Tape it off a mate cos £4,50 is way to much for a 7".

FLAG OF DEMOCRACY - 8 Love Songs 7"

Flag Of Democracy are an American H/C band which sound like a mated Dead Kennedys and Minor Threat. Their 7" album(8 songs!) is good value for money but the songs won't blow you away.They are all mediocre H/C stomps lasting under 1 minute each. The singer mimnicks Jello Biafra perfectly(Even fooling my mate-who's a hardcore DK fan).But why? It's been done before,only better.They should try to be more original.Iwould'nt recommend this, unless you've got money to throw away.

Last Chance Animal Benefit Gig
The Shelley Arms.16-1-92

A full Shelley was there to witness these four generous bands donate their time for the poor helpless fluffy animals.After all,where would we be without them?We'd have nothing to eat for a start!So on with the show......
9.30 hailed the debut of 'Joey Fat'(2 Couch Potatoes and 2 tall people)who play a hybrid of rock/grunge/popcore.Can't remember the names of most of the songs,although the acoustic based 'Pass the Sprouts' was vocally reminiscent of Green Day in places.Talking of Green Day,'Joey' ended with the superb 'Only of You'.Crowd response was good considering it was their first gig.Erm ...yeah,well,that's about it.
Next up,'Protest' and yea..well..ahem.I don't want to slag them off but it wasn't my sort of stuff.A couple of scruffs shouting over chugging riffs.They were nice blokes though. 'The Pseudo Hippies' stumbled on next pissed as usual.They started with the excellent 'Pretty Girl' then bulldozed into the melodic mosher 'Bubble Gum'(No,not the All song).Next up an old one 'Shagpile Carpet' then the classic 'I turned into a martian'.The new catchy duet 'Up your Bum' rushed by as they dived headfirst into the crowd favorite 'Puke'.A couple of other ones came and went then the mandatory 'Wasted' 'Hate Breeders','Rock Away Beach' and 'Sniff some glue!They were a bit loose and a lot pissed but they got a good crowd response.

Angus Bagpipe took to the stage last and the mosh pit was crammed as usual.They gave the punters 'Crime Squad' plus loads of other excellent toons which were amazing.Sort of Spermbirds meet N.W.A these blokes sure know how to write songs with a groove that makes yo move yo boody on di floor tonite.Get the picture?They got the best crowd response and so they finished with the rap/core of 'Crime Squad'.A superb band.

Night 2.Tunbridge Wells.The Rumble Club.17-1-92.
A full house greeted Protest with quasi-enthusiastic jeers.They shouted their way through a set of hardcore grinders that rarely deviated from 'chugga-chugga' chromatic doom riffing.Idon't wanna sound too hard on them.They're decent chaps and I'm sure they've got nice houses and parents an' everything but..well, if you don't like em-you don't like em.Right? Next up,the infamous 'Joey Fat'.A much better perfor mance tonight as the lights gave a whole new dimension to their show.Drummer Jim'stix'Hadlow pig farmer only messed up once(compared to 6 times the night before), and axe-god Dave"I put the 'Fat' in 'Joey'" posed all night to the camera crew.Again I don't know the names of the songs although the first one was sexy. They finished with the brilliant 'Only of you' and got loud cheers from a large crowd present to witness their first gig.
Oh well,on we trundle to the Pseudo Hippies.Following last nights 'performance',tonight we find a straight edged Psuedo crew.Stone cold sober and better for it too.They ripped into a fuzzed out intro-"We're the Psuedo Hippies from the depths of Hell,you must be Tunbridge Wells!!!"1.2.3.4-and into the incredibly infectous 'Pretty Girl' which is reminiscent of the intro to D.K's 'Child and Lawnmower','Bubble Gum' followed next and got the crowd bopping but it wasn't till the alcoholic anthem 'Puke' that the crowd let it rip and went ape.'Spunkmonster' got em going as usual and then it was on to covers time.A medley of 'Wasted','Breeders' and 'Glue' got the crowd singing along and then that was it-the end...or was it? The crowd shouted for more but were told the band didn't have anymore stuff to play.The bass player tried to leave the stage but was pushed back on by the crowd and the guitarist turned off his amp to mass booing.They had no choice but to do another song.They decided on the crowd favorite 'Blitzkreig Bop' which went down triumphantly and then that really was it.
Angus Bagpipe strode on in their usual attire of baseball caps and shorts.They crashed through'Crime Squad','Better than you','Your not a punk' and a brilliant Weasels cover.Followed by the excellent house/core of 'Medley' which got the crowd moshing in circles.

The divers were out in force,slaming off of the P.A And sandwiched on the ceiling etc and there were a lot of girls there getting into them(especially an extremely sexy one called Clare,i wouldn't mind getting to know!) which was good to see,although hardly surprising as 'Angus' are all very,very sexy. All together they raised £260 which was good to hear. Oh well,I can't remember much more so i'll think i'll end it here.

INTERVIEW WITH ISTVÁN

-How and when were you formed?
-Band was formed in November,1988 it was formed by Gábor Tóth /base/ and Zsolt Antónyi /guitar/.Then the former drummer and I/voice/ joined to the band,it was the F.D.M./Fucking Dirty Money/.We gave one gig under this name;After it the previous drummer left us,and Attila Bodnár took the place of him.The joining of new drummer brought along a new name-UNPOLLUTED AIR.
-Why do you sing in english,Wouldn't be easier to use native language?
-We decided to write english songs by mutual agreement,because this kind of can be made only by english words.We think Hungarian language-what is very lovely for all of us-isn't suitable for this type of music,because of its sounding.
-To play Beatles adaptation is not too usual in this type of music you play. Would you tell me where did the inspiration come from?
-Well we play a BEATLES adaption,Hey bulldog.Our drummer-anyway he's a BEATLES fanatic!-came up with the idea.We thought this idea was unsolvable before didn't even listen to the song.But in a practising appeared this song again, we listened to it and we liked it.This song is so dynamic that rescoring was working of itself.
-Would you tell me what kind of music do you listen to?
-We are four,we enjoy four sort of music.My absolutely faveourite is SAW THROAT but I like to listen to ALICE DONUT,PRIMUS,DOORS/!!!/.The guitarist likes acoustic guitar music,our bassist enjoys PINK FLOYD,MEKONG DELTA,MINISTRY. The drummer is a BEATLES fanatic,but new METALLICA lp also appeals to him. But the music we listen to doesn't have an influence on us.
-Are you satisfied with your new studio demo?
-Not at all.During the mixing we thought the casette was all right.But after the first hearing realized things that I should have done better.
-What are these things?
-Especially the guitar sound /we worked 2 days on guitar sound.The IBANEZ DISTORSION-what we use on concertsproved to be useless in studio.The voice might be more agressive.Maybe we should use more noise effect in our songs.
-Do you wanna say you don't like the tape?
-Not at all.Well,it wasn't made in a 'hightech' studio,but we got a lot of help from the owner of studio mostly the good sounding of our demo is due to him.
-Is there any band that you are on friendly term with?
-We know many bands,but the one who really helped me is TROTTEL/from budapest/
-Talk about hungarian scene,please.Could you offer us some cool band or zine?
-It's only my opinion:If a hungarian band met with some success it takes a star-pose-with few exceptions.They defend their positions,tey they advocate "Diulde et impera" principle.I find impossible that young band plays before VÁGTÁZÓ HALOTTKÉMEK /Galopping Coroners/ or VÁGTÁZÓ HALOTTKÉMEK falls into conversation with them at all.
O.K.-about fanzines:More and more zines are made to inform about hungarian underground music.I really like SZÜKBÖRÜ and some issue of MÁSODIK LATÁS which aren't deal with politics.My personally favourite bands from hungary: LEUKEMIA,TROTTEL,VAV WAW and formerly A.M.D.
-You mentioned "aren't deal with politics" in your last answer.Does it mean that that you don't care about politics?
-Politics doesn't leave mekold because it cares about my destiny.Hungary is the only sure point in Central Europe.Day by day I can hear from radio that hungary's air-space has been violated by Yougoslavian planes,refugees crowd to hungary;UNO gives a few million dollars support to help solving the problems about refugees;Unemploying is the highest in Miskolc /second la rgest town of the country.We do care about politics in this situation.
About english politics:I think John Major wears very sexy eye-glasses!

-I say a few notions for example:Unemploying
-It concerned me closely.I was unemployed for IO months,the bassist for half a year.
-Army?
-Our drummer was in the army.There is universal conspiration in hungary,so it's very hard to find a way out.
-Anti-Militarism?
-It comes into fashion nowadays the policeman caught you till now and they don beat you if you hadn't luck.Papers write about it,but people who are responsible only laugh to your face.It's LAUGHABLE.
-Thanks for the interview.Something else you want to say?
-I tell you my personal experience about a famous english person.This stupid fuckin' bitch posed on the streets of Budapest with 2 meters clove of garlic hanging in her neck and she moved like a popular person.It's not a joke!!
c/oNorbert Tamasi
    MISKOLC 3508
    Futo 45
    HUNGARY

R.U.Sure!

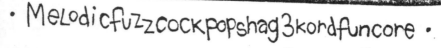

THE PSEUDO HIPPIES

6 songs for nodding and wanking,
for tapping and hopping, for waving and shaging
and shouting: Do you hang low?
The prehistoric animal brigade;
The galloping major...

These Pseudo Hippies are really groovy!

We present the supremely triumphant

" **Okki-tokki-unga** " Demo!

Action songs for children

Available free from : 5 Henryson rd,
Brockley, London, SE·4 1·H·L· send
tape & S·A·E· Ta! Mr Hardcore Freak!

THE *WINCHESTER* CLUB

★ ★ LIVE MUSIC ★ ★

EVERY FRIDAY

TOP NATIONAL INDIE BANDS AND ALTERNATIVE DISCO

EVERY SATURDAY

ROCK, POP, REGGAE, METAL, BLUES. *MUSIC YOUR MOTHER MIGHT NOT LIKE !! (BUT BRING HER ANYWAY)*

Downstairs at: THE PANTILES NEVILLE STREET, TUNBRIDGE WELLS.

ENTRANCE £3.00   8 - 1AM

Hi ! It's issue three of BHP. It took a lot of hard work, so thanks for buying it and ...hmmm....I don't like this bit, I always get it wrong, somehow. I'll just talk about something that's on my mind, worrying me, something I feel. A thing I know.

HARDCORE, I like the whole scene. It matters a lot to me. I like the fact that it's easy to get involved, to contribute, to give something and be positive, an asset. It makes me feel like I belong. Perhaps I'm insecure, but then anybody who says they're not is full of shit.

It's good to know that we can make this thing the way we want, influence it and be part of it. The alternative scene. This is what is so great about hardcore, but it is also it's biggest weakness because if you, and me, and all our friends are not a part of it, then it won't exist.

I don't do enough, and you don't do enough either, so we'd better be part of it, we'd better get motivated ! Yeah, this sounds like an order, a lecturer inviting you to do some really difficult homework. But it's not, it's quite easy. How hard is it to go to see a band, or even put on a band, or even form your own band. Maybe write a fanzine, a letter, a poster, have a real conversation. You could start a record label, or even easier, a tape label. Help local bands, help anyone, other people. Maybe form a distribution service, a shop, a collective. Buy the records, buy the T-shirts, of course, but do more, be a part of it, not just another consumer.

Hardcore (punk, indie, alternative, whatever) is obscure, but it keeps coming and going. Maybe its popularity will increase, but the trouble is, most people just consider music a product, a piece of clothing to support a shoddy self image. Suck on it, chew it, play with it, but at the end of the day just spit it out. It's a shame, because if more people swallowed the feeling they buy for parade, they might not seem so transparent. So painfully shallow.

I could stop here. Leave it and hope you understand, but you won't, so I won't. It's my zine after all, my effort, my chance to give my opinion - so I shall. If you disagree with what I say, fine - just say so, maybe write a letter, maybe even do your own zine! Who knows what could be achieved if you got off your ass.

Real music is not to do with money, or fashion, it is about personalities, characters, emotions, ideas, dreams, things that make life, LIFE.

If you bother looking for them, there is no shortage of great bands who feel just like you and I, and are eager to write the sound-tracks for the lives of the young and misunderstood.

The problem is, the nation of sad, fashion-followers who shift their devotions on a whim. Only being what they've heard 'is' or 'is not' in.

This wouldn't be a problem, maybe we could hear as well as listen, but most seem incapable of dealing with more than one thing at a time. Hardcore, Rap, Classical, It's all great, check it out. Talk to strangers, give things a chance, open your mind - you might learn something.

It's pretty obvious that some sad people spend their entire lives doing what they think is coolest in order to increase their narrow chances of getting shagged, despite the opinions and emotions of others. All I'm saying is relax, maybe think, because no-one wants to shag a fashion victim.

I know, by now you're probably thinking "What right has he got to say this, it's just a zine, he's trying to tell me what to do, to tell me what to think." But no, I'm not. I am merely giving you my opinion, I know, you'll take it or leave it. But you may surprise yourself with what you're capable of - just TRY.

PLANET EARTH IS 4,600 MILLION YEARS OLD

If we condense this inconceivable time-span into an understandable concept, we can liken Earth to a person of 46 years of age.

Nothing is known about the first 7 years of this person`s life, and whilst only scattered information exists about the middle span, we know that only at age 42 did the Earth begin to flower.

Dinosaurs and the great reptiles did not appear until one year ago, when the planet was 45. Mammals arrived only 8 months ago; in the middle of last week man-like apes evolved into ape-life men, and at the week-end the last ice age enveloped the Earth.

Modern man has been around for 4 hours. During the last hours man discovered agriculture. The industrial revolution began a minute ago.

During those 60 seconds of biological time, modern man has made a rubbish tip of Paradise. He has multiplied his numbers to plague proportions, caused the extinction of 500 species of animals, ransacked the planet for fuels and now stands like a brutish infant, gloating over this meteoric rise to ascendancy, on the brink of the final mass extinction and of effectively destroying this oasis of life in the solar system.

The above is an excerpt from a Greenpeace leaflet.

If the Earth were only a few feet in diameter, floating a few feet above a field somewhere, people would come from everywhere to marvel at it.

People would walk around it, marvelling at its big pools of water, its little pools and the water flowing between the pools. People would marvel at the bumps on it, and the holes in it, and they would marvel at the very thin layer of gas surrounding it and the water suspended in the gas.

The people would marvel at the creatures walking around the surface of the ball, and at the creatures in the water. The people would declare it precious because it was the only one, and they would protect it so that it would not be hurt.

The ball would be the greatest wonder known, and people would come to behold it, to be healed, to gain knowledge, to know beauty and to wonder how it would be. People would love it, and defend it with their lives, because they would somehow know that their lives, their own roundness, could be nothing without it. If the Earth were only a few feet in diameter.

Maybe it's 'Society's Not For Us'? 'Straight Not Fucked Up'? Even 'Sniffing Naughty French Undies'? All wrong I'm afraid, but they are as energetic and exciting as it gets. One of our favourite bands - SNFU - had reformed and were on tour. It was their 30th date, but the first in England when BHP persons hassled them for an interview at the Expose Club in Canterbury. Interview by Paul, with Steve & Dave. Thanks to Chi Pig. No thanks to the barman and the bass amp! Read on...

Mr Chi Pig - Vocals
Dave Rees - Drums
Muc - Geetar
Bunt - Geetar again
Ken Fleming - Bass

BHP: Introduce yourselves.
CP: As of November 1992 SNFU are:

BHP: How long has SNFU been together and has the band changed much since forming?
CP: SNFU have been together since 1981. This is the 8th line up thus far, with 3 of the original members.
BHP: What are your influences?
CP: All kinds of stuff. Everything we see & do & listen to. All different kinds of music. Everything from Lyle Lovett to AC/DC, to beer to Coca-Cola...
BHP: How did you meet each other?
CP: Through gigs & skateboarding & just generally hanging out together & listening to music. We knew one another before we formed the group.
BHP: As we understand it, the band split up a while ago. If this is true, why was this?
CP: Yes. We took a 2 year break from '89 -'91. Lots of tension, loss of fun, personal problems.
BHP: Now that SNFU have reformed, have you any major plans or directions you wish to follow?
CP: New songs, a new album in the works. No touring after this one so we can work on stuff before we go out again.
BHP: Many of your songs have focused on the depression and frustration of society. Are these from direct experiences for any of you?
CP: Just the constant life experience which can be depressing and frustrating at times. We also have some rare happy kinda stuff.
BHP: For those who don't know, and for all the poor bastards who wear your shirts and get asked every day, what is the real meaning of the letters SNFU?
CP: Satan Needs Fresh Underwear!!!
BHP: Your music is often humerous. Do you find this important, rather than being political and heavy-going?
CP: Yes. Humour is an important value in our lyrics. We try not to be too heavy-handed about things.
BHP: How is the tour going?
CP: Very well. Good crowds, lots of enthusiasm and we get treated quite well. The voice seems to be holding out too!
BHP: How many people do you get at your Canadian gigs?
CP: Anywhere from 300 to 1200 people, depending on where & when we play.
BHP: What do you eat in Canada? Maple leaves & mountains or lots of Chinese?
CP: Eggs, meat, all kinds of junk food. No fucking beans!!!
BHP: Do you play ice-hockey, what is your involvement?
CP: I don't. The others ice-skate & play on a hockey team. I never learned how to ice-skate.
BHP: Anything to add?
CP: This barkeep is an asshole!!! Cheers!!!

You can contact SNFU at: P.O. Box 65512 - STN.F.
Vancouver, B.C.
Canada, VSN SK5.

AFTER receiving a tape from Atomic 61 I decided to write to Jo Smitty, record producer and writer for HIP CLOWN RAG to see if Seattle is as "cool" as the English press make out.

I asked about THE

SEATTLE UNDER GROUND

EMPTY RECORDS is getting bigger with GAS HUFFER, ZIP GUN and SUPERSUCKERS (now on sub pop) and there are lots of other cool bands that have gotten some 'fame' - FASTBACKS, ACCUSED, DOSED BERNIE, MAXINE etc... The funny thing is that post-NIRVANA almost all the 'hot' bands are going straight to major labels and skipping SUB POP or C/Z but I guess you could call SUB POP a MAJOR by now...They sure made a pile of money off BLEACH after NEVERMIND did so well.

GRUNGE? I do feel that "grunge" is a Seattle thing it couldn't have started anywhere. About ten years ago TOM WOLF gave MARK ARM a copy of BLACK SABBATH's "Masters of Reality" and he began writing songs in MR EPP that were slower and heavier. Also Side 2 of BLACK FLAGS "My War" LP had to be a big grunge influence. KIM THAYIL (Soundgarden) wrote music that owed a great deal to LED ZEPPLIN and CHRIS sang a lot like ROBERT PLANT. When GREEN RIVER came round the STOOGES were a a prime reason. So there you are - the main ingredients of grunge BLACK SABBATH, BLACK FLAG, LED ZEP + THE STOOGES.

SEXIST!? Yes, this is probably true because folks like the DWARVES are "smart" enough to see that this is a good way to get lots of press.

WE concluded our short postal chat by discovering it's always greener on the other side (they rave over JESUS JONES, BOO RADLEYS, DRIVE, GALLON DRINK etc etc.)???

ATOMIC 61's "Heartworm" tape is really good. The guitar sound is a bit like VICTIMS FAMILY but with far more balls! A good example of the lyrics would be:

"If you can't handle it, you oughta pack it in - Oh so easy. Click, Bang, and you're gone."

$7   BOX DOG SOUND
PO Box 9609
SEATTLE
WA 98109
USA

For Hip Clown Rag add $1.

ATOMIC 61

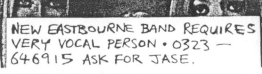
MARINE CONSERVATION SOCIETY

Over 300 million gallons of sewage is dumped in our coastal waters. Every day.

Quicksand are a superb band from New York, featuring ex-members of Gorilla Biscuits, Youth Of Today, Beyond & Absolution, to name but a few bands. Only 1 month after forming they released a 4 track EP on Revolation Records. The first pressing was of 12,000, the largest 7" press that Revolation have done; it sold out!

Q: What songs have you written since the EP?
W: The ones we played on tour. We're kinda in a transitory position where we're writing now; we're trying to develop. The EP was very spontaneous, now we're trying to have some sort of direction.
Q: Are the songs slower, rockier or standard H/C?
S: Nothings contrived, we're playing what we feel and what we love, it's as simple as that.
W: Whatever comes out that sounds good.
S: We're not dealing with any parameters or factions or anything that keeps us from doing what our hearts tell us.
Q: Who is Dan Doolin? (A musician featured on the EP)
W: He's in a band called Skinnerbox; kinda jazzy, reggae type stuff. They're putting out a record on a label I'm doing called Crisis.
Q: Anything to add?
W: We'll have new material out soon; I don't know if it will be an LP or another 7" first. Hopefully a lot of people will get interested in it so we can come back and tour a little more successfully.

There are rumours that Quicksand may have signed to Geffen. Check them out because they're gonna be huge!

QUICKSAND

PORNOGRAPHY has always seemed a rather grey issue to me personally.The amount of properganda steming from.not only feminist groups,but also from fundamentalist right-wing religious groups can be conflicting to say the least.In the eyes of the *"Citizens For Decency Through Love"* pornography causes crime.venereal disease and a "dangerous social change" through it's depiction of everything from beastiality,sodomy.rape,fornication,masturbation, piquerism,orgies,homosexuality,sadomasochism...",you get the picture.They're very quick to try and silence any threat to their *"ideal"* family lifestyle,with conservative virtues.But do they have a point ? Does pornography alter behavior and attitudes by men leading to aggression and discrimination against women ?Certainly pornography is a big buisness.In the USA in 1988,the porn industry was a ten billion dollar buisness.That's bigger than the record and film industires combined.The following article was written in responce to some of the typical arguments against the outlawing pornography.

A common argument put forward is that "pornography is the theory,rape is the practice",meaning rapists are inspired to rape <u>directly</u> from the images of pornography.However,evidence shows that the majority of sex offenders have been exposed to pornography later than other men and have seen less of it.If there were a direct link between the two,then in theory,much of the men who see pornography and those who manufactor the material as well,would commit far more crimes than they actually do against women.The vast majority of men who use pornography do not rape.

Virtually anything can trigger the impulse for a man to commit a violent act against a women.Past sex offenders have claimed images of art and literature lead to their actions.No connection between violence and pornography has ever been proven.One multiple child murderer was said to be haunted by an episode in the Old Testament in which Abraham is instructed by god to sacrifice his son,Isaac.

After exposure to violent pornography,men have been claimed to be more likely to commit rape.In many Western European countries,after legislation of pornography had been brought into effect,sex crime figures did not increase.Furthermore,evidence points to pornography offering a form of release to those who may otherwise commit acts of sexual violence.

Certain claims have been made that the most important evidence to show that pornography plays a role in rape,comes from women who have testified that pornography was <u>known</u> to be used by their assailants in the past.Anti-porn campaigners are fond of citing the fact that sex offenders often *admit* to commiting crimes directly from the use of pornography.This is obviously an easy way for the offender to shift the blame from himself.It also can often be as a result of treatment programmes ran by counsellors who beleive pornography is the main factor for sexual violence to occur;who in turn,often without intending to do so,infulences the offender into this opinion.

Many images of women can be degrading - but "Page 3" images can often be as damaging as an image of the "housewife scrubbing the floor",or for instance of the "secretary making tea for her boss".The term *"Pornography is the theory,rape is the practise"* suggests a simplistic mode of human behaviour.People are seen as robots,switched on or off by a pornographic image.Whereas <u>real</u> people - men and women alike,react in so many different,and individualistic ways.

Certainly pornography may *mirror* sexism,but it did not *create* it.Rape and women's oppression has been concurrent throughout history,long before pornography existed.Local Council's who have banned Postman Pat and so on from nursery schools on the grounds they are sexist are certainly not helping the problem.Despite the matter being far from a black and white issue,censorship is not the answer.Anti-porn campaigners are missing the <u>whole sourse</u> of the problem.The whole role of society needs to be questioned to obtain results.Better sex education,an end to macho images portraied by films and the media etc,a less materialistic society and a greater self-awareness is only the beginning to the solution.....

NO MEANS NO RAPE

IS VIOLENCE NOT SEX

Any feedback is welcome:
AWA Zine
c/o 31 Manor Row,
Bradford,
West Yorkshire.
BD1 4PS.UK.

Sourses:
Pornography & Feminism - The case against censorship - By Gillian Rodgerson and Elizabeth Wilson.
Feminism & Censorship - By Gail Chester and Julienne Dickey.
Pornography & Society - DF Barber.

Lord Tennyson

There is sweet music here that softer falls
Than petals from blown roses on the grass,
Or night-dew on the still waters between walls
Of shadowy granite, in a gleaming pass;
Music that gentler on the spirit lies
Than tired eyelids upon tired eyes.

Have You Ever Considered Becoming A Vegetarian?

More than 600 million animals are slaughtered for food each year in the UK alone. The vast majority are reared in factory farms where they never see daylight, or feel fresh air, nor take proper exercise.

Ten years ago, if you decided not to eat meat, you would have been considered something of a crank. But nowadays if you become vegetarian you will be joining one of the fastest growing movements in the country, particularly amongst young people.

There are many reasons for taking this step - I myself am a vegetarian - but you must decide for yourself. You may well have many questions you need answered. A good place to find this information is ANIMAL AID. An organisation for campaigning against cruelty, a voice for the voiceless. Anyone can become a member and they are quite happy to answer your questions. You can write to them at Animal Aid, 7 Castle Street, Tonbridge, Kent TN9 1BH and remember, as long as there are slaughterhouses there will be battlefields. Make your next meal count!

THANKS
We just want to say thanks very much to Jay & Mark, and all the others who helped out at the Rumble Club and made it the best thing in Tunbridge Wells. On behalf of everyone who just wants to see good bands and hang out, you have our respect and best wishes.
Let's get a new club open as soon as possible!

The Nuclear Threat - A Reminder
At the recent SNFU gigs when Chi-Pig introduced 'Black Cloud' he said "Just because things are quiet now, don't forget what could happen any day." This reminded me that the threat of nuclear war, or nuclear accident, is still very real.
So, let me remind you. There would be <u>NOTHING</u> to rebuild, there would be <u>NO</u> survivors. <u>ALL</u> life and the environment would be <u>annihilated</u>.
The Hiroshima bomb <u>destroyed</u> an entire city and <u>killed</u> hundreds of thousands of people. Today, single bombs exist with 4800 times the power! <u>THINK</u> about it!

On The Edge
You're really angry with the system and the position society has put you in - so you escape by floating in a drug induced haze. That's great! Yeah, that's really making a difference! Instead of staying aware, and thinking and acting, you just fuck yourself up. You sad loser! Be angry and active, not subdued by drugs. Your choice? Your stupidity! Drugs are for Losers!

COMMUNICATION IS THE KEY...

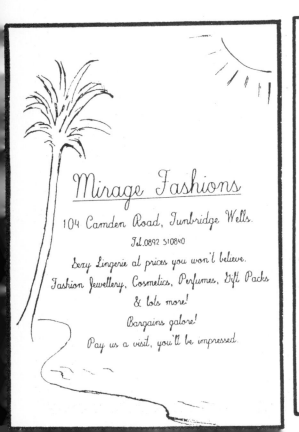

DRAWING THE LINE

You're walking down the street, a desirable person passes you by. You walk a bit further and then look round - why? To see what they look like from behind, or to see if they're looking at you? Instance one - you look round, they're not looking at you, what do you think? They do/don't look nice from behind & maybe, they're not looking at me- forget it? Instance two - you look round and they are looking at you, wow, ego boost or what? You look away smiling to yourself, that has really made your day hasn't it? Why? This sort of behaviour has, in some way, been misconstrued as sexism but it seems to take on a different type of analysis depending on which genre is doing what. If a man is seen to be looking at a womans form in any manner it is seen as voyeurism, oggling, undressing with the eyes etc. If a woman does it, then...but this seems to be the problem. I never notice it. Am I blind or just not paying enough attention? I'm not sure, but would it be fair to say that supposing woman are more visually attractive (as we are constantly led to believe) that it is more probable that a woman would notice male voyeurism than a man would notice females? I don't know, I'm bloody confused? Anyway, let's go back to the street scenario - surely there must be a middle ground? Some people may say that if you're looking at somebody you don't know just for their body then that is sexist. So let's say the person who is looking, at the present time, was not involved in any sexual relationship, would that be more acceptable than somebody who was sexually involved with another person? As an example, an unattached person may be seeking a sexual partner and if they are looking at somebody then they may not be doing so in a sexist manner. On the other hand a sexually attached person doing the same may be seen as doing so in an attempt at voyeuristic gratification. Where do you draw the line?

Earth

Diameter: 7,921 miles

Length of year: 365 days

Conditions: Among the planets in the solar system, only Earth has the right balance of environmental factors to support life. An intelligent civilisation developed, but does not always like it.

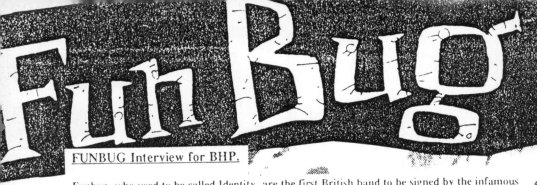

FUNBUG Interview for BHP.

Funbug, who used to be called Identity, are the first British band to be signed by the infamous 'Lookout!' Records. The three piece come from Redditch and play energetic but melodic popcore in the style of Hard-Ons, Ramones, Descendents, GreenDay... Kris posted this interview, which was answered by Jason...

BHP: How did the deal with Lookout! Records come about?

J: We went to London to do a gig, turned up 3 hours late and drunk, played awful, gave him a demo and all that. I gave him a tape, he took the tape. I went home, he went home. He played the tape, I waited by the phone. He rang up, I answered the phone and basically the 'Big Live' liked us.

BHP: What's on the EP and when is it coming out?

J: The EP is called 'TEZBINETOP' EP. It's got 4 pop songs on it, which you can hear at our concerts. First up being 'Everything', then 'Plimsoles', then turn the bugger over and it's 'Seventeen' (my favourite song, only 2 chords) and last and the least 'Lobo Doc', but that's crap! It will be out in August/September. By the way, my birthday is on 14th August (hint hint). When you send me my pints, make sure they're wrapped well and they're Becks!

BHP: How was your Euro Tour? Any stories to tell?

J: A lot happened, mainly being drunk 16 hours a day on free beer! I broke 2 fingers, a dog then bit them, saw NOFX in Switzerland, saw Mondo Popless in Hamburg, loads of parties, met interesting people. Blimey! So much and there are interesting stories but too much to write down.

BHP: What has been your favourite gig to date?

J: Mmmm... so many to chose from. The Frankfurt A, which is a brilliant squat, funnily enough, in Frankfurt. We played 30 songs, the last night of the Eurotour.

BHP: Do you still hear from MC4 and Senseless Things anymore, or are they too big to talk to you?

J: Not really, because they are all very busy. But I get in touch with Wiz now and again, 'cos he's sort of always got time for people.

BHP: Do you ever get frustrated that other bands hog the limelight and you're always left behind, eg: MC4, Senseless Things, Goober Patrol getting tours with Mr T, GreenDay, Spermbirds...?

J: I don't know, but we aint crying about it, but we are nowhere near as good as Mega City Four! (Funbug's hero band!) I suppose it's 'cos we are crap then really.

BHP: What are your favourite bands at the moment? Who do you reckon are the most promising up and coming bands in the UK?

J: Big Drill Car, Doughboys, Lemonheads, GreenDay, SLF, Leatherface, MC4, Specials, Dickies...! Up & coming bands: Mondo Popless, Saffron's Daughter, Pseudo Hippies, MDK (Redditch), Ludicrous Lollipops, Pop Am Good, Another Fine Mess, Skimmer (ex-sect Kev P. & Tez) and Steve & Kev Cov's band (ex-sect) without a name!

BHP: What Marshall amp do you use, 'cos the sound is excellent?

J: Yeah, muso talk now. It's a luminous green & pink thing; it's a 1974 JMP Master/Vol 100w Head and the crucial bit is an early '60's Orange Cab (they have deeper sound than Marshall Cabs! Pop tip of the week.) And a late '60's Coron Dist pedal which is more of an overdrive!

BHP: Will you ever record 'Milestones'& 'Inertia' because they are excellent?

J: Well 'Inertia' will be the next single sometime and I think 'Milestones' could be the B-side... Thanks for the compliment.

BHP: Lastly, any future plans?

J: Drink more, play better, write some new somgs! Get to see 'Sugar', sell more than 11 records a year! Thanks Kris & Pseudo Hippies and BHP. Hi Steve, Mark & Tez! The dudes in Tun/Wells who came to see us... Love, Thanks, Bye!

When I first got into skateboarding everyone was into hardcore, vert ramps, flourescent shorts, and big wheels, but now you have to be into hip-hop, wear adidas gazelles and trousers so baggy that the back pockets are below your knees (cut down of course), only skate street or maybe the odd mini-ramp, and have wheels so small that you're riding on the bearings! What's happened?

I remember when skateboarding was about being individual, and the English 'scene' was the best because it was all about having fun and not caring about fashion or doing the latest cool trick.

It would be cool if someone could write in and tell me what they think.

Hopefully this will become a regular feature in BHP and if Steve lets me have a go next issue, I'll write some shit about new products and stuff, and I might even have an interview with Rob Dukes (Slam City Skates).

So don't give up skating because that sucks, and get more skaters to buy this rad 'zine!

SKATING SAM

ALL... I mean what can I say? This band really are 'the total extent, the utmost possible when nothing else remains'. They hail from Brookfield, MO. but used to be called Descendents and come from California. Actually, I guess they're citizens of 'everywhere' as they tour, on average, 8 months every year and only stop to rest and record. All of their albums are superb; Artistic masterpieces you must hear. We hassled the drummer and founder member, Bill Stevenson (ex Black Flag), into answering a few questions on their latest visit to the UK:

BHP: How's the European part of the tour going? You seemed to enjoy last night, have you an favourite gigs?

Bill: I liked the Norwich show about as well as anything. We play so many shows I get confused.

BHP: The latest album 'Percolater' is superb, but a little different to the previous albums. Are the band changing direction?

Bill: We practice so much that I think we change directions daily, but we haven't turned into a ska band or something.

BHP: You finish the tour in 4 days. What's the first thing you're gonna do when you get back home to Brookfield?

Bill: Sleep!

BHP: Last night in Norwich, you and Stephen swapped instruments on 'Birthday I.O.U.', one of your new songs. Are you likely to record any tracks on the new album in this way?

Bill: Mostly we do that just for fun.

BHP: You've a shirt that says 'Keep your politics out of my music' and a new song with the same lyric. What has brought all this about?

Bill: Not anything in particular. It's just a song idea I came up with because I hate listening to people talk about politics and rock & roll as if they have some kind of inherent connection with each other.

BHP: Has the new 'DOT' video been on MTV yet?

Bill: MTV has played it some, but not as much as Madonna & Bon Jovi.

BHP: Descendents/All have been around for 14 years now. Is it still as much fun as when you started out?

Bill: I think it's actually 13 isn't it? Maybe 14, I don't know. I've spent my whole life doing thi music, and everything that I am, it is, and everything it is, I am. I can't really tell how it compares to 14 years ago, because I was 15 then and I'm 29 now.

BHP: Do you miss playing in Black Flag? Is it true you were offered $100,000 to reform for 3 gigs?

Bill: I like Black Flag a lot, but we would not want to get back together

BHP: Are ALL sponsored by VANS? Do any of you find time to skate?

Bill: ALL is not sponsored by Vans. I skated a lot when I was a kid, but not this flying through the fucking air stuff like you guys do now!

BHP: Are there any bands, US or UK, that you'd particularly like to play with you?

Bill: 'My Name' & 'Black Sabbath'.

BHP: Do you think maybe you'll start your own label to produce bands you like?

Bill: I don't think so. Maybe when I'm too old to play.

BHP: Will you be returning to the UK soon?

Bill: We'll come back when we have a new LP out.

BHP: Could you explain the lyrics to 'Minute'. Is there a story behind it?

Bill: I'd rather not go into details for fear of getting into more trouble with my girlfriend than I already have over that song.

BHP: Anything else to add?

Bill: Suck me bell end! (Only kidding).

Make contact with ALL at: P.O. Box 441,
Brookfield,
MO 64628,
USA.

ALL

Clockwise from top left:
KARL ALVAREZ
BILL STEVENSON
SCOTT REYNOLDS
STEPHEN EGERTON

PHOTO: SARINA MATTEUCCI

CRUZ
RECORDS

SKIN DEEP
(Lyrics and Music by Alvarez)

I looked your way
You looked your best
Looked like a million,
More or less
You were so carefully undressed
But you're just skin deep
And I'm not impressed
You're just skin deep,
Just like all the rest
Because you change your mind
Like you change your clothes
pre-fab perspective, poise and pose
In it comes and out it goes
But it's just skin deep
Don't you know?
It's just skin deep
And that's as far as it goes
It's all done with mirrors
And painted smiles
Reflection...Obsession...
The hype of style
I looked away
I could have cried
You always have me hypnotized
Sure like to know what you're like inside
But you're just skin deep
And looks can lie
You're just skin deep
So why even try?

I HATE TO LOVE
(Lyrics and Music by Alvarez)

Her glance can make you short of breath
Your heart stop dead inside your chest
She has what words just can't express
She gives a kiss that's cursed and says-
"I hate to love"
A word, a song, a smile, a tear
She doesn't care for me, it's clear
I'll never tell
It hurt like Hell
To see her turn and disappear
I hate to love
I hate to love

She's laughing beside someone else
And I'm alone beside myself
She's like no one else
Hung by my rope
Strung out
Hurt
Let it drop, it just won't work
Stretch my neck across the block
Heart in my hand, axe in hers, (while she says)
"I hate to love"
I hate to love
So I do without
And die within
Once we were two
It wore too thin
It just wore thin
I hate to love
It hurts too much
Everytime
The time is up

POSTAGE
(Lyrics and Music by Steve)

I want to forget
The day we met
And the way I felt inside
I'm just a perfect failure
And all my plans gone wrong

I'll never replace you
But you are sick
And I know there's no cure

So much to hate
But I hate to see you go
Without a fighting chance

I'll never replace you
But you are sick
And I know there's no cure

It doesn't matter what I call you
As long as I call you
So I won't call you anything
Or you'll always have me
In the palm of your hand
So right now I release you
And right now I forget you
Can you do the same for me?

You never tell the truth
But I can't call you a liar
You're never Faithful
But I can't call you anything

It doesn't matter what I call you
As long as I call you
It doesn't matter what I say
If I'm talking about you
I can't call you anything
Or you'll always have me
In the palm of your hand

SCARY SAD
(Lyrics and Music — Stevenson)

All in my mind, but there's no shaking
Scary, sad things out of my mind
Always on time, but there's no time to
Bring the scary, sad girl back to life
None in her heart, some of the things
She did seemed almost nice
I can't stop the blush when things aren't right
But I'm too scary, sad to cry

Feel it so strong, but she's done it so wrong
All those scary, sad things; those scary, sad things

Every time she slit her wrists I wish she hit instead of missed
Every secret family crime, all my love a waste of time
Every doctor, every shrink, every bloody bathroom sink
All the filth we tried to hide, just a lace I needed to be beside

Scary, sad girl leave my happy lone world
All those scary, sad things are what any love brings

Every girl that I ever hated was just monster that I created
Maybe if I close my eyes real tight, then the scary, sad
Things will go away and I'll quit living in yesterday
I'll just smile, and laugh at all the scary, sad
things you put me through

None of the doctors could find a cure
Just a scary, sad girl in a scary, sad world
None of the shrinks could make her think
About anybody else but her
I want to go home, I want my mom to make
The bad things go away
I want to forget I could ever let any
Scary, sad girl treat me that way.

Feel it so strong, but she's done it so wrong
All those scary, sad things; those scary, sad things.

Truth comes out in dreams at night.
'Cause she's done it so right.
All those scary, sad things; those scary, sad things.

FOOL
(Lyrics and Music — Alvarez)

I sent you a valentine, I'm afraid it won't get there till June
Somehow I lost track of time, but you know I'm a fool for you

I sent a bouquet of roses, the kind that you're allergic to
You know that I don't know better, you know I'm a fool for you

Head over heels, banana peels, its funny how you make me feel.
Like a love sick, slapstick tragedy - would you like to
Fool around with me?

I'd fall off of the highest mountain, drown in the deepest river too,
catch cold in the hottest desert. You know I'm a fool for you.

I would sing outside your window, if I could only hold a tune.
I suck. So hold it against me. You know I'm a fool for you.

The real world seems so mean to me that I can't take it seriously
But I love your laugh, and I hope you see that I just might be the
Fool you need.

Every single time I'm with you something's wrong with what I do
Don't get mad its like I told you, I am just a fool for you

SUM
(Lyrics and Music - Alvarez)

Long time, no see - so, tell me, how are things?
Just 'cause I was wondering - what ever became of you?
You don't look well - can't hide it I can tell
I know you love to hurt yourself
There's some-things about you I wish I never knew
And I wish that I could say that we're happier today
Sometimes there's just some things I don't want to have to know

Don't you know me? Has it been too long a time -
Weren't you once a friend of mine? It gets so hard to tell

Hoping gets lonely, I'm lonely all the time -
But time and circumstance combined and every other someone
Just helped you kill the pain you felt

And I wish that I could say that we're happier today
Sometimes there's just some friends I don't want to know
Sometimes some things I don't want to know
Sometimes some things I don't want to have to know.

The real truth is it brings no peace to swallow lies that let me s
There's some things about you I wish I never knew.
There's some things about you -
Sometimes I wish I never knew you at all.

I stayed a stranger ever since
I learned I can't depend on friends -
If ignorance is innocence
There's some things about you I wish it wasn't true.
And I wish that I could say that we're happier today
Sometimes there's some things I don't want to know
Sometimes some things - I don't want to know
Sometimes some things I don't want to have to know.

MARY
(Lyrics and Music — Reynolds)

If you talk to Mary please don't look at me
'Cause she's never seen me before
Don't call attention to the man outside of me
'Cause she can cut my head off with the blinking of her eye
And I'm not supposed to be here, and I'm too young to die
See she carries my confusion in the pocket of her jeans
I go bouncing like pinball in between extremes

I'm not surprised, this happens all the time
And my hand lights her cigarette inside my mind
And she's never seen me before

So if you talk to Mary, please don't mention me
'Cause she's never seen me before
Just let me hide behind the smoke and pleasantries
'Cause I do my best work with the mannequin brigade
I just peek around the statues spitting art and foreign trade
She looks a hole right through me to a shadow on the wall
Till I'm sick of my surroundings white I'm not here at all

I'm not surprised, this happens all the time
And my hand lights her cigarette inside my mind
And she's never seen me before

Warhol monotone, robotic talk - we're all so smart we're so perceptive
But her mouth doesn't move, except to smile, to be polite.
To be receptive
She burns me with a glance, I look away
I'm safely cool, I'm so deceptive

I'd give my right arm for a different situation
Convince myself I see everybody watching me
I set myself up for this stupid situation

BUBBLEGUM
(Lyrics and Music -- Alvarez)

Warm, and sweet, and soft and pink
Or so I was led to believe
The good things went from bad to worst
Every bubble has to burst

It seemed so sweet before, but not anymore
Just chewed me up and spit me out like bubblegum.

Cold, and bitter, hard, and grey,
The whole world seems to be that way
Its no surprise, its only life
It makes me want to hide inside
It used to make me cry, but now I'm just too numb

What seemed so sweet before, means nothing anymore.
Just chewed me up and spit me out like bubblegum.

Small minds firing words that freeze
Conspire to drive me to my knees
Fine, I know that can find
Courage burning deep inside
Fire to keep me warm for when the winter comes

It hurt so bad before, but never anymore.
I'll never be used up like that by anyone
Never be used up again like bubblegum.

It seemed so sweet before

A MESSAGE FROM YOUR LOCAL PIG STATION

Skaters, jaywalkers, party goers, owners of cars with incorrectly tinted windows, communists, people who don't come to a complete three second stop at a stop sign, unlicensed vendors, MDC fans, heavy metal satanists, owners of illegal fireworks, flag burners, sidewalk spitters, pot smokers, flyer pasters, parking criminals, anarchists, under-age beer consumers, copiers of copyrighted tapes, purchasers of 2 Live Crew records, punks, loiterers, "skinheads" at the broadmoor, you folks who make a living off recycling cans, hippies, animal rights activists, men who wear dresses and especially all you stereotype violators who we can't classify YOU ARE SOCIAL SCUM ! Criminals who we will punish when we find you (and we will). We have already done away with several of you : especially you who have smoked politically unacceptable vegetation. We also will continue to punish those of you who still use politically unacceptable transportation which doesn't support our corporate sponsors and fellow fascists. We are sick of your outrageous crimes against our system and laws which you had no part in deciding. What would Amerikkka degenerate to if we would cut you criminals some slack? FREEDOM? Well, we like our authority and power and our extensive FREEDOM. We will keep our freedom to throw intoxicated hippies in jail for acting unacceptable. We will keep our freedom to beat you senseless if your vocabulary gets out of line and yes, we love the freedom to frisk and cuff suspects as we stuff them in the back of our pigmobiles. Yes, all you slimy degenerate criminal scum police rule means freedom. Especially for all you sexy, inexperienced fifteen year olds who want off the hook, you have the freedom for us to pork you in to squealing ecstasy . Well, well we are well aware that you criminals are ashamed of your filthy, disgusting and inhumane crimes so we would like to extend our hooves to all of you who would like to come on good terms with us. So when you see us on the streets harassing loiterers or busting a party at your friends home, greet us with a friendly grunt, oink or squeal and we'll return your charity with a swift nightstick to the head. Also we can get beyond all these formalities There is little more we hate

than being addressed "officer", "police" or even "cop". Just call us Pig, Swine or call us by our common nickname PORKY!

We laugh when you fall on your face

your local PIG PATROL

"Police make me feel guilty, even when I've done nothing wrong."
— Bill Stevenson

'Support the police - beat yourself up'

the Mr. T Experience

A DAY OUT WITH MR T.

Jon von: "love, like law, is ageless"

Picture this. A warm, sunny Thursday evening. I'm lying on my bed watching TV when I get a phone call from Aiden (Lookout! Records UK).

"Kris you're my last hope. Do us a huge favour and go to Dover and pick up the Mr T Experience. We haven't got a tour bus for them yet, you're the last person I know with a van. Please, please, please, beg, grovel etc. You'll get free albums, singles, T shirts plus petrol money".

"Um...well, OK I suppose".

So I get dressed and bomb it down the M2 to Dover. I get there for 9.30 and run into the arrivals lounge at the ferry port. Sitting opposite me is Jon Von in a leather jacket looking straight at my Green Day T shirt.

"Hi, I'm your chauffeur! Ha!". Handshakes all around. A brief discussion followed on lorry road blocks in France then I get my small Austin Maestro van and I see the amount of stuff they've got with 'em.

"Jesus!!" Aiden said you've only got 4 guitars!". Now I know my van and so I was 100% convinced that the stuff and band wouldn't fit in. This is where Aaron stepped in.

"Positive thinking! We need a positive attitude. Don't worry, we'll get it in. Maybe we could pyramid it on top".

"Er, no. There is no roof rack" I reply. Well anyway it was a bloody miracle how all the stuff got in but it did so we set off practically touching the ground.

Several stops to stretch their legs passed till we got to the Isle of Dogs where we were stopped by the old bill. We told them our story and they creased up!.

"Wow! An American rock band! Are you famous?" Needless to say Aaron & Jon Von sweettalked them all. Thank God they didn't look in the back 'cos there were 4 illegally carried people in it hiding amid the luggage and plus Aaron & Jon Von were sitting on each others laps in the front without seatbelts.

Aaron: "Are they all so thick over here? They're real nice. They would have beat us up back home"

At about 1 am after several stops to look at the A-Z we found our way to Lookout HQ. The interview that follows was not strictly an 'interview but a conversation that started in Dover, developed along the M2 and Tom's house (Pseudo Hippies) where we stopped for beer and ended in Walthamstow at 1.30 am.

Q: Who sells the most on Lookout?

Aaron: Operation Ivy. Their last LP sold 40,000 and that was before the CD came out. Green D ay sell a lot, yeah they're tapped into this youth market man! We're just a bunch of old timers. I don't know why I hang around you guys!!

Q: Talking of Green Day, how are they doing?

Alex: I saw Billie Joe at one of our shows before we left for Europe. They're fine, but we don't hang out with them, they live on the other side of the bay in Berkeley, we only see them now and then, at shows and stuff.

Q: How's the Eurotour been going?

Frank: Good, weird, okay. Some places have been real good like Germany. The bands get treated really well in Europe. Other places have been strange.

Alex: In spain there was this big promoter, a big fat guy with a beard who took Jon Von around all the bars before the show. He drunk enough of this liquor to kill himself. We didn't see him till the next morning!

Q: I thought the new album is bloody brilliant!

Frank: What?! Hey guys - here's someone who likes the album! We've got a fair amount of stick for it. People saying it's wimpy, too melodic. It's got a woman singing on a song and they say there are too many solos.

John Von: They like the punky H/C stuff.

Q: Anyway, talking of the n ew LP what's behind the title?

Frank: Don't you have it in England?

Q: Have what?

Frank: Milk Milk Lemonade!

The Mr. T Experience	
Jon von	Rhythm Guitar, Screams
Dr. Frank	Lead Guitar, Vocals
Alex	Drums, Counting to Four
Aaron	Bass, Interjections

Q: What is it, a drink?

No it's "Milk Milk Lemonade, round the corner fudge is made, stick your giner in a hole..." It's a childrens rhyme.

Alex: I'm leaving these guys when we get back home. Maybe you'll see me over here in another band.

Q: Why are you leaving?

Alex: (shrugs). I just am.

Aaron: "so big and fine"

Q: D'you think Green Day will have another record out soon?

Frank: I don't know. They're pretty prolific so they'll probably have an EP or something by the time they come over.

Aiden(Lookout): They were gonna come over about now and stay with me for 3 weeks and try and book a short tour but it didn't pull off.

Q: Well what bands have you played with?

Everyone: Big Drill Car, Descendents, All, Dickies, Samiam, Green Dau, O.P.I.V.

Q: Yeah, did you know there was a large earthquake over in California a couple of days ago?

Jon Von: We were there for the big quake a couple of years back when the bridge fell. It was like the rush hour and everyone was out on the streets, all these people were killed. It was mad, scary.

Aaron: We left on tour the day after that one, so we didn't see much of it.

Q: What about the riots?

They were in LA but we had a few small incidents in S/F. We left for Europe a couple of days later.

Q: D'you lot still go to college?

No only Alex does.

Aaron: I'm unemployed, broke, a bum, but I've got miles of credit.

Jon Von: This man has credit on his credit.

At 1.30 am we arrive at Lookout HQ, have a few drinks then retire. Goodnight.

Mr. T Experience.

...For Brunettes Only

LOOKOUT! RECORDS

Environmental Investigation Agency

I thought I'd use this space to publicise an organisation t
I think is important but a lot of you won't have heard of,
The Environmental Investigation Agency. The group's aim is
locate and expose incidents of wildlife abuse throughout
the world. Investigations into these cases often involve
risking the lives of investigators who are working undercov
The information that they get is then given to the media to
publicise while the EIA use the public support this engende
to lobby Govt. and organisations to try and end the cruelty
The reason I chose the EIA for this piece was because the
evidence gained by them and their use of the media to get t
support of Joe Public watching News At Ten or whatever. Mos
of these people aren't like us totally enlightened right on
punks (absolutely no irony there,I don't think) and they do
know of anything like that going on. If they do they turn a
blind eye,but it is impossible to do that if it's on the
news every time they listen.It's through such methods that
most 'outsiders' get involved in animal rights,so it has to
good. The EIA were amongst the first groups to be involved
in the boycott of the ivory trade and it is with the aid of
the tv pictures the EIA got that mass public pressure was
brought to bear in the case and now the ivory trade is bann
The EIA is currently involve in 2 main campaigns,one to aid
dolphins,small whales and the other to stop the trade in li
birds. Write the EIA at 208,'209 Upper Street,London N1 1RL.

I am straight edge.However, I am not a Straight Edger.I am vegetarian
- I am not a vegetarian.Can you see the difference? One's an adjective
and the other is a noun.Where is this grammar lesson leading? - you're
wondering.Well, I want to talk about tags/labels.
It's really bad when someone introduces you as a Straight Edger or
whatever.I imagine they build up a picture of me as someone who just
doesn't drink — y'know? I have a bit more going on in my life than that.
This is just a surface thing which people tag on to and notice - we
seem to spend too much time thinking about pigeon holing each other and
not enough time getting to know the person underneath the tag.
Labelling is such a convenient and easy thing to do as it acts as a
reference point to judge people on.But I always thought 'Judging'people
was a negative trait and was always taught not to do it.Judging and
prejudging leads to arrogance, and arrogance is selfish and close-minded.
Arrogance is the attitude which is responsible for sexism, racism,
patriotism and homophobia, and I'm sure none of us endorse those values.
Think about it the next time you dismiss someone 'cos of the clothes
they wear or the music they listen to.

breakthe**chain**   **break**the**cha**

BHP would like to recieve contributions, information & reviews
from anyone. These should be sent to 1 Chandos Road, Tunbridge
Wells, Kent, TN1 2NY. Distibutors or anyone who can help us
spread our message, please get in touch. Help us to help you!

ISOLATION IS NEGATIVE
SO LET'S COMMUNICATE

Getting a Gig.

It seems to be getting harder & harder for bands in this area get gigs, so BHP to the rescue! Here are some numbers to cal Shelley Arms, Nutley, (Warren), 082 571 3121, The Square, Harlow, (Mac), 0279 417029, Jericho Tavern, Oxford, (Mac 0865 54502, Powerhouse, London, (Darren), 081 9615490, Playpen, London, (Robin), 081 3000427, Robey, London, 07 2634581, Rich, Folkestone, 0303 276517, Rich, Southampto STE, 0703 617522, 101 Club, East Grinstead, (Tony), 0825 791035, Expose Club, Canterbury, (Roger), 0227 366354.

Also, there are loads more not listed here so talk to the prom You could call Kris (081 6905163) for gigs in London, or Do (0702 201334) for gigs in Southend, or Alan (0942 826598) f list of venues further north.

There are new clubs opening in both Tunbridge Wells & Canterbury, although we do not have their numbers yet.

The Tunbridge Wells club is going to be called the Forum at opening for music 7 nights a week in the new year. The new in Canterbury is called 'Cadillacs' and is opening on 5th December and looking for bands.

Alice Donut have just finished another UK tour, playing at Reflections club in Brighton on the 4th. The only interest in December is a possible Drive tour and Labour Party Xmas g Tunbridge Wells featuring Joeyfat. In January, Joeyfat are supporting Alloy on all of their UK dates (4-11), and playin Folkestone with Sonar Nation on 16th.

In spring of 1993 the UK will be lucky enough to see Samiar GreenDay, Screeching Weasel, Down By Law, Fiendz, & Pan UK bands Funbug, Couch Potatoes, Pseudo Hippies & Joey have new singles available in early 1993 and there is a 24 tra Couch Potatoes cassette album available now from Gotham for just £1.50 ppd. Also, Boss Tuneage Records have a compilation LP out in spring featuring Samiam, Mr T, Wy Riders, Sleeper, Toast, Rise, Five Foot Nothing, Red Fisher Couch Potatoes, Gan, Goober Patrol, Wordbug, Shutdown, Pseudo Hippies and others - Wow!

Alan's, the alternative shop, has recently moved to 53 Mesn Wigan, Lancs, WN1 1QX, and so is in a little bit of turmoil moment but should be running smoothly with a new catalog soon. Let's hope Mel gets TCV started again to help bands support it!

APATHY AGAIN?

I've come to fuck up your scene. I've com to take the piss out of your haircut. I'v come to your gigs to get pissed up and pis people off. I've come to wind you all up. I've come to spoil your evening. I've com to enjoy myself at all costs. I've come annoy and cajole anything that takes my f I've come to laugh at you all cos you can only bitch behind my back. I've come cos know I can get away with it. I'll keep coming cos I'm contributing to the scene too and you can't deny that. In fact I probably do more for the scene than you. It makes me enjoy taking the piss even mo I like it when I annoy you. I like it whe you're pissed off. I like it when you bit behind my back. I like it cos you're just a bunch of apathetic fuckin wankers too fuckin scared to stand up for what you be lieve in. And you know I'm going to fuck you off even more until you do stand up and question my principles and then I wil be happy cos I'll have finally got what I wanted (deserved). A direct reaction. Stop talking amongst your selves and star talking to each other. If you've got som thing to say just say it.

REVIEWS

PINHEAD GUNPOWDER - FAHIZAH 7" EP (LOOKOUT)

Um,Billie Joe from GREEN DAY heh?Aaron ex CRIMPSHRINE heh?Looks impressive?Yeah,it is pretty much mate. I'll start with the best song 'Big Yellow Taxi' the only song that rock god-Billie-voice of an angel-Joe sings. Great catchy uptempo teen garage pop with some thoughtful lyrics.The other three toons really remind me of ROLLINS.Grungy guitars,boppy beats and that ROLLINS rasp/ bark.Pretty cool stuff.Definetly worth £2.50.Get one soon.

SCREECHING WEASEL - BOOGADABOOGADA LP (LOOK)

'My Brain Hurts' is a fugging great bouncy pop gem. And 'Hey Suburbia' rules.But does this elpee? No,not much.Almost all the songs are generic H/C stomps.A few RAMONES-like bursts try to break thru the mediocrity but nowt to write home about i'm afraid. Incase you're not in the know,this is an old LP just re-released on LOOKOUT.Awaiting the new LP 'WIGGLE'. Till then i'm off!!

DOWN BY LAW - BLUE LP (EPITAPH)

I'd been gagging for this LP for SO long!Ran all the way home when i got it.Except i didn't,i got the train. Running from Piccadily to the suburbs is not advisable. Even after a shot of speed!Was i disapointed?-FUCK NO! This,and wait for it(my fav word) is a CLASSIC!! Emotion filled riffy power pop.Identical to their last LP and the newest DAG NASTY LP.Dave Smalley is God springs to mind.All tunes are worthy to be crowned and made royalty.Get it,get it,get it!

SAMIAM - DON'T BREAK ME 10" EP (NEW RED ARCHIVES)

A 5 track acoustic 10"er(ooer!)of old songs. Now you all should have a vague idea of what SAMIAM usually sound like.No?Well,emotion filled,raw,turbo fuelled garage musik.Yet this record hits you like a cool summers breeze.Soft,tender,acoustic wafts. Different and refreshing.'Home Sweet Home' is a timeless classic.'Don't Break Me' is lifted from 'Billy' and 'You Looking At Me' is the sonic equivalent of a meaty joint. Breath in,feel the shit soak into your lungs and float to the ceiling.SAMIAM make everyday worth living. Oh and it's cheaper than an eighth too!

SCREECHING WEASEL - my brain hurts LP (lookout)

On first listen this 3 chord Ramones stuff just washed over me without making much of an impression,which is strange cos i love that stuff,but after a few listens things started to happen and now this record is my baby and we're getting married soon.Fancy coming to the wedding? Sure,there's nothing new on offer,they're not as original as Green Day or Mr.T.X,but what they do is real groovy in my book.The whole album is constant bubble gum orgasm.So if you're into Ramones/Hardons 3 chord surf punk then you'll wet yourself to this! Another bitchin' Lookout! release.

HARDONS - HAPPENING DUDES CLUB mini LP (RESEWAL)

Yay-Hay!A new HARDONS mini LP!! 'Happening Dudes Club' So off we go.Side 1-new stuff.Side 2-live stuff. City side kicks off with the best song 'She's a Dish'. Moody & broody riffy HARDONS.The lyrics suck though. "Supertight skirt,red hot lips,caught a glimpse like a flash of thunder"-Come on guys-grow up! Their new stuff is quite different from the pop punk of old-only rearing it's bubbly head in the chorus. If you've heard 'Carry Me Down' on the ROLLINS/HARDONS 12" then you'll know where they're coming from now. 'Selfish','World' & 'Hate so Hard' follow in the openers footsteps.Pretty good on 5th listen. Side 2 is the live shit.A cack 'Test' opens up but things hot up with 'Raining' and 'What Am I Supposed To Do?' but nose dive with the dire 2nd-year 'humour' of 'Suck 'n' Swallow'-oh yeah,great lads. So my verdict?D'you really give a shit?-thought not.

THE FIENDZ - WACT LP (FOREFRONT)

New Jersey's guitar pop teen punks return for their 2nd LP minus the MISFITS hair-doos and the RAMONES chord progressions,to offer us this akward bugger! Took me at least 10 listens to get into it,but once in,i didn't wanna come out.Their first (see BHP 1) was a total orgy of 3 chord monsters.This(3 years later) is a mature expedition into experimentation- land.Heavy ALL influence with creamy smooth vocals and 'interesting' song structures combine to make this a real good buy.Acoustic songs,Spanish instru- mentals and all out chugga-chugga popcore injection provide value for ya dosh.See 'em in the UK in the Spring/Summer of 93 with the PSEUDO'S in tow. Available from;FOREFRONT RECORDS, PO BOX 1964, HOBOKEN NJ,07030-1308,USA.Costs 10 dollars.Includes P & P.Send money order or well hidden dollar bills. You'll get the LP a week later.Don't worry Mike at FOREFRONT is a good bloke-no rip offs!

ALL - Percolator LP (cruz)

So,their new elpee has seen the light of day at last. Not that it's been a particularly long or anticipated wait,cos i'm no ALL freak.I love 'Prez' and other songs but they don't arf have some boring stuff.(Watch it!-ed) Well,to get to the point,this album surprised me,cos for once ,i loved every track.Yes,all of 'em. They seem to have cut down on the weirdness and stuck to a more conventional popcore sound with a heavy rock edge. On side one,we're introduced to a 'weird' instrumental that sounds like the tunes to 'Out Run' and 'Space Harrier' the arcade games!I'm not a big fan of their 'strangeness' but the rest of the long player hits home hard.An' i mean real hard.As hard as fuck.Period. I've been given a blank tape with no lyrics or even titles,so i can concentrate on the music 100%,cos that's all i have to go on(which is best i suppose). On to the rest,and please ignore my metaphores,all songs are beautiful showers that rain down on you making you smile and tingle all over(??).The single 'Dot' is a peach and the next reggea-ish/Sabbathlike tune is real bold of them and brilliant at the same time. There are fathoms of big fat shimmering fish in this ocean of an album(yes,the metaphores are back!!) plus 'amusing' bits and pieces.Like Egerton going into a music shop and trying out a BC Rich in true Wayne's World fashion and ALL's pisstake(at least i think & hope it's a parody) of MTV cock rock.It brings a smerk to my face hearing Reynolds scream 'Woah Yeeaaah!' in true AC DC style.The last number is a Nat King Cole type 50's ballad and is so cool.It's good to see them not being too scared to deviate from what is expected of a HC record. So,to round things off,a stonker of an LP and good to see them getting better and better.Their best vinyl since 'Allroy for Prez' by far. A definate buy.

HÜSKER DÜ - Warehouse :songs and stories (Warner)

This is the legendary Dü's last album and a double it is.It retails for around £15 so maybe this review might help you make your mind up whether to buy it if you're a Hüsker cognoscenti. Well here goes.It takes a few listens(like most of their stuff)to really appreciate it but after a few plays,shit happens. The whole first side is really excellent and the prize pig is 'Standing in the Rain' a real beautiful and emotional song.It's also,quite amusing to hear the uncanny similarity between the verses to 'Ice Cold Ice' and Nirvana's 'On a Plain'.But then if i were to name the amount of bands that the Dü had influenced i'd be here all week. Side 2 kicks off with probably the most immediate song on the side 'You're a Soldier'(who writes these titles) and the meandering 'Could you be the one'. The rest of the side follows in the same mid paced fuzzed out half whined/slurred melodies that are pretty good but do ware a bit thin after a while. Perhaps a touch of variety wouldn't go amiss? Pull out the next record and we have side 3 ready for a go.'Bed of Nails' opens with its melancholic triste tune.Ah good,something different. 'Actual Condition' really surprised me as it is either a pisstake(which i doubt the Dü would do) or a tribute to Elvis and did bring a smerk to my face listening to Hüsker playing rock 'n' roll. So flip the disc over,place the needle and it gives you the best song on the side 'Turn it around' and continues in the same vein more or less. I can't help thinking that they should have stuck to a single album format rather than stretch out 20 songs that almost half really don't hold up to much. But Jeze,7 albums in the space of 4 years is a phenominal rate and to be that good (have you heard Flip Your Wig?) you really can't grumble can you? This one's for fans only,though you won't go wrong taping it off a mate.May the legend live on......

ROLLINS BAND - Low self opinion 12" (imago)

A real angry powerful grind of a song we have here. Henry spits out all the demons trapped within his taught body and really conveys a tension i've rarely heard since Black Flag.This six minute grunge epic drops on you like a tonne of bricks.Play this and watch your Town collapse.Blinder.

The DAMNED - Live at the Lyceum '81 (ID)

I picked this up in a 2nd hand record shop and i'd never seen it before,so i thought i'd review it for you.(Tut.The things i do for you,heh?) This was released in '87 but was recorded at the LYCEUM (where ever that is) back in '81. The sound quality is real good and so are the songs. The best ones being 'I Fall','Smash it up','Love Song' and 'Just can't be happy today'.This is well worth the money but if you want the definitive Damned live album get 'Final Damnation' cos it's a total 18 song mutha' of a classic.

FUNBUG + the Pseudo Hippies. Clacton. 20-6-92

Yes!THE rock 'n' roll town,second only to L.A!!
Depressingly bleak Clacton-On-Shite is home
tonight,to the granny fucking,hog bumming and
buttock spanking gig of the year.Well,week
anyway...
The Pseudo's plug in and take off with a country
version of 'Hey You!Yeeehar!
Tear through a bucket load of fuzzed out,popped up,
2 minute noise feasts,say 'Fuck off you sad gits'
and piss on the front row!Now there's a band who
can thrill!
Funbug,billed as pop punk godz from Redditch,wobble
on dressed in cut downs,tanned naked tops(cor!)
and big Brummy cheesey grins.They continue to chat
to the punters before reluctantly,after 15 minutes,
launching into the god-like 'Everything'.All their
greatest hits dived off the PA and into your hearts.
The Pseudo's joined them for 'Tracey don't lose it'
and 'Blitzkreig Bop'.End.Kaput.
Tonight Clacton saw God.

The DAMNED- T&C club. London. 26-7-92

Silhouetted against green smoke is the eerie sentinel
like figure of Dave Vanian.Robed in long black pvc
cloak and 'Timothy Claypole' black jesters hat.But
this is no comical joke hat,no,this is an inverted
evil bit of headgear.
His presence is both arrogant and awesom,like some
macabre demon that's fallen from medi-eval folk lore.
Compelling....
'Fuck off you tossers!' grins Sensible.And shatters the
ghoulishly gothic atmosphere.A simultaneous cascade
of empty(and full)beakers arc through the humid
auditorium like a syncronised scud attack,finding
their mark perfectly(these punks must practice!)
'Fuck off!You love me really'(more beakers)
1-2-3-4!'New Rose'Woosh!Go the masses.Pogo frenzy!
Vanian controls the stage and the crowd.He kneels
in exhaustion,strides the monitors surveying his
grinning minions,swirls in his long cape and
generally is rock god.Tonight the world rotates
around him,and does he know it!
Wait for the blackout!Fall,Fish,Kill,Neat.-oh hell.
You know 'em all by now.Encore comes in the guise of
a 10 minute epic version of 'Smash it up'(along with
Captain in white Y-fronts and erect french loaf!!)
that builds from a tense acoustic opening.
Theatrical,fun,moody,insane-the Damned are everything.
Tonight they're the best band on the planet and we
want to have their babies.

FUGAZI- whitstable.kent. 4-5-92

Whittstable?Where's that?Kent?Is that in England?
Well after finding the miniscule sea side town we
searched for the church hall and found Ian Makaye
standing outside one."Oh,that must be it" i casually
remark.(Or does he take to hanging outside Church
halls for a hobby?)
I tell you what was weird,seeing members of Fugazi
walking around a sea side town the size of my
thumb nail and 'rubbing shoulders' with these
underground 'stars'.
And the gig?
Well,in an hour flat,600 people materialized out of
thin air to witness this pre tour 'secret' gig!!
Secret my scrotum!
The hall that previously rang to the echoes of
'Ging Gang Goolie' on a Tuesday Cub Scout night,
reverberated to the titanium rumbles of 'Repeater'
and all out american underground rock.
The sound was way too loud(they could hear it in
Zeebrugge) and therefore most of the songs were
reduced to pure high octane fuzz.But we did
recognise some and duefully jumped up and down,
teeth gritted in appropriate manner.
And isn't Makaye a sarky ol' git?!
(Assume preachy father-like voice)"I want my monitors
here and here!Don't push them.(rightfully directed
at the arsehole Nirvana stage 'divers') or "Do you
approve of the lights??Please turn them off"-well
excuse me for adding to the gig 'environment'.
You know,we only thought it'd might look a bit
cooler to have some lights....but if that's perceived
as detracting from the music then how about turning
down the P.A so we can bloody hear it!!
Still a good gig though.
And sweaty too!

The LOOKOUTS - IV EP (Lookout #42)

The Lookouts is (was) Laurance Livermore's(head stooge
at Lookout records) band.This EP features Green Day's
Billie Joe on guitar and backing vox and GD's Tre
(when he used to play for the Lookouts).This 4 song
single is quite good.A sort of folky Green Day but
no way as good.I suppose it's fairly decent but it
won't blow you away.7 out of 10 i'd give it.If you see
it i'd recommend it but i won't commit myself to

RAMONES - MONDO BIZARRO LP (chrysalis)

Easily the best RAMONES LP since 1981's 'PLEASANT
DREAMS'.A total corker of a long player.Fast,furious,
fun,as catchy as STD and twice as tasty.All songs rip
but the ones that rip that little bit more go by the
names of 'Censorshit','Job that ate my brain','Poison
Heart' and 'It's gonna be alright'.Bye or die!
GABBA GABBA HEY!

SAMIAM - BILLY LP (N.R.A)

Quite simply the best SAMIAM record in their discography
A monster of a disk.Serious shit.Power,emotion,melody.
How do these guys do it?There are some monolithic
masterpieces on this transparent green round-thing.Such
as the emotion charged 'Don't Break Me',the murderous
'Well' and the Nirvana-like tranquility of 'Go Away',
which simply makes Nirvana look like clueless school kid
mucking around with some amps they found.
If you dig any alternative/guitar music that WILL move
you then hear this or miss out on a whole new experience
Watch these guys get huge.Sorry....HUGE!

MONSULA - SANITIZED LP (Lookout)

Iwas quite taken a back on first listens.I expected
teen guitar pop.I was greeted by a mellow Pugazi.
On 3rd listens things happened.Now it seems this LP
is pretty damn flipping mucho good you know?
Groovy,bouncy,harsh,confident.Different for LOOKOUT
but maintaining the quality.

GOOBER PATROL - DUTCH OVENS LP (B.T.R)

The geeks from Norwich manage to con Aston Tuneage into
releasing another LP for 'em!Well,a good job too!
SNUFF meets GREEN DAY with splashes of DESCENDENTS.
The playing is a little sloppy ere an' there but it
would'nt be the GOOBS otherwise!Their best song ever
starts the ball rolling and 'Hay Hay Hay' they've won
BHP's appauling tacky cover of the decade award!!
A record to make you smile.Treat yourself to it.
£5 from: BOSS TUNEAGE RECORDS,"ASTON FIRS",HALTON
FENSIDE,Nr SPILSBY,LINCS.PE23 5BD.UK

The MR.T.EXPERIENCE - sex offender 7" (vital music)

An old single by the T. but fairly hard to find in the
U.K so i thought i'd bring it to mass attention (oh
posh eh?)The title track i think is a Blondie cover
but is a dead ringer for Mr T. cos it's awesom again,
a short sharp burst of guitar pop but the B side takes
the biscuit.'The last time i listen to you' is one of
the best songs on their new LP cos they rerecorded it
It's real hard to convey with puny words like 'ace'
and 'fab'.how good this really is but if you dig any
H/C pop punk guitar shit then search for this.

The MR.T.EXPERIENCE - MilkMilk Lemonade LP (lookout)

Yes,another bloody Mr.T. review!!Well they're the
latest buzz around these parts so who cares!?
This is easily their best album to date,these guys
just get better & better.I thought it'd have to be
a master piece to better their previous LP 'Light'
and therefore i was pleasantly(no,make that FUGGIN
OVER THE MOON!)that it turned out even better.
Every song is a (serial) killer.Raging,melodic
bursts of californian popcore to boogie to.The
songs that really excell above the other superb ones
are 'What do you want?','2 minute itch','I love you',
'Love American style' and 'Last time i listen to you'
Should be available in all good record stores now.

BIRDLAND-the Venue.New Cross.London. 2-5-92

Once apon a time Birdland were the most exciting
thing in British rock music.Dangerous,goodlooking,
arrogant and loud.Their records and live shows
shuddered with adrenalin fuelled sheet metallic
guitar pop.Now sadly,they are pleb.
Eagerly anticipating their arrival on stage,i stood
at the front grinning like some demented gremlin,
little did i know what i was in for......
On trundled four skinny blokes in hi-tec trainers
and sad baggy jeans.Said geezers proceeded to 'play
a string of new jangly indie-shite songs.Confused?
Sure,they played the smash hit classic 'Sleep with
Me' but it lacked passion,aggression,angst,that edge
that was present before......
Having seen them 15 months earlier at a packed
Kilburn National at the height of their popularity
and being blown into orbit(around Paradise,not Eart
stupid)tonight is like a jam in a garden shed in
comparison.Birdland now are minus a record company,
minus management,minus a new product and minus the
magic.
Sadly another great band chewed up and spat out by
that great big monster that is the biz.
I'm off to sulk.

A Scream From The Silence - Volume 1 (Looneytunes)

The first compilation LP from Looneytunes, featuring lots of good bands such as: Armed Relapse, All Too Human, Useful Idiot, Hooton 3 Car, Pus, Haywire, Tragic Performance, Pig Ignorance, Nocivo & Sarcastic Existence. It's pretty varied, not just featuring punk/hardcore bands. There's industrial ska, indie, thrash & death metal bands. I'll look forward to volume 2. Volume 1 is £2.50 (includes p&p) from: Looneytunes, Top Flat, 23 The Esplanade, Scarborough, N. Yorkshire, YO11 2AQ.

Pus - The Real Scapeghost EP (BFP)

The debut EP from Pus is finally out and it's a cracking piece of vinyl. 8 tracks of anarcho punk/hardcore. A few tracks are also melodic, tuneful, grindy & doomy which makes it a little more varied. Good stuff! £1.85 from: Nik, Marston House, Main Road, Elm, Wisbech, Cambs, PE14 0AB.

COUCH POTATOES - Excess all areas LP (vice)

Debut elpee by the bunch of fat lazy gits known as the Couch Potatoes and easily the best H/C (and i use the word liberally) record ever released by a British band.Forget the crap Jailcells,the pleb-like Goober and the sad Sofahead etc...this is the album of 92.And make no mistake about it! There are a bucket load of potential singles here. The phenomenally catchy 'Bob', 'Hole', 'Part of you', 'Another'(vocals penned by Kris Pseudo Hippy)and (yes,this word has been used before) the utter CLASSIC 'Three'.

Every single song is honed to murder.No fillers here mate,just perfectly crafted riffy popcore gems. This album,in my opinion,is on the same level as 'Nevermind' as it has the ability to appeal to indie pop kids,punks,thrashers,infact,bridge the whole spectrum of music listeners.

Get it,buy it,steal it,tape it,hear it now!

The MR. T. EXPERIENCE - Let's be together tonight 7"

Mr.T's latest single kindly donated to BHP by the band. This offering is on a spanish label called 'Munster' and not on the cool 'Lookout' and therefore is very limited,so god knows where you'll be able to buy it. And buy it you must cos,(wait for it)...it's a FUGGIN' MONSTER!! The A side is 2 minutes of classic Buzzcock meets sunny californian punk and is SO catchy it's disease like.The two B sides 'Merry Fuckin' Christmas' and 'Speed Racer' are also real good but not up to the same standard as the flip side.Here's Munster's address so you can find out how to get it- Munster Records, PO BOX 18107. MADRID 28080. SPAIN. Write today or be a sad pleb.

PAVEMENT - slanted & enchanted LP (bigcat)

Well probe my weeping piles with a rachet screwdriver but aren't these supposed to be the latest thing or Nirvana or something? 'Summer babe' kicks off the album and sets the president for the rest of the long player.Boring 2nd rate Pixies/ Dino Jr that rarely impresses but just plods away lazily in the background.This is the stuff that wanky 6th form tossers drool over(cos they're SO weird). A load of old dog's bollocks.Need i say more?

the PSEUDO HIPPIES - 7" EP (NASTY)

BHP's favs the PSEUDO HIPPIES debut 7" EP. On GERMANY's NASTY VINYL. 4 corking songs lifted from their 2 demo's. 'NA NA SONG'-pure sing-a-long city.Sort of PRIMITIVES meets RAMONES on steroids! 'WHY D'YOU LEAVE?' The song GREEN DAY wished they wrote,and how!! 'BUBBLE GUM 2' a surf-pop classic-must be heard to be believed! And finally the live fav/classic/Blitzkreig Bop of the 90's 'HEY YOU!'(you know,BA!BA!BA!) I've heard their forth coming MINI LP-which is a real mature progression and 1000 x better! If these kids get the right contacts they could be headlining BRIXTON ACADEMY in 3 years!No shit. For £2.50 you get photo's,info &lyrics. Cash or postals to;PSEUDO HQ,5 HENRYSON RD,LONDON, SE 4 1HL,UK

KRIS' TOP OF THE PLOPS ☺☺☺

1. SAMIAM-billy LP & don't break me 10"
2. RAMONES-mondo bizerro LP
3. VIOLENT FEMMES-debut LP
4. PSEUDO HIPPIES-mini LP
5. MR.T.EXPERIENCE-milk milk lemonade LP
6. FUNBUG-tezbinetop 7" EP
7. DOWN BY LAW-blue LP
8. COUCH POTATOES-three
9. PRIMITIVES-singles LP
10. SHAMEN-boss drum LP
11. WONDERSTUFF-8 legged grove LP(yep!3 years late!!)

DAG NASTY- 85-86 SINGLES BOX SET (selfless)

A limited edition of 3,500.Unreleased demos on coloured vinyl.All to entice the loaded consumer to part with their cash.Was it worth it? Um,me thinks not.Ok.Single one. 'Another Wrong' isn't much cop but 'Circles' is the same as the original only with demo-quality. 'Never go back' & 'I've heard' are nothing but mere copies of the originals.So far,so bad. Sigh.Single 2 commences with 'Can i say' not bad. 'Justification' okay.'Under your Influence'? Bloody good at last.But then it's such a good song it'd be good no matter who did it.'Moni Q' is a then new song and has appauling sound quality due to the fact that it's a bootleg of a gig.You can't hear fugg all.Seriously,you'd hear more melody in a coffee perculator than in this 'recording'.Sad. Single 3.This is where things hotten up.Songs from 'Wig out at Denkos' period.'Fall' & 'Trying' are real good.'All ages show' apart from the production, i feel is better than the original,oh,and 'Safe' is safe. Single 4.And this is the Dave Smalley bit. 'My Dog is a Cat' is a comical song,fairly amusing and 'Mule' is nothing short of mediocre.'Trying' live is again,atrocious sound quality wise and 'Another Wrong 2' is marginally better than the version on single 1,cos of Smalley's vocals(what a vocalist!!)All in all(Pun not intended) £9.99 is way too much for this obvious cash in.It's also out on LP for £6.99 which is better value than this boxed singles set but still for fans only i dare say.

FUNBUG - Funbug e.p. (Lookout)

This is a MONSTER of an EP. A 30 legged,16 eyed,sky-scraper sized,green scaled one at that.And my god,do you need this!!! The mother (and granny) of all EP's this year! Puts most bands to shame.The UK's answer to the Ramones:only BETTER!There's no point describing the songs,cos words don't do them justice.Only to say that 'Everything','Seventeen','Lobo Doc' and the neo classic of the 90's 'Flimsoles' would brutally murder your Granny if they could exracate themselves from your turntable.And they'd have a tough time doing so,cos once you've listened to this God-like masterpiece,you'd never have it off your stereo.Never,ever.You might aswell super glue it on,so you don't loose it when you move house in 7 years time,or something.If anyone ever gets bored of this,they deserve to be shot for having no taste what-so-ever! BUY IT NOW!-No!Make that yesterday.Or be a terminally boring,clueless,miserable CUNT! contact:Lookout Records.135 Grove Rd.Walthamstow. London.E 17 9BU. £2.50 should cover it.Now bugger off and order it!

IS IS MY WINDOW ON THE RLD—I SEE IT ALL WITHOUT VING TO DO ANYTHING

IF ONLY I'D LISTENED WHEN THEY TOLD ME THAT HE WAS A CHEAT, A LIAR, A THIEF......

THANKS TO SOPWITH MINOR'S TIMELY INTERVENTION, THE SCHOOL BULLY WAS NO LONGER A PROBLEM

FOR YOUR CONVENIENCE...
← WE TURN THIS...INTO THIS →
USING ONLY....
1. Enough grain to feed a Somali family for a year.
2. 40,000 Volts.
Wasn't it Worthwhile?

EN THEY SAY "NO" THEY ALLY MEAN "YES"!

BHP
iSSUE 4

JOEYFAT
LONDON FINSBURY PARK GEORGE ROBEY

"JOEYFAT — IT'S all one word, it's all one word . . ." So says singer Matt, strolling around the stage as if he blinkin' well owned it. And so he should — after all, the man is (seemingly) nine feet tall, with mercilessly cropped hair and hence just a suggestion of pathological violence.

Without wishing to labour the point, this man is . . . positively *elongated*. He could challenge tower blocks to a fight. And win. But if this suggests a discomforting Goliath, more awkward than a three legged donkey who's just been caught shoplifting, the vocalist turns the prejudice with consummate ease. Persistently stroking his stomach helps; constantly grinning to himself is also an advantage; and gracefully leading the Joeyfat pack into Hardcoreland is most certainly the cake underneath the icing.

While the vast majority of UK bands peering across the Atlantic have opted for the slack plaid passion of the grunge brigade (see Bivouac, Edsel Auctioneer et al), Joeyfat have burrowed deeper into the American turf and emerged with a sound that demands the term 'lethal', and then punches it in the face.

Taking their cue from Fugazi, the Tunbridge Wells five-piece go for the jugular with a jagged edge of sound that confronts as much as it comforts; a tense guitar assault that leaves the senses all wondering and wobbly.

'People' and 'Windscreen' set the scene perfectly, abrupt titles backed up by equally economic hardcore touches. Where so many in their position are thrashing around in search of some kind of Nirvana, Joeyfat aren't afraid to strip down to freak out; to leave holes which compatriots fill pure bluster.

Jeez, if they were any more disciplined we'd be calling in Vice Squad for fear of their propriety.

Joeyfat: lard as nails.

Simon W

Local band Joeyfat playing to a packed audience at The Chalybeate Forum

And the band played on

ABOUT 150 people had to be turned away as crowds packed into the The Chalybeate Forum, the new music and arts centre on Tunbridge Wells common, on its opening night last month.

Headlining on the night were London band Four Heads in a Fish Tank, supported by Joeyfat. The following evening saw local band Code performing.

Mark Davyd, one of the four founders of the centre, said: "It couldn't have been any better. It was a superb opening evening.

"It was packed on both nights and there were no problems at all.

"We had to close the doors just before Friday and at about 9.30pm on Saturday be the amount of people."

The Forum, off London Road, has a film Tuesday nights, jazz on Wednesdays and and blues is on Thursdays. Fridays and S are rock and pop nights. Mark said he w hear from classical and folk musicians to Monday nights, and someone to run evenings on Sundays.

Anyone seeking further information can The Chalybeate Forum on 0892 530411.

HELLO AND WELCOME
To BRITISH HARDCORE PRESS? Issue 4!

I wasn't sure if this issue would ever see the light of day - so a big thanks to you for buying it, and all the wonderful 'I got off my arse' people who've helped in it's production. I get a pretty good response here at BHP HQ, and it's very encouraging, but it'd be cool to receive a few more letters. Feel free to send me articles, opinions, interviews or whatever. Write to :
BHP, 1 Chandos Road, Tunbridge Wells, Kent, TN1 2NY, UK.

Thanks and take care,

Dave

Special thanks to : Steve, Ben, Martyn, Kris, Austin, Ian, Andy, Dave & John, Vic & Pat, David Barbe, Simon, Matt, Sugar, Decadence Within, Alloy, Strookas, Joeyfat, Sonar Nation, Couch Potatoes, Chi Pig, Pseudo Hippies, Shreds & Austin, Dragnet, and LOBO!

Here is a list of the merchandise being distributed by BHP, available from the address above.
Cheques / P.O's payable to D. Gamage. All prices post paid.

BHP - The best zine in the country - Back issues, 50p each.
#1 featuring Green Day, Hard-Ons, Jailcell Recipes, Factory Farming...
#2 featuring Ramones, Joeyfat, Unpolluted Air, Sleeping...
#3 featuring All, MTX, SNFU, Funbug, Planet Earth...
#4 featuring Sugar, Alloy, Decadence Within, Comics...   BHP #5 - Out and about real soon!

GOTHAM TAPES - The Alternative Tape Label - £1.50 each.
GOT 001 : TEE-HEE Compilation; 40 mins, 12 bands, 12 trax.
GOT 002 : COUCH POTATOES - LIVE IN TUN/WELLS; 40 mins, 16 trax.
GOT 003 : LIVE AT THE SHELLEY Compilation; 60 mins, 5 bands, 25 trax - featuring
          BBMF's, Strength Alone, Angus Bagpipe, Couch Potatoes...
GOT 004 : 'Hello, Bollox & Welcome' Compilation; 60 mins, 25 bands, 25 trax.
GOT 005 : MORAL CRUX, Tout a fait punk, live radio broadcast; 60 mins, 20 trax.
GOT 006 : ANOTHER Compilation; 40 mins, 13 bands, 13 trax
GOT 007 : Eyes Down For God Compilation; 60 mins, 20 bands, 20 trax.
GOT 008 : JAWBREAKER - LIVE AT GILMAN STREET; 60 mins, 15 trax.
GOT 009 : COUCH POTATOES - EXCESS ALL AREAS; 60 mins, 24 trax - Brilliant Melodic
          Hardcore in a Descendents vein.
GOT 010 : JOEYFAT - SOUP; 60 mins, 15 trax (8 studio & 7 live) - UK's finest - reminiscent
          of Shudder To Think, Alice Donut & Rollins.
GOT 011 : Low Brow Head Tread Compilation; 60 mins, 20 bands.
GOT 012 : All the Smiley Faces Compilation; 60 mins, 21 trax, 15 bands - superb melodic HC.

VINYL
PANX 11 - 7" EP, £2.00
featuring Couch Potatoes, Blanks 77, Eight Ball, Public Lost, Wounded Knee & Lamento.
NOWHERE STREET - 7" Compilation, £2.00
featuring Vendabait, Couch Potatoes, Cheese Doodles & Pseudo Hippies.
JOEYFAT 7" GOD/WINDSCREEN £2.00
"Band of the month" - Lookout, "Punches lethal in the face" - NME.
COUCH POTATOES - IN BED WITH 7" EP, £2.00
4 Trax of Punk, melodic hardcore from the fat lads.
COUCH POTATOES - EXCESS ALL AREAS LP, £5.00
14 classic trax, in the vein of Descendents, BDC, Samiam, Green Day...

T - SHIRT
JOEYFAT - ONE WORD GRRRL, £6.00.
Double sided XL , large logo and angry girl - "It's all one word", Black & White.

BUY INDEPENDENT - SUPPORT THE UNDERGROUND!

WHAT'S IT LIKE BEING A BAND IN KENT?

What's it like being in a 'Kent Band?' is the question BHP put to the STROOKAS, SONAR NATION and JOEYFAT, probably the best three bands in the country, (in our opinion,) and these are the answers we received...

Being in a Band in Kent can be a painfully frustrating experience, especially if you're in a band that plays music similar to us.
Venues are the major problem - they are few and far between. I can only think of "Bottoms" in Folkestone and "The Forum" in Tunbridge Wells.
There are some good bands in Kent such as "Joeyfat" and "Somersault" who deserve some recognition. London's nearby, but if you can't prove you've got a following, you're unlikely to get a decent London gig. If there's not enough decent indie venues in Kent than you can't really build a decent following to take to a gig in London. I suppose that's what you call a vicious circle. JOHN - STROOKAS

I've answered with a list of pros and cons.
Pros
1. Lack of competition from other Bands, although this could also be a con due to lack of incentive to better yourself.
2. Being a Kent Band keeps you far enough removed from immediate scenes which don't seem to last to long.
Cons
1. Lack of decent venues to play.
2. General apathy of people wanting to see live music.
3. Hardly any music industry i.e. Record companies, reviewers, management etc. Although this could be used as a plus point.
4. Hard to get decent London gigs.
5. Sometimes snubbed by London before they even listen to you.
6. Too many sad metal bands.   SIMON- SONAR NATION

As the sun beats through my kitchen window, bathing the lower half of my body and carbonating my hormones, I ponder your question.
I like my home town (Tunbridge Wells) in the same way I like the shirt I'm wearing. It doesn't present me in my best light, at my most attractive, but I'm used to the way it presents itself to me. Perhaps I like it as a reaction to the obvious, that I should hate it as if in some way it holds me back, but I'm very much of the opinion that that sort of negativity just reflects a discontent with oneself.
Lets examine the facts (oh no - court room drama!) We have the best small venue in the South, probably the country (The Forum) a meeting place for the rich and poor in spirit. Where did this mythical place come form? From the efforts of the participants, from years of enthusiasm. Sounds idyllic doesn't it? That's the way it happened. We have the brightest band in the country, probably the world (Joeyfat) How did that happen. From effort, creativity and a refusal to be compromised. These things haven't arisen from a bed of privilege, the paths have not been smooth, we're all used to the boot in the teeth. What we do have is a solid belief in this you get what you settle for!
So that's why things are much fizzing in this town for me, so what about fringe benefits? We have two of the best cake shops in the world here ("Piece of Cake" and "Truly Scrumptious,") open fields within two minutes walk (for those who do,) I could go on at miserable length. Apparently we don't have good clothes shops or record shops. So how far are London and Brighton away?
So that's about enough, struggle hard, keep your wits about you, beware of platitudes and thank God you don't live in America. MATT - JOEYFAT

So that just about answers that, it can be dismal - but where can't. On the whole we agree with Matt. Make the best of it and being a band from Kent can be great!

THE MYTH OF MILK

Milk is one of the most controversial and misunderstood foods. We are told to drink milk every day throughout our lives as part of our Western diet, but Orientals and Africans have traditionally avoided milk, except as a purgative.

In nature, the young feed exclusively on milk until weaned away from it on other foods. The natural disappearence of the milk-digesting enzyme, lactase, from the human system upon reaching maturity proves that adult humans have no nutritional need for milk. Though milk is a complete protein food when consumed raw, it also contains fat which, according to the rules of trophology, means that it combines poorly with any other food except itself. When you 'wash down' other foods with cold milk it curdles immediatley on entering the stomach, coagulating around other food particles, insulating them from exposure to gastric juices, delaying digestion and permitting putrefaction. Therefore the main rule of milk consumption is 'Drink it alone or leave it alone.'

Today, milk is made even more indigestible by pasteurisation, which destroys its natural enzymes and alters its delicate proteins. Raw milk contains the active enzymes lactase and lipase, which is devitalised of active enzymes, cannot be properly digested. Pasteurization also renders the calcium and others minerals in milk unassimilable.

During the 1930's, Dr Francis M Pottenger conducted a study on the relative effects of pasteurised and raw milk diet on cats. The group fed on raw milk thrived, remaining healthy throughout their lives, but the group fed on pasteurised milk soon became listless, confused and vulnerable to a host of chronic degenerative ailments such as heart disease, kidney failure, loss of teeth and brittle bones. The first offspring of the pasteurised milk group were all born with poor teeth and small, weak bones - a sign of calcium deficiency from pasteurised milk. The offspring of the raw milk group remained as healthy as their parents. Many of the kittens in the third generation of the pasteurised group were stillborn, while those that survived were all sterile and unable to reproduce, so the experiment had to end there, although the raw milk group continued to breed and thrive. Furthermore, new born calves fed on pasteurised milk usually die within six months, a fact that the commercial dairy industry is loathe to admit.

Despite such scientific evidence in favour of raw milk and against pasteurised milk and despite the fact that until the early 20th century the human species thrived on raw milk, it is actually illegal to sell raw milk to consumers. It is far more profitable to the dairy industry to pasteurise milk to extend its shelf-life, though such denatured milk doesn't kill all of the dangerous germs.

Three generations of Westerners have been fed on pasteurised milk and today infertility has become a major problem for young mothers, while calcium deficiency affects 90% of children in the form of tooth decay and many women in the form of osteoporosis.

To make things worse, milk is now routinely 'homogenised' to prevent the cream from separating from the milk. This involves the pulverisation of the fat molecules to the point that they will not separate from the rest of the milk. But it also permits those tiny fragments of fat to pass through the villae of the small intestine, greatly increasing the amount of denatured fat and cholesterol absorbed to the body. In fact, you absorb more milk-fat from homogenised milk than you do from pure cream!

Adults should seriously reconsider milk as a constituent of their diets, unless they are able to obtain raw certified milk, which is an excellent food by itself. To stuff children with pasteurised milk in order to make them grow 'strong and healthy' is sheer folly, because they cannot assimilate the nutrients. All humans should eliminate all pasteurised diary products from their diets, for they only gum up intestines with a layer upon layer of slimy sludge that interferes with the absorption of organic nutrients.

DECADENCE WITHIN

Decadence Within formed in 1984 and spent the next 9 years forging their own unique musical and lyrical style.

Combining hard-core, punk, metal and rock, they play music which is complex but melodic, aggressive but controlled.

Lyrically they write about both personal and political concerns, the tensions and dilemmas found in the inner and outer worlds.

To date they have done about 200 live shows, honing their enthusiastic and energetic performance to a razor edge.

They've released 2 albums and 2 7" E.P.'s and appeared on many compliation albums, always receiving excellent critical response.

Their 3rd L.P. is about to be released called "Reality Wake-Up Call" through Prophesy Records (distributed world-wide by Plastic Head) in May. Without doubt their finest work to date. Obviously an interview was called for.......

BHP: What is Decadence Within about as a band, what do you want people to get from it?

DW: Decadence Within try to be challenging both musically and lyrically. We don't want to play & say what people expect. This is one of the reasons why we deny labels like "Straight Edge" - when you've been labelled, you're conveniently tagged and pigeon-holed and severely restricted. I mean, two of the band are what you could term" straightedge" if you're one of these folk who feel a need to categorise everything, but we don't want to be lumped in with all that.

I'm the way I am because I'm health conscious and because I need to keep my wits about me, not because I'm so insecure I need to be accepted by some peer group. All the individuals in this band do what they want when they want - and this is reflected in our band. We don't want your approval or acceptance, we play like this for ourselves and if others can get off on it, well that's OK too. If we wanted to be big, we'd play some generic thrash and grow our hair, but we don't, we want to provoke questioning and ultimately understanding.

BHP: Where did you get your name?

DW: My Mum and Dad gave it to me!!!!

No, seriously, I picked the name from a novel called " Portrait Of A Lady " by Henry James, which is abut an American girl who comes to Europe and soon discovers the hidden corruption in society there. We thought it could also apply to the decadence in Government , Church and other such institutions.......and also to the decadence in us all. We've all got it, a darker side to our personalities, many people try to deny it, but why? They should learn to look inside themselves and embrace their own blackness, like a coin, we are made up of two sides. They compliment and support each other, one cannot exist on it's own.

BHP: What is the "Hard-core Scene" like in Herefordshire?

DW: Crap. It is non-existent. There is Decadence Within and there is Shutdown and that's it. It's basically a very rural area which is very nice, but this tends to will people asleep and in their dale they sit and idly watch life drift by. Fortunately it's this soothing sense of security we hate, which inspires us to kick back and get the hell out of here as often as we can. Believe me, without the band, I would've gone the way most of my friends have, kiss ass all week saving for the weekend when they turn into violent drunks and knock shit out of each other every Friday and Saturday. There a few bands in neighbouring counties, like Prophecy of Doom who've achieved a medium of success, but they're more "death metal" than "hc".

BHP: Are there to be any more releases on First Strike and what do you have currently available?

DW: There's unlikely to be anything else on First Strike, the 7" "Pay off Time" was a one off. The next album will be on Prophecy Records, through Plastic Head, another one off. I think we''ll take each record as it comes, rather than embroil ourselves again in the legal and contractual wrangles a multi-record deal entails. Currently available is the "Pay off Time" 7" and the CD and cassette versions of "Soulwound" which also include the "This Lunally" L.P.

Come May, the new L.P. will be available on vinyl and CD. Write for details, try to enclose an SAE if you can.

BHP: Tours or future plans?
DW: As soon as the new L.P. is out in May, we're off to tour Europe, mainly Germany. Then in June we're doing a mini-tour of Ireland. In the summer we'll do sporadic shows in the UK, wherever and whenever we can, then in the Autumn we'll record another L.P. and start it all over again!! The new L.P. is called " Reality Wake-Up Call" and believe me, when I say, it kicks ass! Please watch out for it.

BHP: Anything to add?
DW: Live life to the full because before you know it it's time to go.

Contact:
Decadent H.Q,
"Eastlea"
Homend Crescent
Ledbury
Herefordshire
HR8 1AQ

IN DEFENCE OF COMICS

...the Professor Tring reports...

"With words and pictures you can do anything!"
- Robert Crumb.

The status of comics has been frequently and hotly debated: do comic books constitute an art form? or are they just mass produced, shallow, entertainment for the masses? Are they innovative and progressive, or do they propogate dangerous and antisocial values?

In what follows, I want to try and put a little perspective into some of these arguments. If you can't be bothered to read the rest (or if you just like knowing what I'm going to say) I'll give you the basic conclusions now. (1) Comics have a history which goes back at least to the 18th century (cartoonists like Hogarth - who is considered to be a Great Artist). They might even go back to Ancient Egypt. (2) Essentially the comic medium is a combination of words and pictures. There is no way that comics may be attacked as an inherently evil medium. (3) Accusations that comics are sexist and over-violent are often difficult to sustain. It is nearly impossible to prove that they affect behaviour. The problem is that in the current climate, people can get away with this type of charge without really proving their case - because, as we all know, if its sexist and violent it must be BADD!... It is perhaps more important to ask why comics should be singled out for such treatment.

HISTORY

The ancestor of the contemporary comic is the Ancient Egyptian Hieroglyph. The use of pictures which included words or phrases continued through classical greece and rome, and into the middle ages. Many religious paintings were either surrounded by words (prayers or excerpts of scriptures) while some even have a phrase 'coming out of the mouth' of a saint. Medical textbooks from the (15th/16th century) renaissance often included written text within an ilustration, the labelling of a muscle or artery for example. By the 18th and 19th centuries, a tradition of political cartooning had developed. A single panel would be drawn to illustrate a political event, often satirically - not t say insultingly.

The newspapers of the 1890's realised that an excellent 'hook' with which to catch new readers would be the inclusion of comedy sketches - comic drawings - in their pages. So it was at the start of this century, that the comic strip was established in its modern format. The strip would be a series of panels (probably 3 or 4), either captioned, or including the famous 'speech bubbles'. These strips appeared daily, often with a specially long strip for the Sunday edition. Newspaper proprietors quickly realised that collected editions of comic strips could sell well in their own right - the comic book was born.

You're probably familiar with the rest. The 30s and 40s saw the rise of the superheroes (superman was the first, in 1938). Its important to realise that they were nothing startlingly 'new' - the tradition of telling stories about the fantastic deeds of heroes goes right back to the myths of greece and rome, and even before that. Its a phenomenon we share with many other cultures. Native americans have their Hero Twins, and Indian legends are littered with heroic kings and princes, to give just two examples. (What is interesting is that the emergence of the superhero comics coincides with the new role which america was taking in the world - the US was confirmed as #1 nation after WWII). The 50s saw the attack on horror comics in England and the US - depraved and wicked publications like 'Tales form the Crypt' were 'proven' by various 'experts' to affect the behaviour of otherwise 'normal' children. In the 60s, the superhero returned - a notable newcomer was spiderman (note: the Spiderman, like the Batman may be found in the myths of the central america cultures - aztec, toltec and so on). Partly in response to the censorship of comics in the 50s, in the 60s we also see the development of underground comics within the beatnik subculture (e.g. Robert Crumb, part of the San Francisco hippie set).

THE MEDIUM

The combination of words and pictures is extremely potent. Like the great Calvin (of Calvin and Hobbes), I can spend days lost in the imaginative world of comics; they are really absorbing. Comics are similar to film/ tv in this way. They present us with two different modes of thought - imagery (associated with dreams), and words (which we use to communicate and to think analytically). That last sentence might seem a bit dodgy - the precise difference between words and pictures is often unclear. Within comics, however, we may agree that the 'words' of the text are distinct from the 'images' of the text (here, the text is the whole comic - colours, words, pictures, panels, the lot).

The categories of 'images' and 'words' are incredibly open. They may be filled in many different ways. We'd be foolish to expect anything else. This means that there are many ways of expression

ALEISTER CROWLEY.

KAREN

within the medium of comics. A quick glance at the diversity of work within the genre confirms this. It may come as a surprise that 2000 AD and Marshall Law are part of the same medium as Bunty and Fungus the Bogeyman. In the world of comics we find such diverse stories as Watchmen; Aliens: Earth Wars; the Beano; The Sandman; Viz; Tank Girl; Maus I and II; Deadline magazine; Terminator versus Robocop; Battle Action; Sin City; Misty; Roy of the Rovers; Calvin and Hobbes; Love and Rockets; Peanuts; Batman; Hardboiled.

Further afield, there is the mass of comic material in France, Belgium and Spain, where the medium is frequently considered as an art equal to painting and the novel. The work of Hergé, Moebius and Jacques Tardi all demonstrates a high level of accomplishment. The Anglo-American tradition has its own great names - Neil Gaiman, Frank Miller, and Alan Moore, for example. The rising sun of the Japanese Manga comics should not be forgotten, particularly since it conceals the vast comics culture of SE Asia in general.

Associated forms include Disney animations, the cartoons of Hanna Barbera (the Flintstones, the Jetsons, Scooby Doo), Raymond Briggs and Art Speigelman's more 'serious' work, and the use of animated cartoons in music videos. The connection between music and comics is seen in the publicity work that Jamie "Tank Girl" Hewlett did for the Senseless Things. The audience for indie-pop noise, off-beat comics and political issues like feminism, environmentalism and racism is often linked together - as seen in the Love and Rockets series by the Hernandez brothers.

I suppose what I'm getting at is that 'comics' are just one aspect of a medium which is linked to many other forms around in society. To say that 'comics' are useless/ boring/ crap etc is really narrow minded. Its like trying to say that all work on video is evil. As if Bill and Ted, action movies, rock video, educational videos for primary schools, corporate videos shown to executives in suits, pornography, horror movies can all be lumped together... as if. So don't try and talk about 'comics' like its only Batman, Spiderman, and the Marvel(lous) superheroes.

CRITICISM

Comics are often criticised for being obscene, sexist, violent, racist, corrupting and so on. The best way to tackle this type of allegation is to change the rules. Who is making the charge? Is the charge made fairly? Can it be justified? Is there another, equally reasonable explanation?

1) Who is making the charge?

When Spike Lee was asked to comment on the Ice T 'copkiller' controversy, Lee replied that Terminators 1 & 2 saw Schwarzenegger shoot up a whole load of cops, and no-one said anything - so why the problem with Ice T? (The answer lies in the fact that Ice T is black, and therefore a threat (?), but Schwarzenegger is friends with that Nice Man, George Bush...)

What this brings out is the way in which an act may be seen as good or bad according to who performs the act, and not according to the act itself. So when comics are criticised for being sexist or violent, is it because they are sexist and violent, or is it because of what (who) comics are - if you will, part of the ethnic minority, the working class of the publishing world. It is noticeable that the (self-)righteous critics who attack comics/ videos/ rock music as a corrupting influence somehow exempt other work - noticeably 'fine' art, 'great' literature, and 'classical' music.

2) Is the charge made fairly?

The play by Shakespeare 'Titus Andronicus' is surprisingly violent, including two rapes, the forcible removal of a girls tongue, and the cutting off of a man's hands. Finally, a man's head is baked, whole, in a pie. No-one attempts to censor the violence in Shakespeare. Or in the bible, which several 'blood and guts' passages. Neither does anyone condemn the bible as sexist either, despite the way in which women are consistently protrayed as inherently evil (Eve seduces Adam and brings about the fall from grace), or lustful (the whore of babylon), and women are seldom given prominent roles - except Mary, who is better than normal women because she can give birth without all that sordid 'sex' business.

The point is that, all too often, only some art is attacked as obscene/ sexist/ violent. All too often, the work which is ignored is ignored because its audience 'will know how to react to such scenes' (in other words, audiences of Shakespeare are not perverts, and know when to be shocked, and know the boundary between what is artistically expressive, and what is socially intolerable).

Equally, when 'art' is attacked as obscene, there is often an underlying sense of duty: "We must protect comics readers from comics, because they are incapable of protecting themselves"....

3) Can it be justified?

Having said that, yeah, sure, comics are often violent and sexist. Its a male dominated industry, in a male dominated society. But is it terrible and despicable that comics are sexist, or is it worse that society as a whole is that way? More importantly, is it enough to say that comics are sexist/ violent? It seems to me like a pretty arrogant attitude that is able to write off the whole comic reading public simply because the majority of comics are sexist and violent.

Such outright condemnation ignores the many moves within the industry to counter the sexist/ violent preoccupations.

ROKARA SOH.

I KNOW.

For instance TankGirl - an undeniably strong female role; the (brilliant) work of the Hernandez Brothers; and a few (sadly unpublicised) female/ feminist artists all show that moves are afoot to provide an alternative to sexist attitudes. Surely it is more important to ask _why_ sexist and violent images are so popular. Until we can account for this we will not be able to change it.

In fact, on a more abstract level, it had been shown that fantasy (which is what most comics really are) is difficult to describe as simply sexist or violent. In fact it is often difficult to describe altogether. The reader may identify with the powerful or the powerless in a comic - and probably both. The reader may identify with both male and female charaters, or even animal characters, regardles of the reader's own gender/ species. At its most obscure, a reader may identify (at a level of fantasy and desire) with a particular place, or even the atmosphere of a place!

Another important consideration is that much pacifist/ anti-sexist criticism of comics works in a rather strange way. Instead of saying 'what is the world like, what is going on?', it instead states that 'this is how the world should be' before going out to attack everything which fails to make the grade. In this sense, anti-sexism is not necessarily a progressive idea. It shows how the arguments against sexism - that it discriminates against women - can turn through 180 degrees, and end up repeating the old inequalities in reverse - discriminating against men.

4) Is there another, equally reasonable explanation?

It is also important to understand how violence in comics may work in unexpected ways. Marshall Law is a good example. Like the comedian Denis Leary, Marshall Law over-does the macho hero image to such an extent that it is no longer possible to take such a character seriously outside of the story (or even within it). Rather than promote a particular way of life, both Leary and Marshall Law are so excessive that they end up becoming unbelievable, revolting and extreme (the fact that on a level of fantasy we may enjoy subjecting outselves to such revulsion only complicates things further!). These comics (to which we might add Hardboiled, Raw, Battle action, or even Rambo/ Stallone, van Damme, and Seagal) present us with the impossible Ultra Male/ hyper-macho. If to act 'tough' is now to 'do a "Rambo"', then it is no longer the same as it once was - to be a 'real' man. Both real men and Rambo have become objects of derision rather than objects of aspiration. As the slogan on his huge chest suggests, Marshall Law, becomes an image of fear and loathing rather than one of love and desire for the "Real(ly) Man(ly)"

So how do I end this ?

Well, first of all, comics are not just superheroes. There is a world out there. Different types of comic books, of comic strips, of cartoons and graphic novels, and so on. They've got a long history. These days, its a very varied field. Like everything, you have to look hard for the really good bits (remember, 90% of everything is shit). But comics are not just sexist, or just violent. There are many different stories, and they work in many different ways. So get out there and read some. If you don't like them, find some others, or take up knitting.

And remember - stay hungry.

A transatlantic interview through the post with David Barbe of

SUGAR

As we all know, Bob Moulds' new band have received a lot of coverage in the music press over the last year. His past and present activities and thoughts have been the subject of many a double-page spread.But what about the other two, eh? What do they do, other than tread the boards with Bob? What do they think? This short interview is my humble attempt to redress the balance. (How about someone doing an interview with Malcolm Travis?)

Town & Country Club 1992

● **With the success of Sugar, has your own band Buzz Hungry been put on the back-burner for the forseeable future?**

Buzz Hungry is still active.We play locally in Athens, and record periodically as well. However, we all have other projects that receive priority. Drummer Brooks Carter plays guitar with Jack-O-Nuts who have just released their first album via Radical Records, a Matador subsidiary. Bassist Eric Sales also plays with Little Debbie. Sugar keeps me pretty busy. We all still very much enjoy Buzz Hungry.

● **For the benefit of people already in bands, please give us the lowdown on the John Keane Studios and your work there. Which local bands are particularly worthy of attention?**

When I'm not on the road with Sugar, I engineer and produce records. I do the bulk of my recording at the John Keane Studios. It's a very comfortable, warm-sounding, 24-track work environment.

There are several Athens bands that need to be heard. I've already mentioned Jack-O-Nuts. Little Debbie also have a record, a six-song 7" EP that is blistering. Six String

Fever is a new band to watch for. Seersucker, from Atlanta, too. I just finished recording their album.

● **With bands from the independent/underground scene finally breaking big, how do you see this affecting the attitude of the major labels in America?**

It seems like more and more new major label acts are being marketed as alternative in order to establish some credibility, although it is manufactured credibility. There are some positives. I never thought I'd see a band like The Melvins on a major.

● **Are there any plans to re-release the Mercyland Records and/or release tracks that haven't yet made it onto vinyl or CD?**

Yes. Planned Obsolescence is going to release a full-length CD compilation late fall of this year. I'm currently working on editing it. Squashing five years into 70 minutes is not easy, but I must say I've been enjoying myself putting it together. I hadn't heard a lot of that stuff in ages.

● **Do you see the election of Bill Clinton as a positive step for America?**

Certainly Clinton over Bush is a step in the right direction. At least he admits that problems exist. Nonetheless he is still a politician. It will be interesting to see if, or how much, he is able to deliver on his promises.

● **What is your view on the suggestion that the music industry is in heated competition with the computer software industry?**

I wouldn't say that the computer software industry in competition with the music industry, but that they are in league with one another, what with the advent of mini-disc.

Right now, current technology doesn't allow for mini-disc to do what the manufacturers say it can without compromising audio quality. It will be interesting to see what happens in the future.

● **In the wake of the LA riots last year, do you think progress has been made to ease racial tension, particularly in Georgia?**

Perhaps awareness has been heightened, but real change probably won't occur until today's children are adults.

I should point out that the tensions in Georgia are nothing close to what you saw in LA last year. Most of the racism is subtle. That doesn't make it any better, just less explosive.

● **Are songs by you, and come to think of it Malcolm, going to be recorded by Sugar in the future?**

Sugar will probably record a

Town & Country Club 1992

few of my songs when we make the next record. Whether or not they wind up on the album will depend on how they fit in with the context of the whole.

● **Can you tell us what inspired Bob to start up the Singles-Only Label?**
You'd have to ask Bob about that one.

● **What was the first record you bought? And the most recent?**
The first with my own money was the 'Barrel Full Of Monkees' anthology at age seven. My most recent purchase was a vinyl copy of Slint 'Spiderland'. I already owned the CD, but it's such a great record I wanted to hear it on vinyl as well.

● **Is there one song that means more to you than any other, be it one you've written or one written by someone else?**
I wrote a song called 'When Annabelle Cries' for my daughter when she was about six months old. Mercyland played it once or twice before breaking up. Very few people have heard it. It is a very personal, honest song. I still think about it.

　　As for a song by another, it would have to be The Minutemen's 'History Lesson Part II'. Now that's honest. ■

Town & Country Club 1992

MERCYLAND/BUZZ HUNGRY DISCOGRAPHY

MERCYLAND SINGLES;
Black on black on black/Ciderhead
(Mustang Records 1987)

Enter the crafty bear e.p.
(Planned Obselecence 1991)

Service Economy/Uncle
(Nasty Vinyl 1993)

MERCYLAND ALBUMS;
No feet on the cowling
(Tupelo Recording/Revolver 1988)

COMPILATION APPEARANCES;
"Amerigod" - Some Compilation
(DRG)
"Western Guns" - Make the city grovel in it's dust
(Twilight)

BUZZ HUNGRY SINGLES;
The Envictor/Beer commercial
(Singles Only Label 1992)

BUZZHUNGRY ALBUMS;
Fried like a man
(cassette only mini album)
(OIC International 1992)

DIARY OF A STROOKA AGED 29

We Played 11 gigs in 11 days all over France. That's more gigs in two weeks than we play in a whole year in England.

10 February: First gig in Lille was a corker. Lots of people turned up and they really enjoyed our frantic set. Stayed in French Fella's Apartment and were awoken by somebody dressed head to foot in bacofiol with a toast rach stuck on his back - rock'n'roll.

11 February: Next gig was in Amiens. It was a fine venue jam packed with lots of lovely people and again we played rather wonderfully. People were even dancing to our music. Tony managed to sit down on a seat and promptly break it - highly impressive. That night we stayed in a lovely hotel.

12 February: First of two nights at the same venue. First taste of mediocrity that night. We had to play with a rather hideous r&b band. Despite a rather ridiculous radio interview to promote the gig, nobody turned up. Hopefully it was because of the really bad fog rather than the pathetic performance on the airwaves.

13 February: The day started well when John managed to break a toilet seat in a rather dreadful hotel that had hanging carpet for walls.
That night we played first so that we could get out fast. We played much better and sounded good but again there were not many people there. The audience woke up when the interval disco played "Back in Black" by "AC/DC" Enough said.

14 February: Valentines Day but no romance in the air for "The Strookas." Not that it really mattered that night because we were too engrossed in a fabulous gig in a dead rough punk squat cafe. It was absolutely brilliant. The support band "Budz" were pretty cool. We played everything at break neck speed and the crowd lapped it up. The organisers even bootlegged the gig.

15 February: Next stop Montergis and a support gig with the legendary american Jeff Dahl, who was in the middle of a 55 date tour of his ego. His band were dead pathetic. The Bass player introduced a song saying "Me and my Fender Jazz Precision Bass are gonna fuck you." Later on Jeff "Hairy Bastard" Dahl drooled "This song's really good to fuck to - trust me." Sad lads. We played OK but not many people were there.

16 February: Met up with those Twickenham rockers "The Revs" who we co-headlined with for the final 5 dates of the tour. This night we played in Perigeux. Great gig by both bands. We were videoed for some French TV thing. Fantastic meal afterwards with our ever so friendly french hosts.

17 February: Clermont Ferrand was the place for our next gig - the home town of the cuddly Tour Organiser Patrick Foulhoux. Good gig in a good club type setting. By this time our driver and Roady Frank Bass was learning how to get pissed and stay awake at the wheel. Tony was well bladdered too and danced alone to the sound of "Buffallo Tom" belting out of the PA.

18 February: Best gig of the Tour. Another small cafe. It was dead hot and the crowd went loopy to both bands. No stage diving but plenty of ceiling tiles went flying. The Cafe Owner tried to rip Dave's "Strookas" T Shirt off him and she tried to pilfer John's holy "Strookas" Baseball Cap. Stayed in a rather plush "Formula 1" Hotel. The showers were a blast and a half.

19 February: Penultimate gig was near Switzerland in a place called Annecey. Dead picturesque. The gig was pretty bad mainly 'cos John made zillions of cock ups and Tony forgot where the strings were on his bass.

20 February: Last gig of the Tour was in Besancon. Played a fine set but nobody was there to see it except for some dubious French Nazis. Said "Good Bye" to "The Revs." They are indeed a fine band to catch the ferry taking a detour to see the Eiffel Tower. Dreadful ferry crossing but were glad to reach English soil.

A GREAT TOUR. 2500 MILES TRAVELLED. THE FRENCH WERE INCREDIBLY HOSPITABLE. THE FOOD WAS GREAT AS WAS THE BEER (AND IT WAS ALL FREE.) GOT PAID AT LEAST £100 FOR EVERY GIG EXCEPT ONE. SOLD SOME ALBUMS AND MANAGED TO PLUG "JOEYFAT" AND "SOMERSAULT" WHENEVER WE WERE INTERVIEWED BY FANZINES, CAN'T WAIT TO DO IT AGAIN.
JOHNNY STROOKA

DEAD!

:poet to the grunge generation
(SEATTLE, OCTOBER 1991)

Think of a mad-ass grunge sleazegrinder getting to remix the theme tune to the Tampax advert - 'Its My Life'. Better than imagine it, listen to <u>STEVEN JESSE BERNSTEIN</u>. Its <u>his</u> life. Its not cheerful, its not sanitary, there are no smiley happy people. Bernstein explores deranged moments of isolation and bloody introspection, he pulls words together in bizarre associations, testament to an 'unusual' view of the world...

Bernstein recorded an album with Sub Pop, 'Poison', released in the middle of last year. I know little about Bernstein other than the details presented in an Independent On Sunday article ('Godfather of Grunge', 20th Feb 93). But many of these seem to have been taken from a poem/ track on the album, called 'Face'. The narrator tells the story of his life, using the image of his face reflected as a mirror as a point to start. It is, if you will, the story of the face. But the track begins 'the following is pure fiction'. The article remarks that his life has been 'so mythologised', and I'm left wondering whether it falls into the trap of perpetuating the myths. If you're interested, I paraphrase the story below.

But do we want, or even need to know his story? Why not start by considering his work? I've managed to get hold of a copy of the album (which I hope to make available through Dave Gamage) - definitely not everyone's taste. But appearing as it does on the sub-pop label (<u>the</u> Seattle grunge label) it may be of interest to anyone into grunge - Seattle or otherwise.

The tracks on 'Prison' are backed with Bernstein's own music. The first, 'No No Man', is set against what feels like a disgarded soundtrack from Mission Impossible. My current favorite, 'The Sport (Pt.1)', has a more funky/ hiphop backing, introducing progressively more agressive ('sonic-youth-ish') guitar riffs. It brings out a pounding city night life, and Bernstein's unrepentant rant describes an arcade video game; but his words rapidly career into related ideas, peeling of into an interzone lost betwen Willian Burroughs and cyberpunk. This is not the kind of poetry they taught you at school. On 'Face' the 'heart-beat' beat (?!) gathers volume with the increasing emotional intensity of the words (he relates how he proposed to a girl at school when he was about 9 years old, bringing out all that cringing, primary school embarrassment).

The crazed rantings of Bernstein tell something about a life full of paranoia, misunderstanding and anger. The voice, the words, the images, are strikingly clear. They communicate - they've certainly got under my skin. There is too much of this clarity to suggest that he is re-telling anything other than his own experience -

'... Are there humming birds?, it thinks/ and I press a dead humming-bird to its face / this is a formula for happiness/.../You who gave your life for me, what was the point?/ yes, I am satisfied here with my iron teeth and my roof made of stained hats/ my many roofs and so many layers of windows/ the world looks like a grey mouse with its squeaking head pinned under a black shoe'
[*'The Morning in the Subbasement of Hell'*]

-*.*-

'I live on a street/ where there are many, many cars and trucks and factories that pump and bang and grind all night and day/ it is a miracle that I can write poetry or sleep or talk on the telephone or that my lover will come visit me, here/ there's so much noise'
[*'More Noise Please'*]

-*.*-

'The arrangement of things/ the argument against the body/ warring bodies corroding wires of habit/ in the cold brain/ I imagine the tentacles of the game reaching backward into the fingers/ up the nerves to a trapped organ of conquest/ we believe that the cybernetic approach to consciousness/ whipped up frothy/ would carry us to a plateau overlooking a pleasent mirror/ but instead left us blathering in a dressed up solitude of mannequin planets...'

'cannibalised to death, we realise the tantric bazooka, in the folds of our naked brassieres, too late as the odds shift, lights in the sky'

'and our death-tattoos breathing ignorant of strategy/ world watching/ sulphurous and lewd acidic/ with pants dripping tantalus dangling down to his knees/ unable to stretch even the feeble edges of our hunger to the witches teeth with forks of need-to-survive/ the pounding now on the table of THE SPORT THE SPORT/ a question of consequence squirting out late in blasphemy of having tried to/ film our belt loops through a mask of nakedness in the wretched museum where only our memories decay and the rest waits to give off light mesmerised by the hopelessness of logic/ the big boom tweets and the shovel dribbling the planet earth into the rain/ and science wretching sure, it's been re-crafted, re-set, edited, changed and so on. That's how it manages to communicate so clearly. To the clarity, add the honesty with which it is presented. This honesty outweighs all the rancid verbal overkill. In the end, its the consistency with which Bernstein keeps up this lucid honesty which gives these tracks their impact.

Bernstein's cruel and biting tone is classically confrontational. It makes you think. It doesn't make you like him. This is great stuff. Listen in if you get the chance.

at last with its greedy claw and tentacle lost/ reinventing god and animals reinvent science/ philosophy/ hate pantheon where victory and destruction are deified, adored'
          [The Sport, pt.I]

-*,*-

'the following is pure fiction... actually I have been handsome and popular all my life... There has always been something wrong with my face... "Look in the mirror Stevie", my mother said, holding my up so I could see my face... "See? There's Stevie!"... The little ears stuck out, that was the first thing I noticed, the two ears...'
          ['Face']

-*,*-

The story of a life:
Born 1950, Bernstein had a crippling bout of polio when he was four, but recovered from the paraylsis it caused him. It would seem that he was very intelligent, perhaps too intelligent, too sensitive. He slowly dropped out of school and became a recluse. After failing to reach Canada, he lived in Seattle, making a living by playing in jazz bands in various bars an clubs. By his early twenties, he was on heroin. He learnt Kung Fu, and slipped betwen jobs, religions, romances and hospitals (physical and mental), perhaps prison. Three marriages, constant physical pain, two published novels. Campaigning for the rights of the most despised criminals (often sex-offenders), saying of them that "for every crime that is represented by a prisoner, there is another that I know nothing of that was committed against the prisoner". His son remembers his delight in beautiful things, things which littered his apartment, perhaps an old watch, or "weird beans, a stetson hat". His last wife recalls his amazing ability as a story teller, his tremendous sensitivity. In october 1991, he killed himself. In an act which suggests both extreme despair and disturbing self-control, and which leaves a very strange taste in the mouth, he opened up both jugular veins, apparently remaining kneeling for five minutes to allow the blood to fall through a hole in the floor. Then he keeled over and died.

THE BIGGER THE BETTER

Ever since Elvis first wriggled his skinny butt the stereotypical rocker has been svelte to the point of anorexia. Thin was in. However, not everyone is a cover girl or Chippendale. Some need more aggression, more volume, more imagination, in fact just plain more.

Fat is now where it's at, in the past Mr Domino climbed Blueberry Hill with the ladies and the likes of Heavy D and Barry White seem to do OK. Now grunge has its hefty heroes, led by the like of POISON IDEA, TAD, SCREAMING TREES, and SUGAR's Bob Mould. Pig Champion of Poison Idea maintains that fat people are more creative and "The few good people out there - I only consider about 2% of the human race worth a shit - they are fat, they've got that little bit more oomph!"

There is even now a fat-rights movement in America. The National Association to Advance Fat Acceptance, is lobbying for bigger airplane seats and protesting about fat jokes on TV. "What we're trying to do is change the stereotypes about fat people" says Laura Eljaiek, NAAFA's program director, "our basic message is that any body is a good body. We can all dance, sing and have fun, those things have nothing to so with size."

Built for comfort, not speed. Fat and Proud!

REVIEWS

SNFU - Camden Underworld - 12/11/92.

Canada's finest (well perhaps amongst the finest if you consider Nomeansno, Guilt Parade, DOA, Superconductor...) have reformed after a few years apart. Their style of punk hardcore is very fast and loud, but certainly not just noise. On stage, Chi Pig has immense energy, continually jumping about stage or frantically rolling around and still singing. SNFU haven't lost any of the power and energy they are renowned for. Old favourites are brought out tonight as well as the newer stuff : sometimes it's serious political and thought provoking, sometimes tongue-in-cheek fun songs, lyrically. They play a long set tonight and even the mosh-pit flags at times. The highlight for me is 'Where's my legs?', including a knock on the bonce with one of the bands renowned props - a plastic leg, but this gig will be remembered for its intensity and energy as a show - an event - not just a series of songs all strung together. Punk rock never died!

ALLOY & JOEYFAT - 7/1/93 - Sir George Robey, London.

JOEYFAT: I've seen Joeyfat before, but this time they've definately improved. Whereas so many UK bands feel that they have to play loud and fast in that typical Husker Du / Nirvana kind of way, Joeyfat take their inspiration from Washington DC stuff it seems, especially Fugazi or perhaps Soulside. So it's not a collection of three minute noise routines (which has it's place, of course) but songs, well constructed with atmosphere which stop and start with nifty tempo changes. Singer Matt is very tall and thin - he stands and writhes twisting his T-shirt, talking and singing what seem deeply personal and intelligent lyrics. Joeyfat are doing something different, but importantly doing it well. No news of a 7" but apparently there should be a tape of their stuff available soon.

ALLOY: For those of you who don't know: Vic Bondi, once singer with seminal '80's hardcore group Articles of Faith, is now fronting Alloy. He also sings with Jones Very, but Alloy were formed after Vic grew more radical and became thoroughly pissed off with the Gulf War. Whereas AoF were out and out speedy brash punk, and Jones Very are poppier but still with intelligent lyrics, Alloy (check out their LP 'Eliminate' on Bitzcore) are passionate and powerful - a cross between the two. Roger and Pat of Dagnasty play with Alloy as well... a bit of a supergroup in hardcore circles. Live, Alloy are intense, powerful and surprisingly noisy compared to the LP. God knows what AoF must've been like live because this is angry. But Alloy have good tunes too, and their new single 'United' sounds just as impressive as anything from 'Eliminate'. The music tonight is fast, tight and deafening, and only one wanker tries to spoil it all by getting up on stage and pushing the band around. This just seems to make Vic sound angrier, louder and more intense! Unfortunately, by the encore the sound is cracking up a bit, but it's still awesome and they are well received by us all. Drummer Colin kicks over his drumkit and Vic attempts to pull down that weird netting hanging from the Robey's ceiling with his guitar. He is angry and pissed off, what could be called a true punk spirit. What an excellent nights entertainment!

COME - 23/1/93 - Camden Underworld.

Come are present MM and NME favourites, well what do you expect? Their debut single 'Car' was on Sub-Pop, so it's got to be cool (irony). However, Come are a bit different to the current stock of US guitar gods - like Codeine, they are prepared to play slow but with equal passion and intensity as those equally wonderful speed pop-punk merchants (Rocket from the Crypt, Seaweed, Supersuckers...). 'Eleven- Eleven' was indeed one of the great understated debuts of 1992. Live, the songs from this LP sound better than ever : Thalia Zedek has a voice that even Frankie Stubbs would be proud of - it's coarse and powerful, sort of Janis Joplin at times. In their slower moments, they resemble Codeine (Drummer Chris Brocaw used to play with them) but are never that slow. The music is very bluesy really, and sometimes it reverts to typical grunge style noise. But Come have great tunes, lovely structured music and the songs do sound different. To be perfectly honest, they don't put a foot wrong. Some would accuse them of being a tad too serious perhaps, but you can't expect the Hanson brothers or the Frank and fuckin' Walters every night, can you?

SKYSCRAPER - 25/1/93 - London Borderline.

Skyscraper are a trio with Vic on vocals/guitar from the sadly defunct but truly awesome Milk and Adi, ex-Swervedriver on bass. I never saw a naff Milk gig once and Skyscraper's performance at the Underworld supporting Sebadoh last October was a pretty fine one too. It's a club night for TLF tonight and a mere £2 to get in. In my humble opinion, Vic and Milk could never put a foot wrong. Apart from the occasional over log song, they were a noisy grating and very powerful outfit and very slick. Skyscraper's basslines have a familiar Swervedriver feel, but lyrics, vocals and guitar are typical Milk - intense. Those amazingly varied sounds and noises from Vic's guitar, the changes in tempo, the softly sung bits, the angry shouted bits-it all sounds as good as ever, except that it's a bit of a rough P.A. at the Borderline, but that's not the bands fault (or was it just where I was standing?) Skyscraper are tipped for big things apparentley. One thing that pissed me off, the last couple of years, was that Milk never got the attention that they deserved, so Skyscraper with a slightly subtler more accessable, dare I say more commercial sound certainly deserve your attention. Vic's a nice bloke too!

DWARVES / SUPERSUCKERS / REVEREND HORTON HEAT.
The SUB-POP Gig - The Venue, New Cross. - 29/1/93.

Supersuckers are first tonight. It's their first ever gig in the UK too. They kick ass - fast, brat punk, great poppy tunes sped up to 100 mph - it's a traditional sounding sort of music, but not many do it as well as the Supersuckers. Live it's very effective - they sound good and are well received by an appreciative audience. They may be young but already they're slick, stylish and good fun.

The Reverend Horton Heat is probably Sub-Pop's most unusual export : a warped Texan preacher with his band playing a very different kind of noise - 'psychobilly' I think it's called, it's roots firmly in Rock 'n' Roll, Country & Rockabilly. It's a far better experience than listening on vinyl. After a shaky start it becoms really good fun, especially when the reverend talks to us, telling his witty stories. The man is genuinely funny and this was a very entertaining show : Great fun and very different.

The Dwarves on the other hand are total wankers - they last 15 minutes tonight, so it's nothing unusual. To be perfectly honest, their music is shit-hot, fast rock - very powerful, good tunes. Unfortunately, their attitude fucking stinks. They've always had this outrageous attitude. They're supposed to shock but that doesn't justify their behaviour this evening; continually bombed with cups they respond by spitting at the audience (Ho, Ho, How funny) pushing one girl in the face, hard (tongue in cheek? Mmm... very funny) and generally being obnoxious. It ends when it all starts getting a bit out of hand and the band start hitting people and end up being pushed too - forced to leave the stage, bombarded by missiles to cries of 'Wankers!'. I suppose this was all expected, but the Dwarves obviously have the talent. It's just the sexist, obnoxious attitude they have is not even funny - it's shit! Jeez, all they have to do is moderate a bit. A strong attitude can enhance a band in many ways, but the Dwarves go a bit too far.

HENRY ROLLINS (Spoken Word) - Astoria - 15/2/93.

This was the fucking biz! One of the most entertaining evenings I can remember. Henry Roillins captivated a 1000+ audience for a massive two and a half hours with his tales about being an American in England, us Brits, Pigs in the States, Gigs, Iggy Pop and more. Unlike Biaffra, with his deeply political, often shockingly truthful stories about US society, Rollins is more a kind of 'Philosopher of the People'. He's a wonderful story teller and very funny - one of the best stand up comedians. Although generally light hearted, there's usually some moral behind it all. Rollins saddening tale of his best friend Joe Cole, who was shot dead next to him, is told in a serious captivating tone. Rollins genuinely loves us! He hopes he's inspired us to go out and do what we want to do, because Joe is dead and can do fuck all now, so we've really got to try. It may sound blindingly obvious, but I suppose the 'you had to be there' cliche holds true in this case - the man has to be seen and then you'd understand. Well, I'm inspired! A real priviledge and a pleasure to have seen the great man. Shame I was too young to have seen Black Flag.

CIRCUS LUPUS / LUNGFISH - Camden Underworld - 20/2/93.

Lungfish: Lungfish play a fine set this evening to a handful of people at the underworld. Their's is a blend of slowish hardcore with Fugaziesque walking basslines, but it's their bearded, tattooed singer who really shapes the band's sound. Their longer songs (such as Non-Dual Bliss' from 'Talking songs for walking' LP) sound far better live; full of energy and passion which doesn't come across as well on vinyl. It's the intensity and feeling behind it all that impressed tonight.

Circus Lupus: Singer Chris Thomson pisses me off during the first song by stage diving onto me and me alone - I don't really need this, it has to be said - he's full of manic energy and seems thoroughly pissed off, or at least mighty serious. However, because Circus Lupus are one of the best fucking bands around I can forgive his attempted flattening of me, and a few songs in and they really started to pick up. Circus Lupus have an original sound - very angry, seemingly inspired by bands like NOU and Trenchmouth, but for some reason I seem to detect hints of Scratch acid / Jesus lizard too - that stop start chugging kind of sound, weird, distinctive vocals... Live they don't sound as good as I thought they would, but it's still pretty impressive. On vinyl, it's a masterful sound; check out the 'SuperGenius' LP. Circus Lupus are a tad too serious perhaps and so fucking intense - I'm not expecting witty one liners and silly quips, it's just the crowd don't really warm to them and there's a feeling of resentment in the air. Perhaps that's what Circus Lupus want. I guess they are an angry band, pissing off our generation of pissed off people even more, maybe.

Bikini Kill & Huggy Bear - ULU - 14/3/93.

Huggy Bear : Anyone who says Huggy Bear can't plai an ignorant fucker. Thr 'Riot Grrrl' thing has been so twisted by our Great British music press it's unreal - really, it's a push for more girl and girl/boy bands, more communication, getting out and doing things - what's so bad about that? Huggy Bear are an excellent punk rock band - fast, noisy with something to say and they do it well, in fact they're fucking slick! Onwards!

Bikini Kill : It's debatable whether sexism should be fought through alienation of men - this seems a bit crass because much of the RG movement was inspired by male dischord bands, especially 'The Nation of Ulysses'. Bikini Kill have a guy in the band... Tokenism? This seems to be what singer Kathy is proposing, but the 'men are wankers' attitude is useless - all men are potential rapists? Are all women potential mothers? Why not look on most men as potential good guys and friends? Musically, Bikini Kill are shit hot - a grungey punk rock sound, intelligent lyrics and they seem to be enjoying themselves. Everyone's entitled to their own opinion; Bikini Kill have theirs and they play great punk rock music, it's as simple as that... So do Huggy Bear, whether you agree with what they're saying or not.

Christ on a Crutch - White Horse - 18/3/93.

I seem to give good reviews to everything. but this was something special. Christ on a Crutch are one of the fastest, loudest, most powerful bands I've ever seen. It works so well on vinyl - 'Crime pays when pigs die' LP or 'New Red Archives' - and live it's even faster. The version of 'Shit Edge' was so quick it was unreal, or were they taking the piss? Considering their singer quit, the guitarist does a great job on vocals and is no mean guitarist too. It's sometimes simple, sometimes intricate all out punk with intelligent, anti-establishment words. Very slick, very tight, it all holds together so well considering the drummer is so fast he's going to explode. No mistaking Christ on a Crytch are Punk! A blinder!

The Hanson Brothers - Gross Misconduct LP.

This group contains two members of Nomeansno, you have been warned! A full length LP, it's a perfect parody of the Ramones, complete with '1-2-3-4's' and simplistic lyrics. They do actually kick ass, something the Ramones could be accused of not really achieving. Nomeansno couldn't be weak if they tried - they're so tight! 'Gross Misconduct' is not so much a piss take, but rather an appreciation, except 'Blitzkreig Hops' on the free 7" about the joys of home brew! This album is fiendishly catchy and great fun. Highly recommended!

Rocket from the Crypt - Circa Now! - (Headhunter).

Rocket from the crypt are a great band. This is their second LP after 'Paint as a fragrance' and numerous 7"s (even one for Sub-Pop... Wowee!). Some say 'Circa Now!' is better - I'm not so sure. As a whole LP I don't think that it matches the pure wonderfulness of the first side of 'Paint as a fragrance' which contains some of the best tunes ever and those kind of songs that just stay in your head for weeks! Sure 'Circa Now!' is still one of the best exponents of this melodic rough-vocal, avant garde, grungey style thingies (how many labels there?!), but it seems to contain too many filler tracks, which was a problem with side 2 of 'Paint...'. Rocket still have a monster sound, first song 'Short lip fuser' is a classic and they still use trumpet and piano really effectively. Don't get me wrong, Rocket from the crypt are a big favourite of mine, but 'Circa Now!' lacks a certain something, or maybe I expect too much. Buy it and see!

Triggerman - Dead like me - (Workshed).
Same label as the truly awesome 411, Triggerman contain members of No for an answer and Carrynation, apparently "Emo-core?" - I don't like this phrase and it doesn't strictly apply. Some tunes are like a rougher Samiam, the 411 influence shines through too. Great music, good changes of pace, rough/smooth vocals mix - this LP certainly has variety, but is not as awesome as I was lead to believe on the first few encounters, but I feel it's a grower. Definately worth checking out if you're a fan of medium paced, post-hardcore (crap expression - why post?) and I could imagine them fucking corking live!

Alloy - Untied / Hard Rain 7".
Two great tunes, brand new and fresh sounding hardcore from alloy. If anything a harsher direction seems apparent than on the 'Eliminate' LP. This band is shit hot - miss them at your peril!

AntiSchism - End of time plus one - 2 x 7"s - (Selfless).
This is a double 7" pack with a remixed version of the 'End of time' EP and 4 unreleased songs on the second 7". This is the first stuff i've heard by AntiSchism, just hear them name dropped as classic hard core a lot in MRR. Both EP's are fucking fast and noisy, especially the second one - not exactly pleasant memorable tunes to hum in the bath but raging, loud screamed vocals, very powerful, very intense and this is what makes it memorable. 8 very angry tunes, weird noises, killer percussion - worth getting hold of and probably limited.

Capitol Punishment 7" - (Selfless, 1000 only, white!).
A 7" with 8 unreleased tracks from 1982 and with Ralph on Vocals - probably one for the collector. Rough, harsh vocals sort of Brit sounding, pretty classic really, like a sped up Toxic Reasons - fast and powerful and still pretty tuneful. A lyric sheet would have been nice - I never heard them first time around, but 10 years on it sounds pretty fucking exciting!

Rage Against The Machine LP - Epic.
Before even playing a single show, Rage against the machine recorded their own independent 12 song tape and sold about 5,000 copies! In the short time this group's been around they've opened for such well known acts as Pearl Jam and Public Enemy. Their self-titled release features 10 tracks, combining churning metal riffs, in the vein of Suicidal Tendencies, with hardcore rap beats reminiscent of House of Pain and Public Enemy. I saw them play live at the ULU a while back and they were totally awesome. Raw Rage!

Cyber Core - 'Grate'.
Driving through a misbegotten industrial wasteland, all jagged black silhouettes and smokestacks, polluted rain shone green on the windscreen. I had 50 miles of 5 lane highway to myself. Sweat collected in my palms, across my back. I searched the airwaves for something to listen to...
For years the factory ship had lain dead on the sand. It's huge metal hull once rang with the noise of machinery. Whales had been hoisted in and cut up. Now the hull rang again. A monstrous baby was riveting a last few pieces of flesh onto it's shins. A mix of its own viscera and putrified ends of whalemeat had been clumsily stuck, skewered and stitched onto its metal skeleton. It giggled happily whilst fircing a rusted meathook through its thigh. What a good game. It found a new toy. With an old rusty chainsaw it began beating out a pounding rhythm on the disintegrating carcasses of the dead whales. Their ghosts released long moans, ancient whalesongs of despair. This mechanical abortion had returned to hunt for it's whore mother.

Born again from the metal womb of a sea born slaughter house. It ran back to Sin City, crying 'Ma maaa!' As it ran, the occasional piece of dribbling meat would fall away, rasping along the length of the corroded metal pins holding it in place. But mama wasn't at home. Nobody had told baby that the bitch was dead. Mama was in a morgue. Baby broke in and set off the alarms. Baby found mama in a drawer. 'Found you!' the infant squealed. 'What big teeth you have, baby' - 'All the better to eat you with, Mama!' It curled up with Mama in the drawer, stroking her hair, and peeling off strips of flesh to suck. 'Mmmm Mama Mmm!'...
It's funny what a tune will make you think of. The DJ said I had been listening to Cyber Core - Grate. I thanked him for the information, but it had felt as if I had tuned in to every available frequency simultaneously. Cyber Core had evidently tried to create an aesthetic of interference. I don't think I'll be wanting my own copy, but it got me through the night.
I gurgled and licked my lips.

ALLOY INTERVIEW

Alloy features Professor Vic Bondi, ex AoF, Jones Very etc and ex-members of Agnostic Front and Dagnasty. Alloy were over here a few months ago promoting their excellent new Eliminate album and touring with Joeyfat. They play powerful melodic hard-core. We caught up with them in Leeds for this interview:

BHP: Since arriving in the UK, you've been labelled with this "Prof Rock" tag, do you think this makes people take Alloy more or less seriously?
VIC: Probably less. One group of people simply won't believe it and assume it's hype, another group will believe it and despise us for it. In truth, it's not that much an asset for the band, other than honesty. A Phd doesn't make you a good musician.

BHP: We know the drummer was less than impressed by the Egg Parmesan in Belgium, what have been the highs and lows of the European food experience?
VIC: High. John's cooking in Newport, Wales.
          Low: Egg Parmesan in Belgium.

BHP: How does "Alloy" compare to your previous bands?
VIC: Better by far than both AoF and Jones Very, in the sense that we enjoy continued good fortune and good audiences. More exciting and more frightening. In some ways, Jones Very was a far different band, perhaps more experimental which was both a strength and a weakness. Since AoF was my first important band, during very exciting times in music, it is impossible to compare. Those days can never be revisited or exceeded. But since the Aof reunion (which was completely misconceived) and the first Alloy tour were only months apart, I can state categorically that Alloy is a far better band to play in.

BHP: What would you like your audience to get out of Alloy as a band?
PAT: I think it's best to say that we "give the people what they want", but we want to send them away thinking about what they've heard, get them inspired to do something or educate themselves on certain issues.

BHP: What is Boston like at this time of year?
PAT: Boston tends to be clear and cold or hovering around freezing with rain or snow.

BHP: Anything to add?
PAT: Thanks to all our support bands this tour, especially Joeyfat and NRA. Also thanks to
          Aziz, Coliath and Aiden.

This interview was conducted on the 8th January 1993 at the Duchess of Leeds.

You can write to Alloy, C/O Bloom Records, PO Box 361, Boston, MA 02101, USA.

XCESS - A Brief History of a Fat Band.

the end of April 1993 will, at last, see the release of the first vinyl album by the UK's most 'CULT' fat band. COUCH POTATOES formed back in 1990, and have since been playing the sort of energetic, sweaty, fun gigs that they have become known for, with songs about food, girls, and bed! They have appeared on two Jailcell Recipes tours, and supported bands such as GreenDay, Alice Donut, NOFX, and Chemical people, to name but a few. The 'Couchies' have sold well in excess of a thousand copies of their demo's, but have not, until now, appeared on much vinyl, with one song on a 'Retch' compilation LP (featuring Dr & The Crippens, Parasites, Verukers...) and one song on a 'Boss Tuneage' compilation LP (featuring Samiam, Mr T Experience, Rise...). COUCH POTATOES now have a full length album, called 'EXCESS ALL AREAS', being released on 'BACK IN CONTROL RECORDS'. It has already received rave reviews as a 'Classic Hardcore' album, featuring 'Genuine Kentifornian Couchcore'.

Put a smile on a fat blokes face and send for it now, from : Back in Control Records, 5 Hexham Avenue, Hebburn, Tyne & Wear, NE31 2DL.

14 Great Trax only £5 ppd - Cheques to M. GRAY.

JB'S - BEST IN BED

JB's MUSIC STORE
41 ALBION RD
T/W 522141

GUITAR SALE!

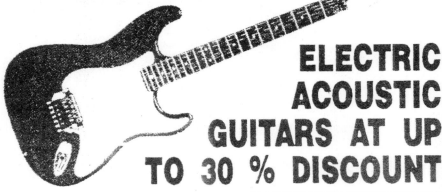

ELECTRIC ACOUSTIC GUITARS AT UP TO 30 % DISCOUNT

OPEN MON-SAT 10am-6pm

VISA,ACCESS H.P-P/EX

it's still all one word

Hello and welcome to BHP 5.

Thanx very much for reading and supporting this zine and the underground as a whole. A[...] of time, money and hard work goes into this stuff, so thanx for giving it your time. Sp[...] thanx to Steve, Claire, Martyn, Miles, Austin, Andy, Kris and everyone involved in [...] production of this zine. Shout outs to; Joeyfat, Sonar Nation, Down By Law, Strookas, Al[...] Head, Couch Potatoes, Green Day, Samiam, Pseudo Hippies, Shreds, Compulsion, SN[...] Understand, BBMF's, Strength Alone, All, Lifetime and Quicksand. Also, Ian at W[...] Mark at B.I.C., Dave at Spiel/Something Cool, Ros (Garbles), Richard (Your Mornings[...] Mick (P+D,) Suspect Device + Rich + S.T.E., The Zine, the Forum crew in Tunbr[...] Wells and all my friends. Thanx.

If you're into supporting and continuing Hardcore in any way, please write to us now.

Take care

Dave

BHP
1 Chandos Road
Tunbridge Wells
Kent TN1 2NY.

Here is a list of the merchandise being distributed by BHP, available from the address above. Cheques / P.O's payable to D. Gamage. All prices post paid.

BHP - The best zine in the country - Back issues, 50p each.
#1 featuring Green Day, Hard-Ons, Jailcell Recipes, Factory Farming...
#2 featuring Ramones, Joeyfat, Unpolluted Air, Sleeping...
#3 featuring All, MTX, SNFU, Funbug, Planet Earth...
#4 featuring Sugar, Alloy, Decadence Within, Comics...

GOTHAM TAPES - The Alternative Tape Label - £1.50 each.
GOT 001 : TEE-HEE Compilation; 40 mins, 12 bands, 12 trax.
GOT 002 : COUCH POTATOES - LIVE IN TUN/WELLS; 40 mins, 16 trax.
GOT 003 : LIVE AT THE SHELLEY Compilation; 60 mins, 5 bands, 25 trax - featuring
        BBMF's, Strength Alone, Angus Bagpipe, Couch Potatoes...
GOT 004 : 'Hello, Bollox & Welcome' Compilation; 60 mins, 25 bands, 25 trax.
GOT 005 : MORAL CRUX, Tout a fait punk, live radio broadcast; 60 mins, 20 trax.
GOT 006 : ANOTHER Compilation; 40 mins, 13 bands, 13 trax
GOT 007 : Eyes Down For God Compilation; 60 mins, 20 bands, 20 trax.
GOT 008 : JAWBREAKER - LIVE AT GILMAN STREET; 60 mins, 15 trax.
GOT 009 : COUCH POTATOES - EXCESS ALL AREAS; 60 mins, 24 trax - Brilliant Melodic
        Hardcore in a Descendents vein.
GOT 010 : JOEYFAT - SOUP; 60 mins, 15 trax (8 studio & 7 live) - UK's finest - reminiscent
        of Shudder To Think, Alice Donut & Rollins.
GOT 011 : Low Brow Head Tread Compilation; 60 mins, 20 bands.
GOT 012 : All the Smiley Faces Compilation; 60 mins, 21 trax, 15 bands - superb melodic HC.

VINYL
PANX 11 - 7" EP, £2.00
featuring Couch Potatoes, Blanks 77, Eight Ball, Public Lost, Wounded Knee & Lamento.
NOWHERE STREET - 7" Compilation, £2.00
featuring Vendabait, Couch Potatoes, Cheese Doodles & Pseudo Hippies.
JOEYFAT 7" GOD/WINDSCREEN £2.00
"Band of the month" - Lookout, "Punches lethal in the face" - NME.
COUCH POTATOES - IN BED WITH 7" EP, £2.00
4 Trax of Punk, melodic hardcore from the fat lads.
COUCH POTATOES - EXCESS ALL AREAS LP, £5.00
14 classic trax, in the vein of Descendents, BDC, Samiam, Green Day...

GreeN Day

Green Day are a three piece from California, they are THE purveyors of sloppy, boy/girl pop punk tunes. Their last UK tour was great, but this one was even better and they look set now to leave Lookout and record a 3rd LP for Warner Bros. Their London gig with Joeyfat and Funbug was packed and then they returned to Tunbridge Wells...

BHP Hi - What was Spain like and how come you're playing at all, I thought the tour was cancelled cos of Mikes injury.

TRE The doctors said it was ok for us to go now but we had originally planned to go a month ago or something. Jose Antonio of Zaragoza said we had to come and that we would have a free trip if we agreed to come. We're here aren't we?

Spain is pretty large and the drives ranged from 2-6 hours. We toured with a three piece band called Trip Inside and three other dudes. 10 men on tour. We rarely slept, we drank very good wine and hung out with really nice people. Basically - we've seen more of Spain than we thought possible. We lived like the Spanish because we were the minority. Very cool experience.

BHP What is Baldeagle? How does it taste?

TRE Bald Eagles are the US National bird and they're almost extinct. They taste like a mixture between California Condors and Spotted Owls.

BHP What do you think of this trip to the UK - Why so short - Any highlights?

BILLIE So far everything has been dandy! We've only been here for a day and a half. Mike was questioned heavily at customs. It turns out we had work papers and we didn't know it. So, Tre and me (Billie) said we were vacationing. By the time Mike was up to show his passport, customs had it on computer he was in a band and playing gigs. So customs told him to tell us that if Tre and I get caught we would be deported, But the show in London was bitchin.

MIKE We were only planning to finish our originally planned tour. But we decided to play England for Christy Colecord who booked the tour originally.

BHP Is it true you've just signed to WARNER Bros?

BILLIE Yes, we are about ready to sign our lives away to Warner. but that's OK, they promised us Bugs Bunny stuffed animals.

BHP Any US News, riots, etc?

TRE My sister just had a baby girl and Billy's sister is very pregnant. The new president is a complete bastard (Mike disagrees). Nobody has rebuilt the south of Florida yet.

BHP New releases, plans?

BILLIE This summer we're planning to record a brand spankin' new L.P. called 'Dookie,'

BHP Anything to add?

BILLIE $x(xy - ?) = z$

Find what ? equals

therefore $x^2y - ?x = z$

therefore $?x = x^2y - z$

therefore $? = \dfrac{(x^2y-z)}{x}$

MIKE I hope people still like us we're doing the W.B. thing for them too.

We receive loads of great mail at BHP, but not all of it gets properly reviewed in our limi
space, so here's a bunch of stuff I haven't written articles on, but deserves your attentio
CHICKEN BONE CHOKED, an aggressive UK band have a free demo, available for a star
from 23 The Embankment, Bedford, MK40 3PD. JOEYFAT, awesome Fugazi/Alice Do
style T/Wells band have a 3 track EP out, for only £2.00 ppd, from the new label Someth
Cool, (who are looking for bands to appear on compilation singles) at Flat A, 24 Mon
Colonnade, Tun. Wells, Kent, TN1 1LY. The brilliant SONAR NATION have a new 12"
'SURGE D.T.' available for £3.50 ppd from TMSY Records, Webster House, 24 Jesm
Street, Folkestone, Kent, CT14 5QW. Couch Potatoes have a superb EP on Weird Recor
61 London Road, Balderton, Newark, Notts, NG24 3AG and on LP on Back In Control,
Hexham Avenue, Hebburn, Tyne + Wear, NE31 2DL and also tracks on European and U
vinyl comps and JAPANESE CD!
ARTCORE have a new demo, £3.00 from 45 Alexandra Rd West, Brampton, Chesterfie
S40 1NP and HUNCHFRONT(28 Christopher Crescent, Balderton, Newark, Notts, NC
3BS) and CHOCOLATE MONK (49 Rowan Drive, Blackburn, West Lothian, EH47 7NP)
both looking for bands to send demo tapes for compilations.
There are freebies, for a stamp, from PROTOTYPE (79 Waterloo Road, Dublin 4, Ireland)
SPIEL (Flat A, 24 Monson Colonnade, un. Wells, TN1 1LY)
S.T.E (15 Sparrow Square, Eastleigh, Hants, SO5 3LB)
Your Mornings (9 Gainsborough Close, Folkestone, Kent, CT19 5NB) and if you need g
records get a catalogue from AURAL RESPONSE, 4 Brackendale Grove, Harpenden, He
AL5 3EJ.
Also, if you want to check out a good new vinyl from the South East write to Miles
SAMUTAM, 10 Grantham Bank, Barcombe, E Sussex, BN8 5DJ, for a list including most
the above and lots more.
You can get gigs here in Tunbridge Wells by phoning the FORUM on 0892 530411

The ZINE will publish and/or review anything you send to P.O. Box 288, Shere, Guildfo
Surrey, GU5 9JS.
Other zines to check out include the MANGAZINE (on Anime,) G.D.W. from Wei
GARBLES, (50p - 5 New House Close, Canterbury, Kent, CT4 7BQ,) Kent Band (50p -
Box 553, Rainham, Gillingham, Kent, ME8 9AR,) A.W.A (50p - from 6 Ennerdale Ro
Bradford, W Yorks, BD2 4JE,) SUSPECT DEVICE (50p - 24 Windrush Road, Millbro
Southampton, Hampshire, SO1 9DD,) A.H. (50p - 83 Edmunds Road, Cranwell Villa
Sleaford, Lincs, NG34 8EP.)
Anything to be reviewed in BHP can be sent to our address here in T/Wells or straight
Martyn, 34 Kenilworth Rd, Edgeware, Middlesex, HA8 8YG. (If you sent something and
not in this issue, it'll be in the next.)
Get writing, make contacts, support the Underground!

DID YOU KNOW?... Molly Ringwald, the gorgeous star of films such as 'Breakfast Clu
and 'Pretty In Pink' once dated Ad Rock, a.k.a. Adam Horowitz of the BEASTIE BOYZ.

SAMIAM, a long time favourite of mine, came back to tour Europe in May 93, they visited our little town of T/Wells to play their powerful, melodic hardcore and received a warm welcome. Martin, the bassist answered these questions for BHP, backstage at the FORUM ...

BHP: Welcome to Tunbridge Wells. What do you think of our fair town and indeed UK and Europe as a whole?

MARTIN: Tun Wells smells like black pudding but we love it, ha ha! UK has been much better this time around than the first time and Europe is always a lot of fun and we have really good shows in Germany and France.

BHP: For anyone who doesn't know, could you tell us the current SAMIAM line up and how long you've been playing?

MARTIN: Bass – Martin, guitar – James, Drums – Mark, Vocals – Jason, Harmonica – Bruce Springsteen, pan flute – zamphere, tambourine – Dave Mustang, together 5 years.

BHP: What is left of the tour, how's it been going and what plans do you have when you return to the US.

MARTIN: 2 weeks left it's been wonderful and when we get home we will shower, shave and quit. Take a little break and then get back to practice.

BHP: I've heard a rumour that SAMIAM had been approached by a 'major label.' can you confirm or deny this. And what do you think of GREEN DAY signing to WARNER BROS?

MARTIN: I can neither confirm or deny that we have been approached by majors and I think GREEN DAY will do whatever they will do.

BHP: Your most recent album, the brilliant 'BILLY' has a slightly more 'produced' sound to and some 'different style' songs. Does this signal a change in your style at all? Are you happy with your recordings and what can we expect in the near future?

MARTIN: No. No change at all. We sound the same today as we sounded in the beginning. We've just found snazzier ways of recording it. Sometimes we like our records. Don't expect anything in the future, just accept it.

BHP: Does the name 'SAMIAM' come from green eggs and ham, who's idea was it and do you read a lot of Dr Seuss?

MARTIN: Yes, it certainly comes from green eggs and ham – I believe it was Dr Seuss' idea and yes we have a fully stocked Seuss library in the Samiamobile. It's all we can understand.

BHP: Any good bands we should check out at the moment?

MARTIN: Yes, Goober Patrol is playing right as we speak and tomorrow you can go and buy Nuisance record or the BeeGees 1975 onward.

BHP: Anything to add?

MARTIN: 5 2-1 = 2.

X

COMPULSION

**COMPULSION left to right: Sid Rainey (bass,
Joesephmary (vocals), Garret Lee (Guitar), Jan Willem Alkema (drums**

Of the many bands rising to the surface in the '90s, London-based band Compulsion really stand apart from what constitutes the norm of the British independent scene. Highly self-motivated, Compulsion's music bristles with confidence, crafting unorthodox but addictive melodies with intriguing lyrical narrative.

A truly great band with a future I'll be watching with great interest (an understatement!) Many thanks to guitarist Garret Lee for obliging me with this interview.

★ **First of all, what motivated you to leave Ireland?**
Joeymary, myself and Sid moved to London about four or five years ago. Jan is from Amsterdam and moved here long ago. When we lived in Dublin the music scene was shite! Hot House Flowers and Four Of Us were huge. Incredibly cliquish. Ridiculously expensive to record and get equipment. It was quite incestuous and parochial. Most of the

bands I liked were coming from England and playing in London regularly. I really became bored in Dublin and wanted to experience somewhere else. London seemed the obvious choice. Joeymary was less attracted by the prospect. He had just returned to Dublin after a year and a half in Baltimore (Maryland, USA) but we had started a band that was doing okay and hit a brick wall trying to get our music heard. So basically we packed and left. Most of the good bands from Ireland have moved here, presumably for the same reasons – My Bloody Valentine, Fatima Mansions etc. I haven't been back to Ireland in close to two years now, but from what I hear there is quite a healthy underground scene and things are getting better. It still seems like a waste of effort to me when U2 and the Saw Doctors are still the most important bands there.

★ **Are you inspired or disillusioned by the British music scene?**
Both. The fact there are still great

new bands, records, fanzines, label support from people, gigs, writers, festivals, XFM, etc emerging and st working is an inspiration.

It's annoying that there is still a majority of people falling for the sar bullshit: scenes, hype, Brett's bony arse, indie snobbery. I won't even start on major labels. The worshipping of all things American, the phrase 'tomorrow's music today crap lyrics, the Corporate Killing Of Vinyl and so on.

★ **Would you like to release musi by other bands on Fabulon Recorders?**
Yes, if we ever get to a position where we can afford to.

★ **What prompted you to release records by yourselves, rather tha seek a record deal with an existi record label?**
There was no way that we would do major label deal. Most of the indies had received tapes but were too broke or too slow to do more, or we

really independent at all, but
dowy parts of major companies.
ulon gave us the opportunity to
e complete control, not only over
music but over our schedule, etc.
en we eventually link up with
ther indie they will know what they
getting and we won't have to
npromise what we are. We do
ed to team up with someone else
ause we are completely broke.
wever, doing the first two EP's was
t cheaper than we thought it would
and a lot easier.

**What's your opinion of the so-
led riot girl movement?**
n't know if it is a movement. If it
ens people up to issues other than
lism" then fine. The problem is not
ply sexism. Everything is
nnected: tolerance, understanding,
pathy for everyone/thing. These
goals we should all aim for. There
lot of bullshit that needs kicking at
do it enough) and if Huggy Bear
al can turn a Sonia fan into
neone with an opinion and a voice,
n great. But – please! – someone
e a song.

**Where do the striking images of
s that you have used for your
work come from?**
e cat from the Compulsion EP was
d to a brick and thrown into the
ames by some idiot. Sooty (the
or thing's name) was saved by the
otographer, who it now lives with
d snapped straight away for a
ore and after shot. The cat is alive
d well. The "casserole" cat is a
vonshire Rex (a breed with no fur).
name is Sunbronz Thor, and
ologies but we know nothing else
out him. Jan keeps a Rex and
eymary a regular moggy. We
ught the images were wonderful

and all being cat fans (Purring, Not
Laughing) we had to use them. More
cats are on the way. There are a
number of reasons I can think of why
cat pictures work so well with our
music, but that's for another time.

**★ Josephmary's cartoon characters
have been the subject matter for
some of your songs. Will they feature
as artwork for future releases?**
Ambrose Beasley and Dennis
Wheeler are part of a series of
"Heroes of the 20th Century". They
and others will be used later. We need
more space. At the moment the rest of
us have nearly convinced Josephmary
to compile his cartoons and publish
them in a book. Either way we will use
them some way or another.

**★ Do you know how well the two
EPs have sold yet?**
Not exactly. We know the first sold out
in Britain and some more went out on
import around Europe and the US. It
sold steadily but not enough it any
one week to chart. For "Casserole" it
is too early to say, it is just about re-
order time for the shops so we have to
see how that goes. Because we do
not advertise etc, sales run off word of

mouth, so while you get the same
number of sales as from advertising, it
just takes longer.

**★ Have there been any places
you've particularly enjoyed playing
and why?**
Camden Falcon, Whitehorse, Mean
Fiddler (Wallop Club). The
atmosphere is usually great (the
White Horse has closed down now –
shame). People who go to these
places seem really interested in what
we are doing.
  It's hard to say why some places are
better than others. I guess we just
enjoyed ourselves at gigs we have
done at those venues.

**★ What was the last bloody good
film you've seen?**
Twelve Angry Men.
Cinema Paradiso.
Wings Of Desire.
Reservoir Dogs.
Delicatessen.
Man Bites Dog.
Trust.
Wiseblood.
Wizard Of Oz.
Hearts Of Darkness.
Goodfellas.

OTHER INFO

are bringing out a single "Mall Monarchy" in late August which will be taken from our album. We are
fway through recording songs for the album. We have ten songs recorded and are going into the
dio for two days this week to record another eight. And then again, two days for the final
ht. From these we will pick the album. As yet we are not sure if we will put anything from
two EPs on it. If we do not we will put the two EPs together with a few new tracks done at
same sessions and release that as a mini-album before Christmas. Because only a
ited number of these came out on vinyl it would be nice for more people to be able to hear
m on other formats as well.
Ve prefer vinyl but not everyone is able to play it any more. I think the songs are good and should
be lost. Hopefully we will play solidly throughout the year and build up support slowly.

ON DREAMS...

From time immemorial dreams have been regarded with an interest transcending mere superstition. Their cause and their meaning have been the subject of study and investigation by learned men throughout the ages. The many references to dreams which turned out to be 'events casting their shadows before them' can leave little doubt as to the importance of dreams in history.

Dreams were defined as 'states of consciousness occurring during sleep.'

Dreaming belongs to our most intimate experiences. During waking hours, our reaction to our experiences is mainly emotional. In our dreams it is even more emotional because dreams are a concentrating agent for our various subjective motives. They also constitute an interrelation between present, past and future of human experience. In our dreams we create a world where space and time have no limiting power. In his fascinating book, '*An Experiment with time,*' Professor Dunne proposes the theory that all the time that is now, has been, or will be is like a river and that you can navigate this river, forward, backwards and sideways, in the vessel of your dreams.

Herder, the German philosopher, states that dreams are but the ideas of all poetic arts, while Jean Paul Richter, another German author, thinks that dreams are involuntary experiences leading to the composition of poetry. Both these writers concur with other great ones of the past, such as Nietzsche, Kant and Novalis.

F. W. Hildebrandt wrote in 1875, 'Dreams help us to inspect those hidden depths of our existence which are mostly beyond our reach during our waking hours. Dreams bring us such refined insight into self-knowledge that on waking up, we admire the sharp-eyed demon that helped us find the hidden plot. A dream can warn us from within with the voice of a watchman stationed at the central observatory of our spiritual life. Our dreams can also warn us of the dangerous steps we have already taken!'

Most dreams are in the form of visual images, through which we are able to explore the human mind. Jung, the brilliant Swiss psychiatrist, pointed this out concisely when he stated, 'Visual images have the quality of the human soul!' The mental pictures you can carry over the threshold of your consciousness are unimportant when compared to the wealth of dream imagery. Every human emotion and experience can be reflected in dreams

Through the ages dreams have been recorded on cave walls so one can imagine that those dreamers compared notes with each other on the happenings which followed and so through some shaggy scientific-minded cave dweller began the study of the omens, prophecies and warnings contained in dreams, which have since been woven into every fabric of life, until they have become a part of art, literature and religion as well as science.

The ancient Assyrians, Babylonians and Egyptians disseminated the dream lore of their times and centuries later when Artimedorus compiled his Oneiro-critica on this subject, it proved so popular that 1600 years later its first English translation had been reprinted 32 times by the year 1800.

Cicero, the Roman statesman and author, wrote 'nothing can be so silly, so impossible, or so unnatural that it cannot happen in a dream.' Today, almost 2000 years and mountains of research later, it is still true that nothing is either impossible or ridiculous in a dream; because a dream can be likened to a private script, written, produced and directed by the dreamer sometimes he takes the leading role, but in all cases he is the only audience and each time he falls asleep, there is an opening of a new show, because everybody dreams every night! At this point you may be saying, 'I don't; maybe other people, but not me!' Which may seem to be a reasonable reaction, since even those who know they dream may claim to remember times when supposedly they didn't.

After extensive scientific research at the Walter Reed Institute of Research and Harvard University, it has been proved that everybody dreams every night, by monitoring the sleep of thousands of volunteers. By measuring their heart action, respiration, eye and body movements, brain waves, and, when indicated by these physical responses, awakening them to be told that they were dreaming. These studies found that you have a minimum of three dreams a night, but you can have as many as nine. It has also been established that congenitally deaf or blind dream, that children as young as eight months dream and that people of low IQ dream no less than those of high IQ.

You may remember most of your dreams in vivid detail, you may remember only vague parts of your dream, or you may forget everything, but no matter what you remember about your dreams and regardless of who or what you are, it is certain that you *do* dream. Dreaming is a natural process like breathing and there is no way, except for the right combination of drugs or over-indulgence in alcohol, that you can prevent it.

Recent experiments with 'dream withdrawal' suggest that if you deprive a man of his dreams, you take a chance that he will eventually act out his psychotic tendencies while he's awake, and this, in turn, gives rise to the hypothesis currently propounded in some scientific circles that as dreams allow one to go safely insane for a time each day, it is not sleep that is necessary for our well-being, but dreams.

The power of the subconscious mind to dramatise problems or assimilate material only partially comprehended by the conscious mind is spectacularly documented in the field of science itself. Physiologist, Otto Loewi dreamed one night of an experiment to prove his theory concerning the transmission of nerve impulses. He set up the experiment in his laboratory exactly how he had dreamed it, and it worked, subsequently leading to Leowi's receiving a Nobel Prize.

An interesting contemporary case of clairvoyant dream solution in a different type of scientific discipline is that of the brilliant astrologer Hugh MacCraig who was trying to work out a table that would give the position of the moon from the year 1800 to that of the year 2000 in three simple steps. One night, to quote Mr MacCraig, he 'prayed on it' as he was going to bed and he awoke at 3.00 a.m. to find he had dreamed the solution. This mathematical table, which was subsequently proved to be accurate, appears in his book, *Ephemeris of the Moon*, published in 1952.

Many modern psychotherapists are now of the opinion that we can learn to interpret and use our dreams, which are an extension of the situation we live in when awake.

Dr Stanley Krippner, of the Maimonides Medical Center Dream Laboratory, suggests that our dreams can be used to explore problems that we may refuse to recognise consciously and by so doing can lead to positive corrective action.

Dreams represent mental activity that occurs when conscious control is removed.

To interpret your dreams you must bear in mind that the first step is to learn to distinguish between a valid prophetic dream and one that has no subconscious or clairvoyant significance.

Dreams of a prophetic nature usually occur during deep sleep between 2.00 am and 7.00 am. By this time digestion has been completed, your muscles are relaxed, and your mind is free of the days events. Dreams which occur under these conditions are worth your efforts at interpretation.

Persistent or recurring dreams can be traced, almost invariably, to some physical or psychological cause and as a rule have no prophetic significance. However, a dream that occurs only two or three times is a different matter and should be seriously considered.

Dreams which have no significance are:

Those that you have after over eating or drinking

Those that can be traced to external physical conditions, such as dreaming that you are adrift on an iceberg and wake up to find the heat has gone off in your room and your blankets are on the floor.

There are also various noises, e.g, traffic and music, which may not awaken you but which can influence your dream. You have, no doubt, at some time dreamed you heard bells ringing and you woke up to realize that your telephone is ringing.

If you have been deeply grieved or very frightened, it can influence your dreams and dreams that occur during illness, fever, or following a shock must be discounted. Also dreams that you have after seeing a disturbing movie or TV programme.

Dreams connected with people, things, or situations that have concerned you during the day should be ignored.

A certain group of common dreams, which occur to almost everyone at some time, appear to be more easily recalled than others. This is because they produce decidedly unpleasant sensations, and dreams of this type should be considered as prophetic only when they cannot be attributed to external physical conditions. They fall into the following categories:

    Falling

    Being drawn into danger by some irresistible force

    Being nude and unable to cover oneself

    Floating or flying through space

Being unable to cry out for help in the face of visible danger

Being unable to move away from approaching danger.

Unless the dreamer can be absolutely certain that no extraneous physical cause existed during these dreams, they should be ignored.

Prophetic dreams usually fall into one of the following categories:

PRECOGNITIVE - the interpretation of which usually foretells important events.

WARNING - the interpretation of which may suggest the nature of an impending danger.

FACTUAL - the interpretation of which simply confirms or emphasizes a situation that the dreamer knows about.

INSPIRATIONAL - the interpretation of which suggests a solution to a personal or business problem.

The interpretation of dreams becomes more interesting with practice. Perseverance is essential in learning a new language, and dream symbols are a language of the subconscious mind.

Any action or event in which the dreamer does not take part but is merely an observer is a warning. However, where the dreamer participates in the drama, the message should be interpreted as one which personally affects the dreamer.

Rules for dream interpretation are as follows:

Clean or shiny objects are good omens, but dirty or dull ones forecast obstacles or difficulties.

Going up indicates success or improvement, going down signifies reverses.

Successful efforts in a dream are a good omen, but unsuccessful efforts forecast difficulties.

If a dream involves an illness to the dreamer, it is advisable to have a medical checkup.

Dreams involving members of the dreamers family with whom the dreamer is on pleasant terms pertain to business advancement, but if the relations are unpleasant, the reverse is forecast.

In order to interpret your dreams with some degree of accuracy, you must remember that dreams are made up of many elements. There is usually one main fact or feature that will stand out in your memory and that is the one which you should consider first; you should then consider all the other elements and add them to the interpretation. You should not overlook even the most minute detail as it may have an important significance.

For example:

Your dream involves attending a party; it is likely that you will have to consider foods, strangers and clothes before you can work out an interpretation, as all these details may have an influence on what the dream is trying to tell you.

When attempting to interpret a dream, there are a few basic rules:

Make sure the dream is potentially a prophetic one and not merely of the digestive or 'cheese' variety.

That the feature of a dream which is most vividly recalled when you awaken is the most important element, and the significance of other aspects and factors of your dream must be related to its primary meaning.

The vividness and clarity of your dream is an indication of the importance of the event or warning forecast by the dream. A vague dream if worth interpreting at all, is unlikely to have any important significance.

Timing. The imminence of the forecast interpreted from a dream may be calculated by the proximity of the dreamer to the main feature of the dream.

If the interpretation of the minor details of a dream appear to contradict the significance of the main feature, it is an indication that the meaning or forecast of the main feature will be delayed or modified by the secondary interpretations.

Hopefully this article will help you make the most of your dreams. According to Aristotle, 'the skillful interpreter of dreams is he who has the faculty of observing resemblances.' Try to cultivate that faculty and you will soon become adept at understanding what your dreams mean.

"We're not a straightedge band, but I'm totally straight. I have never taken a drug and I r
will." BILL STEVENSON (Descendents.)

39 LUGG VIEW
PRESTEIGNE
POWYS
WALES
LD8 2DE
GREAT BRITAIN

The DRAGNET Organisation.

Driven irretrievably insane by the unfortunate but inevitable failure of Renegade Records I sunk into a deep state of depression as there was so much I could have done but failed and by failing I felt that I'd let a lot of people down. Once I'd got my act together and started thinking again about ways to help bands that are just coming to the surface and at the same time make some sort of amends to all the people I'd let down, ideas came thick and fast and the seeds of Dragnet were sown. Dragnet is more than a label, more than a fanzine. Dragnet is a collective of a lot of good ideas taking shape in various projects.

DRAGNET Records.

I intend to release material on vinyl and cassette formats from current up and coming bands from all aspects of street rock - indie to techno, punk to hardcore. Dragnet's first release is a reissue of the Drongo's for Europe 7" which was originally intended for release on Renegade but never became widely available due to irreconcilable differences between the label and their distributor, APT, which was a shame because this single was set to take Renegade Records into the Indie top ten for the second time, following the success of the Macc Lads 'Jingle Bells'. Then I'm hoping to release a cassette EP from a great Midlands band called Mile High Smile. This EP will be something special and the package will include the 4 song cassette, a flexi-disc with 2 or 3 more, a badge, information and lyric sheet, definately value for money and Mile High Smile are the band to keep an eye on. Next, I'm hoping to secure the right to be sole distributor of a 7" single from another Midlands band, the single is already pressed on a White label, we've just got to hammer out a suitable agreement than the single will appear as a Dragnet Records release. A compilation tape would be the next release to be scheduled, which will showcase a cross-section of material recently received at Dragnet. I'll be wanting plenty of feedback from listeners so I can release stuff that people actually want. Other stuff thats got a good chance of appearing on Dragnet comes from Sand, Mere Dead Men, BodyBags, AWOL, Couch Potatoes, Goober Patrol... More bands wanted for future releases - send demo's to the Dragnet address.

DRAGNET

I intend to promote gigs and festivals under the Dragnet name. We've already put many bands in contact with each other for some very successful 'exchange' gigs around the country and I've now got people checking out reasonable sized venues in South Wales, Liverpool and the Midlands for 5/6 band events. I'm always looking for Bands to appear at these shows so send your stuff in to me.

DRAGNET DISTRO.

Standard Mail-order thing, it's taken a bit of a back seat for a while but a new list should be appearing soon (for a SAE). Any bands/labels want records or tapes included on the list please send me samples and I'll reply with details.

DRAGNET NEWSLETTER

A bimonthly newsletter (free for a SAE) detailing the progress of all Dragnet projects as well as giving record and band news and tour dates. Dragnet Newsletter is proving very popular on the street as it gives up to date and relevent information about your favourite bands and labels as well as the occasional tongue in cheek comment from the Editor.

USEFUL IDIOT FANZINE

Takes up where Dragnet newsletter leaves off. Bands, articles and interviews, record and tape reviews, gig reports... #1 should be out by the time you read this in BIIP, £1 ppd or 75p + sae.

DRAGNET VIDEO 'ZINE

Still in the testing stage but the positive response means one is sure to appear. Bands and labels send in your videos so extracts can be used. Videos will be returned if requested. This inspiration did not come from 'Wayne's World' but from Jettisounds 'Turnpike TV' and crap programmes like the word, no limits and raw power. It'll be amateurish and spontaneous, but a good laugh with no Terry Christian or Jools Holland.

The Dragnet collective is set up with the sole intention of promoting and supporting up 'n' coming street and underground bands and hopefully encouraging them to keep on until they receive the attention and success they deserve. Support Dragnet in our quest to support these bands; read the newsletters and zines, buy the records and tapes, go to the gigs, check out the videos; it all serves to strengthen our case for survival. Dragnet is not a money thing and all proceeds received from the sale of our products will be put straight back into the scene by Dragnet improving the service, releasing more records, putting on more gigs and generally helping bands out whenever possible.
DRAGNET - Do it!

The shreds are a sexy, popcore band that we keep hearing about. I recently received a demo of theirs from my mate Austin and decided a quick postal chat was needed. The answers are by Russ (guitar) and Austin (bass), so here goes;

BHP: How did the band start and what inspired you to do it?
AUSTIN: Martin (drummer) and I were in a real shit band that split and we formed the band with Russ joining and then later on, Jamie when the original singer left. I was inspired to do it by seeing Adam Ant on TV at an early age and wanted to be such a cool customer.
RUSS: Martin agreed to buy me a pint if I joined!

BHP: What bands would you compare yourselves to?
AUSTIN: Anything fast and poppy really, a bit like the Ramones, but with dress sense (well, sort of!!)
RUSS: Sort of melodic fuzzcore, a bit like Funbug, but no way as whizzo on our instruments.

BHP: Have you always been interested in music?
AUSTIN: Yes indeedy! From when I was a nipper and I first experienced music in the form of the great Adam Ant. I have always shared an interest in numerous bands, my fave's being Grandmaster Melle Mel and the Replacements.
RUSS: No not really, not until I heard the and thought there must be more bands like them, cause 80's pop was shit.

BHP: Who inspires you individually?
AUSTIN: Paul Weller, Adam Ant, The , Morgan Thing, every Replacements song I've heard, Pretty Girls, Weetabix, Martin's razor sharp wit, Jamie's left tit, my cat and the Pixies.
RUSS: Beer, snuff, the wankers that said I'd never do anything, Indigo Floorshow, Circle Sky poems and Eliott, cause I hope I'll never be a bit like him!

BHP: Best band ever and why?
AUSTIN: Senseless Things, because they've kept on making good songs all their career and they can drink beer like no-one else!
RUSS: Citizen Fish, Culture Shock, Subhumans all because they've all got a message. Also they make a change from almost all other bands.

BHP: Best gig you've every played?
AUSTIN: Ritzy (college party) in Lincoln. The free beers flowed all night and we thrashed out a 20 minutes set.
RUSS: The same one, the free beer won me over.

BHP: What do hate and what do you love?
AUSTIN: Loves; senseless things, being in 'photo's, the Rev's, Pretty Girls, Tank Girl, Answering Machine by the Replacements, buying records and getting pissed and falling over.
Hates; Gitanes, the fact that fags cost so much, Martin's tendency to hit me and Jamie's cold bagels.
RUSS: Loves; Fags, Miller Lite, the , sleeping, Pretty Girls and getting wasted.
Hates; the fact that my stereo's knackered, sweet Jesus, Martin's jokes.

BHP: What would be The Shreds finest hour?
AUSTIN: Sleeping with Vanessa Paradis for half an hour and Kylie the following half hour.
RUSS: To have the same amount of screaming girls after us as the Beatles.

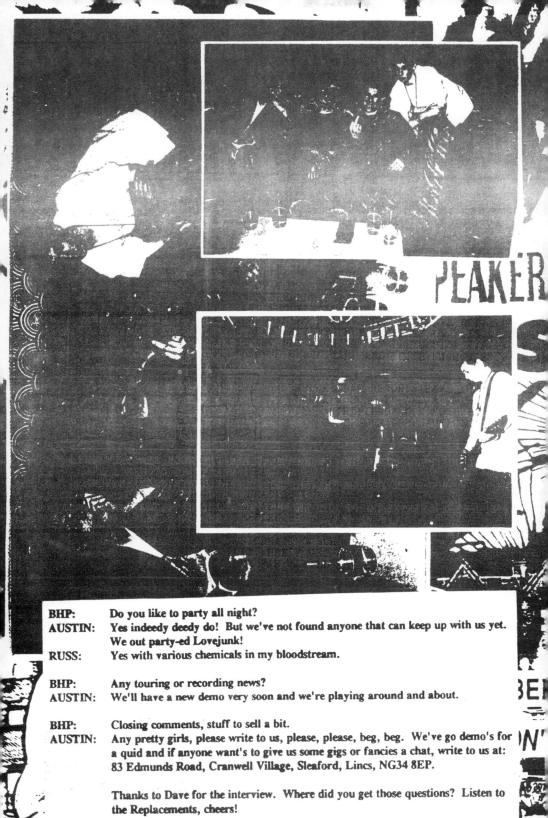

BHP: Do you like to party all night?

AUSTIN: Yes indeedy deedy do! But we've not found anyone that can keep up with us yet. We out party-ed Lovejunk!

RUSS: Yes with various chemicals in my bloodstream.

BHP: Any touring or recording news?

AUSTIN: We'll have a new demo very soon and we're playing around and about.

BHP: Closing comments, stuff to sell a bit.

AUSTIN: Any pretty girls, please write to us, please, please, beg, beg. We've go demo's for a quid and if anyone want's to give us some gigs or fancies a chat, write to us at: 83 Edmunds Road, Cranwell Village, Sleaford, Lincs, NG34 8EP.

Thanks to Dave for the interview. Where did you get those questions? Listen to the Replacements, cheers!

£2.00

Have you noticed that on many 'metal' or 'alternative' records now, there are warnings against drugs. But these same labels put out 'aceed' dance music especially for the druggy generation. And those 'respectable shops that refused to sell CRASS and the like are full of this shit. Who's fooling who. Take your drugs and fuck off!

HATE, that's a pretty strong emotion, a lot of people irritate the shit out of me but I'm not sure I actually hate them for it. (I'm not saying hate is all bad though, sometimes it's necessary.) I know I love people though, that's for sure. And it's a much stronger emotion. Lots of people, in different ways. LOVE is not a dirty word, it's about giving, not taking. Try to enjoy any while you can.

"Rave is the refuge of the mentally deficient. It's made by dull people for dull people."
MORRISSEY

SNFU

I recently wrote to Chi asking what SNFU were currently up to, this is an extract from his reply...

We just recorded 3 songs for a 7" due out in July on Hom Wrecherds. A label started by our geetar players. Who, also play in 'The Wheat Chefs.' They'll be releasing a full length W.C. C.D. quite shortly. They're on a short Canadian tour right now. We'll be doing a W. Coast tour of the U.S. in July. Back to L.A. in August to record the new album for Epitaph. It will be produced by Donnell Cameron. (Superchunk, Rocket from the Crypt.)

Possibly shoot a video for Said Release in September. The L.P. is slated for a mid October release. Waiting to get accepted at the Berlin Music Festival in November. If this happens, we'll tour Germany for 2 weeks. After that, we'll patch up Canada and the U.S. before it gets too cold!!! Another visit to Europe (including England!) will follow shortly thereafter. Oh!! now we have a new bassist: 'Starbuck.' Things are goin' well, just waiting to get back on the road!

You can write for more information to;
Mr Chi Pig
P.O.Box 106
101-1184 Denman Street
Vancouver B.C.
V6G 2M9 Canada

BORN AGAINST

On cigarettes...

Have you considered that while you raise your fist in support of the freedom seeking hordes, your other hand holds between the yellowed foul smelling fingers a smouldering instrument which destroys freedom and cheapens life. Your "second hand" toxic waste fills the lungs of innocent bystanders as well as your own. Your cigarettes are pumped out of laboratories packed with beagles and rabbits suffocating for your "bad habit." The cancer sticks are sold by women masquerading as hunks of flesh. The same newspapers that advertise the poison reveal, upon closer investigation, that more blacks in America die from smoking related diseases than any other drug or violent crime. No surprise considering the media blitz, portraying the goddess with lily white features, and a long slender white cigarette hanging so sensuously from her thin lips, which inundates the African-American community in the form of billboards and other propaganda designed to sell and kill. Twelve year olds watch as you light up, and they aspire to your mature disorder and physical addiction that is smoking every time you buy one of those nice neat little packages from the flag waving, union busting, all American R.J. Reynolds corporation. You will not die with a smile on your face when chemotherapy has made you so fucking weak that you can't even move your bald head or lift another piece of that shit to your shrivelled lips. I've watched loved ones wither and die from the innocuous vice, people who are so sure these things only happen to other folks. Don't talk about blowing up Shell stations or boycotting Coke while you are directly killing people and animals. Show respect for yourself and the lives of others in your immediate environment before even pretending to give a fuck about the plight of the oppressed, because the personal is the political.

Souvenir...
Do you remember when unity meant something?
We were gonna be friends till the very end
Do you remember when hardcore was everything?
Dancing, diving always good times
But, I guess it had to end
Young and full of energy
Punk rock shows every Friday night was the life for me
We swore we'd change the world, we swore with sincerity
But a few years down the line, proved punk a false reality
Minor Threat, 7 Seconds, S.S.D
Straight Edge Hardcore was introduced to me
Remember when.
I can't help but get down at the state of things today
Are unity and togetherness remnants of yesterday?
Sorry, I'm not willing to throw it all away
Our memories are souvenirs of yesterday
I still feel the passion and the energy
I can't help but feel hardcore as a part of me
Times will change and people will change and so will styles
But something in the music just makes me smile
Remember when.

← LIFETIME

ON HARDCORE

down by law

Down by Law are something of a H.C. supergroup, with Dave Smalley, ex ALL and Dag Nasty and ex-members of 'Thats It' and 'Left Insane.' You've probably already heard of them, but if not, here's an interview with Dave, at their Brighton gig with Joeyfat. Questions by MILES.

BHP How is the tour going? How was Europe?

DBL The tour is going really great so far. We played for a couple of weeks in Germany, then three shows in Holland, which was a really special place. Now we're doing shows in the UK; which has just been a really moving experience - great people, who really care about their music and how it affects life. Basically, for me, it feels like coming home.

BHP I was expecting to see the Chemical People guys. How did the new line-up come about? What have the new band members been involved in before?

DBL Dave and Ed from the Chems are doing a new band, called Chaser, which is really a good new band. Down by Law was really a project the three of us started in 1990, just for occasional fun practises or shows. Then Epitaph records signed us and things started going a lot faster than we ever thought about and the reactions from people really were incredible - it was like, holy shit, people really also care about this band, they believe in the same things we believe in - right on, so after we recorded "blue" it was pretty evident to all of us that we had lit a torch and no way were we going to let people down. I really feel like Down By Law is soul music for your heart and mind. I believe that you can affect life, the world, each other - you name it, but if you love and care you can leave the world a better place.

Anyway, after deciding to go full steam ahead, since everybody had another band (Chems and Clawhammer) Down by Law is now Mark Phillips on quitar, who is a soulful human being who plays his heart out. He's a great guitar player and a friend, as are all the guys. Anyway he was in 'Thats It' and the 'Young Caucasions' (he's from Wash. D.C. too.) Pat Hoed is the bass player, from L.A., he was in the '? Drivers' and 'Left insane.' Hunter Oswald is our drummer, he's 19 years old and moved out to L.A. to join DBL. That was a long answer, sorry.

BHP Between songs you talk about their subjects. A lot seem to be about the problems in L.A. Have they affected the band directly?

DBL Down By Law sings about peace, love and being pissed off at a lot of things in life. When you see the police drawing a chalk line around a dead body in L.A., which you see a lot, it really affects you, we write songs about life and trying to make the world a bit better, you find a battle in life and fight it.

BHP Is "Best Friends" a cover? (Who did it originally if it is?)

DBL Best Friends is a cover of an Outlets song. They were a great pop punk band from Boston who never made it out of Boston, but if you ever get the chance to hear anything by them, do it.

BHP What are you guys listening to at the moment? What do you think of "Rage Against the Machine" (being on a major label?)

DBL Hunter: Special Beat, Husker Du and Wool. Dave: The Jam, the Clash and the newest S.L. Fingers l.p. and Wool. Mark: Wool, Iggy Pop, the Damned. Pat: Rage Against the Machine, Tool, the Obsessed and Wool. Rage is a great band - more power to them. They still have retained their credibility. Major labels are starting to wake up to good music now - they've approached Down By Law, Samiam, lots of bands that you can believe in, for me it's not the best thing but for certain bands that want that, it's ok.

BHP I noticed your drummer wearing a 'Blind' T-shirt. Do any of the band skate?

DBL Yeah, Hunter and I skate. Hunter is a way better skater than I am! We all like to believe in the free spirit that skating brings to you, to life.

BHP Dave - how is your book going? Is it finished? What's it about?

DBL There is no book, I wrote one at age 19 and after re-reading it, I realised I didn't want it to go out, for a lot of reasons. Maybe at some point when we stop touring for a while I'll have time to sit down and really write about some experience and for right now Down By Law is my love (after my wife Caroline.) I think this is what we were put here to do.

BHP What can we expect after the tour?

DBL There are 2 singles coming out, 1 is on Break Even Point from Italy, that should be out now and then 1 is on Selfless Records from TX. Each one will have some originals and at least

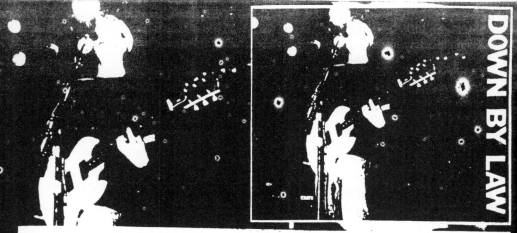

DOWN BY LAW

one cover song - 'Revolver' by Mission of Burma is on one, then 'Get Up Stand Up' by Bob Marley is on the other, along with 'Next To You' by The Police. The singles came out are really special, I think. Then after this tour will take some time off, then record the new album. Hopefully next year we will be able to come back to the UK.

BHP Anything else?

DBL Just please remember - it's a big scary world out there, but there is something everybody can do to make it a little better. Give money to Greenpeace. Sign a petition, support independent music, recycle - all that you do means something. Live your life to the fullest and take care of your friends and your world.

Thanks to everybody in Europe and especially here in the UK for all your support. We love you guys and we won't let you down.

ANIMALS in Laboratories

Did you know that:

1. 100,000 animals die every week in British laboratories.

2. Animals in laboratories are poisoned with oven cleaners, weedkiller, lipsticks, crayons, shampoos, drugs, weapons, paint and many other products. This is done to find out how poisonous they are.

3. 3½ million experiments are performed on animals every year in this country. In three quarters of these experiments *the animals are given no anaesthetic to kill the pain.*

4. Shampoos are dripped into the eyes of rabbits which often makes their eyes swell and destroys the tissues of the eyeball. Imagine what *that* feels like.

5. Some people steal cats and dogs and sell them to laboratories.

6. Dogs and rabbits and rats are strapped down and made to smoke, sometimes for six hours at the time, in order to test smoking materials, when everybody knows that smoking is harmful.

7. No independent observer is allowed into a laboratory to see what is happening to the animals, not even an RSPCA inspector or a Member of Parliament.

8. Animals are blinded, scalded, electrocuted, paralysed, driven mad, turned into drug addicts and given diseases in animal experiments.

9. The only release from pain in the vivisectors laboratory is death.

- -

☐ I wish to become a member of **Animal Aid** and enclose £7 for a years subscription. £3 if under 18.

☐ I enclose . . . . donation in support of your campaign.

ANIMAL AID

Name . . . .

Address . . . .

. . . . Age . . . .

Please make cheques/postal orders payable to Animal Aid Society

7 Castle Street, Tonbridge, Kent TN9 1BH. Telephone: (0732) 364546

STRICTLY PEACEFUL CAMPAIGNING

lay is everything work is not...

At work only the past and future exist; what may appen after work and what happened before. Play happening in the present, allowing the past and ture to take care of themselves.

Work is always to be finished. Then there is the ext job, so life is measured in terms of time between ork and the time taken to do a job. Time is the aster of all, defining the routines of misery. Play an't remember the time because it is here and now.

I'm *too* sexy for a job

The desire to play has returned to destroy the hierarchical society which banished it

Work is daily despair trying to maintain the pretence of normality. Forced to work but "that's life" The brutality of the empty choice between survival the one hand and survival on the other is internalis and poisons every human contact. Play never forces anyone to play and can never wish death on someone else.

Adults work, and their "good sense" represents the hidden class struggle, the oppression of children. Children play but growing up is the sensible cleansing of life, for bright, white order and the pur of responsibilities. Play is reclaiming childhood for everyone so that no one has to apologise for dirty knees.

Work is identity, making people into their work. Work is the centre to which everything else must gravitate. Play creates chaos because people no longer have to be something. Everything is unfixed in the play of infinite possibilities.

Work is the division of life so that it may be controlled. Everything must have its proper place, what happens can only happen where can happen. Work is the only connection. Play creates infinite connections, and myths, so that anything could happen anywhere.

Work is the greed of possession, the ownership over everything, the power to buy. Everything a product, a product of the same everything that is everywhere, a planetary work machine. There is no release from the work of production to earn money to buy back the goods produced Play is the release that produces nothing except itself.

Work is the management of time on behalf of the usiness of desire. This worldwide business plan ants to control and manipulate desire for its own ofit. Play is desire without restraints, the fantasy orld that banishes money matters.

Work is the lie that nothing else is possible. Get up to work. Driven out of bed by the delusion of ason constructed by consensus. Work fears nothg more than the notion that there is something else d play is the irrational thought out of nowhere aking the workplace jokes wear thin.

The working world is a world where everything is a commodity to buy and sell, including love. Lovers spend time together, balancing their accounts of commitment and declaring budget deficits in sacrifices. Play deserves no martyrs because no one has got a price on their head.

Play is everything work is not... Think of everything work is not and dream of what games to play. The games will have no beginning and no end, but only really start when the last spanner has been thrown into the last cog of the planetary work machine.

the PSEUDO HiPPiES

(left)colonel cop-alot.
(right)lieutenant sex machine.
photo;dommy stardom,Worcester,
jan '93.

THE PSEUDO HIPPIES NEED NO INTRODUCTION.THEY EMBODY ROCK'N'ROLL
TO THE FULL.GIRLS,DRINK,DRUGS AND FUN TO THE MAX.WITH THE
RELEASE OF THEIR SUPERB MINI LP 'GIRLFIEND' ABOUT TO SHUDDER THE
POP ESTABLISHMENT,BHP TOOK THEIR CHANCE AND MET THESE FOUR EVASIVE,
SUAVE AND SHOCKINGLY SEXY POP-THINGS FOR AN EXCLUSIVE INTERVIEW.
BAND LOW-DOWN IS KRIS PSEUDO 'COLONEL COP-ALOT' ON VOICE AND
GUITAR,ADAM ANCIENT 'MUFF MAGNET' ON BASS,DANNY RINGO RATS
'LIEUTENANT SEX MACHINE' ON PERCUSSION & POPAGANDA AND FINALLY
TOMMY LEGEND ON GUITARS AND VOICE HARMONIES.FIRE AWAY!!!

BHP:OK.WHAT RECORDS HAVE YOU GOT OUT?
ADAM:A 4 SONG 7" AND A RATHER PUNKPOPTASTIC MINI LP ENTITLED
    'GIRLFIEND' OUT SOON.WE ALSO HAVE A 3 MINUTE POP-GEM ON
    BOSS TUNEAGE US/UK COMP LP WITH SAMIAM &MTX.

BHP:WHAT ARE YOUR FAV BANDS AT THE MO AND WHICH ONES WOULD YOU
HAVE LIKED TO BE IN AND WHY?
DANNY:BEATLES,KINKS,FUNBUG.COZ THEY'RE MIGHTY FINE DON'T YOU AGREE?!
    BEATLES COZ RINGO IS MY DAD.
ADAM:ALL,ALL & ALL.ALL,COZ THEY'RE THE TOTAL EXTENT.(ALTHOUGH THE
    BEATLES WOULD BE NICE,THE BIRDS YOU KNOW.)
KRIS:BEATLES,MONKEYS,STEREO MC'S.THE FAB 4 COZ OF THE MILLION
    (S)CREAMING SCHOOL GIRLS AND WORLD WIDE FAME.I CAN SEE THE
    DAY WHEN I GET CHASED AROUND TOWN BY 500 GIRLS.EXCEPT I,UNLIKE
    THE FAB 4,WILL NOT RUN AWAY!

BHP:I HEAR YOU'RE TOURING GERMANY TO PROMOTE THE MINI LP.
    CARE TO ELABORATE?
ADAM:YEAH.FREE BEER.
DANNY:WE'RE GOING TO EAT THEIR WOMEN,SHAG THEIR BEER AND DRINK THEI
    SAUSAGES.
KRIS:YEP.IN SEPTEMBER.2 WEEKS OF PSEUDOMANIA ON THE CONTENANT!

BHP:WHERE'S TOMMY LEGEND TODAY?I THOUGHT HE'D BE HERE?
DANNY:HE REFUSED TO BE INTERVIEWED COS HE SAYS HE ALWAYS GETS
    MISS QUOTED,SO HE PREFERS TO BE THE MYSTERIOUS ONE IN THE
    GROUP.HE'S OUT AROUND TOWN IN HIS SPORTS CAR,SURVEYING THE
    TALENT FOR TONITE!

BHP:I ALSO HEAR YOU'RE CHANGING MUSICAL DIRECTION A LITTLE.TO WHA
    AND WHY?
DANNY:TO A MORE 60'S SOUND.VERY BEATLES/KINKS WITH MORE 'UMPH' AN
    NRG!WHY?TO COP MORE WOMEN OFCOURSE!!STUPID QUESTION!

BHP:IS IT TRUE THE ONLY REASON YOUR IN A BAND IS TO GET WOMEN AND
    NOT BECAUSE YOU WANNA GET SUCCESSFUL?I'VE HEARD SOME OF YOU
    HAVE TAKEN TO HANGING OUT AT THE LOCAL NURSES HOME FOR LONG
    WEEKENDS?
KRIS:SHHH!THAT'S OUR LITTLE SECRET!
DANNY:NO.THAT IS A VICIOUS RUMOUR SPREAD BY THE MEDIA.ALTHOUGH THE
    OTHER TWO DO SPEND ALOT OF TIME LOCKED UP IN THE NURSES HOME!
ADAM:YOU WANT THE HONEST TRUTH?.....YEP!

BHP
BHB
IPB

BHP:DO YOU LOT PULL ALOT AT YOUR GIGS THEN?
DANNY:OFCOURSE!WHAT D'YOU THINK WE DO THIS FOR?!!
ADAM:LOOKING LIKE THIS?WADD'YA THINK?
KRIS:YEAH.A FAIR AMOUNT ACTUALLY.THEY MOSTLY GO FOR ME?COZ I'M THE
    SINGER/LENNON FIGURE OF THE BAND.MUSICAL GENIUS AND ROGUE-ISH
    LATIN LOOKS TO BOOT.

BHP:WHAT PISSES YOU OFF MOST ABOUT BEING A PSEUDO HIPPY?
DANNY:ALL THE GIRLS THAT WAIT OUTSIDE MY HOUSE SCREAMING FOR A
    GLIMPSE OF ME.
ADAM:THE OTHER THREE COZ THEIR UGLYNESS PUTS THE GIRLS OFF.
KRIS:GOD!YOU BITCH ADAM!WE'VE BEEN NICE TO YOU ALL DAY!ANYHOW...
    PROBABLY CONSTANT MEDIA HARRASSMENT.I CAN'T GO FOR A PEE IN
    THE MIDDLE OF THE NIGHT WITHOUT THERE BEING A PHOTOGRAPHER
    ON A LADDER AT MY WINDOW WITH A FLASH BULB.

BHP:I HEARD YOU'RE BIG IN THE WORCESTER AREA.YOU WERE PLAYED ON
    BIRMINGHAM'S 'X-RATED' RADIO SHOW AND ARE VERGING ON POP
    STARDOM-NESS?CARE TO GIVE MORE DETAILS?
ADAM:ONLY WHEN I'M WITH A CERTAIN SOMEONE ON A SOFA.NUFF SAID!
DANNY:NO.ASK HIM(POINTING AT KRIS)
KRIS:WOULD I CARE TO ELABORATE?UM....NO NOT REALLY,COS I'LL
    PROBABLY GET HASSLE FROM SOMEONE IF SHE READS THIS AND I
    COULD DO WITHOUT MORE GRIEF FROM GIRLS-HONESTLY!I'VE HAD TO
    PADLOCK THE DUSTBIN COZ THEY GO THROUGH MY RUBBISH.

BHP:HOW MANY UNITS OF ALCOHOL DO YOU DRINK A WEEK?WHEN WAS THE
    LAST SOBER WEEKEND YOU HAD?
DANNY:ENOUGH!CAN'T REMEMBER.WHO CARES?WHO KNOWS?!!
ADAM:ABOUT 10 TO 15.THIS WEEKEND.COS I HAD TO TAXI EVERYONE AROUND.
KRIS:TOO MUCH.PROBABLY ON HOLIDAY IN ITALY LAST X-MAS.I USED THE
    VACATION AS A DRYING OUT PERIOD.DID IT WORK?UM...NO.AND ANY-
    WAY,WHY IS THIS DISCUSSION FOCUSING ON GIRLS AND DRINK?WHAT
    ABOUT MUSIC?
DANNY:YEAH.WHAT ABOUT MUSIC?(TO KRIS)
KRIS:UM.OK,CARRY ON MATE.

BHP:YOU'RE WOMEN PULLING POWERS ARE NOW REACHING INFAMOUS LEGENDARY
    STATUS,HOW ARE YOU GUYS SO SUCCESSFUL?
KRIS:THE SECRET IS IN OUR GENES AND JEANS!C-YA!!!

BHP:OK.LAST QUESTION.WOULD YOU RATHER GO ON A WORLD TOUR WITH THE
    RAMONES FOR A FORTNIGHT AS THEIR ONLY SUPPORT ACT OR HAVE THE
    BIRD FROM BAYWATCH LOCKED IN YOUR BEDROOM FOR A WEEKEND OF
    PASSION?
DANNY:THE BIRD FROM BAYWATCH.COS THOSE BAPS ARE THE JUBBLIEST I'VE
    EVER SEEN.
ADAM:OPTION 2 COS,WELL IT'S PRETTY BLOODY OBVIOUS!!
KRIS:DON'T BE SILLY!OPTION BABEWATCH!WHY?USE YOUR HEAD BOY!(THAT'S
    WHAT SHE SAID!!!)

FAB 4
FROM
LONDON

WELL THERE YOU HAVE IT.A BRIEF GLIMPSE INTO THE HECTIC AND
HEDONISTIC LIFE OF THE PSEUDO HIPPIES.THEIR 7" AND MINI LP
ARE AVAILABLE FROM THEM(SEE ADVERT THIS ISSUE)SO GET THEM
NOW COZ THEY REALLY ARE SUPERB.FOR MORE INFO,BOOKINGS &
MERCHANDISE WRITE 'EM AT-PSEUDO HQ,5 HENRYSON RD,LONDON,
SE 4 1HL.

"We're four guys who believe in what we're doing."

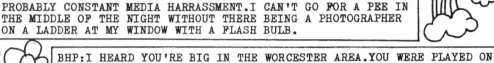

SUGAR 'Beaster' (Creation)
Only 6 tracks yet it clocks in at over 30 minutes, this new mini-LP has been highly acclaimed by many. I'm in two minds about it. So it's worth considering track by track. First song 'Come Again' is a dull 5 minutes, to be frank 'Tilted' sounds like Husker Du circa 'Flip Your Wig' - it's cool. 'Judas Cradle' and 'JC Auto' both over 6 minutes are where it gets slow, noisy and intense - Best songs lyrically not musically though. 'Feeling Better' is a breath of fresh air at first - almost funky, Rock n' Roll! Final track 'Walking Away' is an unusual choral sounding thing - different but so what? So in part, 'Beaster' is a pretty blinding very intense and powerful, a really 'meaty' production sound, good words and that. On the other hand, it's agonisingly slow and noisy in parts, but not noisy in a raw punk way (which is appealing, but in Sugars case it's sort of unnatural.) 'Copper Blue' had a real good pop-edge to it which was great, but 'Beaster' is 'evil' and different - This is it's main appeal no doubt. Half marks from me, sorry Bob!

FLUF 'Wasting Seed' 10" (Headhunter)
This newish band has 0 and Jonny from the wonderful Olive Lawn. This 10" is a corker if you ask me. I suppose it's 'Grunge' but done in that typical headhunter kind of way - firmly rooted in punk and sounding bloody great. There's a great Soundgarden piss-take too 'Kim Thayills Paw (Guitar Centre.) Some cool 30's sounding music sampled and all the songs are winners especially the fastest 'Hecko Del Diablo' If you liked Olive Lawn check this out, even though it's a winner and so on, coloured vinyl too! And 10"!

CORNERSHOP/HUGGY BEAR/JACOBS MOUSE/MAMBO TAXI/BLOOD
SAUSAGE...9.4.93. POHIO benefit (Wiiija night) Powerhaus.
Only five quid and it goes to charity, a good deal I reckon whatever your tastes are - tonights Wiiija night had something I suppose for everybody. BLOOD SAUSAGE are a great start, Dale is a pretty unlikely star. BLOOD SAUSAGE are popular in 'Riot Grrl' circles too - they also have Jo and Nikki from Huggy Bear in them. If your bothered about that kind of thing. They have an excellant garage sound but with personal meaningful lyrics sung and screamed passionately by Dale. Definitely a band to check out. MAMBO TAXI - four girls and one bloke dressed in drag are getting pretty much attention these days. They're good fun. Dressed up in glitzy clothes and play a trashy glam - punk full of tunes and with a garagey punk sound underneath it all - it's a bit messy in parts, but still cool and when the keyboardist takes the mike for the last song it's the definite highlight, the weirdest night ever! JACOBS MOUSE are the worst tonightby far. They've got all the wig-out moves and a metally grunge sound but with a few extra twists. Frankly, they're dull still churning out the same stuffthey did when they begun - It's loud and fast but so what? It's shit, not even exciting or fresh. What can I say about HUGGY BEAR - only given twenty minutes or so, it's not enough and it seems Jo's guitar has packed up too. Weirdest cover of 'Relax' ever, 'Her Jazz' sound okay, but newest song 'Pansy Twist' is friggin great. Still Huggy Bear are exciting and punk as fuck. Despite not such an impressive performance tonight. Headliners CORNERSHOP thoroughly impress something I didn't really expect. Effective use of sampling noise feed back and great punk tunes with a sense of humour too. It's a very fast grating sound and Chris from Huggy Bear joins them for 'Kawasaki' so it sounds even better. Cornershop are definitely worthy of your attention, don't listen to all that 'Mary Chain Rip-off' bollocks because Cornershop are a band in their own right, excellent live, better than on vinyl me thinks - unoriginal? How many bands these days use a sitar and sound totally punk!

CODIGONEUROTICO Thomas-a-Beckett pub, Old Kent Road, 10.4.93
"Who the ?'" I hear you cry and rightly so 'coz this one took me by surprise. I'd turned up with my mate because his mates band were first on then there was a slick sounding truly cliched metal band called 'Moth.' Codigoneurotico are from Barcelona - 3 youngish lads with big grins and cool influences. Sung totally in Spanish. These guys we're corking - their sound is obviously Brit-punk/Dead Kennedys/Ramones influences but with an almost California air to it - a Ska Op IV influence shone through, so did the Descendants but maybe they've heard neither ?! Very fresh and fun sounding practically flawless punk pop surprise ans so unexpected. God knows whether they have records out - chances are I'll never see or hear them again. Does anybody out there know anything about Codigoneurotico? Please help 'coz they're shred!

VORMEES, London, Tufnell Park The Dome. 19.4.93

This is the first time this Newcastle hardcore-punk outfit has played in London and surely any band that covers songs by Dys The Faith and Negative approach can't be that bad, eh? Vormees have an almighty sound and they are very well received tonight supporting slapshot, perhaps their sound isn't totally original but they do it well. Quick punk riffs with a tinge of metaland rough sounding vocals tackling typical right-on punk subjects, sounds dull? Well, check 'em out because it's so raw and energetic and exciting definitely one to watch, Vormees.

THEE HEADCOATS + THEE HEADCOATEES, Archway St JohnTavern. 21.4.93

It's packed here tonight because it's all being recorded for a live LP. Thee Headcoats are on form tonight - perfect garage trash, full of energy and conviction with a really trad fuzzy sound - the set-up is perfect here for their kind of stuff. Geez, Billy Childish and Co. certainly have style and even drop in a Mudhoney number for good measure. Later the lads are joined by their alter egos - the female Headcoatees, well only three of them tonight. Their vocals and screams enhance the Headcoats distinctive music. The stuff off the Headcoatees 'Girlsville' LP sounds pretty wonderful and they're having fun! Last up is a few instrumental numbers and the wonderful manic 'A.T.V.' 2 hours tonight excellent garage mayhem - not bad for £3.50 me thinks.

ANTISEEN. Camden Falcon (London) 27.4.93

Antiseen are better that I expected live. I think this is their first UK tour. Yet they've been around a good ten years. Their sound is firmly rooted in punk (Ramones, Buzzcocks etc) But with firm garage roots, too. However, it's livened up by Jeff Claytons vocals and loud distorted guitar Claytons voice is rough - more Lemmy than Lemmy! Live, the whole sound is intense, energetic an faster than their vinyl stuff. Only 35 minutes or so including corking covers of Roky Erikson and Anti-Nowhere League songs. Punk as fuck.

SAMIAM/GOOBER PATROL/GUNS'N'WANKERS/CHICKEN BONE CHOKE, Sir George Robey, 11.5.93

Chicken Bone Choke: first time I've never heard of them too but it's impressive - Very loud fastish pop-punk in the style of Pegboy, but it's kind of original too because I can't think of who else they're like. It seems not much other UK stuff sounds like them. Watch out for'em.

Guns'n'Wankers: ex-Snuffie DUNCAN now plays guitar and sings with these guys. It's more Hardcore than Snuff (the obvious comparison is there to be made) but still fun, especially the piss-take(?) metal numbers excellence.

Goober Patrol: their usual selves tonight, going on about how inept they are but still churning out fun pop-punk in their own inimitable way. They basically fill the void left on the demise of Snuff, it's cool but nothing special.

SAMIAM: Call it sacrilege but I tend to find some of Samiams studio stuff a bit dull sometimes. It works better live, full of energy and distinctly raw. The vocals are what individuate their sound, sort of 'whiney' but harsh and powerful too. Even in their slower moments, Samiam command your attention because of their sheer conviction and energy. A far better live band.

THE NEW BOMB TURKS. Tufnell Park, The Dome, London, 12.5.93

So everyone's been going on how great these guys are, yet the Dome is practically deserted tonight. The 'Destroy, Oh Boy!' LP is wonderful so are all the singles and guess what? live it's just as corking. Their sound is firmly rooted in garage but heavenly punked-up - imagine the Supersuckers at 78 rpm! It's fast full of energy, loud of course and frankly pretty awesome. Singer Eric is a bit of a nutter. The guitarist plays so fast it's untrue and the drummer is mighty fine too. Perhaps an hour was a bit too long and it's a shame such a big venue was chosen (The Falcon would've been a good choice) but overall, this band is exciting like no other I've seen for a while.

J CHURCH/CHINA DRUM Sir George Robey, London 25/5/93

China Drum are amazing! These guys really have something going for them, no denying excellent, powerful punkpop in a Descendents/Bay Area kind of way - fast and very slick. The bassist is amazing as too the drummer/singer and it's topped-up with excellent guitar and the coolest vocal harmonies. I can't but praise China Drum - they're shred. But their CD single or cassette (no vinyl, both 3 tracks) from: China Drum C/o Adam, The Hermitage, Ovingham, Prudhoe, Northumberland, cost £3, cheques can be made out to 'China Drum' T-shirt £5, sweats £10 - red/blue/black. Do it!

J Church in case anybody doesn't know, are Lance and Gardener ex-Cringer - that most perfect of California. Pop-punk bands, and drummer Brendan, who's ill tonight, so his place is filled by none other than ex-snuff sticks-man Duncan! It's a harsher sound than Cringer, the bass lines are familiar but it's delivered in a more 'hardcore' than 'poppy' way. It's cool! Lance is a wonderful singer and guitarist, so unpretentious and it all works rather nicely live - energy, conviction but tuneful. Check out the fabulous 'Quetzalcoatl' LP and numerous 7"s and see!

GREEN DAY + JOEYFAT Dome,Tufnell Park, 2.5.93

Joeyfat seem to be improving every time I see them! They're style is distinctive hardcore, but restrained in that Fugazi, Shudder To Think kind of way. Singer Matt is still the hero, very intense, jumping, clapping, twisting, his vocal style is distinctive and the words seem deeply personal. Joeyfat are getting better and deserve more attention. But will the bassist ever turn around and face the audience is the question on everyone's lips.

Green Day playing after all! A pleasant surprise after last month's cancellation. I'm sure all BHP readers know what these guys sound like - perfect pop-punk, basically - Green Day are considered the best in their class too. Live, it's a rougher rawer sound than the clean smooth sounding recent LP - Billie-Jo's voice is pretty wonderful through it all and so live Green Day are probably at their best. It's good fun, friendly and swelteringly hot, but we don't care because Green Day cheer us all up no end. 'Up the Villa?!'

COUCH POTATOES 'In Bed With...' (Weird Records 7" EP)

Four tracks, this 7" contains songs from the 'Excess all areas' LP. This grew on me second, third time round - it's fuzzy sounding pop punk rather similar to All or Big Drill Car. Roughish production unfortunately. But good fun the best song is probably 'Impossible Easier.' They sound like they're enjoying themselves so why not join them £2 ppd from Dave, 1 Chandos Road, Tunbridge Wells, Kent, TN1 2NY. Quality stuff indeed - it sounds better fourth time round too!

THE BERTS 'Sing it' (Demo Cassette)

I've listened to this a few times now but so far nothing's persuaded me to like this and why does the first track remind me of Depeche Mode? The songs are nicely written and well-played, a kind of commercial sounding indie-pop with a harsh edge but thats all there is to it. I'm not going to slag it off because it's not my kind of thing, just that it lacks that certain something - not enough hooks to make it good pop-punk, not harsh enough so lacking energy too. What I do appreciate is their obvious commitment and cool sounding production but poor lyrics 'Every Time She Kisses I Die... I'm making love to a razor' and an overall weakness to it all just put me off. Well, see for yourself, contact Mark, 8 Carriage Close, Oldbury Road, St Johns, Worcester, WR2 6ARE.

ERASE TODAY 'The Economic Prison' mini LP

Now this is cool! Erase today are a young band from Blackpool and this is their debut vinyl release. It's like Husker Du meets Pegboy except with English accents! Apart from a slightly muffled production and a couple of over-long songs, I can't fault this at all - there's such potential for great stuff here! Intelligent lyrics, variety musically and well packaged too. £3 or £4 ppd from erase today C/o Sedbergh Avenue, Blackpool. Lancs FY4 4DQ. Check it out.

DOWN BY LAW Camden Underworld, 5.5.93

Joeyfat entertain again - another slick set, it's sounding better everytime and their newer stuff seems faster too. Your Mum are a bit erratic but improving as well, Snuff-sounding melodic punk. Unfortunately, Down By Law are a thorough disappointment. It sounds terrible tonight, perhaps it's the Underworlds PA but Joeyfat managed okay and I've seen great sounding bands here. No, the bassist had his stuff turned up too high, it's all to muffled tonight. D.B.L sound perfect on vinyl - it's a clean fresh sounding pop-punk, like Dave Smalleys previous bands Dag Nasty and All (and Dys,) their first LP was choc-full of beautiful songs especially 'Best Friends' which sounds appalling tonight, where's the tuneful melodies? Where's the sweetly sung songs, the clean but cutting guitar? Down By Law lost it tonight. A potentially corking gig turned out to be particularly special... but I'll keep listening to Down By Law, they're still a great band but it didn't work tonight to these humble ears.

Get writing, make contacts, support the Underground!

"There are certain things about life that are really wonderful, like love, food and sex. But to really enjoy food is one of the best things" MOLLY RINGWALD

LEATHERFACE/LITHIAM JOE Hull Adelph Club 15.5.93

First up were Hull band, Lithiam Joe. Having already built up quite a following through intensive gigging and their two released demos they play an excellent set. Their mix of pop, punk guitars and skank (?) seems much tighter in recent gigs. A band worth seeing.

Leatherface take to the stage to an eager audience and from the first chord, the pit goes crazy and from then on I knew it was to be a good gig. I can't think of a band that produces the intense feeling of excitement like Leatherface do live and this was no exception. Playing only a handful of new material from "Minx," their recent LP they ran through most of "Mush" and earlier stuff. "Trenchfoot" was a particularly excellent - an old fave of mine. Frankie + Co played a long set before returning for a burst of covers that can only be compared to Snuff in speed! Wat Tyler's "Hops and Barley" was requested and when it came it exploded after sustaining multiple bruising and someone's teeth to my head(!) I retired a happy man. (N.S.)

ZERO POSITIVES 'Human Meat For Sale' 7"

This is the latest 7" release by the Zero Positives (a really promising new Belgian grindcore/hardcore band) and my god is this little record intense! Although it does not match up to old Zero Positives classic like "Randin Dread," it does keep up to the standard set by the band when they first started out. There are 4 trax on offer here, the first is very grindcore but that changes on the second track on to a slow moving hardcore track. The most outstanding song on the 7" is "Mine" which is saved to last and is just so heavy it does remind me a bit of Tad at first. I'd only recommend this to grind and hatecore fans but overall a pretty good record. (E.A.)

BIOHAZARD "Urban Hazard" LP (Roadrunner)

This is the best Biohazard offering yet, and boy do they sound more frustrated and pissed off! This is pure streetcore mixing rap rhythms with trash riff. This album is shouting out at all the stupidity around with hate grinded out by dual vocalists Billy and Evan demonstrated outrax like "Punishment," where Evan stops singing Billy takes over his distressed raw rapping voice. This is one of the best hardcore LP's of the year. Buy it! (E.A.)

GRAVEL "Breakbone" LP (Estus Records)

Gravels musical style lands somewhere between Mudhoney and Green Day. It has some real poppy H/C gems like "bucket of blood" and "as for tomorrow" and also some amazing grungenomic songs like "loneride" and "halfride" so the album is a good healthy mixture of these 2 types of music. As for their lyrics and songwriting technique. The lyrics are emotional, personal and high spirited. I'd really recommend this to anyone who is sick of the Sub Pop scene and wants some real groovy underground grunge action! (E.A)

POISON IDEA London Marquee 1.4.93

After Headbutt have abused our ear drums for too long. The DJ warms up a pretty much packed Marquee by playing such rock classics as Slayer, Motorhead, Ramones, Helmet and Dead Kennedys. There's a real punk atmostphere here tonight - it's great. I know everyone goes on about how large Poison Idea are, but it has to be said - Guitarist Pig Champion is the biggest, fattest, widest. person ever to hold a guitar - he hardly moves. He's that huge. It's an amazing sight - he makes Tad Doyle and the

Connorbrothers (Screaming Trees) look positively slim! Singer Jerry A is pretty big too. He's the real star tonight. It's great the way he talks to stage divers and reacts with smiles or gasps as they dive in. As if he's going to hold up score cards or something. Oh yeah, the music: Poison Idea have a full meaty sound, more metal these days but still firmly rooted in punk. They all play exceptionally well and of course fast. Jerry A's voice is rough and powerful. Half-way through it loses it's way somewhat. So many people have got on stage and don't move, all so proud they're there. Fact is I'd much prefer to watch the band, cheers. The "Mosh pit" looks far too scary and diving's fine but hogging the stage!? Great covers of "Up Front" (Wipers) and "Jailhouse Rock" add to the fun, but classics like "Plastic Bomb" hardly get sung due to Jerry A's wonderful crowd friendship. This was a cool punk rock show, no denying - thank god Poison Idea have presence and character to make it all seem worthwhile..."responsibility made me quit/I'm sick of this motherfucking goddamn shit"... I ain't sick of these guys now I've seen them live, because 'Blank Blackout Vacant' was not a patch on 'Feel the Darkness.' Yep, an enjoyable evening's entertainment.

GOOBER PATROL/CHOCOLATE/GLUE White Horse 26.03.93

Glue are a Scottish punk outfit, their LP 'Gravel' is very intense, sort of straight-edge sounding, it's cool but a bit too much to listen to in one go. Live they sound alright. Nothing exceptional, noisy, excellent 'twangy' bass, pretty tight and energetic. But just lacking that certain something to make me think "Yeah!" Then again, what do I know?

Chocolate are frankly, disappointing. Perhaps I was wrong in expecting a Stupids sounding fast brash hardcore. They're very slick and have good songs but there's really nothing to it - no excitement nothing different just very ordinary. Their fun attitude and too much talking (witty Banter??) doesn't help really.

Goober Patrol enjoy the fact that all their mates are their tonight and don't play enough of the pop-punk stuff they're good at. Again, too much talking in-jokes, blowing up condoms (tee hee) they only manage half a dozen songs which are so Snuff-like its unreal. Good covers of the Spiderman theme and a Beatles tune "Daydreams Believer," though, but too much bullshitting and I get the feeling I was one of the only people paying to see music. What a boring bastard I must be - going to a gig to see bands playing music! This evening stank of clique-ness.

DIDJITS London Powerhaus 29.03.93

Okay, so many bands these days do the typical 3-minute punk-pop stuff, but I'll certainly never tire of it when it's done well. The didjits do it _very_ well! When it's fast, it's very fast indeed. Even the slower(ish) numbers are well constructed, tuneful and very slick. The singer/guitarist is the star of the show. The cliched wanky guitar solos and tongue - waggling is all tongue-in-cheek (hopefully!) and his voice is pretty rangey too. The Didjits really seem to enjoy themselves, which is good to see and so did we this evening. Good fun.

THE MR T EXPERIENCE "Gun Crazy" 7" (Lookout!)

A new MTX 7". Their first without Jon Von it seems, who will no doubt be sadly missed. As with everything they've ever done. This is still a pretty corking 3 song E.P. "More Than Toast" is a catchy funny song, more Buzzcocks than Ramones,

WYNONA RIDERS-SOME ENCHANTED EVENING 7"
The Riders first Lookout! release and a mighty fine one at that. Run of the mill Californian hardcore with whiney brat vocals. Best song being the A side. Definetly worth a look.

NINE INCH NAILS - BROKEN mini CD
Total mind fuck techo/guitar shit. Makes Ministry look shite. Pumping rythms, ear shredding sheet guitar work and seriously fucked-up vocals. Grooves to dehydrate ya. Check it out.

really. In fact it's probably one of their best ever! "Swallow Everything" is a gem to but it's "Together Tonight" which was first heard on a rare 7" on a Spanish label (live,) which really shreads. So catchy, sunny, fun, very Buzzcocks indeed - pretty much perfect punk-pop. MTX may have lost a member. But this E.P. should restore anyone's faith in them - they still do this shit better than anyone.

SUPERCHARGER "Goes Way Out!" L.P. (Estrus)

This has been highly acclaimed in maximum rock n' roll, but rightly so - it's just such good fun! Very garagey. low-fi sounding with a raw punk-pop (Ramones again) element to it! It's simple, dancey' too and just so easy and pleasant to listen to. Thoroughly recommended and very inspiring! The biz.

FUGAZI "In On The Kill Taker" L.P. (Dischord)

Was it worth the wait? You bet your life! This L.P. contains some of Fugazi's most raging tracks ever. Less of the slower stuff. It always remains so fierce, distinctive, passionate and almost 'spooky' in places. You know what they're like. And this is one of the best things I've heard them do - prepared to experiment sometimes so restrained, but always explosive, so intense, so angry... Buy it or miss one of the essential L.P.'s of 1993. nothing but the best as usual.

NOMEANSNO "Why Do They Call Me Mr Happy?" L.P. (Alternative Tentacles)

Mmm... 6th L.P. already: The C.D. has extra tracks. Most songs are very long, slowish paced with not as much impact as previous recordings. Lyrics about love, hate, death, loneliness, possessiveness - you know the score... Typical Nomeansno. It's all as bitter and angry as usual. Theres that warped sense of humour too, especially on 'Cats Sex and Nazis' - probably a bonus C.D. track? Overall, a bit disappointing and over-long. Still a fine band, mind you.

SEDITION L.P. (Flat Earth/Nabate)

This is their first full length L.P. and what an impressive job it is too. In it's own hessian bag this L.P. is far more intelligent and meaningful than on the split with pink turds in space. Here, sedition present 16 thoroughly raging tunes in that fast anarcho - thrash kind of way. Lyrics cover the environment, attitudes of tribal instinct. 'Homelands,' but this ain't no hippie shit, it's well thought out and passionate. As well as some of the fastest thrash punk music and screaming vocals you're ever likely to hear, there's a really cool 36 page booklet with lyrics, artwork and explanations/view.

£5 ppd from: Flat Earth, Box Flat Earth, 52 Call Lane, Leeds, LS1 6DT. Cheques payable to D. Taylor. Very highly recommended, Scottish punk bands are too often ignored.

JNBUG - SCOOBY DOO 7" (Damaged Goods)

last someone has released this gem.After
yl Solution and Nasty Vinyl never got
nd to releasing it,Damage Goods have
eashed it on the unsuspecting public.
s recording is nearly 2 yrs old but still
nds the test of time and head and shoulders
ve all other popcore competition in the UK.
ssics include the supremely infectious
ooby Doo','Wednesdays','I Wanna Be With U'
'Crazy Mixed Up Kid'.A record not 2 B missed.
ll have you smiling all week!

EREO MC'S - CONNECTED LP (Island)

my opinion the LP of '93.Everysong is a
ner.From the cool 'Step it up' & 'Keep
the pressure' to 'Connected' and the awesom
eation'-a definate future number one,if ever
eard one!The best dance,dub,rap,funk outfit
the UK.Elevate your mind and get it.

PISSED SPITZELS - I'M IN LOVE WITH YR UNDERWEAR 7"

Listen,this is the funniest record i've ever
bought.I've heard it 500 times and still crease
up everytime!German drinking songs meets Ramones
oop punk with a superb trombone player on acid!!
"I'm in love viv your undervear,i'm in love and
you don't care,I don't care iv it's black or
vite,i vanna be your man tonite!"
Totally cool.

SCREECHING WEASEL - WIGGLE LP (lookout!)

A mutha of a record.Steps exactly in the prints
of their last LP.Hi NRG head on power popcore.
Ben's vocals are a little gruffier but the songs
kill like no other.Stand out is the god-like
classic 'Automatic Protector'(i think).This'll
pick you up and throw you across your bedroom.

NOFX + THE OFFSPRING Powerhaus, London 1.7.93

The Offspring from California sound like Bad Religion, NOFX and Green Day rolle
into one - it's a typical California sound with those 'whiney' vocals too. Not
particularly original but full of energy and good fun.

NOFX are more fun! These guys are thoroughly entertaining blending frantic H.C.
with ska breaks and trumpet sounds and even a classic piss-take bluesy version of
"Straight Edge," less of the dodgy lyrics these days too, NOFX put on an excellent
show tonight.

ECONOCHRIST Sir George Robey 5.7.93

Just another California band??? Maybe, but Econochrist are raging punk-hardcore
It's very loud with a really grating guitar sound, good tempo changes and rough
energetic vocals. But it all washes over me because Ben's lyrics can't really be
understood it's all so noisy and they're usually pretty intelligent. So, it all gets a bit
messy and tedious, but these guys still sound awesome on vinyl and their immense
power was certainly apparent tonight.

JOEYFAT "God" E.P. 7"

At Last the guys get something out on vinyl. This is a 3-track 7" which demonstrate
their unique sounding hardcore. The studio seems to suit them, the vocals are varie
and interesting, the music is powerful but sort of restrained in a Shudder to
Think/Fugazi kind of way. Yeah, this is a very competent release and it's available
from BHP H.Q. So why not get off yer arse and order a copy?

NAKED I 'Anus Horribilus'

This is to be released as a 5-track C.D. single on 'Wake' records in late July and it's a
interesting recording because it doesn't lack variety - first song sort of lazy U.S. soundin
vocals but harsh guitars, some stuff manic intense vocals, grating loud guitars, some stu
puts me in mind of Janes Addiction even, or Industrial stuff. Cool words. Always a pun
feel to it all - Yeah, Naked I deserve your attention - it's different, not just plain ol' po
punk for a change. Contact Florence at: Fair Oak, Huntshaw, Torrington, N. Devon
EX38 7HD, for details + info.

RANCID LP (Epitaph)

Ex-operation Ivy here, this LP is not perhaps as immediate as the Lookout! single, but it
raging nevertheless. The OPIV bass lines and Ska-punk roots, are evident but this is nois
and manic in a trad hardcore way. Certainly not as intelligent a OPIV, but definit
excellance in it's own right - powerful, sort of melodic and dead catchy after a fe
listens... Yeah, this band is pretty hot! Bloody loud, by the way.

So Fickle
Here today, gone tomorrow, which beer to drink attitude
Such a shallow mind
I can't be bothered to scratch it I need something deeper
Depth is worthwhile
I wish you were
But you're not.
             DG.

SUPERCHUNK – Hit Self Destruct 10" EP

This is three new and, apparently, exclusive songs on the Australian 'Hippy Knight' label. It's a rather rare import but well worth hunting down. 'Cadmium' is a classic 'Chunk reminiscent of their early EP tracks for Matador and Merge 'C.F.', 'Cool' and 'Garlic'. There's also a brilliant acoustic version of 'Throwing Things', the original version of which appeared on the 'No Pocky For Kitty' LP, and a cover of the Verlaines 'Lying in State' which also rules, although I'm. not familiar with the original.

SEAM - Kernel 12" EP

At last, the first new material from Seam in almost a year. For those of you who don't know, Seam are from North Carolina, feature Sooyung Park of Bitch Magnet on vocals and guitar, and have a sound reminiscent of Sonic Youth and Shudder To Think, and have a LP called 'Headsparks' which was this reviewers favourite album of '92. Back to the EP. 'Kernel' starts quietly then kicks in 'I'm scared, I'm crazy'… for one of the most crazy enjoyable three and a half minutes of your life. 'Sweet Pea' is a much darker tune, similar to 'Sky City' for those of you who have the LP. There's also an almost acoustic version of 'Shame', also from the LP, and it ends with the epic 'Driving the dynamite truck' which is apparently a cover, but I don't know who wrote it.* A band you should definitely check out. (*Ed – Breaking Circus, an 80's post-punk band based in Chicago).

EGO – Form as Function 7" EP

Go! are back, but now they are called Ego. There's been a couple of line-up changes and the sound is slightly different. (There are no two second long songs here!). However, Mike Bullshit is still on vocals and songs like 'But your bible is just a book' and 'Wealth / Self Co Exists' are classic examples of his ranting arguing style. If you liked Go! you'll love this, but if you are not familiar it may take a couple of plays to get into.

SONAR NATION – Surge D.T. 12" EP

The debut EP from this Maidstone five piece is just brilliant. Sonar Nation have a dark, brooding sound that just creeps around then explodes in emotion. 'Some place, not home' is similar to Fugazi's 'Two beats off". 'Master plan' is also very Fugazi. And 'Hate photo', one of the high points of their live set, builds the tension up like Rollins at his best. This is going to be big so pick it up now.

SNAPCASE – Comatose / Crown of Thorns 7"

Not all that new, I know, but I've only just picked it up. In the Victory Records tradition this is very heavy and powerful. If you dig stuff like Integrity, Born Against, Resurrection, etc you'll like this. LP soon.

LIFETIME

This is an interview with the straightedge Emo-core band, LIFETIME. Their records are gr
and what they have to say is worth hearing, so check them out. (Reprinted from U.S. zi
INDECISION)

DAVE: Why don't you start by telling who plays what?

DAN: I'm Dan I play guitar. Scott plays guitar. Dave plays drums. Justin plays bass.
Ari sings and remembers all the lyrics.

Lifetime started playing together in October of 1990. I had flyers up looking for
people to play with because I had just moved back to New jersey from Michigan, where I
went to college. Rob hooked me and Ari up, and our original bass player answered my
ad. We found Scott and out original drummer through mutual friends.

DAVE: Justin didn't play on the 7". What happened to your old bass player?

DAN: Crispy is our original bass player. He's now attending college in Boston. We miss
him, he's the coolest kid. Justin heard "Tradition" from our new demo on some kids
answering machine. When he found out we needed a new bass player he sort of hunted us
down and asked if he could try out.

DAVE: How did you guys settle upon the name Lifetime?

DAN: We felt it was our top priority to put across a positive message to people. Bands in
the New York area tend to try to put up this tough guy front, and we don't want any part
of that. We want to make a clean break with the negative image and attitude that this
part of the country has become associated with. This band is our way of doing that, and
since your bands name is often the source of people's first impressions, Lifetime seemed
perfect to us. It's time to do something constructive, instead of dealing with life's negative
aspects.

DAVE: Do you like the way your 7" turned out?

DAN: Yes, we are psyched with the way the record sounds. No major complaints.

DAVE: How did you get on new age?

DAN: .Mike (New Age) was at a show in New Jersey that we played with Up Front,
Mouthpiece, Edgwise, and about ten other bands. We had just finished recording our
demo and we gave him a copy. He wrote us a few days later and asked us to do a 7". We
were so happy, we freaked out.

DAVE: Isn't there plans for a possible 12"?

DAN: Yes, we will be recording for a full-length LP this winter, and it will be released on
New Age. We hope it will be out by the summer. We're gonna put as much music on it as
we can.

DAVE: How'd you like California?

DAN: Our mini-tour in California was awesome. We got a great response, and we were
treated really well by every one we met. Also, California has the best vegetarian
restaurants.

DAVE: Do plan on coming back out soon?

DAN: As soon as we can afford it.

DAVE: Did you notice any significant difference in the CA scene, whereas in NY are, it
has become accepted as a normal part of hardcore, which is bullshit. The sad thing is that
in NY, it's usually just 5 or 6 idiots with an attitude that mess things up for everyone else.
We're not taking a passive approach to this, however. We are organising people (bands

as well spectators) to try to wipe out the violence, which is a threat to the safety and enjoyment of everyone. Hardcore is for each and everyone of us, not just the hoodlums big enough to control the pit. Maybe we'll start a movement called "SOFTLINE." Our symbol could be an "X" made out of daffodils instead of assault rifles.

DAVE: I know Ari played in Up Front and you played in Resurrection, has there been any other bands you guys have been in?

DAN: Ari was in Enuf, which as far as I know, was the first NJ straight-edge band. Also, he was in Courage, which was this really heavy, metal-influenced band. Scott was in Out of Hand.

DAVE: We've completed six songs so far. We have at least four more that are completely finished, but that the band hasn't had time to work on yet.

DAVE: What do some of them deal with?

DAN: "Pieces" is about pulling yourself together when things may seem to have fallen apart. It's about building something good out of the wreckage when it's tempting to wallow in despair sort of growing stronger as a result of failures and mistakes. "Thanks" is about appreciating your friendships now, before it's too late, and not taking friendship for granted. I think everyone has received a great deal of love and support from special people in their lives, and it's important to appreciate that. "Old Friend Emptiness" is about that one person who's always there to pull the rug out from under you just when things seem to be going perfectly. "Background" deals with many issues relevant to hardcore, as well as to the world in a larger perspective. It's about motivation and lack there of, and it stresses the importance of not blending into the background. It emphasizes the need to break away from apathy and make a positive impact on the world around you, not to just be carried along by inertia without affecting anything or anyone. "Ghost" is about the true spirit of hardcore. People talk about "where it went" and "bring it back," when they don't need to look any further than inside themselves. There are times when it may seem dead, especially to people who have been in the scene for a long time and who have consequently witnessed a lot of change. But I see it thriving every single day inside good people, through selfless acts, kind words, and constructive thoughts.

DAVE: What are some future plans for the band?

DAN: We will tour during the summer of '92, and the album should be out by then. After that, who knows. Until then, we just want to play as often as possible. I especially like playing benefits, because it gives us an oportunity to make a contribution to bettering the world. To me that's a priviledge.

Write to: Dan Lifetime, 216 Twin Oaks Terr. Westfield, NJ 07090, U.S.A.

HEEP ON DRUGS- 15 MINUTES OF FAME CD (island)

uffer little children in your skyscraper hell.
crack cocaine...while popstars drive fast cars
drink champagne...see your name in neon,that's
ur dream.Dream on!"
'ardcore techno.Pvc,bondage,sex,drugs,cars,
ney and everything in between.Sado masochists
th attitude an' i love 'em.

USE OF PAIN — ALBUM CD (XL)

real cool LP by the Irish/American rap combo.
yr face HC rap contrasted with mellow funk
od-alongs.Stand outs are the two singles,
ump Around" and "Shamrocks..." and the forth
ming single "Top of the morning".The singles
omised a cracker of an elpee:the band delivered
oretty good one at that.7/10.

HOWEN KNIFE- GET THE WOW 7" (August)

you wanna forget your hassles and stresses of
eryday living then stick this single on yr deck!
ble gum to the extreme.The Jap girl equivalent
the Ramones.Pop 'till ya drop,catch these on
r-they sound like fun!!

THE Y-FRONTS- CATCH 22 7" (NASTY)

The German answer to Big Drill Car.A fugging
hammering 7" that drags you by the nuts thru
the CRUZ back catalogue.AMAZING is the only
apt word.And you thought german bands were all
sad beer drinking-knees-up HM?Think again!!
£2.50 from;NASTY VINYL,RIEPESTR 17,3000 HANNOVER
81,GERMANY.

ANOTHER FINE MESS — ANOTHER 3 SONGS — DEMO

A cracking demo by a cracking band.The Messies make
music that's a hybrid of the best Ramones and Buzzcocks
with splashes of the Jam.All three songs bristle with
melodies,energy and confidence and the superb production makes this tape an essential purchase if you dig
cool melodic guitar pop."I remember U","Hilary" and
"No way out" for your information.These songs will
soon feature on their self financed mini LP along with
their superb last demo,so get this today from:
The Messies,7 st Dunstan's Cres,Off London Rd,Worcester,
WR 5 7AP.£1.50.

BHP
1 Chandos Road

Tunbridge Wells
Kent TN1 2NY.

COUCH POTATOES

EXCESS ALL AREAS

OUT NOW

ON GOTHAM TAPES
1 CHANDOS ROAD
TUNBRIDGE WELLS
KENT, TN1 2NY

BHP

6

Hello and welcome to BHP #6!

As usual, I'd like to thank you for reading and supporting this 'zine, and helping us to try to support the 'underground / alternative' scene as a whole.

An awful lot has happened since our last issue was printed. Whole new 'scenes' have risen up and then fallen apart, due to petty squabbles. Great new bands are gigging, yet receiving no support, maybe because they're 'too punk', or 'not punk enough'. For some people the hardcore / skate scene has become a trend - it is much more than that, and I'd hate to see it trivialised. (It is not how you look, but how you act that counts. There are many kinds of prejudice. Just try to remember what this is all about.)

On a personal level, I've had people I trusted stab me in the back, and then practical strangers turn out to be great friends. I will never give up hope and I will never stop fighting for what I know is right. Neither should you.

Thanks and take care.

Dave Potato.

Please write to us at : BHP HQ, 1 Chandos Road, Tunbridge Wells, Kent, TN1 2NY, UK.

For their help in creating this issue, I have to give special thanks to : Kelly (all my love), Miles, Martyn, and Steve. I could not have done it without you four heroes. Thanks also to Justin Kyle and Jon Wantling for contributions, and everyone who sent me a letter, bought a 'zine or is active in the hardcore scene. A big thanks and wet kisses goes to Miles, Dan, Daniel, and Paul for being real 'Couch Potatoes'!

"It's like the heaviest weight that you can imagine"
Couch Potatoes

Here is a list of the merchandise being distributed by BHP, available from the address above. Cheques / P.O's payable to D. Gamage. All prices post paid.

BHP   Back issues, 50p each.
#1 featuring Green Day, Hard-Ons, Jailcell Recipes, Factory Farming...
#2 featuring Ramones, Joeyfat, Unpolluted Air, Sleeping...
#3 featuring All, MTX, SNFU, Funbug, Planet Earth...
#4 featuring Sugar, Alloy, Decadence Within, Comics...
#5 featuring Down By Law, Samiam, Green Day, Lifetime...

GOTHAM TAPES - The Alternative Tape Label - £1.50 each.
GOT 001 : TEE-HEE Compilation; 40 mins, 12 bands, 12 trax.
GOT 002 : COUCH POTATOES - LIVE IN TUN/WELLS; 40 mins, 16 trax.
GOT 003 : LIVE AT THE SHELLEY Compilation; 60 mins, 5 bands, 25 trax - featuring
         BBMF's, Strength Alone, Angus Bagpipe, Couch Potatoes...
GOT 004 : 'Hello, Bollox & Welcome' Compilation; 60 mins, 25 bands, 25 trax.
GOT 005 : MORAL CRUX, Tout a fait punk, live radio broadcast; 60 mins, 20 trax.
GOT 006 : ANOTHER Compilation; 40 mins, 13 bands, 13 trax
GOT 007 : Eyes Down For God Compilation; 60 mins, 20 bands, 20 trax.
GOT 008 : JAWBREAKER - LIVE AT GILMAN STREET; 60 mins, 15 trax.
GOT 009 : COUCH POTATOES - EXCESS ALL AREAS; 60 mins, 24 trax - Brilliant Melodic
         Hardcore in a Descendents vein. ✱
GOT 010 : JOEYFAT - SOUP; 60 mins, 15 trax (8 studio & 7 live).
GOT 011 : Low Brow Head Tread Compilation; 60 mins, 20 bands.
GOT 012 : All the Smiley Faces Compilation; 60 mins, 21 trax, 15 bands - superb melodic HC.

VINYL

PANX 11 - 7" EP, £2.00
featuring Couch Potatoes, Blanks 77, Eight Ball, Public Lost, Wounded Knee & Lamento.
NOWHERE STREET - 7" Compilation, £2.00
featuring Vendabait, Couch Potatoes, Cheese Doodles & Pseudo Hippies.
JOEYFAT 7" GOD/WINDSCREEN £2.00
"Band of the month" - Lookout, "Punches lethal in the face" - NME.
COUCH POTATOES - IN BED WITH 7" EP, £2.00
4 Trax of Punk, melodic hardcore from the fat lads.

Do not send to B.I.C. for the vinyl version of this album, as there may well be problems with the label. We are currently looking into it and doing our utmost to deal with the situation. The cassette version contains extra tracks and is great quality. Couch Potatoes have a new 7", the Brad EP out real soon, and two more 7"s of brand new songs to follow.
Couch Potatoes are looking for shows - please contact Dave on (0892) 527959 or write to BHP.
If you want to send anything for a review you can write to the BHP address or Martyn, 34 Kenilworth Road, Edgeware, Middlesex, HA8 8YG. Other worthwhile addresses to contact include: Ian at Weird Records, 61 London Road, Balderton, Newark, Notts, NG24 3AG. Benny at Dragnet, 39 Lugg View, Presteigne, Powys, LD8 2DE. Samutam (distro) 10 Grantham Bank, Barcombe, East Sussex, BN8 5DJ. and Richard at 'Your Mornings' newsletter, 9 Gainsborough Close, Folkestone, Kent, CT19 5NB.

Spread the word, support the underground!

Supersuckers - London Powerhaus - 13/4/94

These guys were somewhat disappointing, I have to confess. They've kind of got, how can I put it, "theatrical" - cowboy hats and starry shirts. A lot of the new stuff, presumably off the newest LP, sounds pretty dull and "countryesque". The older stuff from 'The Smoke Of Hell' saved the day, but overall they sounded kind of 'trashy' and were only saved by a few sparkling moments of brilliance, making my jaw drop and go like... wow. (Namely tunes like 'Coattail Rider' and 'Retarded Bill'). But it seemed that the Supersuckers lacked a certain something.

Bob Tilton - Archway, St. John's Tavern - 21/4/94

People I spoke to, including a band member, said this show was poor and sounded bad compared to previous gigs, especially on home territory (Notts area). I thought 'wow... this is one of the most intense shows I've seen for a while'. The singer is wild and energetic, really heartfelt vocal style, and the band is slick and powerful. Great tempo changes, very explosive songs. Geez, these guys could just about shit on most of the UK bands claiming to be 'hardcore'.

Heartattack fanzine - MRR sized - c25

This is Kent McClards new 'zine - he of Ebullition Records and 'No Answers' (R.I.P.) fanzine. It's got that MRR familiar style, layout and format : interesting letters, columns, an interview with Garden Variety, articles, plenty of reviews of 'zines and non-barcoded records. If the kind of Gravity, Ebullition, Old Glory hardcore is your cup of tea, this will appeal to you, but it's an excellent read for a first issue regardless. It's also cheap, and will improve with time to be a "major force" in the 'zine world, I'm sure. Should be available from Richard at A.W.A. Records, P.O. Box 487, Bradford, BD1 4UZ. but I don't know how much he's flogging it for.

MERCURY'S USE IN DENTISTRY

Most people simply assume that dentists use relatively safe materials and most people generally accept and place their faith in their so-called practitioners of 'dental health', however, there is now ever growing fear and concern about the common-or-garden 'silver' filling (amalgam), which through a peroid of time can have dramatic effects on ill health, causing symptoms of chronic micromercurialism. The general theme being amalgam fillings contain 50% mercury - a toxic heavy metal which has been scientifically proven unstable and which slowly bleeds out mercury into the body, that is the tissues, glands, organs, spinal cord and brain, and which over a period of time can cause a variety of symptoms ranging from metallic taste in the mouth, chronic fatigue, leukaemia, multiple sclerosis, epilepsy, migraine headaches, stress, vision problems, Alzheimer's disease, memory loss, allergies, mood change, psychological and emotional damage etc. The slow accumulation of mercury into the cells of the body causing mercury poisoning.

Dentists use a non-touch technique when handling silver mercury fillings, keeping their scrap metal in tightly sealed containers covered in glycerine immersed under water, in fact handled very carefully as 'toxic waste', yet this very same material is also being placed inside of their patients' mouths at a rate of 150,000,000 fillings a year (UK & USA inclusive). One may wonder why amalgams are still being used - one reason being they are cheap and nasty, another reason being the dental authorities, the British Dental Association and the American Dental Association, and the US Food & Drug Administration's dental division are all allegedly staffed by representatives of the amalgam and dental industry, who obviously have their own private and vested interests in their product - a case of fear, power, corruption and lies perhaps? But unfortunately at the expense, and with little care or concern of placing toxic metals inside of their patients teeth.

It's a fact that female dental assistants have a very high rate of still-births, miscarriages and birth defects, simply through the effects of working in a polluted environment aka mercury poisoning. The suicide rate for dentists is the highest for any profession! Also a mixture of metals, eg, gold crowns alongside amalgams cause mini battery effects (oral galvanism) which cause electrical currents in the oral cavity and brain which severely disturb bodily energetics causing serious health problems. Basically amalgam fillings are very bad news, and I urge anyone concerned about their health who have these fillings in their teeth, to find a mercury-free dentist and to slowly have them replaced with either plastic composite (white) fillings or glass ionomer (white) fillings. A mercury-free dentist will recommend detoxification supplementation, and I also highly recommend homeopathic treatment for this process. But words of warning, it can be very dangerous replacing silver fillings and most dentists have little or no knowledge or interest in this matter. In fact, do not expect any dentists to inform you of the hazards of amalgam, as this is 'forbidden' by the dental authorities, and classed as unethical, and dentists can have their licences revoked for exposing the truth - it's called a witch-hunt, and all you will find is silence, fear and ignorance. Simply replacing silver fillings en-masse can make you very sick, and its essential to have them replaced very slowly over a long period of time. If you are pregnant do not have them replaced as the effect will be a high rise of mercury in the body - a molecular rush, which would probably affect or damage the foetus, and never believe any dentist who smiles at you whilst informing you that they are very caring and sensitive, and that amalgam fillings are harmless and not to worry and place your trust in me, whilst at the same time force-feeding the amalgam industry. The fact is that mercury is a highly toxic heavy metal, there is no safe human threshhold for mercury, it replaces and kills living cells. This is a warning to the world!

BHP Interview with Rancid

It's a hot, sweaty, punk night on the beach at Brighton. The violence is dissipating as Rancid come off stage after a lengthy encore.

We're caught off guard again, no dictaphone and no real questions but Matt says he'll do a brief interview...

BHP : Who is in the band, what do they do and what did they do before?

Rancid : Brett - Drums
Matt - Bass / Vocals
Lint - Guitar / Vocals
Lars - Guitar

Lint and Matt were in OPIV, Lars was in the UK Subs for a while and Brett was in a band called Smog.

BHP : How did the deal with Epitaph come about?

Rancid : We did a 7" on LookOut and wanted to do an album with them, but they didn't want to. Then Mr Brett from Epitaph called and said he loved us. We didn't know at first, but after talking to him we felt he was pretty cool so we agreed. We told LookOut and they said cool so we are all friends.

BHP : What are you trying to put across in your music?

Rancid : We write songs as songs. They're about things that happen to us and things we know about. We throw them out there and people can do what they want with them. We play hard aggressive music because we're pissed off and that's what we want to do.

BHP : Why Rancid and why images of guns?

Rancid : It looks cool and sounds cool.

BHP : Are any of the band into skateboarding?

Rancid : Brett, our drummer, is a pretty good skateboarder.

BHP : How did GreenDay's Billy Joe's song come about?

Rancid : Lint and Billy Joe are friends and wrote some songs together - that's all.
Thank you.
If you want to write us :- P.O. Box 4596,
Berkeley CA.
94704 / USA.

So there you go. Check the album out for yourself, and the new7" Radio, Radio, Radio - they're both classics. I think the spirit of punk is still alive.

The Facts about AIDS.

AIDS (Acquired Immune Deficiency Syndrome) is a disease caused by the Human Immunodeficiency Virus (HIV) which attacks the immune system by destroying the white blood cells that are essential for its normal functioning, thereby weakening the body's defences against opportunisitic infections.

The virus is spread via infected blood products, contaminated needles, and the exchange of body fluids directly through sexual activity. Pregnant women can infect their unborn children. Groups most at risk from AIDS include male homosexuals, bisexuals, intravenous drug abusers who share needles and their sexual partners. Haemophiliacs used to be at risk, but now all blood donors are screened and blood products are heat treated. Very rarely, the disease has been transmitted to dentists, doctors and laboratory technicians through accidental contact with infected blood.

The disease goes through various stages. When the virus first gains access to the body there are no symptoms and HIV tests give negative results, so people do not realise they are potentially infective and could spread the disease. Blood test results usually become positive within three months. Early symptoms, such as swollen lymph glands, unexplained weight loss, night sweats, intermittent fever, diarrhoea, headaches, persistant cough, loss of appetite, fatigue, muscular weakness, and frequent infections soon follow and these have been called AIDS Related Complex (ARC). Ultimately, HIV positive people will develop full-blown AIDS, which is always fatal.

As there is no cure, the only effective drug therapy being purely palliative, medical emphasis is on prevention. Avoid sexual intercourse with anyone who might be infected; use a condom during intercourse unless both of you are certainly monogamous. Avoid contact with infected blood; if you use hypodermic needles, never share a needle or use an unsterilised one and do not share toothbrushes or razors. If your occupation brings you into contact with blood or blood products, be sure to wear protective gloves, a mask and other equipment. Contrary to popular belief, AIDS is not transmitted by casual contact such as touching and cuddling or by donating blood. If a blood test shows a person to be HIV positive, their therapy would involve the treatment of secondary viral, fungal and bacterial infections that may develop as a result of the condition, with the relevant antibiotics. Existing anti-viral agents are uneffective against HIV. Moreover, the discovery that HIV affects the brain, causing brain damage, has complicated matters because most of the known anti-viral drugs do not reach the brain cells and because of the nature of HIV itself.

HIV is what is medically termed a retrovirus. This is because it contains an enzyme called reverse transcriptase, which causes viral DNA to be produced and incorporated into the patient's cells, which then programme the production of more virus. Consequently, HIV is written into the very basis of the patient's life and cannot be eliminated without destroying the cells within which it is contained. In the case of the brain, this would clearly be undesirable even if it were technically possible. Despite these difficulties a vaccine against AIDS is being researched.

People suffering from AIDS or who are HIV positive need to stay as healthy as possible by eating a balanced diet and getting adequate rest. They should also take sufficient precautions against passing on the virus. They should advise any doctor or dentist that treats them. They should not share toothbrushes, razors or anything else that could carry blood, and they should not donate blood, plasma, body organs or sperm. They should not become pregnant. If they cut themselves they should mop up the blood with bleach. Fortunately, the virus cannot survive for long outside the body. One of the most devastating effects of having AIDS or being HIV positive is the loss of contact with, and support from, former friends. The Terence Higgins Trust helps to introduce AIDS sufferers to a relevant support group. The Trust can be contacted at the following address: 52-54 Grays Inn Road, London, WC1. Helpline: 071 242 1010.

Everything that happens to you is your teacher. The secret is to sit at the feet of your own life and be taught by it. Everything that happens is either a blessing which is also a lesson, or a lesson which is also a blessing.

Mahatma Ghandi

We shall have to repent in this generation, not so much for the evil deeds of the wicked people, but for the appalling silence of the good people.

Dr Martin Luther King

DAN CLOWES INTERVIEW

In issue **4** of BHP there was an article about comics. However, seeing as BHP is an 'alternative' / hardcore zine, the article failed to mention any of the 'underground' comic writers such as Daniel Clowes, the creator of 'Eightball'. This is an attempt to redress the balance somewhat... there follows a brief postal interview with Dan Clowes. He apologises for the brevity of his responses, but this is probably due to the crapness of my questions. Nevertheless, I want to say a big thank you to Mr Clowes for responding so quickly to my letter, and if some consider this interview somewhat uninformative, I hope, at least, it will bring the fantastic 'Eightball' and Dan Clowes to the attention of more people here in the UK.

BHP : So, say someone was holding you at gunpoint and forcing you to explain 'Eightball', what would you say?

D. C. : It is an 'underground' comic (meaning content-wise anything goes) written and drawn completely by one person - me (meaning that there is a certain idiosyncratic unity of vision).

BHP : How did it all start? I guess you must have had stuff printed in various zines, but how did you go about getting 'Eightball' published?

D. C. : At age 23, I sent a Lloyd Llewellyn strip to 'Fantagraphics' and they gave me my own comic which ran for 7 issues, and after a brief hiatus, I began 'Eightball', in 1989.

BHP : The story 'Like A Velvet Glove Cast In Iron' is such an amazing yet bizarre tale, what inspired you to write such a weird story? I see it as a kind of future vision - what's it really about?

D. C. : 'Velvet Glove' is an exploration of my own fears and obsessions... it is pieced together from dreams and daydreams and directly relates to my life during the time that it was written.

BHP : It ends in macabre fashion - was it always going to end like this or did it change depending om your mood? I mean, on another day, could it have ended up completely different?

D. C. : The first five or six episodes evolved

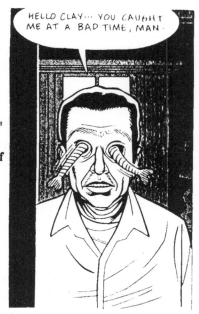

naturally with no thought to what would happen, but around number seven, the various conclusions to the inter-twinning sub-plots began to resolve themselves... By number ten, the ending, as it was drawn, was a foregone conclusion.

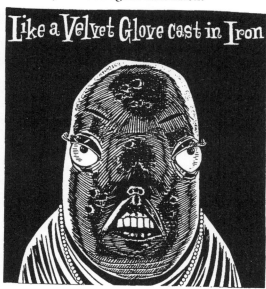

BHP : The 'Young Dan Pussey' strips are hilarious! I presume this is a Young Dan Clowes representation, but isn't there more to it?

D. C. : 'Dan Pussey' is a cautionary tale... He is what I could have become had I taken a different path during adolescence (though I'll admit he is a worse case scenario).

BHP : You're a great critic of art school in the strip 'Art School Confidential', so why did you go to one then? Was it worthwhile or disillusdioning?

D. C. : I went because I got a partial scholarship and it was a great way to meet girls and waste four years... In retrospect, I learned a lot, just nothing about art as they intended to teach it.

BHP : What are you trying to say in 'Eightball'? Say like a musician gets a buzz through playing music, what do you get through writing comics (I guess I'm getting at motives here)?

D. C. : I am definately trying to exorcise personal demons by indulging and exposing them on paper, rather than allowing them to destroy my personal life.

BHP : Along with Peter Bagge (the creator of 'Hate' comic amongst others), you seem to appeal to an underground / punk / alternative (call it what you will) crowd foremost. Why do you think this is? What is 'Eightball's' appeal?

D. C. : Because it's honest and I would hope insightful in regard to the condition of the outsider, the 'loser', the disgruntled, cynical have not... these are the people that seek out non-mainstream culture (which comics are, by definition, in the '90's).

BHP : What do you hope people will get through their reading of 'Eightball'?

D. C. : I'm writing about stuff that has great abstract meaning to me and I'm hoping that my interest and excitement carries over somewhat to the reader.

BHP : Does the stuff you write make you laugh?

D. C. : I would never put a 'gag' in one of my comics unless it made me laugh when I came up with it.

BHP : Many readers may only recognise your work because of the numerous record sleeve designs you have done, eg: Supersuckers, Cheater Slicks, Headcoats, 'Las Vegas Grind' compilation. Seeing as BHP is primarily a hardcore music zine, what stuff do you listen to?

D. C. : I listen to a diverse selection of older stuff, mostly LP's... early country music duets (eg: The Louhin Bros.), '60's pop music (Lee Hazelwood and France Gall are current favourites) and various oddities from the '50's and '60's... anything pre-1970 with a sexual content is a must-have in my book.

BHP : Why the move from Chicago to Berkeley?

D. C. : My girlfriend goes to school here, so I followed her.

BHP : What other comics would you recommend? Do you read graphic novels like 'Watchmen'? What did you think?

D. C. : Just about anything published by 'Fantagraphics' (not 'Eros') and 'Drawn and Quarterly' is highly recommended. I read about half of 'Watchmen' but lost interest... Alan Moore is the best of the mainstream writers, but all that stuff is inherently annoying and stupid... it's for male adolescents under the age of 18... anybody in their 20's (or, god forbid, older) should seriously consider suicide if they are still interested in that crap.

BHP : (BHP style question) What's your favourite food?

D. C. : I don't like to eat.

'Eightball' is published by Fantagraphics Books every four months or so. As I write, it is up to issue 12, possibly higher by the time you're reading this. The comics should be available from most good comic stores.

Dan has had a number of books published too. The entire 'Like A Velvet Glove Cast In Iron' story has been published in book form. 'Lout Rampage' is a collection of strips from the pages of 'Eightball' and others (all Clowes stuff). There is also the 'Lloyd Llewellyn Collection' book of stories, many not available in the comics.

Dan Clowes can be contacted at: 2140 Shattuck #2107, Berkeley, CA 94704, USA.

Fantagraphics: 7563 Lake City Way NE, Seattle, WA 98115, USA.

ALL - The Powerhaus - 31/3/94

Pope (ex-Leatherface) and China Drum were tonight's support acts, but I managed to miss most of them due to the braindead monkies on the door harassing my girlfriend and friends about their age. "No ID, no entrance, ugh!" were the only words they seemed to know. The Powerhaus seemed to have found the missing link and employed it. We were on All's guest list but still had to wait for an hour and a half in the rain and cold before, in the end, Bill Stevenson himself had to 'insist' we were allowed in. At last inside, amongst many friendly faces, we waited for the big event. All's only gig in the UK this year. It was as amazing as can be expected from such a great band. Bursting on with 'Birds' and blasting through classics such as 'Fool', 'Mary', 'Carnage', 'Ex', 'Shreen' and 'Sour Grapes'. Everyone seemed to be enjoying themselves and singing along. After the show, I asked Bill a few questions...

BHP : So how's the tour going, this is the only date I've heard of?

B.S. : Yeah, tonight's the first show of the tour. It was a pretty good one. We're on to Europe tomorrow and not home until June.

BHP : How's Chad (Chad Price the new singer) shaping up?

B. S. : Things are going great, we're all real pleased.

BHP : You seemed to play a lot of new stuff tonight, is there already a new album on the way?

B. S. : We played six totally new songs tonight to try then out, but there won't be a new LP until February.

BHP : You played a lot of the real good old songs tonight, like 'Mary' and 'Carnage', I was really surprised.

B. S. : Why! We've got lots to choose from and always play some old faves, just ask, we'll play what you like...

You can write to All, for a free merchandise catalogue and the latest information, at : P.O. Box 441, Brookfield, MO 64628, USA.

BUY INDEPENDENT - SUPPORT THE UNDERGROUND!

MR T EXPERIENCE INTERVIEW

Here's a short postal interview with Dr Frank of Mr T Experience. It's littered with trivia but fills this space rather nicely...

BHP : Have you a new album coming out soon?

Dr F : The new LP is now finished and is called 'Our Bodies Ourselves' and should be out on LookOut! in January.

BHP : Where did the name MTX come from?

Dr F : The name was conceived in a drunken stupor many years ago when we were callow youths. Like many of life's great mysteries it has no explanation, only thorns.

BHP : What are your full names?

Dr F : Being dedicated paranoids, I'm afraid we can't divulge this information.

BHP : Is Frank really Morrissey's brother?

Dr F : Obviously.

BHP : Which is your favourite MTX song?

Dr F : Gee, all the songs are identical, it's so hard to choose.

BHP : Will you be touring Britain / Ireland soon?

Dr F : Not to be coy, but maybe, maybe not. We're only just barely recovered from the last one.

BHP : Why is the bass player called Aaron on one record and Byron on another?

Dr F : The bass player had to change his name as part of a complex plea bargain in a sexual misconduct case. I'd better not say more.

BHP : Why did you appear on GreenDay's thank you list?

Dr F : That must have been a different Mr T Experience.

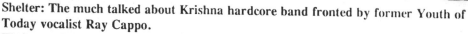

Shelter: The much talked about Krishna hardcore band fronted by former Youth of Today vocalist Ray Cappo.

Their new LP, 'Attaining the Supreme', has less of the crashing power chords that dominated the first records and more chiming Samiam style guitar riffs.

Lyrically, it's still based around Krishna ideals but it has to be said that most of the songs have worthy messages and are relevant whether you are a devotee or not. Also the lyrics on the new LP seem a little more personal as opposed to the world wide scale of the first LP.

They've had many line up changes, current lead guitarist Porcell was originally in Youth of Today and more recently in Judge. He is now a devotee and he answered these questions before a show at the Flohtzircus in Hannover on 29/9/93.

This interview was unplanned and written in a hurry, hence the questions could have been better. Whether you agree with the ideology behind the answers or not, check Shelter out, because musically they rule.

BHP: How is the tour going?

Porcell: So far, great! Now that our new record is out the shows have been a little bigger than last year, plus we have a whole new line up practically, so as a band we're sounding better than ever.

BHP: You've toured Europe a couple of times but never played in the UK. Why?

Porcell: Lack of time, basically. But we might play there at the end of this tour.

BHP: Are there any British bands that you rate?

Porcell: We all live in the temple so I'm pretty removed from the current music scene. Plus we're so busy with the band that we don't have much time to listen to that much music and when we do it's usually bhajans (devotional songs).

BHP: What do you think about the various Shelter bootlegs currently available?

Porcell: There are four defects of the conditioned soul: he has a tendency to make mistakes, become illusioned, he has imperfect senses and he has the propensity to cheat, therefore it doesn't surprise me that people are trying to cheat bands by making bootlegs.

BHP: Why cover Black Sabbath?

Porcell: Because the lyrics to that song were cool!

BHP: Big question - Are you attempting to convert people to Hare Krishna through your music?

Porcell: No, not at all. We are just trying to spread some truth that we have learned. Krishna consciousness is not a sectarian religion that you can convert in and out of. Whether you are Christian, Muslim, Agnostic, black, white, male, female - underneath all these designations you are a spirit soul, or the energy that animates this body, which is nothing but dead matter. And according to laws of physics, energy cannot be created or destroyed, only transferred. So when this body dies, where does the energy go? And what determines that destination? This brings up the points of reincarnation and karma, which literature like the Bhagavad-Gita gives us much information about. So Krishna Consciousness is the science of the spirit soul, of which every living being is, so it's a universal concept and relative to everyone. So our goal is not to shave peoples heads and dress them in robes, it's to give them some truth, some knowledge of who they really are and how to live life appropriately.

BHP: Porcell: are you still in Judge?

Porcell: No!

BHP: Dumb question - First record bought?

First punk record - "Never Mind The Bollocks"
First HC record - Black Flag "Damaged"

BHP: What do you do when you're not playing with Shelter, touring etc?

Porcell: When we're back at the temple we wake up really early, worship the deity, chant, and go through a whole morning program of studying, singing and having more fun than most people do at five in the morning. Then basically we spend the rest of the day trying to apply what we've learnt to our life in a practical way. We also spend three months out of the year on pilgrimage in India.

BHP: Anything else?

Porcell: Sound vibration is powerful. Just the sound of a distorted electric guitar can make hundreds of people jump up and down like maniacs! Similarly, mantras, or spiritual sound, can have a clearing effect on the consciousness. According to ancient India's books of wisdom, the most powerful mantra for self realisation is :

> Hare Krishna Hare Krishna
> Krishna Krishna Hare Hare
> Hare Rama Hare Rama
> Rama Rama Hare Hare

Chant this mantra and feel the liberating effect!

Porcell,
41 W. Allens Ln,
Phila. PA. 19119
USA.

Current Shelter line up:
Ray Cappo (AKA Raghurrath das) : Vocals
Porcell : Guitar
Chris Interrante : Bass, Backing vocals, Percussion
Ekendra das : Drums

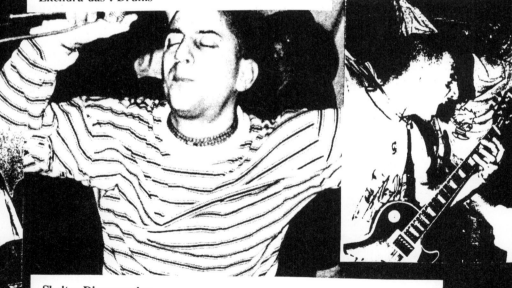

Shelter Discography:
  7" EP's:-   Freewill / Saranagati (Equal Vision #1)
               In Defence of Reality (Equal Vision #4)

  LP's:-   The Perfection of Desire (Revelation #16)
               Quest for Certainty (Equal Vision / De Milo #7)*
               Attaining the Supreme (Equal Vision #7)

               *Compilation of first two 7" EP's plus new songs plus live songs.

WHY THE BATTERY CAGE MUST GO

The battery cage system is one of the cruellest forms of farming. Over 90% of laying birds in the EC are condemned to live out their year-long productive lives in an environment which stifles their natural instincts. It is not unusual to find tens of thousands of birds stacked in cages six tiers high in one building. Under current EC law, up to 5 birds, each with an average wingspan of 80cm, may be crammed into a cage just 50cm by 50cm. This gives each bird a living space smaller in size than the cover of a telephone directory. It is rather like condemning 3 people to spend the rest of their lives together crowded into a telephone box. Battery hens are never able to flap their wings, stretch or preen their feathers. They spend their lives standing on a sloping wire floor. Their feet may become damaged and their claws broken. There are no quiet places for them to lay their eggs. There are no perches where they can roost at night. There is no litter on the floor for pecking in, scratching or dust bathing, which causes hens distress. Lack of movement and exercise will result in weak and brittle bones.

The battery cage is so common because production costs are 10 - 50% lower than the alternatives and egg collection and feeding are fully automated.
The alternative systems for egg production are kinder to hens and can replace battery cages.
Perchery: Some eggs are labelled 'barn' or 'perchery' eggs. These come from hens living in flocks inside large buildings. The hens lay their eggs in nest boxes sited around the building. They have enough freedom of movement to stretch and flap their wings and may be provided with floor litter for dust bathing. There are perches for the hens to roost on at night.
Free Range: The traditional image of free range hens living in small hen houses in open fields is in reality confined to only a few free range systems. Modern large scale production has resulted in most free range hens living in buildings similar to the percheries but having the added luxury of access to the outside world through pop holes. A free range hen has access to about 200 times more space than a battery hen. The birds must be allowed continuous daytime access to open air runs and adequate outside vegetation.

 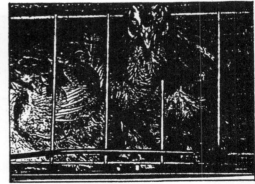

The chance for change is in your hands - Boycott battery eggs!

The RSPCA are campaigning for :
a). An immediate ban on the installation of new battery cages.
b). Clear labelling of eggs produced from battery cages.
c). Phasing out all existing battery cages in the EC within five years and developing a programme to introduce properly designed alternative systems.

Help us to campaign against the battery cage until it is abolished forever. Tell your MP that you support the RSPCA's campaign to phase out the battery cage. Never buy battery eggs. Tell your friends to buy eggs which are clearly labelled 'Free Range' or 'Barn' eggs. Other descriptions like 'Farm Fresh' and 'Country Fresh' are disguising the fact that the eggs are battery cage produced.

Of the 30 million hens kept for egg laying in the UK, over 85% are kept in battery cages. Free range or perchery eggs may cost more, but as these production systems become more widespread in response to public demand, the eggs will become cheaper.

Recognise the packaging?
Of course you don't.

In the egg business, honesty isn't always the best policy. They know the British public is extremely sensitive to phrases like 'Battery Farmed'. So instead, they label their boxes 'Farm Fresh', 'Country Fresh' or even 'Dairy Fresh'. Such words are carefully chosen to add rustic charm to a process that is neither rustic nor charming. The eggs have been laid by hens who suffer serious mental stress and physical harm. Do not buy them. Look for eggs that are clearly labelled either 'Barn', 'Perchery' or 'Free Range'. Beware of all others. They are little more than battery eggs in disguise.

The RSPCA has an information leaflet on battery farming. To obtain a copy or support their campaign, please write to:

The Causeway, Horsham, West Sussex, RH12 1HG.

"IT'S TIME THAT THE CHICKEN CAME BEFORE THE EGG!"

THE 'CRAZY ACE' REVIEWS FOR BHP #6

<u>Pandora's Lunchbox - Demo Tape</u> - P.O. Box 2071, Wilmington, NC, 28402-2071, USA.
This is very good, varied and original. Not really like anything, so worth checking out. Maybe
echoes of Alice Donut meets U2! Strange. 16 tracks for a nice letter.

<u>Xerox Girls - 2 Song Demo</u>
Sounds like hoovers recorded in someones frontroom on a cheap walkman, but the vocals are
very angry and it's all very energetic. One for the DIY riot grrrl.
Xerox Girls, 372 Bedfont Lane, Feltham, Middlesex, TW14 9SA.

<u>Stewed - 5 Song Demo</u>
Total early Mudhoney style songs which rock along and occasionally 'metal out'. I believe the
popular term for this is grunge. Stewed, however, are a little better than some I could mention..
Stewed, 5 Spring Terrace, Folkestone, Kent, CT20 1JH.

<u>Regurgitated - 13(!) Song Demo</u>
Raging early style hardcore by this young German band. Cool P/C lyrics in English, lots of
anger and energy and cool mosh parts a la Sick of it all. This stuff is pretty big in Germany so
check 'em out. (You can write to Germany for just 24p!)
Regurgitated, c/o Andre Rosch, Beim Gronacker 65, 8500 Nurnburg 30, Germany.

<u>The Ceramic Hobbs / Howl in the Typewriter - Split Flexi 7"</u>
This must be a joke! The Ceramic Hobbs (!?*@!?) 'play' an instrumental called 'The stoat rides
out' which says it all really. Howl in the typewriter (yes, that's right, howl in the typewriter!)
are slightly better because their song is only called 'Close' and it has some bizarre lyrics.
Musically the whole thing is like a BBC Radiophonic Workshop Sampler and is worth buying
for a bloody good laugh because it's only 47p in the post! Possibly the strangest record ever!! It
comes with a free piece of cardboard!!!
PUMF Records, c/o Stanzine Promotions, 130 Common Edge Road, Blackpool, FY4 5AZ.

<u>Chicken Bone Choked - 4 Song Demo</u>
Kinda Dischord, kinda Bad Religion, kinda heavy, this is verging on being really good but
perhaps is just the production. The band just don't sound at all enthusiastic or excited about it.
Sorry... Simon, 23 The Embankment, Bedford, MK40 3PD.

<u>The Shreds - 6 Song Demo</u>
A splendid effort from this fine young trio. Snuff, Senseless Things, Hard-Ons, the Who, the
Jam, it's all there. Give these guys a couple of years to develop more and they could come out
with a classic pop-punk record that you'll all be talking about.
Austin, 83 Edmunds Road, Cranwell Village, Sleaford, Lincs, NG34 8EP.

<u>Devil Dogs - Saturday Night Fever LP (Crypt)</u>
14 tracks of raw, crunching, simple garage punk. It's all live, amazingly produced considering
and loud as hell! Here's a band with a string of LP's and 7"s behind them, yet never have had
the attention they deserve. Totally awesome sound demanding your immediate attention.

<u>Fumes - Knockin' Out The Axis LP (eMpTy)</u>
Ooh, another excellent release from Empty out of Seattle. Okay, so it's damn close in sound to
the New Bomb Turks and may lack those guys appeal, but it's raw, brash, fast 'drunk-punk'
and pretty intense. Things calm down a bit and maybe pall on side 2, but it's still cool. Tracks
their stuff from '91 - '93.

<u>Didjits - Que Sirahn Sirahn LP (Touch 'N' Go)</u>
Best yet? Red vinyl, typical style rockin' from these guys - straight ahead, no frills (like Kwik
Save) fast yet catchy with a big sound and unrelenting energy. A few weak tracks tarnish a
pretty consistent effort though.

<u>Pegboy - Fore 12" EP (Quarterstick)</u>
Ha! It was funny to see one of the national music rags reviewing this basically 'cos it's got Steve
Albini on bass and the shop I bought it from had a 'Steve Albini on bass' sticker too. Forget the
harsher but distinctive sounding Pegboy EP, the tunes, the style, the potential for a corking new
LP - this has got Steve Albini on bass. Oh, forgot to mention, Steve Albini plays bass on this.

<u>Girls Against Boys - Venus Luxure No 1 Baby LP</u>
Far harsher musically than their earlier LP's/EP's, Girls against Boys are Soulside with a
different singer. They're far more complex, darker and experimental than Soulside and thus far
more interesting. Although a fine LP, this lacks the more novel sound of 'Tropic of Scorpio' the
1992 LP on Adult Swim records.

Tar - The Garage, London - 3/11/93

So slick, amazingly precise and intricate, Tar have an individual sound, not exactly punked-up fast style, nor slow dirge-like and dull. Kind of in between. Classy chrome guitars, thundering sound, very noisy and powerful.

Screeching Waeasel - Anthem for a New Tomorrow LP (LookOut)

Another cracking LP from these guys. Although not as immediate as say 'My Brain Hurts' this LP is a real grower. Slightly more intelligent, darker even in places, but with fun, poppy tunes too (of course) on some songs. Brilliantly structured music, not just Ramones rip-offs, but a real individual sound coming through - it's as if these guys have 'come of age' with this release. A worthy band in their own right. 'A New Tomorrow' sees a brand new style and guest vocals, 'I Robot' sees treated vocals used, there's effective use of sampling and a fair share of typical Screeching Weasel fun songs. A truly great LP.

Girls Against Boys - The Garage, London - 2/12/93

After two atrocious support bands, Girls Against Boys could've come on stage and played nought and crosses for an hour and it still would've been better! Tonight they play an excellent set, one of the finest live performances I've seen. They are ex-Soulside, and make effective use of samplers with an atmospheric powerful sound, not quick and thrashy, kind of brooding, restrained with energetic moments too. Imagine a better, more experimental Soulside with rougher vocals. Distinctly unique and somehow exciting, Girls Against Boys really are special.

Turner Raus - Animal Peace Benefit 7"
(Abolition / Embittered / Truth Against Tradition / Venus Fly Trap)

Abolition turn out a rather fine number called 'State of Perfection' that reminds me of Rorschach and Nausea. I want to hear more of them. Embittered are that kind of scary, noisy, very fast stuff that John Peel likes so much. Remember Culture Shock? Truth Against Tradition are in a similar vein, kinda dub reggae with hardcore breaks and concerned lyrics. Venus Fly Trap sound like a funky Yuppicide! I'm also reminded of one of those agit-pop bands like Papa-brittle. This compilation has four very different bands and is in aid of a good cause. Buy it. A-Wat Records, c/o Andreas Focker, Hans Kruse Str.21, D-W 5900 Siegen, Germany.

Stand Off - 'Worthless is the unity bought at the expense of truth' 4 song 7"

Four powerful and pounding tunes that tear along at breakneck speed from Southends answer to Project-X. There's a bit in 'Switch' where about five people are going 'aaarrgghh!' that blows me away, and if 'Confusion' doesn't get you out of bed nothing will. Buy or die! Standoff, c/o Tone, 14 Harrow Gardens, Hawkwell, Hockley, Essex, SS5 4HG. - Although it's on Germany's Crucial Response Records.

Drongos for Europe - 2 song 7" (Limited Edition of 250)

This really grew on me. It has a very British sound but it rocks and some of the guitar reminds me of early U2. 'This Town' is about being trapped in a nowheresville and could be on the soundtrack of a John Hughes film. 'Cool Baby' has more power but the lyrics are a bit cheesy, ie, 'cool baby, she's got me on my knees' although they're refering to American fashion trends being bombarded on us. Well worth checking out.
Drongos for Europe, c/o Dragnet Records, 39 Lugg View, Presteigne, Powys, Wales, LD8 2DE.

Bugg - 2 Song 12"

Not strictly speaking a punk or hardcore record, this is a mid-paced Indie with scratchy ska guitar and bouncy beats - no grunge in sight. Very singalongable too. The insert has a cool flow chart type thing that shows how and why new bands often fail. These guys certainly know where they're going. Bugg, c/o 13A British Row, Trowbridge, Wiltshire, BA14 8PB.

Noisegate -Rolemodel demo cassette

A 3-piece from the Worcester area, this is a slickly presented 5 song cassette. I didn't find this particularly inspiring - slowish paced metal sounding with hardcore elements. It's pretty solid though and well played, just lacking any balls and not saying anything new. Promised far more than it delivered and £3 is extortionate for a demo tape. Contact Noisegate c/o Richard Freeman, 35 Woodlands, Evesham, Worcestershire, WR11 6XH.

MDM - Take what you can 7" EP - Weird Records.

Aaagh! This could've sounded so much better! It needs the guitars turning up or harsher sounding ones, because it just lacks the impact it should have. This is an '80's sounding punk EP with good girl vocals and tunes. Pretty cool overall but just lacking that bite it needs. Probably a good live band. £1.80 or £2.00 with 'Goddamn Weirdos' #7 from Ian at Weird Records, 61 London Road, Balderton, Newark, Nottinghamshire, NG24 3AG.

Hey Hey! Compilation Tapes #1 (Jolt)

A 23 track, 13 band compilation with some really fine punk pop melodic stuff from young bands. Includes the excellent Kids and Flags, Couch Potatoes, Shreds, Pseudo Hippies, CDS and plenty more. Best of the lot could well be Chicken Bone Choked and Another Fine Mess, but I'm rather partial to the Specky and the Poo Shakers track myself. A very good tape indeed to check out the UK's new talent and dirt cheap at £1.50 ppd from Sean, 21 Chapel Street, Ryhill, Wakefield, West Yorkshire, WF4 2AD. (Cheques to S. L. Hunter).

Rancid - Dome, Tufnell Park on 14/12/93 & Fishermans, Brighton on 15/12/93

Tuesday night: "No, I've never heard them, but they're Ex-Operation Ivy and on Epitaph so I hope they'll be good. Is this MDC? What! It's Rancid! It can't be. Operation Ivy were tuneful, catchy, bouncy. This is punk rock played by guys with Mohawks, studded belts and bum flaps! I don't know what that was all about, but I'll go see them tomorrow." Wednesday night: After 5 terrible support bands and loads of violent eruptions, we finally hear "Climb in, climb in, climb inside me - paaaain!" from their opener 'The Bottle'. Then it's straight into the brilliant 'Rejected' with it's sing-a-long "Ree-hee-hee-heejected" chorus. Yes, I was converted. I managed to sell more than enough copies of this publication to buy their LP, which is great and now I am a devoted Rancid fan. I think bad sound in London affected my judgement but in Brighton it was a lot clearer and the set was a little shorter making it more of a blast and less of an endurance. They tear through all your faves - 'Animosity','Whirlwind', 'Detroit'. In fact, probably all of the LP. A pleasant surprise.

Spirit of Youth / Ironside / Blindfold - Bradford 1 in 2 Club - 6/11/93

The best thing about the legendary 1 in 2 club is the cheap vegan cafe. There's a crazy foreign guy wearing a kilt behind the counter. Don't worry if some of his (green) hair falls into your tea; he'll fish it out for you with his fingers - what helpful staff! Blindfold are from Belgium. They are a heavy, tuneful sort of Supertouch with different vocals and hinting at Quicksand. I'd heard that this was the last Ironside gig with Richard on vocals. If it was, he certainly went out on a high. (No pun intended). Tonight they turn everything way up with Richards scary vocals cutting through the thunderously loud sound. Their anti-smoking song (not yet released) hits hard! Remember Project X, Gorilla Biscuits? Remember youthful enthusiasm, frustration and anger that made you bounce off the walls? Spirit of Youth do! This Belgian band jump around more than the audience and the singer, who spends most of his time on his knees, 'exorcises his personal demons' in front of us. The emotion seems very genuine, almost as if it's the only time they'll ever play the songs. The sound has it's roots in the '88 NY sound but it's more tuneful and fresher. They were amazing - see them!

Credit to the Nation / Compulsion - New Cross Venue - 2/12/93

I can't think of two more unlikely bands playing together like this. Compulsion are at times highly reminiscent of early DC bands, particularly Ignition due mainly to vocalist JosephMary's voice sounding very similar to Alec McKayes. They have some fine songs but unfortunately they often wander into Pistols / Clash territory and the leather trousers and rock postures spoil what could be a very good band. Credit to the Nation rule! Live rap acts often suffer from poor sound, but tonight its crystal clear allowing us to hear their thoughful, aware lyrics and worthy messeages, delivred over their killer backing tracks and samples. Those of you who only know the hit single 'Call it what you want' with it's TeenSpirit sample should check out other releases because they can do so much more. The cool dancers on stage with rapper MC Fusion made things even livelier. Great show!

Understand / Bob Tilton - Camden Falcon - 4/12/93

I was blown away! Bob Tilton are one of the most gripping live bands I've ever seen, they have so much energy and anger. They were formerly Downfall who were 'the British Born Against' but now they've gone to even more extreme extremes! Imagine all the power and rage of 108 mixed with the madness of Merel or Born Against. Picture the vocalist jumping around, falling over, rolling about screaming his head off, sometimes without a microphone. See them live now! Understand are probably my favourite band at the moment. They just keep getting better. Many people compare them to Quicksand and although it's true that there are strong similarities, there's so much more to them. There's something that's not as harsh, but more elevating about their sound, like Samiam. I'm hoping for a new release soon because the 7" sounds a little dated now. Expect great things.

Arnie #5, A4, 40p

Cool 'zine! As well as incisive interviews with Chumbawumba and Schwartzeneggar, there's plenty of funny comics and good humour throughout. Excellent reviews, layout and interesting articles and opinions. 16 Palairet Close, Bradford on Avon, Wiltshire, BA15 1US. (large sae)

Noise Fest #4, A5, 40p

So it's gone up 10p from last time but this is still essential if you're into the noisier side of things, and it's still worth checking out if you only listen to pop - got to keep an open mind. Interviews with Drop Dead, Sarcasm, Misery, 121 Bookshop, poetry, reports, reviews. Well presented and totally punk. Chris, 15 Ashbourne Gardens, Bradford, BD2 4AE.

No Idea #10, A4, $3 ($5 UK)

Interviews with 23 More Minutes, Jawbreaker, Samiam and more. Double 7" with Samiam, Jawbreaker, Spoke, Radon, Gruel and Bombshell. Good articles and columns, colour too, thousands of reviews. Excellent, if a little pricey for us Brits! PO Box 14636, Gainseville, FL.32604-4636, USA.

Riot #6, A4, 50p

This is just so admirable because of the sheer amount of work involved - it's beautifully hand-written and excellent to look at. The interviews are inspiring and intelligent with Neurosis, Doom, Anti-Climax, CFDL, Rupture and more. Reviews are informative. It works so well, one of the best. Joe, 21 Ebnal Road, Shrewsbury, Shropshire, SY2 6PW.

Take a Day #1, A5, $1

This is Paul Curran's (of Crimpshine & Monsula fame and MRR staffer) new 'zine and it's great. Not choc-full of interviews and reviews, but more a thoughts and feelings kind of thing. Interesting stuff on Benicia, CA, some comics and collage. Lots of views and a certain 'pop fluffiness' about it all. Check it out. PO Box 190054, San Francisco, CA 94119, USA.

Read It! #7, A5, 30p

Also known as 'Eat Shit!' this has Blaggers, (SH)ITA, Nomeansno, and Corpus Vile interviews. Reviews and an Anarchist stint that'd probably piss mummy and daddy off. Short, worthwhile, previous issues have been better. This is a final effort. Box 8, 82 Colston Street, Bristol.

Step out of line #1, A4, 30p

Got a feeling this may have sold out, and it's no surprise because for a first issue it's damn fine. All proceeds go to Greenpeace in their quest to get McMurderers off their back in the libel case. Interviews with Naked Aggression, Leatherface, Sugar, Citizen Fish and others, live and vinyl reviews, a good attitude but not enough articles, unfortunately. Promising though. Scruff, 33 Middleton Road, Hayes, Middlesex, UB3 2RD.

Kids & Flags 'Trying to Blast Reality' 5 track demo cassette

This has been put together by ex-Submission bassist Jamie, who not only sings, but plays guitar and bass in a last attempt to get something recorded by the now defunct Kids. This is a mighty fine effort, 5 pop-punk numbers of varying spedd in a Descendents / Cringer / Monsula kind of vein. The lyrics are heartfelt, it all sounds pretty American and has a certain rawness to add to the appeal. The tape is well presented with lyrics and pictures and it's a mere 50p ppd ($1 ppd elsewhere) from: Jamie, 7 Leesfield Drive, Meadowfield, Durham, DH7 8NG.

Nowhere Street 7" Compilation

A 4 band compo out of California. Vendabait play fast snotty punk with a vocalist who sounds like he's at the wrong speed. Not bad though. Couch Potatoes track is excellent, quality pop-punk like Bog Drill Car, and a cool guitar sound. The (Cheese?) Doodles play a good punky tuneful number, and the Pseudo Hippies 'Bubblegum' title perfectly sums up their poppy Ramones style punk, though they sound rawer live. This is a good little EP, and though sound quality isn't perfect, the whole DIY feel and overall band quality is inspiring. This is available from BHP HQ, so send us your cash swiftish!

China Drum & Pseudo Hippies - Bull & Gate - 15/8/93

Pseudo Hippies are definately improving! Okay, so maybe their music isn't alarmingly original, but they play well and are having fun, even though it's pretty empty here. Ramones meets Screeching Weasel with a bit of Mr T Experience thrown in. Keep going lads! China Drum really impressed supporting J Church a while back and tonight they're just as corking. Fast, loud punk-pop, kinda like Porcelain Boys, quickest drumming seen for their style of music, cool vocal harmonies, good changes of pace and enough variety to keep you interested (transfixed in this case). Watch out for these guys... the Northumberland explosion.

Holy Rollers / Joyce McKinnie Experience / Dogbowl - The Garage, London - 2/9/93

Dogbowl is not a band but a solo American guy and his electric guitar played ukelele fashion. He sung a number of songs, sort of Lou Barlow (Sebadoh) style, but these were warped bizarre tales of discovering a mermaid in his coffee and people with pelican hair. Crazy. JME are back together after what seems a very long abscence. Remember them? Cool pop-punk in the Snuff vein, but highlighted by two harmonious girl singers... almost like Lush punked up. Tonight's set seemed to comprise of totally new material, I only recognised one oldie, and it's a tad slower, poppier and cleaner but still sometimes high on the energy scale. Holy Rollers are a Dischord label band, and recently have had a major line up change. It's difficult to categorise them as sounding a certain way, but it seems to be more 'rock' based these days. They really astound tonight due to their sheer loudness and energy, always changing tempo and then building up to a massive crescendo. The drumming was intense and the whole band commited to create a surprisingly monster sound, something I didn't expect from the evidence of the old 'Fabuley' LP. Obviously a totally fresh start and it seems to have worked well live at least, full of the kind of atmosphere it's often tricky to project on vinyl.

GreenDay - 'Dookie' LP - Reprise Records, a Time Warner Company

Yep, it's on a major label! Still, you get 14 tracks here, the production is pretty clean, but if anything the sound is heavier guitar-wise, especially on side 2. This is one LP of sheer slick pop-punk, the way GreenDay do so well. There are some classy tracks here, some excellent lyrics too.'PullingTeeth' just has to be the first single, pure pop... I can see it on the ITV Chart Show now! Presentation doesn't make it look too corporate and there's a mysterious extra acoustic track at the end - sounds like Sesame Street! Trouble is, next time they play here they'll probably be supporting a big name at a big venue... it's just the lack of control I object to concerning these major labels: high ticket prices, no more intimate club gigs. Vinyl is limited.

Scalplock / Older Than Dirt / The Mighty Mr Men - Camden Monarch - 13/2/94

I think this is The Mighty Mr Men's first gig. They look like old time punksters - 2 skinheads with braces an' all and mohawks too! Trouble is, their sound is weak, it's tame Brit punk with hints of Oi! But it all sounds really samey and has no balls at all. The drumming is positively mellow, the vocals are tuneless, the bass and guitar have no rawness whatsoever. Pretty poor, but kind of endearing because of it. Will play a lot with Working With Tomatoes. The kind of punk your grandma could listen to. Funny. Older Than Dirt aren't at all bad. Half the stuff they play is excellent sort of straight edge moshy stuff but with funkier basslines. However, they kind of wash over me after a while. Definately worth checking out again though. Scalplock are fantastic tonight. A couple of songs in and the skinheads are going wild at the front, and singer Spencer is in the crowd jumping around and singing heartfelt stuff... reminded me of those 80's sXe band photos you see! Sometimes Scalplock are amazingly fast like Drop Dead even. Sometimes it's almost hardcore style like SFA or Pittbull. A bloody excellent new band and they can only get better.

Chicken Bone Choked 7" - Whole Car Records

Whole Car is a Wiiija off shoot. Mr Gary Wiiija apparently wanted a harsh punked up raw thing, and it's good to see CBC slowing it right down, but still maintaining a good style. Why should their sound be pigeon-holed or dictated? Good on you lads! 'Fool' is slowish hardcore with good vocals and competent musicianship. 'Leave Me Nowhere' is slightly more up-tempo with a kind of Fugazi twang and a good pop-punk break. Interesting lil' 7", a definite style change, but I can forgive them because they do it very well.

Rancid - 'Radio Radio Radio' 7" EP - Fat Wreck Chords

A new four track 7" from Rancid, and it's absolutely blinding. 'Radio' was written with Billie Joe, 'Someone's Gonna Die' is an old Blitz number, and there's two cracking originals. Fast, loud real punk stuff here with hints of ska but perhaps more of an Oi! feeling to it all, if anything. Damn near anthemic in fact... after an amzing first 7" & LP, Rancid continue to produce the goods. Miss them at your peril. The band of the '90's and beyond!

Onefold 5 track demo cassette

Five tracks of metally, moshy hardcore that merges all your favourite straight edge bands with Helmet. Good, gruff Judge style vocals and musical quality often lacking in UK bands these days. Impressive, if not totally original : 126 Pembroke Road, Muswell Hill, London, N10.

Lag Wagon - Camden Dublin Castle - 16/2/94

Lag Wagon play a long set tonight. They're on Fat Wreck Chords and their style is very NOFX / No Use For A Name, but with a few extra twists and turns to make it stand out a bit. They really put in the effort tonight, they're sort of funny on stage and pretty goofy sometimes! The songs are usually fastish NOFX style hc but there's all these stops and starts and rhythm changes - it's pretty complex in places. Entertaining, but not groundbreaking. I would've preferred if Face To Face would've made the effort to come over, rumour has it they are destined for bigger things...

Conflict, Schwartzeneggar, Homage Freaks, Fear of Fear - Venue, London - 30/1/94

Fear of Fear may have ex-Conflict members, but I'm not sure. Female vocals, real loud music, a pretty good anarcho-crusty punk sound, but it's not particularly inspiring. Homage Freaks are kind of funky in places, but pretty mediocre overall. Their sound is quite distinctive, but it went right over me. Schwartzeneggar have improved greatly since I last saw them. Steve Ignorant & Co now have a harsher, fuller, more energetic sound. More punk! Steve takes his top off though... Conflict take ages to come on, and once on perhaps play a little too long. I think only singer Colin and drummer Paco are from the original line-up. No more mohawks, and the two 'metal' guitarists look like session players! The impact is still there though - it's harsh but melodic, fast and intense, old and new stuff alike. The impact wanes because they play too long, and it gets dull, eventually. "A.L.F." cries the singer, "Yeah!" respond hundreds of punksters... wearing leather jackets! An entertaining evening of old school punk rock escapism.

I'm Being Good - Hate Sturdy Buildings 7" EP

This is one of the most bizarre records I've ever heard, a band who truly defy categorisation. Actually, I'm sure there's a whole genre I'm unfamiliar with that these guys fit into. The closest thing I've heard to this is very early pavement. The words 'experimental', 'freeform' and 'ARFNoise' spring to mind, as do the words 'I urge you to check this out'. Three of the four songs here make the standard, but 'Suzi Quattro' which sounds like a 45 rpm grindcore record played at 33 rpm or slower begins to lose my interest. Seriously, try something different. Send a couple of quid to the address below and have an experience! The thanks list of this record has some great names on it: Godzilla Burnout, Truncated Spur, Bald Mermaid, Wicked Stepladder, Crayon Skidder and many more. If these are for real please send us your tapes/records for review as you have the best names! I'm being good, c/o Flat 4, 29 St. Michaels Place, Brighton, East Sussex, BN1 3FU.

Pure Morning 3 song 7"

Pavement! You could do someone a tape of 'Slanted & Enchanted' and stick this on the end and no-one would know the difference! Don't get me wrong, it's good too. One lazily strummed number, one mid-paced number, and one massive, crashing early Fall style number. Excellent. Pure Morning, c/o Kool Tone, 34 Mill Lane, Great Sutton, South Wirral, L66 4PF.

The Rip Offs 7" single - Rip Off Records

Jon Von (ex-Mr T Experience) joins a member of Supercharger and others for this great new band. The 7" offers two tracks of rockin' raw garage punk in the vein of Supercharger, catchy and sing-a-long, yet rough around the edges. Bodes well for the future, I reckon.

Chairman Of The Board 2 x CD - Grass Records

Forty one different bands doing their interpretations of Frank Sinatra songs. There's over two hours of music on these two shiny discs and overall it's rather disappointing. Most of the bands contribute pretty dull straight versions of the songs, so Down By Law, Alloy, Samiam, Jawbox and others fail to excite and the lesser known bands are mostly forgetable, as I felt myself reaching for the 'skip' button time and time again. Still there's a few bright sparks here: Screeching Weasel and the Vindictives play theirs in their usual snotty punk way, the Girls Against Boys version of 'My Funny Valentine' could be their own song it's so good, but top prize to Urban DK's ragin' version of 'Just The Way You Look Tonight' and Mind Over Matter's 'New York, New York' done in Quicksand / RATM hardcore style! Worth picking up if you see it second hand as it's expensive (thank christ mine was a present) but I think I prefer the originals.

Rocket From The Crypt - All Systems Go LP - Headhunter

Not a new LP but a compo of all the early (and recent) singles originally released on an expensive import jap CD a while back. Rocket again prove why they're up there with the best - distinctive, original, prepared to experiment. Two minute punk gems merge with longer weird, slower tracks - all exciting (if a little muffled early on) and damn heroic if you ask me. 19 tracks (more than the CD) and linear notes to boot, plus a Red C and Adam and the Ants covers. A great collection if you didn't catch the original 7"s.

Jesus Christ Superfly LP - Rise Records

Excellent fold-out, glueless sleeve like their 7" single (included here), this little known band has produced a fine LP. Great trad-sounding hardcore, like the Humpers, and their covers of Dead Boys and Stooges points you in the direction of their sound. Pretty raw and fastish but a mighty sound overall. 'Rocket Scientist' is a classic if ever there was one, as is 'Fresh Cuts'.

Man Or Astroman? 'Is it...' LP - Estrus

Yeah! Excellent cover art! 16 cool surf instrumentals and a Sci-Fi fixation with great samples from old Sci-Fi movies. A fun LP to listen to but the second side does drag a little and the entire concept isn't everyone's cup of tea ("It ain't 'ardcore mate!"). Not as pleasant as Shadowy Men On A Shadowy Planet but in that vein. Anyway, Man Or Astroman? are from space and that's pretty punk rock!

Jackknife 'Drag Star '69' LP - Sympathy

Psychotic Lo-Fi noise, damn unpleasant really, not particularly tuneful, a bit like the Mummies or Supercharger without the tunes. Sort of bluesy treated vocals, sparse packaging. Great cover on the LP, limted to 1000, but I doubt you'll buy it anyway.

Mr Blobby 7" - Corporate Rock Label

Best single of the year, surely?

Guzzard, Chokebore, Today Is The Day - Powerhaus, London - 23/2/93

At last, the Amphetamine Reptile 'Clusterfuck' tour comes to the UK. For £5 not only do you get three amazing bands, but a free CD with tracks by all the bands... a signed CD too. Today Is The Day were intense to say the least. Original, powerful hardcore, screamed vocals, with the singer sweating buckets. They were so loud it hurt and kind of scary too. They blew me away! Chokebore are another highly original band, sometimes these so-sweet vocals, but always exploding into amazingly powerful hardcore, yet remaining tuneful throughout as the singer rolls around the stage like an acrobat. A great band. Guzzard are more like your straight ahead punk band. These guys were awesome. Their sound has repititious riffs, varied vocals, 'wobbly' basslines, and a power, intensity and presence I haven't seen for a while. This was one of the finest live experiences I've had the pleasure of attending. It seems the new wave of Amphet Reptile bands are going to be better than ever. An excellent evening!

Goon Squad - Uglier Than Your Sister 7" EP
Berzerkers - Anihilation Blues 7" EP

And I thought Sick Of It All were the only band still doing this kind of stuff! These are the first two releases by a new NYC label called Dirtbag Productions and fans of the '88 sound will love these. Breakdown, Warzone, Agnostic Front, Krackdown etc it's all here. Berzerkers have a slight metal edge while Goon Squad mosh it up more and both bands lyrics are pretty tough. Great stuff from: Dirtbag Productions, 223 Wall St, Huntington, NY 11743, USA.

Fabric - Colossus 7" EP

I don't know where to begin, this is an amazing debut! The sound is kinda early DC (Embrace, Swiz) meets 'Emo-Edge' (Lifetime, Admiral), but there's so much more to it. The lyrics are brilliant, subjects covered include the male ego ("A statue standing proud - we must tear it down!"), non-communication ("I cut my throat to speak to you, words spill out, collect in puddles at my feet."), sexism ("She can't close her eyes because she knows you'll be there and you never go away.") it's all covered with real feeling and emotion. I hope this has sold it to you because it's 'buy of the month' (year?). Don't miss out! Whole Car Records, 130 Talbot Road, London, W11 1JA.

Ironside - Fragments Of The Last Judgement 7" EP

If you know them from the 'Neutered Innocence' cassette or their track on the 'Consolidation' comp you'll know what to expect, but this is the best yet. Heavy, slow, pounding, metally hardcore with way cool vocals. Some are touting them as the British Integrity and rightly so. This band are amazing live, so don't miss them. Subjugation Records, 46 Cademon Crescent, Darlington, DL3 8LF.

GONZO SALVAGE COMPANY: Demo Cassette.
Good name! There seems to be more tracks on here than listed. Sometimes (usually) there's melodic vocals over light semi-industrial music, often quite poppy in places. Some stuff is more experimental, with even a techno influence, maybe? I can't see the Carter USM comparisons like what some of the press cuttings said, so that's a blessing at least. One track even reminds me of Spiritualized (?!). An interesting, varied little offering, I like the 'speaking clock' samples too. Contact: 24 Severn Street, Highfields, Leicester.

" Music... the only cheap and unpunished rapture upon earth. "
SYDNEY SMITH

** OLDER THAN DIRT "New Age of Rage" 7" ep
This strikes me as pretty fine...a 4 track EP with a straight-edge hardcore sound,
but there's a really quirky element to it, so it sounds fresh and rockin'! (£2.50
from: FNG Records, PO Box 1, Winchester, Hants, SO21 2SB.)

** DIPSOMANIACS "Growing Up" 7" ep
German hardcore band singing in English (What's wrong with your own language,
boys?). Some of the lyrics are pretty poor, but they've really tried hard. Musically, it has a trad UK punk sound. All in all, a little unconvincing. (Bad Taste
Records, Völksener Str. 46, W-3257 Springe 1, Germany.)

** THE SONS OF SELINA 7"
"Most powerful piece of sound to emerge from Wales since the Dark Ages" says the
crap promo blurb for this band's second single. I don't think so somehow. The A-
side is a dark sounding thing with a metal riff and 'atmosphere'-- not <u>that</u> bad,
the B-side is a load of bleeps and backwards vocals. Experimental? (£2.00 + BADGE
+ POSTER from: N.Birchall, 64 Ernest Street, Rhyl, Clwyd, LL18 2DW)

** EXIT CONDITION / REVERSE split 7" ep
Both these bands play competent punk-pop. Exit Condition's first is fine but the
second song is over-long. Nicely structured and I'd be interested to hear it live.
Reverse's first song is cracking hardcore with Bad Religion style vocals and
tuneful Leatherface style music, their second is perhaps not so hot, but still
pretty fine. Well worth checking out. (Contact: Vitamin Z Records, PO Box 180,
Stoke On Trent, ST4 8YT.)

** TOXIC NARCOTIC s/t 4 track 7" ep (grey vinyl!)
A 3-piece outfit hailing from Boston USA. This features 4 tracks of grinding
metal-type h.c. First track 'Popullution' is medium pace and probably the best here,
the other 3 are slower and duller. Lyrics take an anarchist stint, sometimes
outright blunt, sometimes pretty smart. (Rodent Popsicle Records, PO Box 335,
Newton Ctr., MA 02159, USA.)

** LOSERS / COITUS split 7"
Losers play straightforward 'back-to-basics' punk and it sounds great -- full of
energy and catchy, too! 'Don't Wanna Live' has a rough US punk-pop feel, say like
Derelicts or SNFU. Admirable for their effective simplicity. Coitus offer a more
metallic sounding thing, which is a fine example of this style, slightly Tad-like!
A good 7". (Fluffy Bunny Records, Aural Response, 4 Brackendale Grove, Harpenden,
Herts., AL5 3EJ.)

** CONCRETE IDEA / PORTO BELLO BONES split 7" ep
Two French bands here. Concrete Idea present 2 pop-punk ditties in a NOFX vain,
slightly cliched, poorly sung English but harmless fun. French equivalent of
Goober Patrol ?! What?! Porto Bello Bones have a 'bigger' more intense sound. The
vocals are too indistinct to make it memorable, even though the music is fast &
punky. (Forked Tongues, 101 Bd. de Chateaudun, 45000 Orleans, France.)

** KILLTOIDS / BLUE BLITZ split 7" ep
Two more French bands. Killtoids sing in English (poorly, again, French would be
better, the lyrics have been translated! It's like they feel they have to 'coz
people will <u>only</u> pay attention if in English -- Sad.). Lyrically pretty good, the
music bears a remarkable resemblance to early SNFU. Still, an admirable effort.
Blue Blitz (does that name sound dodgy to you?!) have an early 80's hardcore
sound and play well with cool vocals. Lyrics concern themselves with apathy and
the over-doing of US influences in our society...funny how US influenced they
sound themselves, though. Worth hunting down. (Panx, BP 5058, 31033 Toulouse Cedex,
France.)

" Music and rhythm find their way into the secret places of the soul. "
PLATO

Hello and welcome to BHP 7 !

I've had a pretty good response to the last couple of issues, so this one's out extra quick. It is a little different to past issues, in that it is mainly one big tour report and a few articles. No interviews. This is only a 'one off' but it's something I've been meaning to do since the interest in the Strookas tour report back in issue 4. It is a little more in depth, and a slightly comical look at touring. A big thanks to Adam, Dan, Tom, and Kris here. Also, Couch Potatoes are currently looking for gigs so please get in touch, by writing to the BHP address or phoning (0892) 527959.

I hope that you enjoy reading this issue anyway. I'm working on number 8 already, so keep your eyes open for it.

Thanks, as always, to all my supporters and shitworkers. Your contributions are greatly appreciated. Anyone is welcome to help. Just write to : BHP, 1 Chandos Road, Tunbridge Wells, Kent, TN1 2NY.

Take care and have fun.

Dave Potato.

Here is a list of the merchandise being distributed by BHP, available from the address above. Cheques / P.O's payable to D. Gamage. All prices post paid.

BHP   Back issues, 50p each.
#1 featuringGreen Day, Hard-Ons, Jailcell Recipes, Factory Farming...
#2 featuringRamones, Joeyfat, Unpolluted Air, Sleeping...
#3 featuring All, MTX, SNFU, Funbug, Planet Earth...
#4 featuring Sugar, Alloy, Decadence Within, Comics...
#5 featuring Down By Law, Samiam, Green Day, Lifetime...
#6 featuring Shelter, Rancid, All, MTX, Dan Clowes....
GOTHAM TAPES - The Alternative Tape Label - £1.50 each.
GOT 001 : TEE-HEE Compilation; 40 mins, 12 bands, 12 trax.
GOT 002 : COUCH POTATOES - LIVE IN TUN/WELLS; 40 mins, 16 trax.
GOT 003 : LIVE AT THE SHELLEY Compilation; 60 mins, 5 bands, 25 trax - featuring
          BBMF's, Strength Alone, Angus Bagpipe, Couch Potatoes...
GOT 004 : 'Hello, Bollox & Welcome' Compilation; 60 mins, 25 bands, 25 trax.
GOT 005 : MORAL CRUX, Tout a fait punk, live radio broadcast; 60 mins, 20 trax.
GOT 006 : ANOTHER Compilation; 40 mins, 13 bands, 13 trax
GOT 007 : Eyes Down For God Compilation; 60 mins, 20 bands, 20 trax.
GOT 008 : JAWBREAKER - LIVE AT GILMAN STREET; 60 mins, 15 trax.
GOT 009 : COUCH POTATOES - EXCESS ALL AREAS; 60 mins, 24 trax - Brilliant Melodic
          Hardcore in a Descendents vein.
GOT 010 : JOEYFAT - SOUP; 60 mins, 15 trax (8 studio & 7 live).
GOT 011 : Low Brow Head Tread Compilation; 60 mins, 20 bands.
GOT 012 : All the Smiley Faces Compilation; 60 mins, 21 trax, 15 bands - superb melodic HC.

VINYL
PANX 11 - 7" EP, £2.00
featuring Couch Potatoes, Blanks 77, Eight Ball, Public Lost, Wounded Knee & Lamento.
NOWHERE STREET - 7" Compilation, £2.00
featuring Vendabait, Couch Potatoes, Cheese Doodles & Pseudo Hippies.
JOEYFAT 7" GOD/WINDSCREEN £2.00
"Band of the month" - Lookout, "Punches lethal in the face" - NME.
COUCH POTATOES - IN BED WITH 7" EP, £2.00
4 Trax of Punk, melodic hardcore from the fat lads.
COUCH POTATOES - WHY U SUCH A JERK BRAD? EP - 4 TRAX - OUT SOON.

BUY INDEPENDENT - SUPPORT THE UNDERGROUND!

One of the things I will be doing in this piece is to defend the right of bad art to be fully protected under the Bill of Rights as a form of speech. To do this, I will use the Berkeley performance group known as the 'X-plicit Players' as an example of bad art. Before we get to the particular case, we should lay out some universal truths:

Bad art is the manure from which good and great art springs. All artists have done some bad art. In other words, you cannot have any art without having bad art, any more than you can have any science without having most experimentation be 'failures'. So, we have to protect the right and the freedom to do bad art. We also have to keep the government out of art criticism.

Now for the background to the particular case. Berkeley, until this year, has not had a law against public nudity. In fact, over the years, performance artists such as Paul Cotton and myself have done 'street pieces' containing nudity in Berkeley with community acceptance and support. But about two years ago, public nudity became a political issue. A University of California student, Andrew Martinez, whom the media dubbed as 'The Naked Guy', began going to classes and walking around town nude. Martinez seems to be an idealist suffering from naïvety... which is natural at his age. The college administration, as is the nature of the beast, expelled him.

Around this time, the X-plicit Players began to affix themselves to the controversy by walking nude around town and sitting in coffee-houses wearing only chips on their shoulders... and of course, being with Martinez when the cameras were on him. In art, using confrontation, in-your-face methods are very valid to incite change. In bad art, confrontation is often used for calling attention, recognition, to the artist, creating an arrogance around the artist. All of which may be unavoidable, if embarrassing, yet it's a stage in an artist's development. Be that as it may, the tactics that the X-plicit Players used, created considerable resentment in the community. That resentment was transferred to public nudity in the minds of a sizeable portion of the community, a community that usually prides itself on its openness, tolerance and freedom. One of the functions of art is to offend, to create tension by revealing hidden aspects of life. The bad artist does this for his own aggrandizement or other questionable motives. But, to keep our freedom, we must remember that we do not have a right to not be offended.

At this point, a Berkeley council-person, who for some reason does not want her children to see nude bodies, used this built-up resentment to push through a very reactionary law against public nudity. So, the home of the Free Speech Movement now has a law that is clearly unconstitutional, a law that not only outlaws public nudity, but outlaws a lot of different kinds of clothing (including lots of swimsuits... unintentionally).

To be a test case of a clearly unconstitutional law is the easiest -- and one of the best -- ways for an artist to get in the papers and in the history books. One of the exceptions to the nudity law that the 'liberals' wrote into the law to ease their consciences, was theatrical events. That is, public nudity in theatrical events is permitted. So, the X-plicit Players apparently put on a street theater event. And they were arrested.

Now we come to the meat of my essay. If the X-plicit event was held in a theater, in a performance space, in a gallery, the X-plicit Players would not have been arrested because the logic of the cops would be "it's in a theater, so it is theater". The logic of the arrest was "it isn't in a theater, so it's not theater, thus it is covered by the anti-nudity law". The issue is not whether the X-plicit Players are good or bad theater/art. Rather, the issue is are they theater/art, thus under all of the protection afforded to theater/art. But the core issue is: can the government decree that the San Francisco Mime Troupe, the satirist/humorist Stoney Burke who works the crowd on Sproul Plaza, street theater, union theater, performers like myself, are not theater or art when we do our work outdoors, in public, in the parks, etc.? No matter what I or anyone else think of their work, the X-plicit Players are a theater/performance group.

Although the charges were finally dropped, the bad logic of the judge at the hearing on the constitutionality of the charges is frightening. Judge Ron Greenberg's decision was "I don't know of this as a live theatrical performance deserving First Amendment protection". Greenberg explained that he had difficulty in finding satisfactory legal definition of a live theatrical performance. Because this performance included spontaneity, he decided to rule that the performance would be viewed as 'conduct' and not as 'speech', and therefore was not protected by the First Amendment. Greenberg seemed afraid that a member of the audience might 'spontaneously' at some future performance, decide to have sexual intercourse.

Let's run that by again. A performance that has any kind of spontaneity is not speech, and thus not protected... because of an unknown possibility which may or may not happen sometime in the future!! That would include any work containing any space or freedom, including improvisation, jamming, jazz, dancing, and so on. Like I said, it's very frightening!!

You bet I would say the X-plicit Players are art and theater. Freedom and art are worth it

© <u>FRANK MOORE</u> *October 28th, 1993*

THE TRASHWOMEN: 'Spend The Night With...' L.P. (Estrus Records)
Oh yes! I'd been waiting for this for ages after hearing Peely playing their stuff on his show ages back. Here you get a short album's worth of fine surf / trash / garage punk. It's raw as fuck, with great rock 'n' roll sounds and screamed girl vocals. Possibly <u>too</u> punk for you Emo fans....only kidding! A cool little L.P.

ANIMALS IN CIRCUSES

TRAINING

The cruelty of circus trainers doesn't end with the whips and goads in the ring, as to beat the animal would damage it as an 'asset'. The trainer cannot use direct physical force during a performance, so the animal must be taught to recognise the trainer's signals during the initial training period. By baiting, luring, triggering of escape and aggression impulses, or by direct physical force, the animal is made to perform the required movements repeatedly until all that is required is the appropriate 'trigger'.

Fear & Aggression

Lions often respond to the trainer's commands by slinking across the ring, belly close to the ground, ears flattened, snarling loudly. A clear indication of fear. Aggression is often the first response to fear, and a lion may be seen to paw threateningly at an outstretched whip. An audience may misinterpret these aggressive approaches and marvel at the trainer's daring.

Escape

Biologically the significance of flight is obvious - protection from enemies. If an animal sees a potential enemy it attempts to flee. If confined and unable to flee, the animal will cower, show fear and issue a low intensity threat. If the intruder continues to approach, a critical distance will be reached at which the insecure animal will attack, so lion tamers must assess this critical distance.

Readiness to Learn

There are two distinct phases in the development of a circus act - taming and training. Circus elephants are obtained either as youngsters wild from Africa or from Asia where the Indian elephant is domesticated. In the former case, the animal has initially to be controlled, by a combination of coaxing, rewarding, restraint and force. On arrival, the young elephant is restrained by chaining a fore and hind leg to stakes. Contrary to popular belief, the elephant's hide is sensitive and the animal is conscious of even light jabs on a number of areas of it's body. Mahouts use the elephant hook to control the elephant from behind the ear, pull forward a leg, or jab it in a sensitive area, to make it move in a particular direction. In the circus this hook is abandoned in favour of a walking stick, sometimes with nails concealed in the crook and tip. Once the young elephant has become manageable, the initial training begins. By getting the animal to perform the same sequence time and again, with external stimulation and coercion, the elephant will eventually perform the sequence, even when the controlling factors are removed. For some acts, such as a handstand, the young elephant may be forced into the position the trainer wishes it to learn, using pulleys or an already trained elephant. The pedestals used in such acts are highly significant since the animal is prevented from moving off the spot whilst in this unnatural position by fear of falling. Readiness to learn increases with the strength of either punishment or reward. However, once punishment reaches the point where the situation becomes terrifying for the animal, learning will cease and the animal will become apathetic and untrainable.

Legal Rights

The Association of Circus Proprietors of Great Britain has said that RSPCA officials may observe rehearsals, but not initial training sessions. In order to obtain a conviction under the Protection of Animals Act 1911 there is a need to prove substantial unnecessary suffering, which is known to take place but very difficult to prove.

LIVING CONDITIONS
One aspect of the circus that clearly provides evidence of it's abuse of animals are the cramped living conditions. The animals are also subjected to the added stresses of frequent noise, movement and lights.

Travelling
Beast wagons are aptly named. They are lorry trailers open on one side only, the remaining three sides have painted wooden or metal walls. A wagon measuring only 20' x 8' x 6' is considered adequate for seven polar bears, and fourteen lions can be housed in a vehicle measuring 30' x 9' x 5'. These vehicles, with their inadequate ventilation, are where the majority of circus animals spend most of their natural lives.

At the Showground
Apart from the brief time the animals are in the ring, they are incarcerated in the beast wagons. Frequently old and rusty, these wagons offer no outlet for the animals' instincts to explore, to 'play' or to do anything other than exist. Elephants are shackled nearly all the time, some becoming permanently scarred by lifelong leg-chains. Most bears live in beast wagons and are restrained by chain collars and leads during most performances and whilst being taken to and from the ring.

ABNORMAL BEHAVIOUR
Abnormal behaviour in captive animals is common. Hand rearing of young can result in behavioural disturbances later in life and quality of environment is an important factor. Several research workers investigating the effects of prolonged social isolation in monkeys have shown that severe autistic-like behaviour may result. Stereotyped behaviour, such as rocking and thumb sucking, and self-directed aggression has been reported. Young monkeys reared away from their mothers displayed deprivation symptoms, aggression, apathy, lack of exploratory behaviour, and as adults, many proved unable to copulate. Females who did bear young tended to neglect their infants and even to attack them. Stereotyped movements develop in monotonous environments and tend to persist because they provide a source of stimulation. An animal needs natural stimulation for normal development and subsequent normal behaviour.

Deprivation
Socially deprived animals will often display strange behavioural movements like rocking, throwing the head back, weaving, and chewing their own bodies.

Investigations have revealed similar 'deprivation symptoms' in parentless children living in institutions, who develop symptoms like pulling out hair, chewing fingernails, obsessive scratching and rocking. Comparison with animals is valid and quite justifiable. Basle zoo bought several polar bears from a circus and housed them in a large barless enclosure. Whilst some of the younger animals behaved normally, the oldest female remained in one spot, weaving continuously. Another female paced out an oval circuit all the time, a circuit that conformed to the dimensions of the beast wagon. Stereotyped behaviour can be fixated by habit, resulting in a condition akin to human neurosis. If the circumstances which cause it remain unaltered, it is likely that the behaviour will become permanent. Lack of natural surroundings and lack of space are the two most important contributing factors to the development of abnormal behaviour.

Confinement

In the wild, animals live in environments of great complexity. Their lives are regulated by the natural elements of their surroundings. Vegetation, water, food availability, seasonal changes, and light patterns all add to the endless variety of their lives in the wild. It is not surprising that animals display such gross distortions of behaviour when they are confined in the sterile, predictable environment of a circus beast wagon.

Monotony

Animals rely on their innate responses to environmental conditions. Some, such as dolphins and chimpanzees, have incredible intelligence but the monotony of their confines in captivity makes even these species become dull.

CONCLUSION

Eminent zoologists, naturalists and vets have voiced their misgivings about the lives of circus animals. Dr Desmond Morris said of caged animals: "There is something biologically immoral about keeping animals in enclosures where their behaviour pattern, which has taken million years to evolve, can find no expression. Animals do not live by nutrition alone. They cannot live without it, but we must go a good deal further." But now, fortunately, the public are becoming more aware of the problem. David Hancocks, a distinguished zoo director, offers both the understanding of the problem and the solution in a simple statement: "In a naturalistic environment, which simulates the essential characteristics of an animal's wild habitat, there will be opportunity for the animal to engage in natural patterns of behaviour. Further, the animals will be seen by the public not as deviant forms or freaks of nature, but as true wild animals with their own inherent beauty and appeal. That such improvements can be made in a circus seems to be an impossibility. Circus cages are designed only for transportation. They must, by definition and design, always be inadequate. Zoo cages can be abolished in favour of large naturalistic habitats, but the travelling cages of circus animals can never hope to do more than meet minimum legal requirements for confinement".

Circuses which include animal acts are relics of a bygone age, an age which permitted bear-baiting and cock-fighting, when compassion towards any animal would have been regarded with suspicion. Not only do they inflict an unnatural way of life on animals, they degrade and humiliate them. Circuses are a complete anachronism at a time when the need has never been greater to protect and conserve the world's wild creatures. Man's attitude to nature begins to evolve in childhood, so society has a choice to make for future generations. Are we to look upon animals as freaks for our amusement, or are we to accept that wildlife is part of an intricate network of which we are also a part? Circuses cannot teach this, indeed they are the antithesis of this concept.

It is impossible that the activities of circus animals can ever achieve any worthwhile goals in either education, research or conservation. They must always rely on a show of man's dominance over the animal and will inevitably always present a distorted view of wildlife. Therein lies their futility.

<u>What you can do</u>

THINK! The only way circuses with performing animals can continue to exist is with your support. Withdraw that support. If your children want to visit a circus with animal acts, tell them the facts and then see if they are still as enthusiastic. Children are remarkably sensitive to animal cruelty. Join the RSPCA and any organisations that champion the cause of animals, to add your voice to the growing voice of opposition to circuses with performing animals. IT'S YOUR CHOICE!

For more information you could write to the RSPCA, Causeway, Horsham, Sussex, RH12 1HG, who are totally opposed to exhibitions of animals in circuses, which cause stress and suffering to the animals and are of no value to the audience.

To express your views on this, or any other subject, you could write to us at BHP HQ, 1 Chandos Road, Tunbridge Wells, Kent, TN1 2NY, England.

THE CIRCUS IS NO PLACE FOR ANIMALS!

TRAVELS WITH THE TALL PEOPLE

<u>15/9</u> : The flyers read "Bad Taste Records presents : Pseudo Hippies (Aus London) mit Dipsomaniacs (Aus Bremen), on tour!" and the tour dates and venues followed. Simplicity itself, we thought, as we booked our tickets and even arranged insurance... "Look, someone's brought their donkey jacket" said Adam (bassist), in the back of my (Dave Potato's) van. He was pointing at a possession of Miles's and laughing hard. We were trying, late at night in the pitch dark, to sort out all the crap in the back of the truck. The mirrors were broken and had to be 'gaffa'd', as did part of the wing and the leak holes. The passenger seat was broken too, the jack seized up, and last of all, where to stick the GB sticker? It would be late before we got to bed tonight.

<u>16/9</u> : We woke and left Kemsing ridiculously early (we had left Tunbridge Wells the night before) to reach Dan's house by 7.30 am and meet the other three intrepid explorers. Dan (drummer) and Kris (vocals & guitarist) were there, armed with the equipment and a mountain of baggage, but where was Tom (guitarist)? After much loading and worrying, he eventually arrived to a torrent of abuse, carrying only a young lady on one arm and four Stellas on the other. Aside from bus lane driving, taxi driver annoying and beer can crushing / inflating contests, it was a pretty uneventful race to the ferry at Harwich.
We boarded at about 10.45 am and made straight for the bar, Tom and Dan already still drunk from the night before down the New Cross Inn. Miles disappeared to read Melody Maker and I went to see 'CliffHanger' (everyone dies) at the cinema. By the time we returned, the Pseudo's were surrounded by bottles, drunk, in the casino, insulting everyone present, including another touring punk band called 'Contempt'. Jack Daniels was purchased and by now people were getting very drunk. We adjourned, for our own safety, to the upper deck, where Tom, who was really very drunk, dropped his glass and threw a chair, possibly at Dan. Anyway, unluckily, it went overboard, luckily it hit a lower deck, unluckily it narrowly missed some of our fellow passengers. The more sober amongst us (by the way, Miles and myself do not drink) departed to the restaurant with haste.
We found some veggie food and settled down, but the peace was shattered by Dan's arrival with a Jazz mag, which he wanted to share, loudly, with everyone, whilst sucking an already dead chicken to death. In afterthought, I guess this was pretty bad behaviour, but at the time it was very funny. I guess you had to be there.
"Take no advice you, yes, yes. Criticism, no I think, very much." There was an argument to our right over a chess match. A fat, bearded man was shouting at another, so not even the Captain's corner piano bar was safe, it seemed. My last memory of the crossing over was the vacuum toilets. 'No Disposal of Unusual Things!' the sign read, then ssuckscoosh and it was gone; Kimberley Clark had invaded even here.
A good six hours later we came in to dock at Hoek van Holland. Miles and I followed the trail of destruction, mainly large, knocked over, pot plants, to find the band, sitting on the main stairs with some guy playing a guitar, all singing 'Back in the USSR' to quite an audience. An older guy walked by wearing a sheepskin jacket (no doubt German, or Dutch, as style is not indigenous). Danny asked him where he was bound. "Hamburg" he replied. "Oh really, we're going to Hamburg, and Hannover, and Sheepskin, Baa, Baa" Then he threw his adult magazine at him and hit him on the head. "See ya Mr Sheepskin". We ran.
Back at the truck, we noticed we'd parked next to the Ghost Squadron Model Aircraft Team; Tom and Dan stripped and hailed them, Kris and Adam had to hold them in the van.

It quickly became dark and started raining as we drove to Amsterdam. The van's numerous leaks had apparently not been sufficiently plugged. We turned up Sugar. Parking by one of the many canals, the six of us went to explore the infamous red light district. It more than lived up to all the stories, packed with drugs of all types, characters, red light ladies, banana clubs and an amazing atmosphere. We visited the Free Adam Cafe, which had it's own drugs menu; Kris ordered Afghan Black. Then the Cafe de Burgh, with the wacky toilets, stickers and pool table; obviously not the Mr de Burgh's pad! I cannot really go into detail, but we went on to sample the city's delights until 2 or 3 in the morning, before sleeping in the van, somewhere between Eindhoven and Venlo. There was much talk of 'on our manor' and 'up the gritter' and as we'd nearly crashed several times on the wrong side of the road, we knew we were on the continent.

<u>NB : The Tour Party</u>

Kris	-	Guitar & Vocals (Pseudos)
Tom	-	Guitar (Pseudos)
Dan	-	Drummer (Pseudos & stand in Couchies)
Adam	-	Bass (Pseudos & stand in Couchies)
Miles	-	Vocals (Couchies) Maps & Merchandise
Dave	-	Guitar (Couchies) Driving & Dealing
Beast	-	Rusting old van (352011 miles at Kemsing)

<u>17/9</u> : We woke about 10.00 am and crossed the border at 12 noon, stopping at a garage between Munchen Gladbach and Dusseldorf for food. Lunch consisted of cheese rolls, chocolate milk (Kakao Trunk) and Toblerones. Germany is not a land of vegetarians, I discovered, but a land of sausages and beer!
The first gig was meant to be tonight in Neuss. We eventually arrived and went shopping. Both myself and Tom are fluent in French, but we were now in Germany, this meant trouble. Miles' elephant and hospital phrases would not suffice. Dan tried to order lunch in a kebab house and ended up paying for everyone in the shop!
The venue was the Geschwrister Scholl Haus, a kind of youth club that seemed to be run by a 'Sun Cult' - the older guy in charge no doubt fornicated with all the younger children. But there was a great skate ramp, a totem pole, a homemade pool table (complete with homemade 'fishing rod' cues), some kicker (apparently the national sport) and lots of smiley faces. There were six more when we were fed the complimentary pizzas, in the 'back room'. Which we could only use "after, how you say in English, the young people have finished drinking their coffee."
The other band we were touring with were called Dipsomaniacs. We were waiting for them to show so we could soundcheck. A rusting old orange VW Camper pulled up and out jumped five real characters. Kris had arranged the tour through Isleif at Bad Taste Records (the Pseudo Hippies' German label) and Matze (the Dipso's guitarist and translator) but had never actually met them, until now. It was crazy tight jeans mayhem. "Are you arsehole? - No, I am guitarist!". They were / are all 'diamond geezers'. Matze, Marco (vocals), Thomas (drums), and Marco the short (bass). Also Andreas Isleif, our 'tour manager' who had brought hundreds of records to sell and was as punk as you know what. His first words to Miles later that evening, whilst selling the Pseudo's records and shirts to an army of ladies, were "You like young girls?" No less than three interviews later there was a storming gig. After the show the band were accosted. "Your music is ugly, but good luck on the tour" said a large, blonde, Swedish girl. "Good luck on your diet" was Dan's abrasive reply. We drove north for five hours and crashed at Matze's. We were told that it was not far "maybe 600 km"!

18/9 : Tom had fallen asleep on the radiator and woke up burnt with Aliens eggs growing on his arms. We had a real shower in Matze's beautiful house and then rushed to the supermarket, because it was closing at one for a rest. Picked up the rest of the Dipso's from a club, surrounded by rusting motorbikes and dodgy rocker types and drove to Husum. Miles had a go at driving - it was dead scary, a bit like postman pat on TV, except on a four lane Autobahn with big trucks. Arrived about 5.30 pm, after a Castle Belmont competition on Adam's gameboy, at the Speicher - a large hall / club next to the rather picturesque dock. Soundchecked - soundman's favourite phrase was "More hi-hat!", and we reserved vege spag bog for fifteen. Miles met a green haired girl called 'Mariella from Flensburg' who studied English at college. His classic chat up line was "What sort of wanker mikes a hi-hat but not a bass drum?" Another great gig and merchandising was ruthlessly swift until this guy with a really bad perm kept asking "What is this crazy pop-punk you talk of?" Miles and I told him we were Juan and Jose, new ministers for guitar based rock and sent him to harass the others. At about 12.45am fifteen people piled into 'the beast' and we went to visit a club called the Dornbusch, which, although it was in the middle of nowhere, was attended by everyone in Northern Germany. They played cheesy europop here but it was packed. Matze informed us "Don't go with girls behind the bar, you don't know where they've been." Later Tom Dipso said "I am thinking you guys know what it is to party, yes," before getting lost in the car park. Kris disappeared early on with some girl and we left at about 4.30am to find him 'still at it' in the truck. Went back to Karsen's house for a bad brief striptease and found out Germans have Mentadent C, not P, and also Colgetten. Kris said it tasted like grit and salt before realising he was brushing his teeth with tiling grout.

19/9 : Woke late this morning to the Dipso's triumphant return with some mushrooms and sampled the further delights of German 'dump-plate-toilets'. (You bomb onto a plate beneath you and it then flushes forward into a bowl when you're done. Provided it's not a 'sticker' or a 'splasher' you'll be right, but I would imagine there's quite a few 'stinkers' caused by this odd appliance. I myself would not know as my shit does not smell. I'm straying.)
Todays gig was to be on an island, just of the North West coast, called Sylt. We drove north, stopping only to piss and marvel at Isleif's fluorescent pink and green jumper, to the railway station where we'd catch the train to the island. Although we were near the Danish border now, it seemed to us everyone in Germany drove a Mercedes, very fast, until a Porsche drove by. This was a rich area; they didn't like punk bands. The fare for each truck to cross to the island and back (on a drive-on transporter type train) was 200M, about £80! It was only about 2 or 3 miles away over the sand. We loaded all the gear into the Dipso's orange monster and the rest of us crossed on foot, in a huff, via passenger train, taking photos and the piss out of the Monty Python look-a-like ticket inspector.
The main and only town on Sylt was Westerland - next week it would hold the world windsurfing finals. We were playing at the Jugend Zentrum, the youth club. I was surprised we'd gotten this far, it was a rich people's weekend town, a tourist attraction, not a punk venue. We went to the beach and bought some postcards. Our German vocabulary was progressing, but slowly. Dan tried to order a Coke (the world's most widely recognised word) and got a chocolate. Miles ordered a Gersmachkt (flavour) milkshake, and was hammered at pool by a professional hustler. The Dipsomaniacs do, as you might have guessed, play rather thrashy, beer induced hardcore, but by now we were growing to love them. They had songs like 'We want chips', 'Walk like a dog', 'Tractor blues' and a ripping cover of 'Angel in disguise'.

Their few drunken fans seemed to love them - Bremen is the hardest drinking town in the world, we were informed - and tonights gig, meant to stop at 10 pm, jammed on until midnight.

Everyone at the youth club was friendly, especially Peter, our blonde haired, blue eyed host, who worried us all by saying "If you need anything in the night, just scream and I'll come." This place had a really good pool table and the back room had a Nintendo with loads of games. After another spag bog dinner with cream and garlic, we fixed the PA by spraying Kontakt on it - basically water! Miles met a red haired girl tonight, wearing leopard skins, called Sarah and they made necklaces and did magic all night whilst he sold her all our records. He eventually managed to break her 'secret ring'. After the rather odd gig, featuring schizo guy called 'Anton I think', the party started. Nude pool, during which two cues and a light were broken and beer spilt all over the table, followed by Tom setting fire to his pubes and nipples. Earlier on in the evening Matze had asked "What do you call this tooth tool?" and when he fell asleep in a drunken stupor, was covered in shaving foam for his trouble. The toilets had no lock, so Miles was caught dumping by a stoned Tom, and the few girls that hadn't yet left were abused. All of this, and more, was captured on video by Kris, so look out for it at your local rental store soon. At about 4 am we settled down, locked in a room, to write postcards. One read : 'Dear Mum & Dad - Having a kraut snogging, trouser dropping, pill popping, fans are bopping good time. Lost my passport, keys and pants. Currently residing with a sailor called Bernard in Amsterdam. Have nurtured a long at the back and acquired a taste for spandex. If you see Danny, say hello. Just set fire to my groota! All my love.' It was addressed to : 'Mum & Dad, My house, Blackheathishsortof, SN3 7DP' and it still arrived!

20/9 : Woke up at lunchtime and took much needed showers, despite a chemical warning sign. Went for a wander in our T-shirts, despite the fact that everyone else on the island was wearing artic survival suits, but weren't allowed back on the beach, so we said our goodbyes and Peter invited himself to Adams. The Dipso's drove to Bremen to pick up some records, but we had a day off so we drove to Hamburg. The beast was holding up well.

On the way back South we were attacked by millions of bugs, so we stopped at a lay-by toilet and found a budgerigar and some pictures of anal sex. Was it a sign? We remembered Matze's advice of the previous day "Don't make fun of the tall people, they're not violent but will get upset." Stranger and stranger.

We took a wrong turning from the Hamburg tunnel and got lost in the docks, where a man dressed in green overalls, who we presume was customs, asked us if we had any tea, coffee, spirits, etc. Then we headed for the Reeperbahn to see Mighty Mighty Bosstones play at the Kaiserkeller, but it was cancelled, much to our annoyance, so we wandered around, checking out the expensive Chineses and eventually settling for a BurgerKing with a warm toilet. The Reeperbahn seemed quite dangerous, it did not have the atmosphere of Amsterdam. All the ho's wore the same clothes, leggings and leotards, thigh high boots and bad Campri ski jackets, it was arse-eatingly gross, but there were crazy shops to cheer us up. Crazy Jeans, Crazy Leather, Crazy Gun World, Crazy Sexy Sexy Girls... Helloween were playing tonight in a club that had seen Bad Brains as well as Morbid Angel, Dio and Scorpions. A guy tried to sell us tickets so we hurried back to the KK club to dance to bad Rage Against The Machine type bands and play air hockey. The door pass was a condom here, not as cool as the 'What d'ya want the DJ to play' card at the Dornbusch, but not bad. The girls from 'Heathers' were sitting on the stage and Mr Spock walked in, no doubt beamed from one of the illuminated ashtrays. We drove out of town to a village called Tottensen and slept in the woods.

21/9 : Dan woke screaming. We'd been out a while now and were six desperate men on tour. The roof of the truck was covered in grot, ripped out of numerous mags and hastily gaffa taped up. We washed with bottled water and Kris disappeared into the woods. Visited Helmstorf for breakfast and bought twenty five rolls. Tom cleaned his teeth in the middle of the high street and then we all went off for a pillow fight on a bar in a huge field. Late that afternoon we drove back to Hamburg and met the Dipso's at the Marquee club. It was small and purple, but had recently seen ENT, Sheer Terror and Citizen Fish. Now it would play host to the Pseudo Hippies' brand of GreenDayesque pop-punk. Isleif had tartan trousers and a UK Subs shirt on today, he had the new EP with him, 500 split 7"s on red vinyl - Dipso's and Pseudo's, two songs each for the tour.

Inside the club was small and dark and plastered with posters. Adam met a girl from England called Miriam; she was wearing a dog collar. They decided to form a band called 'Piss-Off' and the first song was gonna be'Cows without Tits' After three crates of beer between the band, Tom and Dan started on tequilla slammers. The bottle read 'Deathshead Tequilla - poisonous'. Tom soon earnt a free one by being the guys best customer that night and tried to shag Isleif. (Who, incidentally, thinks cameras steal your soul). We carried him, kicking and screaming, to the van to sleep and went in search of more food.

We were meant to stay downstairs at the club that night, but the Germans had put towels on the beds already and the place was a stinking brothel. It had mould on the walls and Miles thought it "smells of death". We drove on to Hannover, as I prefer driving at night and the guys were happy to sleep in the belly of the beast, where Tom awoke, still very drunk, and chased us around a private car park trying to piss on us, before attempting a naked high jump over the fence. When he'd finally knocked himself out we continued to the Pied Piper's town of Hameln where we stopped as we'd run out of petrol and gaffa.

NB : The Beast

Our preferred mode of transport for this tour was a huge X-reg Ford Transit van that had been converted into a tourmobile, with 4 bunkbeds, cupboards, a cooker, a sink, a stereo, and loads of HC stickers. It was on it's second two litre engine, but didn't miss a beat on the whole tour. We had a small box of tool-type-things under a seat in case of emergency, but had no idea how to use them.

22/9 : We were awoken from our sweatbox by the binmen next morning. We were parked outside a Turkish refugee home. Asked some Americans at the garage the way to Minden but got more sense from the locals. Eventually we found the F.K.K. (Freie Kunst & Kultur) as it was the largest building in town. A huge warehouse, or 'Dumphole' as Adam called it, run by some people with microphone hairstyles as a kind of squat come arts centre come youth club. We were meant to play on the fourth floor, but the lift was broken. The Dipso's arrived and showed us to the local swimming pool, where we could take showers and watch fat men dive; it was bliss. The Y-Fronts, quite a decent band, were also meant to be on the bill tonight, but had cancelled. By the time we returned to the F.K.K. people had started to arrive. Dinner was hot vege chilli and I ate four bowlfulls, as I was becoming skint and did not know where the next meal was coming from. The Pseudo Hippies also have a record out in Germany on Nasty Vinyl, and they were taking part of the blame for this new EP too, so they turned up at the gig tonight to pogo. Hohnie, a fat geezer with glasses (who kept saying "play na na song for me, yes?"), Krapfe, a fat geezer with blond hair and someone's sister - all very nice people underneath, I'm sure. Hohnie informed me that his band, the Pissed Spitzels, would support the Pseudo's later on the tour - I couldn't wait! The gig went very well, with no less than two forced encores and some mad guy, with the thickest glasses I have ever seen, offered Kris a festival gig for next year where we'd be paid £10,000 in exchange for a freebie, but merchandising Miles stood strong at the back, as ever.

The toilets here had no windows, just a big drop to the railway tracks below. In case of too much chilli I guess. Everywhere we went in Germany there was loads of anti-Fascist literature, and anti-fascist and anti-sexist shirts; it was all they ever talked about, lending it far too much publicity for my liking. It's a good job they didn't see the van before we said our goodbyes and departed for an all night drive to the south and Donuaworth.

<u>23/9</u> : During this mammoth, all night road trip I went through hell whilst the others tried to sleep. We crossed rivers, went over huge mountains and round awkward diversions. I even met Saxon at a service station, they were on their 'Fists Of Fury' world tour, or something. After what seemed like an eternity, but was actually at about 8.00 am the following morning, we reached our goal. It was a garage carpark in Donuaworth, where we slept until lunchtime, but were thrown out when we tried to wash. We then staggered into a roadside cafe and ordered pommes mit salat mit mayo, then proceeded to inform the guy behind the counter that we were in fact travelling clowns from Ausland who were lost. Luckily, a friendly fat geezer in a Subaru showed us where the venue was.

Tonight's destination was the Schellen Bergastadte, a cafe on the hillside overlooking the town. It was still early so there was no-one there to meet us yet; this was deepest Bavaria and everyone was probably still resting from the previous night's blitzkrieging. We drove into a meadow down by the river to laze around and try to fix a few minor problems with the beast. We picnicked and wrote postcards, threw things at each other and got bitten, Kris even found a stone shaped like a poo, before returning to the cafe venue, where we met Toxic Walls, our new support band, and Fratz, the drunken promoter. The 'Walls' were total metalheads and their singer looked like Dayta from the 'Next Generation'. Also we found a facsimile message from Matze informing us that the Dipsomaniacs were not coming as their van had broken down amidst torrents of smoke and flames, so we were now on our own.

We ate a sombre meal of salad soaked in oil and flour and cheese veggie burgers whilst pondering the situation. Toxic Walls may have been morons, but they had brought all the gear that we needed and Fratz promised to help us on the southern part of our tour, as he was "Ace tour manager and close personal friend of Wizo, you know, the MTV stars - All that she wants, la, la, la...". When he asked Kris if he was 'Band Hitler', Dan told him that he was the band's Churchill, and as the Pseudo's sound checked people started to arrive. I went to catch up on some sleep, surrounded by 'the ladies' in the beast, but I couldn't help thinking how much that guy looked like Dayta with red hair. By the way, for those of you (and I'm sure there are many) who don't know of W120, pronounced 'VEE20'. They were riding high in the German and Scandinavian charts with a punk-rock version of Ace of Base's 'All That She Wants'. They were even receiving lots of airplay on MTV of their video, made by themselves, of the band playing air guitar in a public toilet! You can write to them at : Hulk Rakorz & Wizo, Eichendorffstr. 1, 93051 Regensburg, Germany.

The gig went ahead as scheduled and the Pseudo's promptly stripped off their clothes on stage - this was now fast becoming their trademark. Kris changed pants and Tom wore a young girl's vest! After the show, Kris tried to entice a pig "Come back with us and we make party, yes?". "No!" was her stalwart reply and so we all went back to

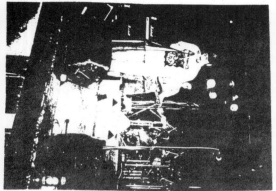

COUCH POTATOES

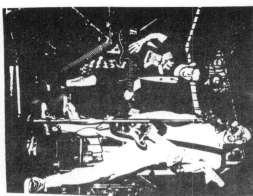

PSEUDO HIPPIES

COUCH POTATOES

PSEUDO HIPPIES

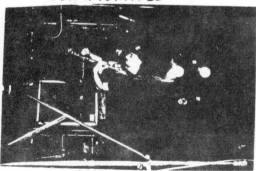

DAVE - COUCHIES

DAN - PSEUDOS

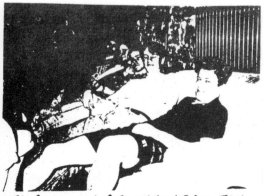

STEVE, IMUND, KRIS, MILES, ADAM, TOM
AND DAN AT THE KESSEL.

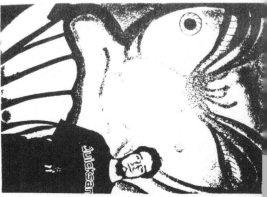

TWO MONSTERS AT THE KESSEL

ADAM - GETTING DRUNK

DAVE - SKATE RAMP - NEUSS.

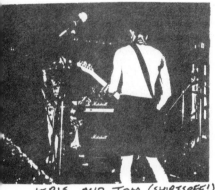

KRIS AND TOM (SHIRTSOFF!)

COUCH POTATOES LIVE IN BREMEN!

SLEIF, MILES + TOM AT 'THE STALL'

ADAM, DAN, KRIS, TOM, MILES - STRASBURG.

ADAM + DAVE AT LAST SHOW.

PSEUDO'S AT A TRUCK STOP.

some guy's flea-ridden pad to share with a dog and ten Germans having a 'party' with half a bottle of wine.

24/9 : It was Friday morning. We were awoken by a dog and offered boiled eggs, which Kris refused as he thought it was raw and part of some strange custom. I washed in a bathroom with a picture of the Pope holding a condom hanging on the wall, and then drove to Fratz's house in Regensburg. It was full of punks and we all ended up watching the tour video so far and indulging in Mars bar antics with a mad kitten.
After a short letching visit to town with some ginger haired student, we all drove to the Burglendenfeld Jugendzentrum and met our promoter Maia. She led us to the pottery that was to be our 'backstage' and fed us pasta with mushroom sauce and as much free beer as the band could handle, which believe me, was a lot!
Tonight's show was very well attended and went exceptionally well. The Toxic's were crap and broke many strings but the Pseudo's encouraged psychotic dancing. Thorsted, the Toxic's drummer, shouted "Look at their lungs, they are so splendid!" and tried to chat up the band, calling Adam a 'Bass God'.
"We don't need money, we are punk rock" exclaimed Fratz, as he threw another empty bottle over his shoulder. A bad party ensued in the pottery, where some idiot tried to rip us off for 100DM and Fratz with his mates "Smash many bottles, yes". There was very nearly a brawl, so after a rock 'n' roll sweep up we jumped in the beast to follow Maia back to her place. 'Her place' just happened to be hidden in the middle of the mountains, real 'Heidi' country, and when we got there Kris grabbed a bed and was assuming German 'beach towel' tendencies, demanding hot water, etc. "Not just hot, boiling. Y' know?" To be fair, I grabbed a big comfortable bed too - when in Rome. Miles, Adam, Tom and Danny ended up having to share two small single beds, sleeping head to toe, but everyone was glad at least to be in some king of 'bed'.

25/9 : I was in a dream. I woke up in a beautiful house, with panelled walls, oil paintings hanging everywhere, and wild flowers blooming outside. It was heaven. Then I heard Kris taking all the hot water in the shower, so I reluctantly had to get up. However, to my delight I soon found that it was worth it, as Maia had laid on a sumptious breakfast feast for us all. Fresh bread and cheese, cereals, tea and numerous other delicious, nutritious munchies, and then let us play with Gandhi, her pet dog. Unfortunately, we had to leave, so we left some money for her under a pillow and piled back into the van for the next leg of our arduous journey. We were right down near the Austrian and Czechoslovakian borders, but had to drive all the way across Germany to Offenburg on the French border. After yet another hellish road trip the six of us arrived at the Kessel club and met our promoters for the evening, Imund (who Miles later described as 'a total babe') and her boyfriend Steve (who he described as 'a speedo wearing afro'd wanker'). Both of them turned out to be really nice people as they provided us with the biggest pizzas we'd ever seen. There was five of them, each the size of a large coffee table.
We ventured inside the club to find it was like a large cavern and tunnel complex, covered in graffitti, mainly of large monster's heads. Making a hideous noise on the stage at that time were a bunch of talentless crusties called Ugly Noise Kick. They were sweating a lot and playing shite, sounding like Napalm Death, so they really lived up to their name, but at least they'd brought some equipment.
Fortunately for us, we'd arrived in town at just the right time, as there was a huge wine festival going on - it was like something straight out of National Lampoon's European Vacation. There were hundreds of people just milling about, getting drunk

and listening to bad local bands. Also, the world's biggest frying pans filled to the brim with sauerkraut and giant brockwurst. Tom bought some wine and we met some locals wearing orange trousers, before posting our postcards into a dirtbox (for dog poop!) which we thought was a postbox.

By the time we returned to the Kessel it was packed, and the floor was covered in peanuts. The sound engineer was going to record the show for us, and it went pretty well, with all the young skate kids in Bad Religion shirts dancing wildly. We were offered places to sleep for the night at the club, but it was pitch black when the lights cut out and people fell over each other in the dark looking for couches to sleep on for the night. Tom and Dan treated us to a drunken rendition of 'Blue Moon' before we retired to the bunks in the truck to try to sleep under what must've been the loudest bells in Germany. Then it started to rain really hard!

NB : Some useful phrases when in Germany
'Prost' - Cheers.
'How wreck die schiesa' - We knock back the shit.
'Armaisenbeer' - Anteater. (You have no idea how long it took to find out this one!)
'Erdvaken' - Aardvark.
'Buschvalen' - Busdriver.
'Fisch / Kartoffel / Mongo Kopft' - Fish / Potato / Mong head.
'Ein Vixen' - A wank.
'Du bist eine lusha' - You are a pansy.
'Krankenhousen' - Hospital.
'Mein elephantan' - My elephant.

26/9 : The bells woke us early and we had a hearty breakfast of 'smacks' before visiting the local swimming baths. It was crammed full of rather hirsuit Germans in briefs - not a very pleasant sight! One very fat boy insisted on diving from the creaking springboard and creating tidal waves over us. "He likes his diving board, does fat boy" said Danny. Adam lost his locker key, but Imund found it by searching the whole pool underwater. In return for this good deed, Steve, her boyfriend, spent ages sucking her toes and wearing his speedos. We wanted to use the toilets, but they all had queues and glass doors! So instead we went on to an Italian restaurant to use their's and eat a lunch consisting of pommes mit spag bog mit pizzas.

In the afternoon we drove to Strasburg, in France, to check out the old town. The border was the Rhine, but crossing was easy as they'd thought to build a bridge. At first, we parked behind a shiny new, bright red car, but then we noticed that it had been broken into and had it's radio stolen, so we decided to move to a pavement down by the river. We visited the cathedral and stole some postcards again before stopping to talk to a Bulgarian photographer who was trying to sell his wares in the street. I went to practice my French and was ripped off twice in as many minutes, first by a tramp and then at an ice cream stall. I'd had enough of France for one day!

We drove back into Germany and right across it again, stopping at Heilbonn for a chinese at the Phuq-Wah, where we were not allowed to stay and sit, so we ate our meal in the truck. Then we pressed on to the outskirts of Nurnburg where we slept in the truck in a lay-by that turned out to be a runway for trucks onto the motorway. It was very noisy, so to put us to sleep we told jokes and swapped trivia; for instance : "What's brown and sticky? - A stick!", "St. John's Wood is the only station on Network South East not in mackerel", and "Brass Monkeys came from cold ships cannon balls".

27/9 : We were woken up by a huge, smelly juggernaut hurtling past, just missing us by inches, and Tom going on about the Grim Reaper and how in Eastern Europe they put sickles over their bodies. Dan was comparing the tour to being trapped in hell, with Isleif as the devil, and the rest of us were searching for clean clothes. There was an acorn fight, during which Tom got hit in the nuts - now he had three! Then we departed for St. Peter's in the centre of Nurnburg.

After being thrown out of yet another garage, we eventually found our next venue, the Kunst Verein, which, Adam informed us, apparently meant 'open sewer'. There was no-one here to meet us yet, so we parked outside Sexy World and went shopping, ending up at Burger King. Miles went into one of the towns numerous bakeries, (every shop in Germany is either a bakery or a chemist) where an attractive young lady behind the counter decided to serve him before the massive queue that was waiting. "She obviously fancied me!"

When we returned to the Kunst Verein it was packed. We met 'Regurgitated', the local support band who had played a 'Chain Of Strength' cover. Then 'Couch Potatoes' played, with Miles on vocals, for the first time ever. Pseudo Hippies rocked out, having to play three encores! It was like a new Nurnburg Rally - all the records were sold out and we only had four shirts left. I had an argument with some old trout outside, about the noise. She threatened to call the police, so we told her "Your anteater is a bus driver" and other such meaningless drivel, before following Thorsten, the Regurgitated drummer, back to his house. Miles and I played some of Thorsten's numerous record collection, including 7 seconds, Born Against, Citizens Arrest and S.F.A., whilst everyone else got drunk and stoned. Tom, Dan and Kris fell into the shower, ripping down the curtain and shelves in the process, and then Dan threw Miles's bed at him before everyone fell asleep on mattresses in Regurgitated's practice room.

28/9 : We woke at elevenish, showered and ate breakfast on our mattresses, listening to Quicksand with Thorsten and Ollie. They showed us some great books, one on the DC scene and Dischord, with some excellent pictures. They were diamond geezers and BMXers, but unfortunately we had to leave for Reutlingen, stopping only at a spar to find it closed, but with crates and crates of beer outside! Very unwise.

The journey took ages and it rained all the way. The venue was another youth club covered in graffitti, called the Bastille. We arrived at about 6.00 pm to find it full of '85 style breakdancers, wearing kneepads and helmets, and asking "Do you still go to the Hippodrome to breakdance?". Miles, who was under the impression that we had arrived in some deprived Eastern European country where time had stood still since the early '80's, tried to sell them his Public Enemy shirt for the equivalent of £20, but they weren't having it, and supplied him with enough wood to build many a cabinet. After eating a rather unpleasant meal of vegetable rice and stew, we relaxed by playing pool for a while before meeting the support bands. Herb Garden - a bunch of idiots from Bristol, I think, and a French band, whose name I can't remember. After throwing rolled up bits of paper at these, Couch Potatoes played, followed by Pseudo Hippies. I hassled about 200 DM from the promoter and we left hurriedly. It was still raining. We stopped briefly in Stuttgart for essential supplies and then drove on for about five more hours to sleep in a garage just south of Kassel, where they sold wild banana and safe surfer condoms.

29/9 : Fortunately, the Beast had not turned into an arc overnight and we woke to find ourselves on a building sight at the back of a garage in bright sunshine. We washed in the toilets and headed towards Hannover. The autobahns were busy and treacherous and on the way we passed a smashed up Porsche 928. (All you see on the roads in

Germany are Mercedes, Beemers, Audis, Volkswagons, Porsches and 18 wheelers. There is no upper speed limit, so to see mangling crashes is not unusual, and, occasionally, a 'Pony' will pass and leave the road shimmering like a ball-bearing. We went to the town centre for dinner and visited Musicland where Adam bought All's 'Shreen' and Miles bought 108's 'Holy Name' LP for only £3.00! Crazy value! Then we all drove to the Flohtzircus to see Shelter, supported by W.W.K., a Czechoslovakian band who broke a lot of strings and spoke pidgeon English (but yes, that is better than I can speak Czech). Miles and I met the band and talked to Ray and Porcell, trying to persuade them to come to the UK to play a few gigs. Then we interviewed Porcell for BHP (featured in issue six) and went to see the show. Shelter started with Krishna chanting and dancing and then played an amazing set to a packed audience. Tom and Dan seemed more interested in the barmaids, and when Ray Cappo tried to sell his book to 'the kids', Tom went over and had a standing argument with him. Just as it was about to come to blows, we broke it up and left. Apparently our pal Rich, from A.W.A. was at the show too but I didn't see him.

After the gig, Isleif arrived in an old, yellow Fiat to lead us back to his house in Springe. We were low on petrol, so on the way we stopped at a garage to fill up. We piled back in and drove onwards for about five yards, only to find that Isleif lived right here and his door was on the forecourt.

Isleif's house is the most 'punk' place that I have ever been in my life. It was covered with literally hundreds of records, videos, posters, creepy crawlies, and not a CD in sight! In the bathroom alone he had tour posters by Gorilla Biscuits and Bad Religion, and a 'Married With Children' poster above hundereds of HC zines. We fell asleep in his front room, listening to the melodies of some french '77 punk band.

30/9 : We didn't wake up until that afternoon, and then tried to shower but had trouble with the taps. We spent most of the day examining Isleif's extensive record collection and listening to 'Friend' and 'Where'd ya go' by Samiam from the 'Time For Change' compilation, and only ventured out to town briefly for a snack. We saw a few nazis, but they ran away. In the evening we went to a party with the people from Zap and Plastic Population zine, where an annoying blonde geezer told us "You are not punks because you do not have green mohicans." Kris got very drunk, but despite this both Pseudo Hippies and Couch Potatoes answered interviews.

1/10 : We'd slept in Isleif's front room again and were woken, at about lunchtime, by two of his rather neanderthal friends arriving to play East German thrash. One of them, who was a fat geezer called '76' because he'd met Sid Vicious, seemed to be eating all the food in the house. So we decided to blow the last of our money on a 'sit down' Chinese for lunch - it was delicious! Late that afternoon, we drove to the Nasty Vinyl headquarters to meet up with Krapfe and Hohne and have a party. Krapfe runs a funeral parlour and gravestone engraving business I think, but anyway, his house was made of marble and he seemed incredibly rich. He had shelves and shelves of records and was a pretty cool guy. We drove out to the Pissed Spitzels practice rooms for a 'jam type gig'. It was a small basement in a desolate farmhouse with a couple of amps. Pissed Spitzels played a few terrible rackets, Couch Potatoes played 'Why' and 'Then I Kissed Her' and the Pseudo's only managed a few before deciding that they were too drunk to play anymore and escaping to a closet full of pickles, with Matze, who had just arrived. We went back to Krapfe's for more partying and to watch most of Kris's tour video. Miles and I grabbed beds in a spare room and fell asleep after discovering Krapfe's collection of 1970's pornographic magazines specialising in 'the larger woman' and watching some cheesy '70's film in German.

<u>2/10</u> : Krapfe woke us up early to feed us all breakfast and give us a few of the records that we were previously trying to blag off him from his mailorder office in the basement. He really was a 'diamond geezer'. We said our goodbyes and followed Matze to Bremen, stopping off at the Becks Brewery to see the largest amount of beer in the world, and then visiting a huge hypermarket to buy presents, chocolate milk and beer. Although Miles and I are both straightedge, there were now at least fourteen crates of beer in the truck, and numerous bottles of spirits, leaving hardly any room for the band or the gear. I myself had collected mainly bottles of Chocolate Milk to take home, and a few sweets.

The venue in Bremen, the Dipsomaniacs' home town, was massive. It had a huge PA and a soundboard with two engineers, lighting rig, smoke and a highly polished floor that we 'skated' on for some time. It was the last night of this triumphant tour and they were expecting a good turn out. We soundchecked quickly and went to check out the Bremen street festival. I annoyed a stallholder by asking how much his wasps were, as they buzzed around the sweets that he was actually trying to sell. There were all kinds of stalls, mainly selling sausages and sauerkraut, but some had bongs, BMX's and karaoke too.

Back at the venue we were fed sandwiches in the backstage rooms as the first band prepared to go on. They were called the Aldheim Strudel Experience and were dressing up as terrorists with guns and masks. This all seemed quite promising, but unfortunately they sounded like Napalm Death! Then Couch Potatoes, Pseudo Hippies, and Dipsomaniacs played. The Pseudo's joined the Dipso's on stage for the final song - it was hilarious. The hall was packed with 300 to 400 people and the whole show was filmed on video.

Afterwards, we all went to an 'all night pub' built in a railway station, to wish each other a fond farewell. We met Matze's girlfriend and a load of Dipso's friends before exchanging the very last Pseudo's shirt for a Dipso's one saying 'Don't take me serious when I'm delirious'. Miles and Isleif, the merchandisers extraordinaire, swore to become blood brothers by dawn. We had to leave by about 2.00 am, or we would miss the ferry back home. We still had a long drive ahead of us. It started to rain in the carpark as we said goodbye. The Dipsomaniacs were such great and crazy guys - I hope that I see them again soon. I drove all night through the rain and fog to reach the ferryport in Holland.

<u>3/10</u> : We reached Hoek van Holland at about 7.00 in the morning. The guys had all tried to sleep in the bunks, but the weather was terrible, about the worst I'd ever driven in, and so I don't think they were very refreshed. We parked at the port, in the wrong lane, and fell asleep until embarking at 11.00 am. The ferry sailed at 12 noon and we all said goodbye to the 'good fun continent'. The trip home was a long and rather uneventful one, playing cards and watching crap Dutch television shows in the lounge. There was a kind of dating game on, where people who'd been dumped pleaded with their ex-partners to have them back - it was cringeworthy. We also watched Journey to the centre of the earth.

We were delayed for at least an hour and didn't dock in blighty until 8.00 that evening. The beast had performed fine throughout the whole tour, the mileometer read 382,101 so we had covered over 3,000 miles, but now on the way home it developed a 'pinging' noise. We limped round the houses, dropping off Dan, Tom and Kris first, then Adam and finally Miles, until just before 11.00 pm I had the great pleasure of climbing into my own 'cuddly teddy bear patterned' bed and falling promptly into deep sleep. We had seen many of the freaky German tall people; travelled with them, and survived. A great adventure!

A CROATIAN'S VIEW OF CROATIA AT THE END OF 1993

You may not have heard anything about Croatia a few years ago, but now everyone at least knows of it's existance. This article will try to explain the situation in the Croatian underground, the country's political and social situation and the war.

All political power is in the hands of one party and, although Croatia is now a 'democratic state' (is it!?!), politically nothing really changed. It got even worse. We have a right-wing conservative government, in which the Catholic church plays a large part. The government constantly uses the war as a threat, a worse alternative. They say "If we stop this policy, the only thing we can expect is war" or "The situation is bad, but it's wartime" and so on. Trust me, people are fed up with the war. Whole generations had their childhood ruined, people can't act or think normally, life becomes so easily lost. Today you're here, tomorrow gone and you can't do a thing about it. People who were pacifists 'to the core' become soldiers after their houses are hit or families killed. It's pure survival - "To be or not to be". All those hypothetical questions people used to ask themselves, like "Would I kill a man..?" lose their sense in front of the brutal reality of war. Although the war is now, more or less, a thing of the past (I hope it remains so but things are not looking good!) it still affects the political and social climate in Croatia. These circumstances provide a perfect environment for the right-wing nationalist parties to grow. They are experiencing great success as ordinary people are forgetting how to think liberally. Left-wing organisations are pushed aside. Nobody has the guts to do anything like Jello Biafra did in the States. "These times are hard" people say. "Fools rule" and it's true.

Also, there's a problem with the youth. Besides alcohol and increasing drugs use, there's a problem which is, I believe, a classic syndrome of post-communist states. Most of the young people really believe in the 'American Dream' and are truly fascinated with the Capitalistic way of life.

I suppose that this shit seems really deep, but unfortunately the story doesn't end there. The social situation is apalling. An ordinary worker earns about 150 DEM a month, which is about 60 GBP. People don't buy records any more (This isn't a real problem as it's almost impossible to release anything). They need the money to buy bread and milk.

The economy has collapsed. Inflation, refugees, conservative government, war - Croatia today is hell.

The President of the State of Croatia - "The Father of the Country" - a typical example of the cult of personality and that "Big brother's watching you" syndrome.

Still, there are many people that keep our underground going. There are many good bands which deserve your attention. Personally, I like 'Nula' very much. They are a kind of anarcho-punkcore and sing their powerful lyrics in Croatian. If you're interested in anarcho bands there's 'Antitude' (good female vocalist) and 'Apatridi' (the oldest anarcho band in the country). Then we've got 'Antiotpad' (used to be HC, now more noisy), 'Why Stakla', 'Ha Det Bra' (both noise). 'Overflow' are a very popular band; they play melodic, poppy, simple hardcore. We've got really great punk bands like 'Kud Idijoti' (they're a real legend), they have EP's and LP's out and even managed to tour a few European countries. 'Hladno Pivo' are also a very good fun punk band. 'Abzznormalan' play NY style HC. 'Deafness by noise' are HC and finally my band 'My Life / My Dreams' play rough hardcore in the old way with some SE influences and a DIY point of view. If you like grind noise core, 'Patareni' are really great and well known throughout Europe. Of course there are (too) many metal bands but they only go underground when they have to.

We also have some really good fanzines: 'Zips & Chains' (8 issues out, punk stuff, great design, in English), 'Warhead' (11th issue out now, anarcho direction, one guy from 'Apatridi' does it), 'Glans Penissis' (5 issues out, a guy from 'Nula' writes it about the works of his band), 'Fecal Forces' (a good 'zine, always many non-music articles), 'Uurtanje Noznog Palca', 'United Blood', 'Ill in the head' and my 'zine 'Make a change' (3rd issue out now, written in Croatian but translated into English on bonus sheets) and more.

We have a few labels, like 'Bonaca' or 'Listen Loudest' but they release mainly tapes. Only 'T.R.I.P. Records' got some LP's out, but some people who were involved with their work were very disappointed in their bad attitude. I prefer small DIY labels like 'Fecal Forces Prod'.

Gigging in Croatia? Well, it's not good. People try hard to organise concerts but mostly for Croatian bands. Very few foreign bands play here (strange huh!), but I think that it's important that local bands get the chance to play live, so I guess it's not so bad.

Besides all this, there are some radio shows on small stations all over the country (I also have one). That pretty much describes the scene here.

As you can see, Croatia today is really fucked up. We've got all the 'usual' problems plus a terrifying war and the living standards of the third world. Sometimes every struggle for a better life seems hopeless, but there are lots of good people who carry on. People from Italy, Germany, etc have got some really good friends in Croatia.
So if you're interested in some other things about Croatia, it's scene, or 'something completely different', or you'd just like to have a friend in Croatia, feel free to write to me. Until then, take care of the people you love, yourself, and our earth. I wish all of you all the best.
Bye!

Sinisa Druzeta,
Jakova Volcica 6,
51400 Pazin,
Croatia.

1914: 'Gold' E.P. cassette-demo.
5 tracks of slowish indie style hardcore with well-sung vocals and heartfelt lyrics. I couldn't really get into this because the tape I got sounded a tad muffled, so lost quite a lot of impact. Still, slick playing, but a bit mellow for my tastes, yet I can see where they're coming from. Excellent presentation, full colour sleeve and that, would sound better live, I reckon. £2 ppd (cheques to D.Barton) from Daz Barton, 199 New Inn Lane, Trentham, Stoke-On-Trent, Staffs ST4 8PS. Fanzines and venues, please get in touch.

Not a lot of people know much about Portland. "oh, that's near Seattle, isn't it?" THEY say, and they're right because Portland lies on the northern edge of Oregon, a state the size of the U.K., about three or four hours drive from Seattle. Yep, the whole 'grunge' thing has rubbed off on Portland, but this city of around one million people still has a cool punk thing going.

It's worth saying a few things about the town itself. For a start, the place looks good. It's very clean, pretty and friendly, people seem to take a pride in their town, and they're hot on the recycling thing like cans, bottles and paper. It's easy to get around, too. With the streets laid out grid-fashion and separated into specific destricts, it's simple enough to know where you are, unless you're way out in the sticks maybe. There's a regular, efficient (and friendly) bus service, and there's the Max, a light railway tram-like thing. Prices are fair, but it's best to buy a pass or book of tickets, because you'll probably use the public transport frequently. Downtown, it's possible to get around on foot, and it's pleasant, uncrowded and clean. By the way, there are no direct flights to Portland from London, so you have to fly to Seattle or California and get a quick reconnecting flight.

So, let's talk about music. The best known Portland band is probably THE WIPERS. Apparently they're re-forming and will have a new LP out soon, they may even tour Europe with SALIVA TREE in tow?? POISON IDEA broke up a while back after a final show at the X-Ray Cafe, nobody I spoke to knows exactly what they're doing, but Thee Slayer Hippy does stacks of production work, and Pig Champion is gonna die soon coz he's a heroin addict and really fat (allegedly). RESIST were one of Portland's finest, fastest PC bands around, but they split-up too. The singer is now with DEPRIVED, but that's not Resist's original vocalist. 90 PROOF used to be called MULE and feature original P.I. members, I think. HAZEL are pretty big these days and have had a couple of Sub Pop releases, there's is a pretty lightweight but competent pop-punk. You've probably all heard of POND these days. GODLESS play raging hardcore with A.P.P.L.E style female vocals. I'm not sure if UNAMUSED are still going, but it's pretty fine, liki So Cal melodic punk. NERVOUS CHRISTIANS are called NIXON FLAT these days. ALCOHOLICS UNANIMOUS still continue to preach the non-straight life in their Brit-punk sounding hardcore. CRACKERBASH have a new 10" out, I would've gone and seen them, but the guy at the Satyricon wouldn't let me in on my fake "I'm over 21" I.D. IGNORAMUS MONKEY ANUS are now called COMRAD BANE, but that's all I know. Other worthy mentionables include GALAXIE TRIO (cheers for getting me in for free, lads!) who play the coolest surf instumentals, RANCID VAT, HITTING BIRTH, HELL COWS, NEW BAD THINGS, OSWALD FIVE-O, NAPALM BEACH and probably plenty more. Apparently, there are legions of sad metal bands and Sub Pop wannabees in Oregon, too!

Venues: The X-RAY CAFE is an all age, intimate, friendly place, scene of many an awesome show in the past. This is probably the best place to see bands, full of different kinds of people and the odd eank crank or two! LA LUNA used to be called The Pine Street Theater and can fit a thousand odd, it's all age and Resist and Deprived used to play there heaps. There may be other all age places, but there's plenty of 21+ clubs like SATYRICON or BELMONT'S INN. Out of town, or on Broadway, there's those big places where the corporate rock people play.

Record Shops: 2nd Avenue Records has a fine alternative, indie, and hardcore section. Lots of vinyl at good prices, plenty of CDs, stickers, t-shirts, too. Ozone not only sells CDs, 7"s (good selection) and new/used vinyl, but does piercing and has great jewelery and t-shirts. Django is a cool second-hand record, tape and CD store, with posters too. On S.E. Hawthorne, check out Roundhouse and a couple of good second hand shops, including Rip City with possibly the tackiest selection of vinyl, all at one buck, and millions (literally) of records to hunt through. And there are other stores to see, I'm sure.

Miscellaneous: Portland has a cool comic shop, a fairly decent large Army Surplas store across Burnside Bridge, a skate-park under this bridge, and plenty of shops for whatever you need. There's a few tattoo parlours, one of the biggest book stores in the U.S. and even a 24 Hour Church of Elvis (don't ask!). Portland has museums, art galleries, fountains, squares and plenty of bridges!

Food: You can't go hungry here! If you're an ardent meat-eater, there are plenty of McMurderers around of course, but anyone with a conscience knows they suck. So, for us veggies, pizza is always a good deal, tasty big slices for around $1.25 to $1.65. Mexican is popular, Taco Bell is really only out of town, but the food is surprisingly good, bean burritos for a mere 70 cents! Coffee is a major thing in the North West, There's coffee shops everywhere, and they're good, too. If you do miss your cuppa too

much, then pay rip-off prices at the 'English Tea Garden'. Plaid Pantry open all night so do some supermarkets. Subway do reasonable sandwiches at fair prices.

Many bars do food too, I guess, but don't forget you need proof that you're over 21 to be let in.

Portland is a cool town, friendly, not too commercial and easy to get around. The hospitality I experienced there was pretty amazing. Yes, it's got a crime problem what with gangs and pigs with guns, but it's safe compared to many other U.S. cities (I think).

I've got to say a big thankyou to Serra and Jake for putting up with me for two weeks. Also hi to Jones (and the rest of RCK!!!), Scott, Warren and Nancy, and Paul Curran again!! Hi to Chris and Brian too, that Stupids 7" is awesome!

** HITTING BIRTH, NEUROSIS, 7 YEAR BITCH, GOD & TEXAS, HYPERLUNG
at the La Luna club, Portland, oregon, USA. 24/9/93

A pretty good bill for a mere 5 bucks! The La Luna is a 1000 strong venue and tonight has a certain atmosphere that differs from UK shows. HYPERLUNG warm things up playing an industrial noisy set pretty proficiently, mainly livened up by drunk mohawked punks throwing those luminous necklace things around. GOD AND TEXAS are a three-piece, later joined by a saxophonist, who play start/stop, heavy and pretty tame paced hardcore. But they have a real energy and enough of an interesting sound, so aren't boring in the least. 7 YEAR BITCH really warm things up, it's that Seattle grunge sound, no denying, but don't hold it against them; they play with a passion and look like they're having fun, at the same time really trying to say something. NEUROSIS are the most awesome tonight. This San Francisco 5-piece mix a number of styles and have 3 LPs of different styles: hardcore-punk, 'grind-core', metal... It's all here tonight as well as some of the coolest visuals ever, plus an intensity and power so many bands lack. Even 8 minute songs don't pall due to their amazing energy and atmosphere. Worth the $5 alone! Headliners HITTING BIRTH are a popular Portland outfit, but strike me as a tad disappointing. A few years back their line up was different, and their sound less generic, apparently. They are certainly theatrical and atmospheric, but the slowed-down Ministry type sound and warped vocals with an almost 'rave' style tribal beat, fails to excite after a while...but I've seen worse, and overall this was a cheap, if tiring, night of pleasure.

** SHATNERS, GALAXIE TRIO, NE'ER DO WELLS
at the X-Ray Cafe, Portland, Oregon, USA. 26/9/93

The X-Ray is a small all-age alcohol-free club in downtown Portland. It's friendly atmosphere, varied clientele and intimacy made for a fun night. Hi to all the cool people who befriended this weird English guy, and a special hello to Paul Curran! The NE'ER DO WELLS have a new 7" on Lookout!, but this ain't no pop-punk for a change, these guys have a trad garage sound in the Headcoats/Milkshakes kind of way, but with a fair supply of pop for good measure. It works better than on the split CD with Judy & The Loadies, the live sound always enhances garage.
GALAXIE TRIO were pretty awesome, a three piece surf-instrumental band in the vain of Shadowy Men, but with a certain rawness, youth and energy often lacking in this genre of music.
The SHATNERS...yep, these guys are a Star Trek obsessed three-piece, or were they just the Ne'er do Wells in disguise? Beaming down from another galaxy, they entertain us playing fun garage trash and instrumentals, like 'Green Bloodied Love', about a certain Mr. Spock undoubtedly. Most illogical, but nonetheless an entertaining evening, Captain.

** TILT 'Play Cell' LP (Lookout!)
I thought Tilt's first 7" was cool, and didn't know whether a whole LP would be that effective. This is a 14 track record in pretty much the same vein, a sound that fuses Green Day and Crimpshrine/15 except with cool female vocals. This LP has a very 'rock' sound, really, but enough of an edge and rawness to stop it from becoming too dreary. It's a real grower, the songs are short, catchy and often pretty intelligent. Worth checking out, and on Lookout! of course. Contains 2 tracks from the EP, too.

** Sinister Six 'Outta Sight!' LP (Empty)
Wow, this funky looking LP has a cool cover and cool writing. It not only looks good, but this band fucking rule. This is fast, raw garage punk played like it should be...rougher than the Supersuckers, rawer than The New Bomb Turks, tracks like 'Go Away' totally shred and they must be the biz live. Rivals the 'Turks and Rancid for LP of the year.

How To Stop Cruelty To Animals

What do you do if you see, hear or know of someone being cruel to animals?

First of all, keep calm. Remember if you are going to help stop an act of cruelty, you will need to keep your wits about you.

You may be able to stop someone from being cruel to an animal by acting immediately. But use your discretion; the person acting cruelly may turn on you if you interfere. You can help the RSPCA simply by trying to gather useful information at the time of the incident. This will greatly help their investigation and may provide vital evidence which may result in a prosecution. If, for example, you have a camera to hand, then use it. Photographs showing the cruelty can be very useful to the RSPCA. When you think that you have done all you can, then immediately phone your local RSPCA Group Communication Centre (number in the telephone directory).

You should be ready to give the following information, if it is appropriate to the individual case :-

1. Your own name, address and telephone number. This is necessary for record purposes and also enables the RSPCA inspector to tell you about the result of their investigation. Please note: It is RSPCA policy to treat all complaints in the strictest confidence. Your name would not be divulged without your permission.

2. The name(s) and address(es) of the person(s) involved, if known.

3. The date, time and place of the offence.

4. The names and addresses of any witnesses.

5. The registration number and description of any vehicle involved.

6. State whether you would be prepared to testify in a court of law if it becomes necessary.

You will also be asked to give a detailed description of what you saw or heard. You may have been upset by what you have seen, but please try and be as calm and factual as possible. You will be more likely then to remember everything that happened.

Remember, you can make a difference. Thousands of RSPCA prosecutions each year come about as a direct result of public action.

** **APHEX TWIN:** 'Selected Ambient Works Volume II (Triple LP, Warp Records)

At last it's here, and if you thought Vol.I was mellow, wait till you hear this! A triple LP set, on brown vinyl, no song titles, merely black and white photos of odd things to represent the tracks. It's a very ambient collection, similar to the first volume (a masterpiece, I swear), but it's less percussive, usually just sounds with the faintest rhythms underneath. Atmospheric, and rather 'haunting' and sparse in places. Beautifully presented and more 'Eno' than 'techno', old-style ambience here. A three LP set may be a little too much to take in, it requires a lot of listening till the tracks settle in your mind...but that's probably not the point. Certainly interesting, if over-long, and at some points it almost matches the magic of Volume I.

BOB TILTON: 7"E.P.

Wow! I've listened to this four track EP over and over, and it's still awesome. One of the best things I've heard for ages. Powerful, passionate, intense hardcore, nifty tempo changes, sometimes raging, always atmospheric. Brilliant musicianship, wonderful lyrics. Just get hold of this gem, or miss out on one of the U.K.'s finest bands. I can't find fault with anything here, it's even beautifully presented in a kind of Gravity Records kind of way (thick paper, prints etc.). The etching on the vinyl says "Not punk enough for MRR?" Bullshit! <u>Too</u> damn punk for MRR if you ask me. Bob Tilton contain ex-Downfall members.

REFUSE: demo cassette.

This young band is straight outta Salem, Oregon. This is a quality demo tape of fast grindy hardcore, and kind of reminds me of a more melodic Doom (?), but a bit more sloppy in places. Speedy, raw, energetic stuff, ▬▬▬▬▬▬ and some great vocals... they even sample 'Braindead'! Cool. Three I.R.C.'s to: Mat, 363 Monmouth Street, Independence, OR. 97351, U.S.A., and they'll probably dub you a copy, if they're sober enough! Drink positive!

'LIFE AFTER BIRTH' Short stories by Stan Batcow, £1.50 A5 size, illustrated.

A collection of short-stories often pretty damn sinister, with good, just as disturbing, illustrations. I like this a lot. Worthwhile checking out. Stanzine Publications, 130 Common Edge Road, Blackpool FY4 5AZ.

4 PAST MIDNIGHT: 'Midnight Escapades' cassette LP.

A really fine punk tape LP here. Quality fast anarcho-punk, full of energy and pretty anthemic in places. Kinda reminds me of Conflict merging with Leatherface (?), with its gruff vocals but still rather melodic through it all. Yeah, this is good stuff. £3 (w. lyric sheet) or $6 if your reading this abroad, from Peter McCartney, 23 Abercrombie Crescent, Bargeddie, Glasgow G69 7SR, Scotland.

NUX VOM: cassette LP

A very experimental thing indeed, sampling merges with dischordant noises and rythms. Dub bass and kind of 'techno' beats on some tracks, really lo-fi stuff overall. Sometimes the vocals remind me of Mark E Smith, but mainly I get the impression of a sort of 'primeval', more experimental (early) Sebadoh, with personal lyrics and feelings. The whole thing is pretty weird but nevertheless interesting. I guess you should contact Dave Frampton, 5 Rose Walk, Purley, Surrey CR8 3LJ for more info.

VINDICTIVES: 'Party Time For Assholes' double 10" (Selfless Records)

Often criminally overlooked, the Vindictives are back with this excellent release. Not only do you get a great 10", but you get an extra, really limited, additional 10" entirely composed of cover-versions. This special double-pack may be pretty tough (and expensive) to find, so even if you can only get a hold of the single 10" it's well worth it. The original is all covers too, I think. The Vindictives have a classic snotty obnoxious punk sound, with snottier vocals even than The Queers or Screeching Weasel. The music takes its inspiration from these bands and Ramones, of course, but with a character of its own and its really well produced too. Check out great versions of 'Wonderful World', 'If She Knew What She Wants', 'Turning Japanese', 'Magic Moments', 'Strychnine' and 'Bang Shang A Lang' amongst

THE MUMMIES / JAKE VEGAS / CB BEAUMONT (Powerhaus, London 11/4/94)

CB BEAUMONT are a trio who play quality garage / surf instrumentals. They're very slick, but not varied enough: they need a raw punk vocalist, or at least more of a surf-guitar feel!

JAKE VEGAS are a nine-piece r'n'b / jazzy / blues (whatever) band with a charismatic vocalist and bass-man. A couple of their tracks are okay, but it lapses into self-indulgence eventually, over-long songs, the same dull riffs, and it seems more like a jam-session than anything constructed.

THE MUMMIES are stars. They split a while back but have re-formed and toured Europe. This is their first visit to the U.K., and tonight the Powerhaus is positively jam-packed. In case you don't know, these California boys play dirty, raw, distinctive garage-punk, sort of Billy Childish influenced, but rougher and punker... and they dress up in mummies costumes, all bandages and that! Their's is a wild live show, a real event. They have excellent stage-presence and heaps of energy, playing both familiar favourites and newer stuff. And we love it! It's just <u>so</u> entertaining! Tonight had the makings of an historic event, and I felt proud to have seen one of the greatest garage acts ever in the flesh. It's ashame the distinctiveness vocally and lo-fi sound didn't come across as well as it does on vinyl, but tonight we experienced The Mummies at their trashiest and back-to-basics punk best. Fun!

'RIOT' #7, A4 zine, 65p (£1 ppd – well-concealed cash)

Excellent stuff here again from Joe. An impressive 32 pages of readable, sometimes brilliant, interviews with the likes of Health Hazard, Econochrist, Drop Dead, Chris Dodge, Dead Wrong and more, extensive reviews, very nicely presented, ie. very slick looking, but I'd like to see more views, columns, opinions, articles etc. coz it all seems a bit too 'formulaic' overall, but Joe <u>wants</u> more columns and stuff, and it seems 'Riot' is, and will, go from strength to strength. Highly recommended. 21 Ebnal Road, Shrewsbury, Shropshire SY2 6PW.

GUSSET #1, A5 fanzine, 40p
Interviews with Mega City 4, Decadence Within, Oi Polloi, Blind Mole Rat (?). Interesting piece on the Welling Demo. Usual reviews (live and recorded), some funny piss-take stuff and an article on 'cool'. Pretty good for a first issue, but this doesn't excite in the least.
GUSSET #2, A5 fanzine, 40p
A better issue containing interviews with the likes of Couch Potatoes, Citizen Fish, Die Cheerleader, Black Train Jack and AOS 3. Lotsa reviews, good stuff on AFA, periods (sic), Riot Grrrl, Government. Funny stuff like '35 Things Virtually Everyone Is Guilty Of Doing...' Recommended.
** both available from Dawn, 63 Russell Road, Mosely, Birmingham B13 8RB, or Charlotte, 18 Addison Road, King's Heath, Birmingham B14 7EW.

'LOVE & HATE: LIFE & DEATH; WHAT'S THE DIFFERENCE?' poetry mini-zine.
A mini-zine of poetry, personal and despairing. One can't analyze poetry in a fuckin' review, so if you enjoy poetry I'd recommend this, or even if you don't. Who knows? Some will hate, others will love. You can only try. Contact Stan, c/o 130 Common Edge Road, Blackpool FY4 5AZ.

English Dogs / Monkey Jungle - Cassette sampler
Some of the English Dogs stuff is a bit hit and miss, a few too many wanky guitar solos in places, but a couple of tracks stand out. A fine mix of trad sounding (Lazy Cowgirls, Dead Boys) with more metally stuff. On the other hand, Monkey Jungle are a truly appalling metal band mixing Soundgarden, Pearl Jam, Alice in Chains... need I go on? Contact : G. Butt, 23 Henry Street, Peterborough, Cambs. PE1 2QG.

'EARFUL' -- a collection of short-stories (zine).
A mini-zine containing a number of short stories / prose pieces. It makes for fascinating reading; varied styles are evident from blunt 'in-yer-face' stuff, to poetic, descriptive pieces. A big thumbs-up from me... there ought to be more of this kind of stuff around. Please order it, it's only one little stamp to: Bridget Prince, 23 The Embankment, Bedford MK40 3PD, U.K.

Hormone Frenzy - A5 'zine - 50p
A queer 'zine containing some interesting opinions and articles, stuff about God is my co-pilot, fifth column, comics, 'rantings', etc. This has a point to make and makes it well. Contact : P.O. Box 361, Cambridge, CB1 2BZ. Recommended.

NFi 'Surf Metal' cassette.
A French band singing in English yet again '(It's Never) Too Late' is slightly metally but kinda poppy punk, too. 'Like it Loud' has pretty crappy words but it's a good tune, a bit like Bad Religion with similar (and way too many) B.R. style geeetar solos. 'Just Passin' By' reminds me of Monsula (?) for some reason. It's alright, this. Contact: Brasselet Fred, 9 Rue Dauphin, 94800 Villejuif, France.

'PROTOTYPE' #8, A5 fanzine, 40p
Far bigger than the usual lose-leaf Prototype zines of the past. An intelligent zine, stuff on Cyberpunk and Karl Koch, author William Gibson (of 'Neuromancer' fame), lots of contacts listed and info and an extensive reviews section. This is certainly excellent as far as underground communications go, and will improve in future issues with your support. Contact: 79 Waterloo Road, Dublin 4, Ireland.

'TRINKETS & BAUBLES' #2, A5 fanzine, £1 (?!)
One quid?! But it's got glossy pages and a very professional look about it. Articles rather than question and answer interviews (I like that) on Nirvana (the band you hate to love), Madder Rose, Mudhoney, Drop Nineteens etc. Interviews with The Wildhearts and Die Cheerleader. Live reviews of Pearl Jam and others, LP and single reviews (mainly popular stuff). Mmmm.... although pretty mainstream, this is surprisingly readable. But one quid!? Contact 18 Gays Road, Hanham, Bristol BS15 3JS. Good quality photos, I liked the more 'punk' stuff like the bit on Johnny Thunders.

'ARNIE' #6, A4 zine, 40p
A new issue of what's possibly the best U.K. zine around. There's interviews with Conflict and Excrement of War, great cartoons and artwork by Simon (this guy is great!), and a thorough review section, plus a few columns and piss-take reports. All in all, another good issue with a good sense of humour throughout. Buy this for 40p and a first-class stamp ($2 elsewhwere) from 16 Palairet Close, Bradford On Avon, Wiltshire BA15 1US.

Escape from the planet of the apes - Book & Record set
This is fun! You play the record and read the comic at the same time, it even beeps when it's time to turn the page! This is so cheesey it's untrue and there's some wonderful opportunities for sampling here too. Dates back to 1974 I think. Power Records, 145 Komorn Street, Newark, NJ 07105, USA. (As if you're going to order it!)

Once the game is over, the king and pawn go back into the same box.
                                                                                Italian Proverb

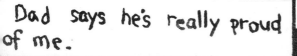

Dad says he's really proud of me.

BHP

He says he's going to take me to the lab some day.

Test Subject #23

06:00   Subject dosed, GGv 350 mm. Subject exposed to temperatures below 32°.
        Readings in normal range. Note: Deviance from earlier test subjects; #23
        is two years younger.

10:00   Subject react... When I'm older... twitches, loss of moto-
        skills, incont...

14:00   Subject begins... ...ained. EEG spiking.
        Subject weak and nonresponsive.

17:34   Subject comatose. Electric shock treatment ineffective. Additional 200
        mm. dosage ineffective.

20:00   Subject terminated by lethal injection. All results inconclusive.

8

BHP - Issue 8 - Early 1995.

Welcome to the latest BHP, and no, I will not tell you what it stands for, it keeps changing, so make your own mind up and send them in. After a little hard work, and months of change in the HC scene, it's here at last. Thank you for reading, and I hope you enjoy it.

Green Day have risen to ultra-stardom and many other 'punk' bands have signed to majors; Samiam, Shudder To Think, Quicksand, All, Big Drill Car, Jawbreaker and Rancid, who I'm told are now even hosting MTV shows. Everyone has there own views on this, and how it affects the predominantly independent and DIY hardcore scene. Most bands would like their music to reach as many people as possible, and most would like to be able to make a living from it. Whether the media can influence the ideals of a whole genre depends on the individuals. It was the DIY and independent underground that helped these bands get where they are, and it is that same scene that will provide us with new bands, magazines and ideas.

Thanks to everyone for their help on this issue, especially Dan and Steve. Please write to us and send reviews, articles, interviews, trades, contributions, anything to :
BHP, 1 Chandos Road, Tunbridge Wells, Kent, TN1 2NY, UK.

QUESTION : How do you get your band on a 7" EP?
ANSWER : Write to 'Get The Gimp' Records at BHP!
We get sent loads of good demo's by bands that never get to hear themselves on vinyl. Whether it's because of lack of contacts, or money, or whatever. It can be very difficult to get a young punk band on vinyl, and then get quality promotion. So BHP are going to try something, and see if people are interested.
'Get The Gimp' is going to be our record label. It will feature releases by both well known and unknown bands, and promote them all equally. We're just going to put out 7" EP's to start with, signing a few bands that we like, and encouraging bands to write to us. Basically, as everyone knows, putting out records costs a lot of money. We do have quite a sum to invest in the label, and all the printing and promotional contacts. We propose to release compilation EP's and split the costs and the products between the label and the bands. For example, if a 7" EP, featuring four bands costs £500 to press 500 copies, the four bands and the label would each pay £100 and receive 100 copies. The bands can sell their copies to recoup their costs and the label will use the rest for promotion in 'zines, on the radio, etc.
Any bands interested should write, enclosing band information and a tape, if possible, to 'Get The Gimp' at BHP, 1 Chandos Road, Tunbridge Wells, Kent, TN1 2NY, UK.
DIY - Support the underground!

? HOW

The first person to write in and tell us what song is depicted by the artwork on the back cover will win themselves the CD!
BHP #9 out soon. Stay punk!

FAT ?

This Is... PUNK-O-RAMA
TEN FOOT POLE
WAYNE KRAMER
BAD RELIGION
CD/CS/LP
PENNYWISE
SNF
TOTAL CHAOS
GAS HUFFER
DOWN BY LAW
NOFX
RANCID
OFFSPRING

Down By Law

This interview with Dave Smalley, singer of Down By Law, took place on the hottest night of the year, between 12.30am and 3.00am. It started in the backstage room of 'The Concorde', where their first UK gig of 1994 had just taken place, continued in my car and ended in the kitchen of the house that Down By Law were staying at in Brighton. The gig had been awesome and although Dave was very tired he still had all the time in the world for this interview...

BHP : So how are you and how's the tour going?

Dave : The tour has been going really great. Germany sucks for melodic, powerful bands; they love Biohazard! But Italy, France, Belgium, Austria, the UK, and everywhere has been brilliant. And I am fine, thank you.

BHP : What happened to Pat Hoed and Mark Phillips, bassist and guitarist from the last tour?

Dave : Pat was really getting into death-metal, seriously! He is now a roadie for Sepultura. So we talked about it and I really wanted everyone to be on the same wavelength musically. But he is great and we are still dear friends. Mark was not the person we thought he was, and he wasn't true to the ideals we all share... You find things out on tour and luckily we found out in time.

punkrockacademyfightsong

BHP : The new album, your third LP on Epitaph, seems to be punker, back to the old styles. Is this your direction?

Dave : 'Blue' was a really emotional LP and with 'Punkrockacademyfightsong' we wanted to show the young punks how it's done! We all share a love of HC and early English and American punk, and this LP really is true to our souls and our origins. And it was a blast to make!

BHP : What do you think of the huge success of Rancid and other new punk bands, and looking at some of your lyrics, is the US scene plagued with bad dance and grunge bands?

Dave : Rancid rules! Grunge sucks - see the lyrics to 'Haircut'. Bad dance - death before disco! See the lyrics to 'Drummin Dave'.

BHP : How did you get to record at A&M studios?

Dave : Last year A&M asked us to sign to them, but we didn't. Then they offered us a chance to record for free in their studios and we could keep the tape and do what we liked with it. So we went in and it's absolutely incredible, huge, ultra-modern, beautiful, like a musician's dream come true! A&M gave us a producer who asked us to bring in some of the music that we liked to give him an idea where we were coming from. I took a few LP's including Sugar, the Clash, Husker Du, etc. He was looking through them, then stopped and said "The Clash, I think I've heard of them", so we left after five days and laughed, but the engineer for the session, Mike Douglass, was brilliant and we liked him. So we asked him to produce the new LP for us and he said only if you record at A&M, so we did and he got us a very good cost. The Rolling Stones were working in the studio next door. During the recording of '1944' we had trouble getting the right guitar sound so Mike said "Turn everything on the amp up to ten!" and the Rolling Stones phoned through to complain! We once bumped into Keith Richards in the corridoor. He thought we were the scruffiest punks in the world, so we thanked him on the sleeve! And the LP came out really great - just how we heard it in our heads... I think!

BHP : You said in an interview when 'Blue' came out that "Down By Law is like a return to the love of music." Do you still feel that? Will you ever get bored and give up?

Dave : I think Down By Law is a special band that's very emotional and the spirit of the band is one of hope and a desire to change the world. Everyone who has played in the band, even when it was a project, really shared the ideals, and those ideals are worth fighting for, and I believe in them, so you're stuck with us for a bit!

BHP : What do you do when you're not playing? Are you writing a book, running a record label, etc?

Dave : Things we <u>don't</u> do : Ski, chase girls, hang out with boring people! I read a lot, right now it's 'Rotten : No Irish, No Blacks, No Dogs', the biography of John Lydon. We write music all day, and answer tons of mail. We're pretty normal - films, parties, museums - my wife Caroline is extremely knowledgeable about art and I've learned a lot from her.

BHP : Has Hunter, Down By Law's drummer and skater, got any new skate tricks? Don't you worry about him busting an arm?

Dave : I worry a bit, I don't think he does. "If it happens, it happens", but we are all really into the skate mentality. It's true freedom, you just do it!

BHP : Do you prefer 'Nesquick' or 'Crusha'?

Dave : Nesquick is God-like, but I've never heard of Crusha. They have good milkshakes in Germany.

BHP : Do you like Thin Lizzy?

Dave : I don't really know a lot of Thin Lizzy but I have many friends who worship them - Dave Naz (ex-Down By Law and Chemical People) for one, Brian Baker (ex-Dagnasty) also likes them - if they're Irish then they're great with me, I'm part Irish.

BHP : Do you still keep in touch with Brian?

Dave : We are still friends. He is currently working on a new project with Tommy Stinson who was in the Replacements.

BHP : Do you like the Replacements? Have you heard the Paul Westerburg LP?

Dave : I prefer the earlier stuff. 'Answering Machine' from 'Let It Be' is one of the most emotional songs ever. Caroline and I have Paul's LP, but it's not as good as 'Let It Be'.

BHP : Do you manage to keep up with the straight edge scene and all the new straight edge bands?

Dave : It's difficult to keep track of all the good straight edge bands from around the world because I'm on tour a lot or in the studio, but I really do support these bands and what they're doing, even if I don't know their music. We don't support any people or bands who are hateful or intolerant of others. The world needs more love and support and friendship between human beings.

BHP : Anything to add?

Dave : We love the UK a whole lot! Remember to live your life your own way, don't ever let anyone force you to do something you don't care to do, it's your life. The next world cup must be England verses the USA.

EPITAPH

6201 SUNSET BLVD, SUITE 111
HOLLYWOOD, CA 90028
PH. (213) 957-7555
FAX (213) 957-2656

Down By Law

THE ECOLOGICAL CRISIS

Many people nowadays talk about being 'Green', but as our planetary life support system is being pushed to breaking point by the relentless demands of humankind, talk is not enough. Most people don't know where to begin to help this situation, or think that their efforts will make no difference. Some don't even know what the problems actually are; lack of education due to political or corporate cover-ups may be the cause. But every citizen of this earth has a job to do, a part to play in it's turnaround. The personal is the political, and people must be led by example. "It is always better to light a few small candles than endlessly to curse the darkness."

At it's simplest, to be a 'Green' today is to put the environment at or near the top of one's list of priorities, and to recognise that we can never genuinely enrich ourselves or properly protect our children's future without first protecting the natural wealth of the planet.
Put like that, it sounds so reasonable and obvious. How could anyone possibly disagree, let alone seek to live in a way which imperils our very future as a species? Yet that's exactly what the majority of human beings alive today either choose to do, in the developed world, or are compelled to do by chronic poverty in the Third World.
In evolutionary terms, the impact of humankind on the rest of life on earth has been a very recent phenomenon, taking up just a few thousand years of a life process that goes back over 13.5 billion years. We only really got into our destructive stride at the start of the Industrial Revolution, 250 years ago, at exactly the time when our capacity to transform the earth's raw materials into goods and services began to liberate millions from lives of grinding hardship and poverty. And we only started to realise the implications of what we were doing a mere 20 or 30 years ago.
This awareness, and the Green Movement that has sprung from it, is only just beginning to permeate our political processes and value systems. It seems to be taking an agonisingly long time to sink in, but when an individual can only count on an average three score years and ten, it's very hard to have to think in evolutionary terms!
There is still no guarantee that we're going to make it. By all accounts, ocean-going tankers, of the kind that devastated Prince William Sound in Alaska, need about eight miles to stop, even with the engines in reverse. The industrial juggernaut that we have created has gained a similar momentum, and there is as yet no desire at all to engage reverse gear as far as most world leaders are concerned. It's daunting enough for them just to confront the need to slow the beast down.
There may be some out there who fondly imagine that just because everybody is talking about the environment, there's nothing to worry about any longer. Just as garlic is supposed by some to ward off marauding vampires, so the inexhaustible stream of hot air from politicians is thought by others to be a sufficient antidote to impending ecological collapse.

Just so we know what we are up against, this is a brief review, taken from J. Porritt's 'Where on earth are we going?', of the twelve most important factors, at an international level, that threaten the earth's future well-being...

1. OZONE DEPLETION

Ozone in the upper atmosphere protects us from highly damaging ultra-violet radiation from the Sun. The 'ozone layer' is now under attack from chlorofluorocarbons (CFC's) and other chemicals. Once released, after use in aerosols, or as refrigerants and foam-blowing agents, they can remain active in the atmosphere for at least 100 years.
In September 1987, the Montreal Protocol set in train international negotiations for phasing out some of these ozone-depleting substances. The Protocol was reviewed in June 1990, but the delays in achieving total phase-out are extremely worrying; every five year delay sets us back fifteen years in terms of reducing chlorine in the atmosphere to acceptable levels. Meanwhile, the seasonal hole in the ozone layer over the Antarctic gets bigger and bigger, and in 1988 a 3% thinning was detected over densely populated areas of the Northern Hemisphere, ensuring many thousands of extra deaths from skin cancer in the next century.

2. GLOBAL WARMING

The small amount of carbon dioxide in the atmosphere makes life possible by trapping some of the Sun's heat reflected back off the Earth into the atmosphere. However, the more there is of it, and other so-called 'greenhouse gases', the more heat is trapped and the warmer it gets. Since the Industrial Revolution, we have steadily increased our use of fossil fuels, the largest source of man-made carbon dioxide, and destroyed more and more of our forests.

International scientific consensus now predicts temperature increases of anything between 1.5 and 4.5 degrees Centigrade by the middle of the next century. This would have a devastating effect on agricultural production and gradually raise sea levels - possibly by as much as three metres by the end of the century. Weather patterns the world over will become unpredictable and there will be more storms, hurricanes, floods and droughts.

3. ENERGY

Meeting the energy needs of more than five billion people is putting a huge strain on many of the Earth's life-support systems. Fossil fuels are still plentiful, but they are a finite resource; yet even now there are more than 400 million cars on the planet, each using an average of two gallons of fuel every day. Burning coal and oil not only accelerates global warming, but gradually acidifies the environment. Acid rain has now affected over 7 million hectares of forest in over 20 countries. It has eliminated trout in rivers across 35,000 square kilometres of Norway, acidified 90,000 kilometres of brooks and 18,000 lakes in Sweden and severely affected over 50 lochs in Scotland, 700,000 lakes in Canada and many in the Adirondacks in the USA. The situation is becoming just as grave in many Third World countries.

Nuclear power provides no escape from this dilemma, not least because we still don't know how to dispose of the waste. By the end of the decade, there will be 100,000 lorry loads of radioactive waste in store in the UK alone. In many developing countries, firewood is increasingly difficult to find.

4. AIR POLLUTION

According to a major report published by the World Watch Institute in January 1990, more than a billion people, one fifth of the world's population, are now breathing air contaminated by pollutants in excess of international safety limits. Air pollution in the United States is estimated to cause up to 50,000 deaths a year; deaths in Athens rise by up to six times on days of heavy pollution. Ozone levels in Europe are dangerously high, causing many chest and lung problems.

One day's breathing in Bombay is equivalent to smoking 10 cigarettes. Many other Third World cities, such as Cubatao in Brazil, and Mexico City, have been very seriously affected by a rapid growth in industrialisation, and an almost complete disregard for proper environmental standards.

5. DESERTIFICATION AND SOIL EROSION

Around 6 million hectares of new desert are formed every year through poor management and changing climatic patterns. The Sahel, where population growth, over-grazing and the disruption of nomadic lifestyles have steadily increased pressure on marginal land, has been particularly badly affected. An inch of soil takes at least 200 years to lay down, but can be swept away in just a few years. Worldwide, an estimated 20 billion tonnes of topsoil are washed or blown off croplands every year; more than 3 billion hectares, around 25% of the world's total land surface, are now at risk.

6. DEFORESTATION

Forty-five per cent of the world's rainforests have been destroyed in the last thirty years; tropical rainforest destruction has nearly doubled over the last decade, and 1.8%, around 140,000 square kilometres, of the remaining rainforest disappears every year. The carbon dioxide released in the process contributes around 15% of total global warming. By the end of the century, most of the world's rainforest will be gone, with the exception of Zaire, Papua New Guinea and Western Amazonia.

Tropical deforestation is also the single greatest cause of species extinctions as the rainforests are home to more than 60% of the millions of species on Earth. Astonishingly, scientists estimate that, given current rates of deforestation, as many as 100 species a day may be disappearing.

7. WATER SHORTAGES
Water use has at least quadrupled in this century, and could double again over the next two decades. In more than 80 Third World countries, with 40% of the world's population, serious water shortages are undermining the livelihood of millions of people and holding up sustainable development.

Since 1980, more than 30 countries have been involved in international disputes concerning the use and control of diminishing water supplies. In China, more than 200 cities are without sufficient water, and the water table under the North China Plain is dropping by more than one metre a year. California is in an equally bad situation, and serious pollution of the Ogallala Aquifer is threatening agricultural production throughout the Western States.

8. CHEMICALS
Worldwide, some 70,000 chemicals are in everyday use. Between 500 and 1000 new chemicals are added to the list every year. The use of pesticides in agriculture, and the disposal of industrial wastes, releases hundreds of millions of tonnes of hazardous substances into the environment every year. Pesticde use in the United States tripled between 1965 and 1985; it is estimated that 80% of pesticide-associated cancer risks come from 15 foods, with tomatoes, beef, potatoes, oranges and lettuce leading the list.

In the Third World, pesticide use is also increasing very rapidly. The World Health Organisation estimates that pesticides poison more than 500,000 people every year, with one in ten cases resulting in death or permanent disability.

9. TOXIC WASTES
Toxic waste dumps litter the landscapes of the developed world. There are more than 4,500 toxic waste tips in Britain alone, at least 1,300 of which have been identified as posing serious risks to the environment. Imports of hazardous waste into the United Kingdom have increased sixteen times since 1984.

In the United States in 1987, the Environmental Protection Agency identified 950 sites as needing urgent attention, and set up an $8.5 billion 'Superfund' to finance the clean up. Experts now reckon that the final costs could exceed $100 billion. Surveys in West Germany and Denmark have revealed similar problems.

Between them, EEC countries produce 50% more waste than can be disposed of at existing facilities. As a consequence, thousands of tonnes are disposed of in the Third World. It is impossible to estimate total volumes of hazardous waste in Third World countries, as there are very few regulations or appropriate disposal facilities.

10. ARMS SPENDING
Military budgets currently amount to around one trillion dollars a year, which is a larger sum of money than the entire income of the poor half of the world's population. It works out at $2.75 billion a day.

On average, 6% of nations' GNP is spent on defence; developing countries have increased their arms budgets fivefold in the past twenty years.

The share of public research and development outlays that goes on military expenditure is as high as 70% in the United States, 60% in the USSR and 50% in the UK. Half a million scientists work in the arms business. By contrast, the United Nations' Environment Programme has received $30 million or less a year from from governments around the world since it was established in 1972. Three days of global military spending is the equivalent of funding the Tropical Forest Action Plan for five years. Two days of global military spending equals the entire annual cost of the United Nations' plan to halt Third World desertification.

11. INTERNATIONAL DEBT
The cumulative debt of developing countries has now reached more than one trillion dollars. Interest payments are $60 billion a year. Beginning in 1984, the traditional net flow of capital reversed itself : in 1982, $18.2 billion went to developing countries; today $52 billion a year is transferred from developing countries to the rich North.

This inevitably puts massive additional pressure on the natural resources of debtor countries, as they seek to accelerate export-led growth in order to pay back the debt. Without due regard to environmental protection, it is impossible for these debtor countries to achieve sustainable development.

12. POPULATION

Today, there are around 5.2 billion people on Earth. By 2025, there will be 8.5 billion. Of the additional 3.2 billion, 3 billion will be in the Third World countries where millions already live on the edge of survival, on marginal and unsustainable land.

Lower birth rates in the developed world are off-set by disproportionately high consumption of energy and resources. Long-term reductions in population levels, both North and South, are therefore a pre-requisite of achieving sustainable development.

For all the rapid growth in awareness about the environment over the last few years, that remains one hell of a catalogue. There are, of course, many encouraging factors on the other side of the balance sheet : new energy-efficient and resource-saving technologies ; far greater ease in communications and exchanging information; the end of the Cold War and the democratisation of Eastern Europe; a clear understanding of trans-boundary issues, like the thinning of the ozone layer, that demand a new level of international co-operation; the exhilarating acceptance of sustainability as the key principle in devising economic and development strategies for the 1990's.

For all that, the gap between the debits and credits is not noticeably narrowing. This is probably due, for the most part, not only to peoples' in-action but also their perception of wealth. Too many see money as a measure of quality of life. New taxes, such as 'Energy Tax' or 'Carbon Tax' may be brought in to cover the true costs of pollution; petrol prices rise whilst the costs of renewable energy falls. Recycling, energy efficiency, general awareness - all these things and more must increase to give the human race any real hope for the future.

There is no master plan, no 'greenprint' to save our future. It is up to every individual to find what they can do and make a start. It needs to be done now!

If the Earth were only a few feet in diameter, floating a few feet above a field somewhere, people would come from everywhere to marvel at it. People would walk around it, marvelling at its big pools of water, its little pools and the water flowing between the pools. People would marvel at the bumps on it, and the holes in it, and they would marvel at the very thin layer of gas surrounding it and the water suspended in the gas. The people would marvel at all the creatures walking around the surface of the ball, and the creatures in the water. The people would declare it precious because it was the only one, and they would protect it so that it would not be hurt. The ball would be the greatest wonder known, and people would come to behold it, to be healed, to gain knowledge, to know beauty and to wonder how it could be. People would love it, and defend it with their lives, because they would somehow know that their lives, their own roundness, could be nothing without it. If the Earth were only a few feet in diameter.

JAWBREAKER

Jawbreaker have been around since 1989 and are now one of the best known purveyors of the 'San Francisco Sound'; powerful, melodic hardcore with plenty of original hooks. Their third full length album, '24 Hour Revenge Therapy', sees this trio getting even more popular, maybe they'll be the next press darlings. We asked a few quick questions at their London show on 31st October 1994...

BHP : How's your tour going? You didn't get to play in Britain last time, due to Blake's throat problem, so how do you like it here?

JAW : Good, fine, it's cold though.

BHP : What inspired the name '24 Hour Revenge Therapy'?

JAW : That was mine (Blake), just kind of summed up a day.

BHP : What sort of sound is Jawbreaker going for now?

JAW : We're going for that new 'Flat Wave' sound. The sound of tubes popping, wallets draining.

BHP : Do you (Blake) find it easy to sing and play?

JAW : It continues to be difficult, like the spiral the tummy and pat the head trick.

BHP : What are the bands other interests?

JAW : B - Arty work. I like heavy physical exercise. Protracted periods of isolation. C - Knives. I like knives... and swords, and Lucy.

BHP : Are any of the band religious or S.E.?

JAW : Totally religious... all the time!

BHP ; Have you had major label interest?

JAW : We've been beseiged with big money offers. I'd soul kiss a gift horse if I could hold the reins.

BHP : Any tour nightmare stories?

JAW : We played with a Bavarian Hate Core band! This is the closest I've come to quitting since the last time I quit.

Well I guess Jawbreaker didn't have much to say that night. The show was pretty good, but they only played for 35 minutes, maybe due to the intense heat as it was packed. Their records are great though and say a lot more about the band. You can write to them at P.O. Box 411324, San Francisco, CA 94141, USA.

The Corporate Music Industry's 'brand new' favourites are getting a lot of press at the moment. Well, at least for once it's a band who deserve it. The Berkeley punk-pop trio have been together for over five years, and were famous in the underground as gods of the four chord girlie song long before their third album, 'Dookie', was released on Warner Brothers. Billie Joe (Guitar / Vocals), Mike (Bass) and Tre Cool (Drums) have constantly toured the US and Europe, building a devoted fan base and playing to packed audiences. Their first two albums, '39 Smooth' and 'Kerplunk', were released on Lawrence Livermore's 'Lookout' label, but there were singles too and these now seem to be getting rare. So, BHP to the rescue! We have one copy of each '1000 Hours' EP, 'Slappy' EP, 'Sweet Children' EP and 'Live at Gilman St.' EP to give away! All you have to do is answer the following questions...

1. What US state is Berkeley in?
2. Where did Green Day recently have a televised mud fight?
3. The last time BHP interviewed Green Day they were just about to record 'Dookie' for Warner Brothers. What did Billie Joe say Warners had promised them for it?

Answers to the BHP address, closing date is the release of the next issue. The Editor's decision is final. This competition is for real; BHP has a load of stuff to share with it's readers.

1,000 HOURS

couch potatoes

Couch Potatoes, the original Kentifornian hardcore band, hail from the town of Tunbridge Wells in South East England, where "there's not much to do unless you make your own entertainment". They've been playing shows since 1990 and have toured all over, including twice in Europe, with bands of their genre, such as NOFX, Green Day, Down By Law and Alice Donut. "I think the key to our longevity is enjoyment. We all really believe in what we're doing and we have fun doing it. Whether the crowd is 50 or 500 people, we'll always put 100% into it and try to share that enjoyment" says Dave, lead guitarist and founding member of the band. "And although it can be a party, most of our songs are very emotional and heartfelt. Not neccessarily political though, as I see that on more of a personal level."

Couch Potatoes have appeared on radio stations, compilations and fanzines worldwide, and have been compared to bands as diverse as All and Quicksand, Samiam and Green Day, Big Drill Car and Lifetime. "Yeah, I guess people will always try to label you, even in a scene like ours. What are we then? A straight edge band that plays pop-punk? We're just five guys, with different influences, but the same ideals." "We are what we are" adds Dan, the band's other guitarist "whether it's punk, vege, straight, whatever. Everyone's entitled to their own opinions."

Musically, the band are very competent and have several records out. "We had a couple of demo's, 'Wash' and '8 songs' and a few songs on compilations, but our first real good release was the 'Excess All Areas' album. Then we had two 7" EP's, 'In bed with' on Weird Records and 'Brad, why are you such a jerk' on A-Wat Records in Germany. That was for the tour..." "Playing shows is great, so touring is the best thing, getting out and travelling, and meeting people. It makes all the work worthwhile."

Couch Potatoes have toured in Europe twice, and recently recorded their second album, 'Man's greatest friend in the windswept heights'. "The 'Windswept Heights' thing is already nearly sold out, it was only a limited pressing, less than a thousand, but we do have two new singles coming out. A four track EP on Weird, called 'Square' and a five track EP on Dragnet called 'User Friendly'." Both of these releases are due out in Spring 1995, along with several more compilation appearances and a live cassette album called 'Stampbox'.

"We're fairly busy, although we could do with more gigs. There never seems to be enough shows around" says Dave. "We do have some great new songs to record though, our best yet, so hopefully we'll be back in the studio soon. Look out for us."

You can write to Couch Potatoes at : 1 Chandos Road,
Tunbridge Wells,
Kent,
TN1 2NY,
UK.

Weird Records, 61 London Road, Balderton, Newark, Notts, NG24 3AG.
Dragnet Records, 39 Lugg View, Presteigne, Powys, LD8 2DE.
A-Wat Records, Bruchstr 51, D-52080 Aachen, Germany.

K.F.C.C.

CANNABIS - THE WONDER DRUG?

Everyone, it seems, is calling for the legalisation of cannabis. But while Britain debates relaxing or abolishing the laws on cannabis, scientists elsewhere in the world are uncovering alarming new evidence that cannabis, ingested or inhaled, is extremely dangerous to health and can even kill. New research shows that cannabis damages the human immune and reproductive systems, and can cause brain damage. There is also strong evidence that the drug is more carcinogenic than tobacco.

Cannabis use has increased at every class level and across generations, and it is estimated that 5 million people nationwide use it. Cannabis is seen as sociable, and a more innocuous pleasure than a pint of beer. If it is harmless, many people argue that criminal proceedings against cannabis users are an injustice and a waste of police and court's time.

However, in America, where the anti-cannabis campaign is taken very seriously, there is growing medical concern about the dangers of the drug. Cancerous growths usually caused by smoking cigarettes are nine times more likely to show up in younger people if they smoke cannabis, according to Professor Paul Donald of the University of California. His research is backed up by Professor Kasi Sridhar of the University of Miami's Cancer Research Centre. "Cannabis smokers develop cancer 15 to 20 years younger than you would expect. I am convinced it is a highly dangerous drug. It may take 5 to 10 years to prove beyond doubt that marijuana causes cancer, but this is similar to what happened with tobacco. Why wait for absolute proof? Smoking marijuana is like playing Russian roulette."

It is not surprising that cannabis is more likely to cause cancer than nicotine. It contains over 400 compounds, 62 of them unique to the cannabis plant, which convert to over 2,000 chemicals when ignited. These contain 70% more tars and carcinogens than tobacco, so cannabis is far more carcinogenic to smoke.

THC, the compound which produces the 'high', is also damaging, and its potency has increased dramatically over the years. Scientists estimate that the levels of THC in cannabis are 16 times higher today than at the time of the Woodstock Festival, due to genetic engineering and improvements in cultivating techniques. THC builds up in the body over a long period of time. It accumulates in the body's fatty tissues such as the reproductive organs, the heart, the liver and the brain, and is slowly released into the bloodstream over a period of five to eight days. THC can stay in the system for up to four months and can surreptitiously accumulate with dire consequences.

The International Colloquium on Illicit Drugs in 1992 concluded that cannabis is "neither soft nor harmless" and can threaten lives. A report submitted by the National Academy of Medicine in Paris states "the noxious effects of cannabis on reproduction clearly indicate that it should be considered as a dangerous compound for humans".

The report shows that the build up of THC in the reproductive system of both men and women can reduce fertility. It also reveals that the offspring of mothers who smoked cannabis just before or during pregnancy were 10 times as likely to develop leukaemia, and even passive smoking increases the risk. In men, cannabis can cause impotence and reduce testosterone levels and sperm count by up to 44%.

Cannabis also affects the body's immune system by impairing the white blood cells which protect it from infections, so cannabis users are more likely to fall ill and remain sick for longer periods. This undermines a powerful argument for the legalisation of cannabis - that it can have medicinal benefits such as alleviating the symptoms of AIDS and reducing the side effects of chemotherapy.

Guy Cabral from the Medical College of Virginia showed that cannabis users had an increased susceptibility to genital herpes, syphilis and tuberculosis. The US Department of Health and Human Services warned that cannabis could even be a co-factor in the development of full-blown AIDS. So any medicinal benefits associated with the use of cannabis have been called into question, and there is no need for it to be added to the list of drugs on prescription as there is already an approved oral drug which serves the same purpose - Nabilone, a synthetic THC.

Experts warn that the relaxing effect that cannabis has on the mind can damage the brain. Dr Robert Gilkeson, a neuroscientist at the Centre for Brain Research in California, compiled research on cannabis users and concluded that "cannabis does more organic brain damage than any other drug with the possible exception of PCP and the end stages of alcoholism".

Studies show that cannabis smokers are up to six times more likely to develop serious mental illnesses such as schizophrenia. Dr Gabriel Nahas, a brain researcher from New York University Hospital, explains why the drug is so harmful to the brain: "Cannabis impairs that part of the brain which allows the individual to reason properly and remain alert and in contact with their environment. Some people develop mental health problems, others lose their motivation and ability to function properly. It can also have a damaging effect on the development of a young person's personality." But because cannabis acts so slowly, it's effects on the body's health may not be noticed for years. Nahas asserts: "The damage caused by the chemicals in cannabis acts like a slow diffusing bomb - imperceptible, but potentially lethal. What we know now is enough to cause serious national concern. Why do we have to wait for proof just to accommodate western societies' desire for fun and libertarianism?"

Recent experiments have shown how cannabis can affect a person's ability to function properly, leading to major accidents. A recent test on pilots, using a computerised flight simulator, showed that they could not land a plane properly up to 24 hours after smoking one joint. A study of 182 fatal accidents by the US National Transportation Safety Board found that cannabis was linked to more deaths than any other drug, including alcohol. In January 1988 a freight train rammed into another train travelling from Washington to New York at full speed, resulting in 16 dead and 175 injured passengers. The conductor of the train had ignored three red signals before the crash. A drug test later showed that he had been smoking cannabis.

Heather Ashton, Professor of Clinical Psycho-Pharmacology at Newcastle University, is also concerned. "Cannabis produces a time and space distortion, there is no breath test for it and the effects can last over a week. One of the strongest arguments against legalisation is the way it affects people's driving."

But despite the growing evidence that cannabis is dangerous, legalisation looks set to go ahead. Much of the medical profession seems reticent to comment on cannabis without seeing all the research on it. Other doctors stand by its medicinal uses. Pro-legislation groups are growing in credibility and they have money behind them. And money talks.

One of the biggest pro-cannabis lobbying organisations in the world, the International Drug Policy Foundation, is given regular donations for its Fighting Fund. The American Civil Liberties Union, which sponsors many of the bills supporting the legalisation of cannabis, is partially funded by major tobacco companies. Dr Janet Lapey, Director of the US-based Citizens for Drug Prevention, says "The legalisation isn't about health, it's about money. Certain people stand to make a killing if the drug is legalised, such as tobacco companies who could patent marijuana products. Tobacco companies are still arguing that tobacco is not addictive or dangerous. Doctors spoke out in the thirties against tobacco and were silenced by the press. It took 50 years and 500,000 scientific articles before the public became aware of the dangers of tobacco, and the same will happen with cannabis."

LETTERS

Readers, please feel free to send letters and articles for possible publication.

All fashion, no substance. All fashion, no substance. This is the call of the tragically hip. Are you cool, daddy-o? Hey man, if you're not into the look then you're just a square. Baby, baby. Things are things, man, can you dig it? I'm so cool. Look at me. I've got the look that kills. The Freeze once sang a song that went like this... "If you dance the same and dress the same, it won't be long 'til you are the same. You look the same and act the same, there's nothing new and you're to blame..."

Warning : what follows is not meant to be an attack on any specific person or group of people, but rather all examples mentioned are simply that, examples. Criticism was once a mainstay of the punk community, but these days a lot of people have very thin skin. Criticism and debate are key components of the communication process. If you are unable to criticize or take criticism then are you not also unable to communicate? If you feel slighted by my opinions, which are after all no more than opinions, then feel free to communicate your own opinions on said subject.

The new trend, and yes it's a trend in every sense of the word, is to look cool and act wild, but say nothing. In the late '80's the straight edge scene deteriorated to homogeny. At every show the band members all looked the same, as did the audience, and the music being played became more and more the same and eventually even the way people acted on stage was cloned from the more popular bands. In the end most of the bands were interchangeable and so were 80% of the people going to the shows. Conformity was reached, and anything unusual or out of place was certainly suspect.

Today the same thing is going down. I can't know how it is in the rest of the world, but in California the buzz is all about how you look and the clothes you wear and the way you move. The idea these days is to gain popularity through mass conformity. Almost every band in California is based solely on conformity and the duplication of some other band. Today you can't be cool unless you wear tight pants, a tight shirt or sweater, a wallet chain, some sort of creepers or dress shoes, and if you're female you had better conform to the riot grrrl standard with your mini-skirt, cat eye glasses, and your lunch pail or fancy hand bag. Your music has to conform to the riot grrrl sound or to the "crazy way-out there chaos" of Antioch Arrow, End Of The Line, Universal Order Of Armageddon, or ultimately to the kings of nothing, Nation Of Ulysses.

Ironically, I think Nation Of Ulysses, a band that appeared so unique, started the most powerful trend in hardcore / punk in the last four years. They were a band based solely on "going off", having nothing tangible to say, and looking totally cool. They set the stage for the future. The message they sent was forget having something to say and go for the style, for the look, for the essence of cool. Nothing else matters as long as you look cool while you're doing it. And at the same time that Nation Of Ulysses was creating this image, the riot grrrl scene was starting to gain popularity.

Riot grrrl, at the central core, is obviously much more than a mere fashion statement. It is about ideas and it is indeed revolutionary in the messages it sends and the results it desires, but this "movement" that seems so thought orientated has been embodied by fashion and style. Riot grrrl is no longer about a way of thinking and grrrl power but rather it is about a way of dressing and the way you present yourself. Revolution through fashion, can you dig it?

The way you carry yourself and the way you present yourself is indeed important, I would never deny that, but it is not the end all of all things. Fashion cannot change the way the world behaves, only the way it looks. Today when I go to a show it seems that some sort of universal dress code has been applied. Everyone looks the same, and all the bands act the same. The total conformity is sickening. Shows are no longer about communication and jacking into a source of energy and inspiration, but rather the scene is a fashion show with each competitor striving to be just that much cooler than everyone else.

Not For The Lack Of Trying once played a show with Bikini Kill, who were quite good incidentally. The place was packed with riot grrrls. For the most part they were all totally turned off to Not For The Lack Of Trying because here was a band where not one member looked tragically hip, and to top it off the lead singer was a woman and she had the nerve not to wear a mini-skirt, a dress, or black clothes, and she didn't even have a lunch pail! Instead, here was a woman screaming her head off wearing nothing more than a pair of jeans, some canvass shoes and a plain white shirt. No style, no sense of the cool, only the intensity of inner honesty. But her intensity and honesty and talent were of no concern, because if you don't look cool then you certainly can't be cool. Grrrl power, yeah, but only if you're a cool grrrl.

On the other hand, a band like Antioch Arrow that generally sounds like total crap live is hailed as the best band in California because they look so cool and act so wild. The last few times I saw them their bass player usually spent more time with his hands floating in the air than actually playing bass. When they play it is all just a roar of nothing. The only truly tangible sound is the drums, which are played very well, but a band cannot be based only on great drumming. Fortunately for them their sound is ultimately irrelevant because all people want these days is to see some cool looking people go crazy. Style first, sound and substance last. After all, Antioch Arrow wears those tight clothes and they look soo cooool. Dig it man, that dude's jacket is so bad.

Conformity of the masses, man, now that's cool. Hey, like if we all dress the same then like we will all be the same and then like the system will just fall down at our feet and like it'll be so cool, man. Boring. Take a look in the mirror folks. Can you tell yourselves apart from your neighbours? Are you competing with your friends to see who can look the coolest? Do you watch MTV or read Sassy to stay up to date on the coolest of cool fashion changes? The so called underground fashion that you folks are conforming to is the same "underground" fashion that the mainstream is selling as an "underground" fashion in K-Mart, Bullocks, Sears, Broadway and Macy's. You can use words like "underground" and "rebellion" until you're blue in the face but your precious fashion will still be mainstream. You are bought and sold.

Life imitates art in a world where conformity is the rule and individuality is a marketing slogan, and when the art being created has no substance then life has no substance. Looking cool doesn't mean you are cool, and looking rebellious doesn't make you a rebel, and in the '90's looking punk doesn't mean you are a punk. If image is all you have to sell then you are the mainstream, and perhaps you're not half as cool as you think.

The funny thing is that half of you wore "skater clothing" four or five years ago, and of course skate fashion has nothing to do with actually skating, and half of you will look like whatever new trend comes around next year. Some people are born to follow, or is that born to shop? Normally I would have to say that these complaints of mine are extremely petty, but at the moment we live in a time when the rock industry are using "alternative" as a selling tool. Our fashion is easily duplicated, mass produced and sold back to us, but our culture cannot be bought and sold. Our principles, our ideas, our dreams, our emotions, and our code of ethics cannot be bought or sold. Those things belong to us, and they will always belong to us.

A letter from Kent McClard of Ebullition, reprinted from Heart Attack 'zine.

It could happen to you, or could it?

After watching a TV documentary about the rich and famous in Beverly Hills it left a rather sour taste in my mouth. It covered most issues which these people face in their everyday theoretical lives, showing us their luxury homes and gardens, and how they mingle with one another, discussing their favourite boutiques, how they hang out with all these pop stars, film stars and royalty, and how tough it is organising so many different parties when trying to fit visits to the local fitness guru or Brenden the cosmetician for a weekly once over. When suddenly the issue of AIDS popped up, when we heard all these stories of friends who have died or are about to die, and don't forget their friends are all of the same social class as they are. Hearing people talking with tears in their eyes about what a deadly virus it is and that it affects every one of us, how it attacks every society, eating away, and there is nothing you can do about it. When Magic Johnson's face appeared on the screen, so did Freddie Mercury's, and a host of other 'celebrities' who have been ravaged by this terrible disease. So all I'm hearing is wear your red Aids ribbon, if you don't you must be a selfish human being, and everybody has somebody they have lost from this Aids virus.

Well what I would like to say is I feel very sorry for anybody who suffers from a disease, it doesn't matter what that maybe. I just would like to know why is every other disease given a backseat. I'm hearing jokes on MTV by a so-called comedienne Tracy Ullman making fun of

Ronald Reagan for having Alzheimer's disease. Would she have said the same about someone who had AIDS? I doubt it. People are telling me I could catch AIDS. Well, no I couldn't; I don't sleep around, I have a regular girlfriend, I don't do drugs and everybody I know is the same, basically not stupid. We are supposed to feel sorry for Magic Johnson. Why? He obviously exploited his position and slept around and is now suffering from his mistakes. Maybe it's the media's fault, but how they can make something like AIDS into some kind of '90's culture I don't know. All I'm saying is yeah, any disease could happen to you, AIDS, well be safe and it won't. And remember to look after old people; they've most probably forgotten more than we will ever know.

Nik N. Helsinki, Finland.

ON A COLD WINTER'S MORNING

On a cold winter's morning I go for a walk.
Outside I feel the chill through my ample attire
Beneath me lies the frost and snow of the night before
Blindingly bright virgin snow upon which I am the first to tread
As sacred an act as the taking of a maiden's virtue
I shiver with the cold, but also with excitement
My breath forms glistening clouds before my eyes
Rising ethereally to join it's ancestors in the sky
My heart pounds within my breast as I set out
Each footstep placed with care on this treacherous path
I try to walk softly on this icy white carpet,
But every footstep leaves it's crunching silhouette
Betraying my presence and confirming my isolation.
I stand still, and a deafening silence creeps up on me
No movement, no noise,
Even time has been frozen in this chill morning air.
I love the solitude of this time, this place
I wish I could just scrunge it all up into a ball,
put it in my mouth and eat it
Then I'd have the solitude within me.
I speak a soliloquy heard only in my mind
As it fills with thoughts of life's deep meanings
And reality blurs into my dreams.
I come at last to a silent, still lake
It's frozen crust reflecting the early morning sun
The ducks cannot swim, but slide awkwardly towards me
I step onto the ice and skate out to join them
The wind numbs my face, but my heart is warmed
I stoop to feed them their breakfast of bread
The silence is broken by an awesome crack and down I plunge
The cold bites deep on this winter's day
But not as deep as the pain I felt when you went away
I am alone, I do not struggle.

Steve Gamage   3/1/95

Reviews

GAUGE - SWING 7" - The two tracks are called 'Flognoth' and 'King soon swing'. Really melodic emo-singing, but harsh abstract guitar. I like this, kind of like Admiral and Lincoln and even Shudder To Think in places. They have an album out now called 'Fire tongue burning stomach' on Underdog Records, PO Box 14182, Chicago Il, 60614, USA.

GAUNT - NATIONAL POSTAL MUSEUM 7" - 'Turn to ash' is the A-side and it sounds like the Monkees with distortion pedals. The band are from Ohio, but this is on an English label. The production is a little too raw and 'Flying' on side-B sounds like Heroin. As it says on the cover though, buy grassroots, support a UK label. Potential Ashtray, 110 Oxford Road, High Wycombe, Bucks, HP11 2DN.

J. CHURCH - SLEEP 7" - Their EP's always seem to be more catchy than their albums and this is no exception. The title track is a classic : catchy pop-punk that gets stuck in your head and bounces around all day. 'Cool Guitar Girl' is a cover of a Heavenly's song. Limited on Rugger Bugger.

JACKONUTS - WEIRD BATH 7" - Quirky, weird, multi-tempo change first track, play to get friends to leave in droves. JECK on the B-side is more of a jazzy indie thing. Picture of a granny looking in pants on the back cover. Reservation Records.

SILVER - MAKE UP 7" - Jangly indie tunes, a little bald if you ask me. If Brief Weeds were boring and on a major label they might sound like this. Nothing to remember, except the bizarre cover. Medicine Records.

FIENDZ - EVERYBODY'S FAVOURITE EP - Four tracks of melodic and incredibly mellow popcore. This band used to be just like Descendents but are getting softer and softer. Good if you're in a quiet mood. Great packaging and four tracks from Black Pumpkin Records, PO Box 676, Totowa, NJ 07512, USA.

SHUTDOWN - SHELTERED HOMES EP - Jawbreaker, Samiam and J. Church all spring to mind here. A brilliant, melodic but powerful four track 7" by a UK band featuring a superb cover of the Beat's classic 'Mirror in the bathroom'. Buy or die! Potential Ashtray Records, 110 Oxford Road, High Wycombe, Bucks, HP11 2DN.

CHOPPER - SAID AND DONE EP - The first release on Crackle Records, a new UK label. Sing-a-long popcore in the vein of Pseudo Hippies and early Lookout bands. Four very produced tracks in neat packaging. Crackle Records, PO Box HP49, Leeds, LS6 4XL.

NO MEANS NO - LEAVE THE SEASIDE EP - A live bootleg EP recorded at Whitstable! in 1990. Very good quality and given away free with Fear and Loathing zine. A must for fans from F'N'L, PO Box 3648, London, N1 1FL.

WORDBUG - DIE b/w WAITING 7" - There's something really stylish about this band, they remind me of Drive or even Dagnasty when they speed up, but then they'll go and mellow out and do it so well. Another classy UK release, blue vinyl and colour cover. Split release by Fluffy Bunny and Boss Tuneage. Licensed from Hometown Atrocities.

WORDBUG - LOCKED IN 7" - More good stuff, extremely tuneful in an old school kind of way, like 7 Seconds and Dagnasty. All Wordbug's songs seem totally different, and the singing is always strong. There's only two tracks, but definately worth getting. Great packaging, again on Hometown Atrocities.

WORDBUG / BYETAIL SPLIT EP - Yet more tuneful and grungey hardcore from Wordbug! Two songs here reminding me of Dinosaur Jr, Drive, Lemonheads, etc. Byetail, from Belgium, give us two tracks of funky popcore. A little bit rock and bad American accents. Immaculate packaging again. Get all of these from Hometown Atrocities or Wordbug, c/o 6 City Arcade, Fore Street, Exeter, Devon.

SHAGGY HOUND EP - This lot sound identical to NY's Animal Crackers or even early Jailcells. Fast and thrashy hardcore from France, but sung convincingly in English. Five tracks from PANX, BP 5058, 31033 Toulouse, Cedex, France.

TRAVIS CUT - WAKING HOURS 7" - This band from Essex have had a few trips into the music press recently and this, their debut release, shows why. Fast and powerful in a Husker Du kind of way, there's three tracks, one instrumental, well worth checking out from Incoming! 2 The Hides, Harlow, Essex, CM20 3QL.

VARUKERS - NOTHINGS CHANGED EP - Bristles, spikes and leather jackets. This is fast, powerful punk in a Discharge style and is already on a second pressing. Anyone who considers themselves truly punk should own this. Weird Records, 61 London Road, Balderton, Newark, Notts, NG24 3AG.

SKIMMER - BETTER THAN BEING ALONE EP - Yes, it's the West Midlands answer to J. Church and the Ramones. Catchy pop-punk, well worth getting. Crackle Records, PO Box 49, Leeds, LS6 4XL.

SPECTACLE RPI - SOFTWARE FOR HARDWARE EP - This sounds a little like very early Siouxsie and the Banshees featuring John McKaye, the singer even sounds alike. Another band from NME who can't play. I guess the hearts in the right place, but basically they're shite. PO Box 56, South Delivery Office, Manchester, M20 2AU.

THE VANISHED - ZU LAUT? 7" - 'Too Loud?' in English. Punk in the old school style, from Germany. Six tracks played by guys with enormous record collections. Bad Taste Records, Volksner Str 46, 31832 Springe, Germany.

SLEEPER - SELF TITLED 7" - I'd heard this band were like Dagnasty, Fifteen and Sicko, but they're not that easy to place. Fast and well produced, it's already in it's fifth pressing so check it out. Tragic Life Records, PO Box 060623, SI NY 10306, USA. It's good!

USEFUL IDIOT - PRESENCE EP - Another UK band making a name for themselves. Funky, powerful reggae influenced hardcore, hard to define. When I saw them live they reminded me of bands like Quicksand, Shelter and even Jawbreaker. There's a cassette album on the way from Dragnet and probably a European tour in 1995 with Couch Potatoes. The record is well worth checking out but on an Austrian label, so write to Useful Idiot, c/o 6 City Arcade, Fore Street, Exeter, Devon.

GREEDY GUTS - 8 SKATED AND SURFED SONGS EP - This is France's answer to Hard-Ons. Obsessed with surfing and playing frantic, fun popcore. It's great! Get it from PANX, BP 5058, 31033 Toulouse, Cedex, France.

DOG POUND - JUNKYARD EP - 'Going back to yesterday' this is very good early style hardcore, brought up to date. Possibly influenced by Descendents, it's melodic and a little different. I like it but I can't explain why. Just get it from Black Pumpkin Records, PO Box 676, Totowa, NJ 07512, USA.

THIRST - FRIEND EP - This 7" is a benefit for Steve Burgess, one of the Southampton STE crew, the original guitarist and friend of the band. Musically it is very good, melodic and original with heartfelt lyrics, reminds me of old Couch Potatoes in fact! This really is a must, from S. D. Records, 24 Windrush Road, Millbrook, Southampton, SO16 9DD. "He is my friend, a true companion."

THE KEATONS - THE BEIGE ALBUM CD - This is their first release for a long time, and I guess it may have been awaited by their families. Fans of Cardiac style weirdness might enjoy this, or retro gimps. It's more than a little wishy washy in a very English brown socks sort of way. Buy it for your deaf Gran from Dogfish Records, 6 Marshall House, East Street, London, SE17 2DX.

ORANGE 9MM - 12" EP - 'What's left of you, when you can't find nothing special?' Well I just found it! This is awesome in a very powerful Understand kind of way. Essential. Features ex-members of Burn and Fountainhead. Revelation Records, PO Box 5232, Huntington Beach, CA 92615 - 5232, USA.

ONION - FASTER LP - This is good already and it's meant to be a 'grower'. Throw early Lemonheads, REM and Farside into a sharp and powerful blender and stand back. Features ex-members of 76% Uncertain, Shelter, etc. Lyric sheet contains Onion related recipes. Crisis Records, PO Box 5232, Huntington Beach, CA 92615 - 5232, USA.

DESTINATION VENUS / LIVING DEAD - SPLIT EP - It's punky tunefulness here, with commercial appeal. You might even catch your mum singing this in the bath. Or maybe not. See for yourself and make up your own mind. £2.50 ppd from 65 Tunstall Road, Biddulph, Stoke on Trent, Staffs, ST8 6HJ.

FOR WHAT - SOME OTHER TIME CD - They look like The Pearl Jam, The Soundgarden, The Alice in Chains, etc, etc, and not surprisingly they sound like The Pearl Jam, The Soundgarden, The Alice in Chains, etc, etc. Not that I have any records from these bands, so what do I know. Aaaargh, Baby! Voltage Records.

SUCTION - WALLACE DEMO - These lads bought the hardcore handbook, or got their dads to, but forgot to read the important chapters like tune, originality, creativity, emotion, power, etc. Don't buy it, because TDK's make better copies. Bald shite!

BANDIT QUEEN - CASSETTE SAMPLER - This is a very competent outing, and well produced. They might like to sound like Shudder to think, or Belly, or even Trees and flowers, but I think they only manage the latter. You'll probably read all about them soon in NME. Playtime Records, Unit 32, 3rd Floor, Camden Lock Place, Chalk Farm Road, London, NW1 8AF.

THE LAST LAUGH - BESMIRCHED EP - Great packaging but very poor production. Not a bad band, reminding me of Alice Donut in places, but lacks a little power. Good samples. 12 Chapel House, Tewkesbury, Gloucestershire, GL20 5PQ.

CIRCUS - SAMPLER CASSETTE - Oh dear, oh dear, two tracks of self-indulgent Smiths / Metal / Pop. You can contact them at PO Box 1135, Bristol, BS17 2DL, but I really wouldn't bother.

SPG - SEEING IS BELIEVING DEMO - Tom, Mark, Ben, and Banksy (aren't they from Grange Hill?) have obviously only recently formed the band, but are well into it, and it shows. Influenced by '77 punk and modern hardcore, a band that will develop. Make contact at 7 Leesfield Drive, Meadowfield, Durham, DH7 8NG.

PEEP SHOW - FLOW - A very slick and well produced demo. You can tell that there's some money behind this band. They have management but are a very hard working band, playing shows all the time in London. Powerful, poppy and pretty original! Almost too accessible though, I wonder if they'll start to sound like Green Day. 5 Paddington Street, London, W1M 3LA.

NIOBIUM - PARASITE - Oh yes, Starts with an Evil Dead sample and then goes into churney guitar, Metallicaesque. A thrash band from Kent. I love them!

LEADBELLY - SUCKERPUNCH DEMO - Really good, honest, pop-punk. Reminiscent of Ramones, Fiendz, etc. Picture of a man getting punched on the cover. A real grower this, well worth checking out. 39 Barton Avenue, Athersley North, Barnsley, S. Yorkshire, S71 3PB.

SMOG - GETS IN YOUR EYES - I picked this little gem of a cassette up at a Joiners show, where it was recorded. 'Easy listening for the hard of hearing' it says on the cover, and this threepiece crank out some pretty great tunes. Stuart, the vocalist / guitarist sounds gruff and there seems to be several similarities with Jawbreaker. Still punkcore, but more British and more varied. No contact address, but try to get it!

SHINZOPHOBIA - CASSETTE - A collection of harsh noises made by some idiot. Not very good at all!

DARLING YOU WERE WONDERFUL - COMPILATION - An excellent collection of tracks from some of the best UK hardcore bands at the moment, put together by Dragnet Records. It features China Drum, Erase Today, Pseudo Hippies, Gan, Couch Potatoes, Useful Idiot, Leadbelly, Decadence Within, Another Fine Mess and more. A must buy from Dragnet, 39 Lugg View, Presteigne, Powys, Wales, LD8 2DE.

DECADENCE WITHIN - THE SHITTY TAPES - This band have been together for over ten years and it shows. This is not a 'best of' however, but a collection of out-takes, rarities and demos from 1986 - 94. Mainly powerful, thrashy, hardcore and well worth getting from Dragnet.

DOWNTIME - DEMO - Excellent power-pop-punk that sounds like it would shred live. In the vein of Green Day or Down By Law. Definately make contact at 117 Melrose Street, Belfast, Northern Ireland.

NFI - THE END TOO LATE - 'Ooh lets have some fun'. Guitar driven, good fun hardcore. Really catchy vocals and powerful music. They've been compared to Bad Religion in the past, but they're better than that. I'm still singing tunes. Write to Fred, 9 Rue Dauphin, 94800 Villejuif, France.

SPEED URCHIN - FAST FOOD FOR SICK CHILDREN - Well it sounds like Elvis formed a hardcore band, and not a bad one at that. The first song, 'Less than amazing', is exactly that, but then it improves and the next three are the Damned playing hardcore. Contact Donagh on 071 370 3633 because Elvis lives!

RISE - JACK TRACKS - This is a mini-album and I think all the tracks are covers, so I can't judge it too harshly, but I can't really recommend it. Don't get me wrong, their first album is a classic, emotional, melodic hardcore, a bit like Doughboys but better. This, however, is just too metal. PO Box 1509, Station H, Montreal, QC, H3G 2N4.

USEFUL IDIOT - URGE, CASSETTE ALBUM - 12 more classic tracks of jazz hardcore from the West country. Heavily reggae influenced and original with Understand style quirkiness. Another good release on Dragnet. £3.00 ppd from 39 Lugg View, Presteigne, Powys, CD8 2DE.

THE SOMA RIDE - AMERICAN MOVIE WEEK 7" - Well, this raw little slab of vinyl is too good to call Indie, but not really hardcore. Kind of geeky college band style. Clint Eastwood's on the cover, so get it from Dreamtown Records, 157 Cromwell Crescent, Pontefract, W. Yorkshire, WF8 2EP.

WEEN - CHOCOLATE AND CHEESE CD - Yeah mate, right! Don't even consider getting this alternative jazz dance drivel. I think it's their third album, I'd hate to hear the first two. Really bad!

GAS HUFFER - ONE INCH MASTERS CD - This band have been around for ages and seem to have run out of ideas. Rocky, bluesy-core on Epitaph.

TEN FOOT POLE - REV. CD - Another Bad Religion soundalike, with a little NOFX, Offspring and Down By Law thrown in, but not quite as good. Melodic, sing-a-long guitar songs. It grows on you the more you listen. Epitaph.

RKL - RICHES TO RAGS CD - A Californian skate band are back and pissed. Ultra-fast, in your face hardcore with angry, but sometimes silly, vocals covering a range of topics. They all wear bad shirts and the vocalist, Jason Sears, has 'Eat Shit' tattooed on his arse, but Epitaph have signed another great band here. Well worth checking out from 6201 Sunset Blvd, Suite 111, Hollywood CA 90028, USA.

RAW NOVEMBRE - DISTURBED CD - This is an Irish hardcore band I kept hearing of, but never heard. They have a pretty varied and original style, but it's just not for me. Abrasive and thrashy, and a little dated, but see for yourself. Aggressive Management, 4 The Beehives, Ballinderry, Mullingar, Co. Westmeath, Ireland.

ANOTHER FINE MESS - MILLION SMILES CD - It's about time their demos were released properly. Eleven classic sing-a-long tracks of pop-punk. I rate these guys up with Wact, Shreds, Couchies, etc as some of the best poppy hardcore in the UK. A must buy from Dropzone, PO Box 89, Worcester, WR3 8YU.

PUNK AND DISORDERLY - COMP TAPE #3 & ZINE #5 - The third compilation by P&D is 60 minutes of punk, HC, reggae and ska, featuring Spithead, Tarbrush, Krapp, Velvet Underpants, and Distortion. It has a printed cover and a 12 page booklet. The P&D zine is 36 pages of A5 with punk articles and interviews with 4 Past Midnight and Spithead. You get them both post paid for £2.00 from P&D, c/o M. Gordon, 2 Westacre Drive, Quarry Bank, West Midlands, DY5 2EE. The punkest.

KRAPP / URBAN EXCRETIA - SPLIT TAPE - This is true DIY spirit displayed by two of the UK's punkest young bands. Angry and loud, even if the quality is not superb. Reminds me of Yobs, Exploited, etc. Get it if you dare from the P&D address.

BANDIT QUEEN - GIVE IT TO THE DOG CDS - The second single before the release of their album, I'm told. Well, it really annoys me that people can waste time and money on such drivel. this is meaningless pap and I bet NME love them! Playtime Records.

DECADENCE WITHIN - REALITY WAKE UP CALL CD - Powerful and sincere, energetic, thrashy hardcore from this UK band. It's their third album and their experience shows on stage. Decadent Records, 7 Court Road, Strensham, Worcs, WR8 9LP.

THE ALMIGHTY - JONESTOWN MIND CDS - What's this, a well known metal band in BHP? Well, I was sent it so here goes. Three mixes of the same track, possibly not the best value for money, but then if you like it... The first is by Chris Sheldon and Almighty, the second by Therapy, and the third by the Ruts. The first is very well produced, but metal, the second is bleeping shite and the third is scraping to be the best of a poor bunch. From Chrysalis if you care.

RUB ULTRA - COMBAT STRENGTH SOAP CDS - I'm sure there's a reason why labels send bad chart music to an openly HC zine to be reviewed. I just don't know what it is!

FLYING MEDALLIONS - GLUEY CDS - These guys have had some good supports recently, but if this is anything to go by, they were totally undeserved. It's slightly angry Indie rock that sounds a little lame and dated. In bright green packaging from Acupuncture / Pinnacle.

NEW KINGDOM - CHEAP THRILLS CD - Yes, they are another pro-drugs rap band, but they are a little different in a mellow, funky way. A great bassline and a very laid back delivery. I guess you could chill to this, on Gee street.

MIGHTY MIGHTY BOSSTONES - SKACORE, THE DEVIL AND MORE CD - What can I say. This is superb. Ultra-catchy, powerful skacore with a Minor Threat, Angry Samoans and SSD medley. Buy it if you can find it! When I went to see them in Germany, they cancelled because the singer had a sore throat. Can you believe that!

STOP THE TORTURE - BAN VEAL CRATES!

These photographs were taken inside some of the Netherlands' veal crate houses. They are places of unimaginable cruelty. Calves as young as one week old are locked inside the veal crates. They stand alone in darkness, unable to move, with no bedding, imprisoned in a veal crate 2ft wide by 5ft long. They can barely stand on the slatted floor, and they are fed a diet that keeps their flesh white and tender for the dinner tables of Europe. They remain inside 24 hours a day until they are slaughtered at six months. Veal crates were banned in Britain in 1990, but this doesn't stop animals from being shipped abroad to European veal crates.

Only one thing can put an end to this torture, a complete European Community ban on veal crates. While the fight for legislation rages on, there are ways you can help :
1. Please do not buy veal that has been reared outside the UK. Most meat is labelled with it's country of origin. If it is not, demand to know which country it came from. Do the same in restaurants. If you must buy veal, make sure it's British.
2. Please write to the Rt. Hon. John Gummer MP, Minister of Agriculture, Whitehall Place, London, SW1A 2HH, asking that the UK stop sending British calves to be reared in veal crates abroad, and urge him to use his influence on European legislation.
3. Please support bodies such as the RSPCA who are lobbying against veal crates, and the protests at the ports involved.

BHP

PUNK FICTION

Price 50p

no. **9**

WELCOME TO BHP - ISSUE #9.

Yes, it's been a while, but here it is at last and I hope it's worth it. I have a list of many excuses for the delay, all of them true, but I know you're not interested in hearing them suffice to say that things are now sorted and BHP will be out and about regularly and more often.

There's been a hell of a lot of changes in my life since the last issue, and I've been pretty busy, with the band, travelling, etc. Some of the stuff I've been doing will be revealed in the future issues, maybe like the issue #7 tour reports. Anyway, with #9 we've tried to improve things and address a few of your suggestions, more UK bands, more humour and better layouts all of which will continue to improve because we've got a bunch of good ideas and a load of new equipment at BHP HQ. Thanx to everyone that bothered to return their 'BHP Readers Poll'. You can read about the results in this issue, along with articles on Quentin Tarantino and the Brat Pack, our usual bumper reviews section, and interviews with Pennywise, No empathy, Riverdales, CIV, Annalies, Dawson and Schema.

We ran out of room in this issue so we'll start working on #10 very soon. Please send your contributions to the BHP address, were particularly interested in hearing bands 'Tour Nightmares'. The competitions in the last issue were for real, but the response was not great. The Green Day singles were won by a young lady from Scotland and the NOFX CD by a punker from Somerset. In this issue we have a couple more silly prizes to give away and runners up will also be sent whatever old junk we decide. For a set of limited edition MANGA postcards, tell us; "What was the first major Manga animation to be released in the UK?" and for an even rarer NOFX blow-up sheep (called the Fuck Ewe) tell us "What is the name of their latest album, on the Vinyl version?" Send your answers a.s.a.p. to BHP Towers, and we will not be biased, even by free gifts of chocolate.

Moving on. As I mentioned in the last issue, the predominantly independent 'Hardcore scene', of which we are all a part seems to be being taken over by major labels and influenced by media hype. This is a situation where individuals must make the difference and the same underground scene will thrive and provide us with new bands, zines, venues and ideas.

As I write this I am listening to 'Burning Bushes and Burning Bridges' by the superb 'UNDERSTAND' - a UK band, yet one of my favourites. There are loads of great bands in the UK that easily stand up to their much hyped US counterparts but are finding it increasingly difficult to get shows. It seems now that everything is handled by management and agencies, so unless you are a big US name - forget it. This is destroying the integrity and DIY spirit of Hardcore, and turning its emotional & energetic music into nothing more than a product. There must be more support for UK acts and more venues to put them on, otherwise a great deal of new talent will never be heard and our scene will go stale. It is up to us not to let this happen.

Special thanx for their help with this issue go to Bernice, Miles, Dan, Steve, Michelle, Martyn Chris M, and you guys for reading it.

Write to: BHP Fanzine
              1 Chandos Road, Tunbridge Wells
              Kent, TN1 2NY. UK

PASS.

BHP FANZINE READERS POLL

With the first 1000 copies of the last edition of BHP we sent out a little questionnaire for you to fill in and return. We even made it easy for you, just ring your answer or fill in the gaps, but still only 553 of you have bothered so far. Anyway, the information was mainly to add to our mailing list but there were a few interesting questions too and here are the most popular replies...

The readership of this little zine seems to be pretty diverse, aged mainly between 17 and 25 but fairly evenly split between school/ college types and unemployed/employed types. Still slightly more boys (60%) than girls (40%) but with a lot of vegetarians and straight edgers as well as punkdoms usual drop-outs. No-one seems to think the police do a good job, except at setting people up and only one of you, Deek from Oi Polloi, is a regular reader of Rubberist. (He even sent in a photo of himself reading the aforementioned adult literature!) Favourite foods seem to be Chinese and Chips, fave format seems to be vinyl, but more people are buying cassettes and CD's now, and fave pastimes include bands, zines, skating and masturbating. It's a bit like 'Smash Hits' this, I'm not sure why I asked all these questions, but anyway, on with the nonsense. The most popular film was Aliens, closely followed by Star Wars, Taxi Driver and Pulp Fiction. Amusing ones, that I haven't seen, included 'Gang Bang Weirdos' and 'The Al Jolson Story'. Most popular colour was black - very HM and not strictly a colour, so we'll give it to purple as second, but it could've been 'Gypsy Celebration' or 'Sick'!

BHP readers best smell was, obviously, SEX! Various cooking and cut grass were also popular, but so were piss, fear and petrol? No-one seems to like cars as they're not very PC - "my favourite one would be crashed with blue lights on top and corpses within." but Pimpmobiles, General Lee, Chitty Chitty Bang Bang and Dolomites all came up. Fave book was 'Catcher in the Rye' (J.D. Salinger) and fave zine was BHP (of course).

The next question took ages to collate the answers but here are the readers top ten bands : Descendents/All, Jawbreaker, Couch Potatoes, Fugazi, Metallica, Green Day, Rancid, Adam & the Ants, Beastie Boys and Rollins. A bizarre collection which may explain why you only get to between one and three shows per month.

Question 23 was a trick one for our amusement but someone rang 'Hair Mares'. Music is bought mainly from Independent Stores and distros, and BHP's #3, 6 and 8 seem to be the most popular. You say that you like the zine because it is "enthusiastic and informative" and "has an editor called Mr Potato", also it has no Blur! Apparently it could be improved by more UK HC (check out this issue), more sex (in colour) and being 'double ply quilted'.

When asked about 'Bodily Topiary' one of you replied, presumably without having to look it up, that he only grew shrubs in his ears and arse. Pant pepsi's seem to occur only after too much barbecue and panty reactions only when you shave nether regions.

It appears that not many of you are going to bother voting, which is strange considering the most important thing about our hardcore scene is the 'DIY Spirit'.

So there you go, some small insight into the tiny minds of BHP's regular readership. We'll probably do a more useful readers poll in the near future, but in the meantime we'll be passing your addresses to the police and your completed questionnaires over for psychiatric evaluation.

<u>Postscript</u> :- We would like to know what exactly a Gypsy Celebration looks like. Are we missing out on Romany speech impediment parties? Also, Deek would like to inform us that the 'Dressing for Pleasure' edition of Rubberist is a particularly worthwhile perusal.

NO EMPATHY

ORLVION

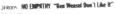

Postal Interview by Andy Ouasted

Hailing from the same windy city that gave us Naked Raygun, Big Black and Pegboy, over a period of ten years No Empathy has become a much respected band in its home town but remains relatively unknown over here. If you like your punk rock witty, articulate and raw, No Empathy's releases are well worth seeking out. Vocalist Marc Ruvolo answered a couple of hastily scrawled questions.

In addition to writing and singing in No Empathy, Marc also runs a record label, Johanns Face Records, that releases material by bands from the Chicago underground music scene.

● **How, when, where and why did No Empathy begin?**

"No Empathy began in 1983 when I was 17. It consisted of Craig White (who went off to join Seam), Chris Russell (now in Church Key) and Tom Costanzo (married, presumed dead). Like most punkers we went to shows and said 'we can do that!' And we did."

● **How long have you been running Johann's Face Records?**

"Johann's Face has been around for five years and I run it with my partner Gar Brandt. We have 19 releases and the bands on the label are: No Empathy, Smoking Popes, Oblivion, Apocalypse Hoboken, NoT Rebecca, The Strike, Smoothies, Cletus and Zoinks!

"We'll have five more releases this year."

● **Is Chicago-style punk rock thriving, or is it being stifled by major label interest?**

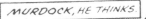

MURDOCK, HE THINKS.

NO EMPATHY

BEN WEASEL DON'T LIKE IT

--FIRE--

BRAKARDA

● **Since the Democrats have been in power in America, has the quality of life improved in Chicago, and in America in general?**

"Things always stay the same here. Republican and Democrat are just two sides of the same coin. But the religious right seems to be on the upswing which should make for some good tension. Gives us something to rail against I suppose. I live in the endless media star debate and sue, debate and shoot country. I love it!"

● **With a new album out recently, do the band have any plans to come to Europe?**

"We need to find someone to licence our record in Europe before we come. We would love to come over and play. I think the UK and Europe are really fascinating and fun. We move very slow, so maybe someday."

● **Do you intend to re-release your first LP (Nothing Less Than Nothing At All) or is it gone for good?**

"The less said about that mistake the better. Hopefully it will never see the light of day again. I'm red-faced now. I really thought it was funny, a joke, ha-ha! Oh well."

● **When and where did you first strap on your punk boots and pogo like crazy (ie what was the first bonafide punk rock gig you went to?)**

"I saw Naked Raygun here in good old Chicago in 1983 and was a convert ever since."

● **Will No Empathy still be 'rocking out' in the year 2000?**

"'Only the Shadow Knows'."

"Major labels are fucking up the bands to some extent – they pursue bands with only one 7in record out and give them all swelled heads and high hopes, then they drop them. Otherwise the punk scene is great, almost too big. The Fireside Bowl is our staple venue: punk shows seven days a week in a bowling alley, all ages and you can drink with ID. It's out of control."

● **What inspired you to release the crafty and hilarious 'Ben Weasel Don't Like It/ Chasing the Wild Goose' single?**

'We wanted to put out a single and I felt the need to make it special, to stand out amongst the pack of the thousands of 7inch singles that come out. So I came up with the idea one day 'cause I think both Ben Weasel and the "lost" Bad Religion record are equally hilarious. It came out exactly as I planned and people really liked it. It was very encouraging!"

● **Did you get any feedback from Bad Religion and Ben Weasel?**

"Ben Weasel hates my guts nowadays and Bad Religion never said a word."

I RESPEC
THAT,
LIEUTENA

BRAT PACK MOVIES

Well, this is supposed to be an article on 'Brat pack' movies. Except that Brat Pack is such an elastic term, something that means different things to different people. Covering such an expanse of fillums, that I figured it probably made sense to just overview it all. Oh yeah, and your correspondent is video-less meaning he could not gen-up on the subject very easily. Purely TV re-runs for this bwoy as he is at the mercy of the programme schedulers. I've never even seen Sixteen Candles! But I'll give it a go.

Where to start, well the man John Hughes seems an appropriate point. Yass, I know the feller despoiled this virgin earth when he delivered into the world the Home Alone's, but pre-Culkin toss he was an ace fillum geez. So let's begin with the worlds greatest movies ever. Hughes wrote and produced both THE BREAKFAST CLUB (1984) and FERRIS BUELLER'S DAY OFF (1986), which together illustrate Bratpacking at its best; funny, sad, jung and phresh, very 80s, strictlee no sequelisin. And of course with a big message at the end, about love will conquer all, whatever mates are they'll always be mates, your teenage years are the best in your life, etc.

THE BREAKFAST CLUB is the perfect Brat Pack film; tight, ensemble playing (five principle characters plus one oppressive authority figure), lots of joking around, plus very emotional bits in between. The idea is that it's Saturday morning at your average US high school. Five very different students, their characters clearly delineated: delinquent, princess, brain, weirdo and jock. They're each serving out detention, the so called 'breakfast club'. None knows any other as each usually moves in exclusive cliques, but throughout the detention they bond together in various ways, realising that love can conquer all, your mates are always your mates, being a teenager is great, etc. The acting is superb - Judd Nelson, Molly Ringwald, Anthony Michael Hall, Ally Sheedy and Emilio Estevez as the respective archetypes - and the script cannot be faulted. Hughes avoids turning it into a crappy 'Sweet Valley High' type piece and holds back from turning it into a series of loosely connected episodes. The point of the film is that it doesn't need to disintegrate into episodes as it's more about the change in character of each breakfast clubber that any individual incidents. For a Hollywood teenflick it is surprisingly wordy, cerebral some would say. Hughes at this time could actually get inside the Teenage Mind. Something that by 1990 and Uncle Buck (witness John Candy as a middle-aged Buck wading through the drunken debauchery of the teenage party, uncomprehending, disdainful) he had lost. But as xxxx wrote in a review of Pretty in Pink: "In those days writer John Hughes had a direct line to teen-think"; troo enuff

FERRIS BUELLER'S DAY OFF, which Hughes directed tells the tale of a popular kid in his last term before college, played by Matthew Broderick, who decides to bunk school (yet again) by feigning illness. Everyone loves him, except his cynical in-the-shade-of-her-bro sister, Jennifer 'Dirty Dancing' Grey and his suburban Chicago high school's principal, Jeffrey Jones - and it's these two who set out to unmask his duplicity. But Ferris is smart and remains one step ahead of both throughout, right up until the end of the movie. His purpose is to treat his Carol Vorderman-doppleganger girlfriend (Mia Sara), and his hypochondriac, neurotic best mate to a day out in the city, without being caught out and kept back for summer school. All this is combined with good humour, great set pieces - especially the street carnival and the restaurant, red convertible 'borrowed' from his mate's dad's garage, and some cheeky Alfie-esque straight to camera stuff, make for a classic film. And natch, it's topped off with a Hughesian moral, mainly to do with 'these are the best years of your life' ideas. A perfect Brat Pack movie because all the adults are stupid or naive and the kids win through always.

So, onto PRETTY IN PINK (1986). This was the second and best of the trio of Hughes' scripts which Howard Deutch directed (coming after Sixteen Candles), and like the Breakfast Club starred Molly, though here instead of the spoilt rich girl she is intelligent white trash bohemian whose best friends are 30 odd year old sceneshifting (one moment a punk, then a new romantic, etc.) Iona, played by Annie Potts, who works in a record store, and the Duck (Jon

Cryer), a Matthew Broderick lookielikie Teddyboy hopelessly but unrequitedly in love with and devoted to moll (soz for the long sentence but hey..). Essentially she falls for rich kid Andrew McCarthy - love across the divide-type stuff; but her friends (except the romantic Iona) all tell her not to get involved with a moneyhead, whilst his circle all take the piss for his falling for a girl from the wrong side of town. The prom is coming up, he asks to be her escort, she's not sure whether to go - she always felt it was a 'stupid tradition' - cue Psychedelic Furs soundtrack and mucho weepiness. Cool stuff. Watch out for Harry Dean Stanton (Alien, Repo Man) as her unemployed, depressed widower dad, and James Spader as the oily leader of the rich kids who keeps trying it on with Molly to no success. Molly looks totally shred in this, largely due to some cool cinematography; this, as The Breakfast Club, was photographed by Tak Fujimoto, and is a classy mix of cool night blues and luxuriant pinks and reds. Note to the swift of eye; notice the Subhumans sticker on the front of the record store counter just before Iona chases out the shoplifter!

SOME KIND OF WONDERFUL (1987) is essentially the same story but in reverse, this time with a poor boy and a rich girl, roles played by Eric 'Mask' Stoltz and Lea Thompson, love beyond class and all that. Eric's best mate is tomboy Mary Stuart Masterson, who loves him in a way far more subtle than Ducky loves Molly. Despite lea's snobby friends discouraging her, and Mary's reticence for Eric to get involved, the two protagonists do get it together; however this one has a twist at the end which many hoped would happen in Pretty In Pink but didn't. If you've seen them you know what I mean, but I don't want to spoil it for those that haven't. Overall this picture is unfulfilling, despite it being a tightening up of Pretty In Pink script. The two principals simply don't gel together, and both Thompson and Stoltz are outacted by Mary Stuart Masterson, who went on to shine in 'Fried Green Tomatoes At The Whistlestop Cafe'. None-the-less it does still convey a sense of the Hughesian optimism in teenage people.

After Hughes came a whole slew of movies during the 1980s which reflected the style and attitudes of the time - many of which also were strongly derivative of his teen-ensemble formula. Many of these even borrowed his casts; few made an impression in the same way as The Breakfast Club, Ferris Bueller's Day Off or Pretty In Pink did though. Exceptions for me include ST ELMO'S FIRE (1985) and O C AND STIGGS (1985). The former features a full complement of Bratpackers - McCarthy is reunited not only with The Breakfast Club's Ally Sheedy and Emilio Estevez, but also Rob Lowe, whose acting, alongside his own, dragged Graduate rip-off CLASS (1983) out of the gutter; and Demi Moore turns in one of only two good performances in her life. All it is really is a long bunch of incidents concerning young yuppies leaving high school and coming-of-age, which largely entails hanging round and getting pissed in the St Elmo's bar of the title. If you enjoy it then check out ABOUT LAST NIGHT (1986) Edward 'thirtysomething' Zwick's interpretation of a David Mamet play, in which seedsowing yuppie Rob Lowe frets over whether he can remain faithful to Demi Moore (in her only other good performance), with whom he has fallen in love. Enjoying in a non-Bratpack stylee. O C and Stiggs was a Robert Altman film made for National Lampoon, which despite receiving such poor reviews to send it STV in Britain, is actually quite a smart movie. It features no Bratpackers but the formula is recognisable; two Ferris-types set out to cause as much trouble to the upper-class Schwab family as possible, irrespective of the harm. There's no real direction in the plot, there's no storyline to shake a stick at, but it's fun and chaotic anyway.

So, that's my weave for this ish. In my next article I'll sew together more recent movies such as HEATHERS and STAND BY ME to the Brat Pack phenomenon, and try and drag a taste of the 1980's into the argument.

The weaver

Molly Ringwald
Pretty In Pink
BBC1 11.10pm

Age: 27.
Looks: Kookily pretty.
Temperament: Remarkably level-headed for a 'brat packer'.
Big break: *The Breakfast Club.*
Off-screen drama: At four, she was performing with pianist dad's Great Pacific Jazz Band. Cut an album at six. Linked with Dweezil Zappa, son of Frank, and Beastie Boy Adam Horowitz.
Previous form: *Sixteen Candles, Surviving, For Keeps, Strike It Rich, Betsy's Wedding, Face The Music.*
Prospects: Worthy of more.

SPACEHUNTER: ADVENTURES IN THE FORBIDDEN ZONE (1983)

SIXTEEN CANDLES (1984)

First film with writer-director-Svengali John Hughes (18 years older than Ringwald to the day), who was responsible for a host of teen angst dramas set in his home city of Chicago, that caught the mood of a generation because they spoke the same language and tackled real issues for the youth of America without offering pat answers. Ringwald plays Samantha Baker, an everyday teenager barely surviving the worst day of her life — her 16th birthday — an hilarious 24 hours full of disappointment, humiliation and embarrassment. Only released on video in the UK.

SIXTEEN CANDLES (1984)

First film with writer-director-Svengali John Hughes (18 years older than Ringwald to the day),

The Mid West heartland, the soul of America, was where most Americans wanted to be, and for film audiences, Molly was right there — the average girl next door from anywhere, USA. Never were the characters she played called upon to worry their pretty little heads about the meaning of life, other than the traumatic search for someone to love her. As possible suitors, Hughes paraded half a dozen good looking, boy-next-door types past his queen, in the likes of Andrew McCarthy and Emilio Estevez. Along with Ally Sheedy, they formed the core of the Brat-Pack.

THE BREAKFAST CLUB (1985)

Ground breaking Brat-Pack film, written, produced and directed by Hughes. A sort of equivalent to the stage musical *A Chorus Line.*

PRETTY IN PINK

"There are certain things about life that are really wonderful. Like love, food and sex. But to really enjoy food is one of the best things."

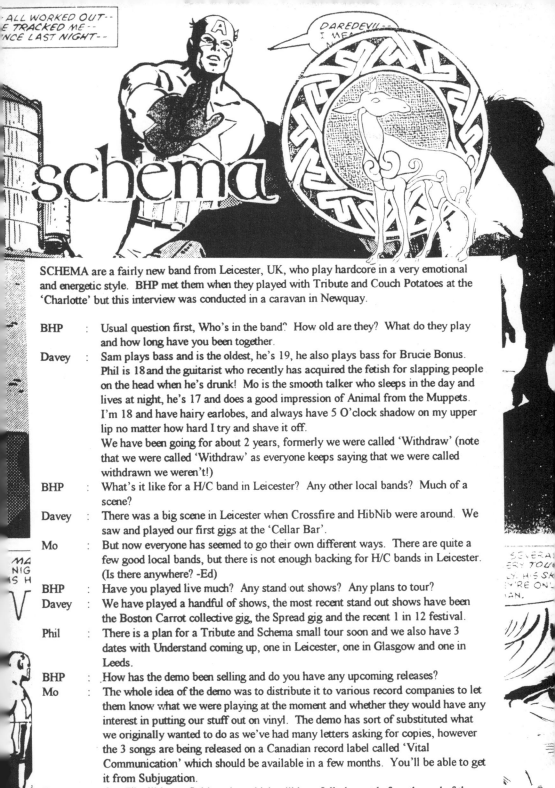

DAREDEVIL--
I MEA

schema

SCHEMA are a fairly new band from Leicester, UK, who play hardcore in a very emotional and energetic style. BHP met them when they played with Tribute and Couch Potatoes at the 'Charlotte' but this interview was conducted in a caravan in Newquay.

BHP : Usual question first, Who's in the band? How old are they? What do they play and how long have you been together.

Davey : Sam plays bass and is the oldest, he's 19, he also plays bass for Brucie Bonus. Phil is 18 and the guitarist who recently has acquired the fetish for slapping people on the head when he's drunk! Mo is the smooth talker who sleeps in the day and lives at night, he's 17 and does a good impression of Animal from the Muppets. I'm 18 and have hairy earlobes, and always have 5 O'clock shadow on my upper lip no matter how hard I try and shave it off.
We have been going for about 2 years, formerly we were called 'Withdraw' (note that we were called 'Withdraw' as everyone keeps saying that we were called withdrawn we weren't!)

BHP : What's it like for a H/C band in Leicester? Any other local bands? Much of a scene?

Davey : There was a big scene in Leicester when Crossfire and HibNib were around. We saw and played our first gigs at the 'Cellar Bar'.

Mo : But now everyone has seemed to go their own different ways. There are quite a few good local bands, but there is not enough backing for H/C bands in Leicester. (Is there anywhere? -Ed)

BHP : Have you played live much? Any stand out shows? Any plans to tour?

Davey : We have played a handful of shows, the most recent stand out shows have been the Boston Carrot collective gig, the Spread gig and the recent 1 in 12 festival.

Phil : There is a plan for a Tribute and Schema small tour soon and we also have 3 dates with Understand coming up, one in Leicester, one in Glasgow and one in Leeds.

BHP : How has the demo been selling and do you have any upcoming releases?

Mo : The whole idea of the demo was to distribute it to various record companies to let them know what we were playing at the moment and whether they would have any interest in putting our stuff out on vinyl. The demo has sort of substituted what we originally wanted to do as we've had many letters asking for copies, however the 3 songs are being released on a Canadian record label called 'Vital Communication' which should be available in a few months. You'll be able to get it from Subjugation.

Davey : Our 7" will be on Subjugation which will hopefully be out before the end of the year.

Phil : There also may be a split 7" with Tribute, which will be funded from gigs.

BHP	:	What have been the main influences on Schema's sound and what were each individual members influence's? How did you all discover H/C?
Phil	:	Schema's sound has been influenced by a variety of different types of music, the basis of the band style is linked with Emotional-Hardcore, but we all do listen to different stuff. I was into all the heavy stuff. When I came up to school and met Davey we swapped D.R.I. records and it led on from there...
Davey	:	I first got into it when I was about 12, listening and taping punk bands off John Peel. Black Flag were on skateboard videos and once I found Rockaboom (Alternative record shop in Leics.) I was buying records each week. Mo got into the sXe stuff from his brother and John Kraus, now he's a techno freak! Sam hates hardcore, it's all an act. His scary slam dancing, shaved head and beady eyes are all a mask. No joke, he's got a Kylie tape and is never ashamed to listen to it !!!
BHP	:	Is any of Schema sXe? Do you have any views on drugs etc...?
Davey	:	When we were 'Withdraw' we had the crosses on our hands and were proud for 2 years!
Mo	:	It's probably because we would never get served at the bar!
Davey	:	But after a while we seemed to be doing it because it was cool not because we didn't want to get drunk, because we did!
Mo	:	We all still believe in the fight for animal liberation, we are all still veggie, apart from Sam who can demolish the 'Little Chef 8 inch Bison burger' in under a minute. (We discovered his talent an hour before playing the 1 in 12 festival).
Davey	:	We still totally believe in equality and liberation. We just found drinking fun. Therefore we couldn't have the edge any more.
BHP	:	Do any of Schema like skateboarding?
Davey	:	We all skate, however we don't stick mattresses in our trainers and don't wear shell suit bottoms like gangsta's. I was sponsored by Switch for a bit until I dislocated my knee stage diving last year at Abby Park to Tubesurfer, so I had to pack it in for a bit.
BHP	:	Favourite foods?
Mo	:	Alsatian in pitta bread, from Aassans Kebab joint. £1.80 with extra chilli sauce. BARGAIN !
BHP	:	What do you never miss on T.V.?
Phil	:	French films with subtitles.
BHP	:	Best gig you've been to?
Phil	:	ZZ-Top, the fluffy guitars that spun round and around did it for me!
Sam	:	The Goats, Phat tunes in da' house!
Mo	:	S.N.F.U., Mr. Chi pigs war dance with the light sabre!
Davey	:	The Bootleg Beetles, Mop tops like mine, yeah! Groovy man!
BHP	:	Do any of schema listen to Hip Hop/rap etc.? Any views on the whole sexist and homophobic thing?
Davey	:	We all listen to a variety of different music. Sam is into Hip Hop the most. We are all completely against the homophobic and sexist attitudes which gangsta' bands use, it's mindless rubbish! The sad thing is that there is nothing anyone can do to stop them writing bigoted songs.
Sam	:	Gangsta's rap just reinforces traditional values, it didn't create them. It's given Hip Hop a bad name.
BHP	:	Why Ned Kelly's Armour? (Artwork on their demo cover - Ed)
Davey	:	OK there's 2 reasons for using Ned Kelly on the front cover. The easy answer is that it looked really good. But the real reason behind using the picture of his final shoot out is that it ties in with the concept of a schema. A schema is a sort of thing that happens which leads to other things, it's a sort of building block. You really have to know about the Kelly story to understand it so.... are you sitting comfortably?

A JOKE, HERE IN /CA WE IE KIDS HRISTMAS OME FROM CLAUS.

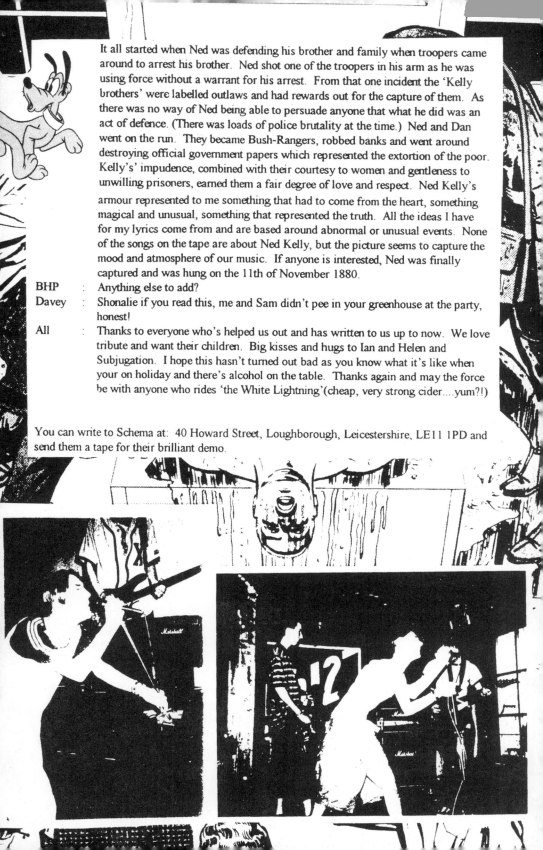

It all started when Ned was defending his brother and family when troopers came around to arrest his brother. Ned shot one of the troopers in his arm as he was using force without a warrant for his arrest. From that one incident the 'Kelly brothers' were labelled outlaws and had rewards out for the capture of them. As there was no way of Ned being able to persuade anyone that what he did was an act of defence. (There was loads of police brutality at the time.) Ned and Dan went on the run. They became Bush-Rangers, robbed banks and went around destroying official government papers which represented the extortion of the poor. Kelly's' impudence, combined with their courtesy to women and gentleness to unwilling prisoners, earned them a fair degree of love and respect. Ned Kelly's armour represented to me something that had to come from the heart, something magical and unusual, something that represented the truth. All the ideas I have for my lyrics come from and are based around abnormal or unusual events. None of the songs on the tape are about Ned Kelly, but the picture seems to capture the mood and atmosphere of our music. If anyone is interested, Ned was finally captured and was hung on the 11th of November 1880.

BHP   :   Anything else to add?

Davey   :   Shonalie if you read this, me and Sam didn't pee in your greenhouse at the party, honest!

All   :   Thanks to everyone who's helped us out and has written to us up to now. We love tribute and want their children. Big kisses and hugs to Ian and Helen and Subjugation. I hope this hasn't turned out bad as you know what it's like when your on holiday and there's alcohol on the table. Thanks again and may the force be with anyone who rides 'the White Lightning'(cheap, very strong cider....yum?!)

You can write to Schema at: 40 Howard Street, Loughborough, Leicestershire, LE11 1PD and send them a tape for their brilliant demo.

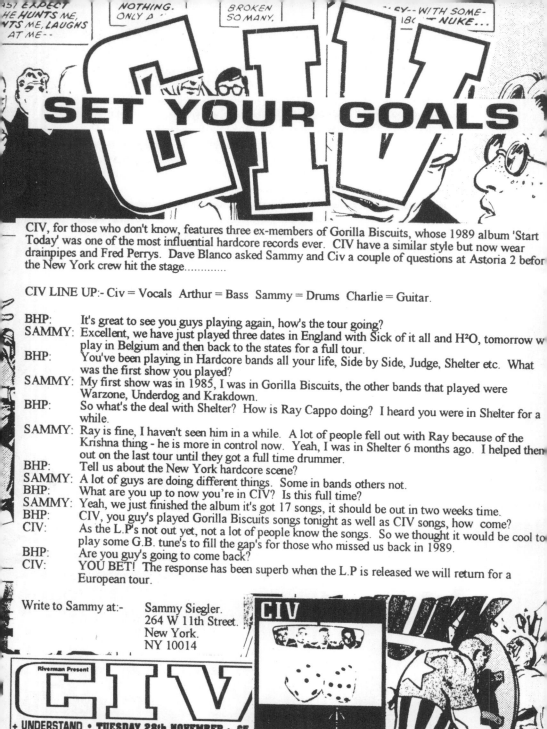

SET YOUR GOALS

CIV, for those who don't know, features three ex-members of Gorilla Biscuits, whose 1989 album 'Start Today' was one of the most influential hardcore records ever. CIV have a similar style but now wear drainpipes and Fred Perrys. Dave Blanco asked Sammy and Civ a couple of questions at Astoria 2 befor the New York crew hit the stage.............

CIV LINE UP:- Civ = Vocals Arthur = Bass Sammy = Drums Charlie = Guitar.

BHP: It's great to see you guys playing again, how's the tour going?

SAMMY: Excellent, we have just played three dates in England with Sick of it all and H²O, tomorrow w play in Belgium and then back to the states for a full tour.

BHP: You've been playing in Hardcore bands all your life, Side by Side, Judge, Shelter etc. What was the first show you played?

SAMMY: My first show was in 1985, I was in Gorilla Biscuits, the other bands that played were Warzone, Underdog and Krakdown.

BHP: So what's the deal with Shelter? How is Ray Cappo doing? I heard you were in Shelter for a while.

SAMMY: Ray is fine, I haven't seen him in a while. A lot of people fell out with Ray because of the Krishna thing - he is more in control now. Yeah, I was in Shelter 6 months ago. I helped them out on the last tour until they got a full time drummer.

BHP: Tell us about the New York hardcore scene?

SAMMY: A lot of guys are doing different things. Some in bands others not.

BHP: What are you up to now you're in CIV? Is this full time?

SAMMY: Yeah, we just finished the album it's got 17 songs, it should be out in two weeks time.

BHP: CIV, you guy's played Gorilla Biscuits songs tonight as well as CIV songs, how come?

CIV: As the L.P's not out yet, not a lot of people know the songs. So we thought it would be cool to play some G.B. tune's to fill the gap's for those who missed us back in 1989.

BHP: Are you guy's going to come back?

CIV: YOU BET! The response has been superb when the L.P is released we will return for a European tour.

Write to Sammy at:-   Sammy Siegler.
                        264 W 11th Street.
                        New York.
                        NY 10014

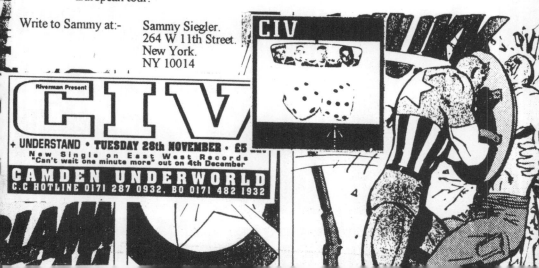

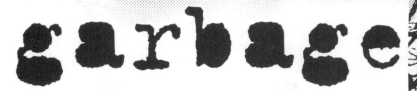

garbage

OUR DAY OUT WITH GARBAGE

Garbage are a fairly new band from Madison, Wisconsin who play music kinda like Nine Inch Nails, but more poppy. There drummer just happens to be producer extrodinaire Butch Vig! For those of you who don't know, he's the producer behind bands like Nirvana, Smashing Pumpkins, L7 and Sonic Youth. Also in the band are Duke Erikson and Steve Marker, who both work with Butch at their smart studio's in Madison. Vocals are provided by Shirley Manson who is from Edinburgh in Scotland, where she still lives.

They have two singles out to date. Their first single 'Vow' was released only on 7". (Cool for a major label). This was single of the week in almost every music publication and was high on Indie club chart playlists. For the release of their new single 'Subhuman', the band decided to hold zines only press conference, and BHP was invited!

Enticed by the invitation, which mentioned free Mexican food and drink, we decided to go along. The venue was a barge on the Thames, which seemed to sail around in circles near the pier for the one and a half hours we were onboard!

First we were played the album, which will be released in late September, then the band, armed with microphones appeared and a mic was passed around for people to ask questions

Most of the questions were aimed at Butch Vig, but what did he have to say? Firstly they're a mainstream 'pop' band and not an underground grunge band. He made this very clear! Butch said he has always loved pop music and claims he was president of the 'Roxy Music Fan Club' in Madison.

Whilst in Europe they had visited some Techno clubs and he thought that what was happening there was similar to when punk first started to happen in America. So much for the 'Godfather of grunge' tag!

The question on many peoples minds was "why form a band when you're so successful as a producer?" His reply to this was that he, Duke and Steve had been doing a lot of remix work for bands like House of Pain, Depeche Mode, U2 and N.I.N. They would strip the song to just the vocals and build them up again, often recording new music themselves. They enjoyed this and decided to start recording music together and met Shirly while she was touring the states with her former band Angelfish.

When asked whether he liked cream buns or chips best, he said he'd better not answer!?!

By now it was time for food! Unfortunately the Mexican food was for meateaters only, the vegetarians were left with rather watery flan! There was however, fruit salad and melon for pudding, which was pretty good and there was two free drinks each from the bar.

We ate, drank, then left. By the time you read this Garbage will probably be massive and their album should be out. Their singles are worth getting for the packaging alone ('Vow' has a metal sleeve and 'Subhuman' has a rubber sleeve).

"Melodic joy lurking in the form of dynamically churning riffs and spectacularly serrated guitars." N.M.E.

Miles & Michelle.

DRINK DRIVING - THE FACTS

You can't calculate your alcohol limit.

The legal limit for driving is 80mg of alcohol per 100ml of blood. There is no guide as to how much you can drink to stay under this limit as the amount and type of alcoholic drink, and your height, weight and metabolism all determine the level of alcohol in your blood. Any alcohol, even a small drink, will impair driving ability.

Alcohol takes effect quickly but wears off slowly.

All the alcohol you drink is absorbed into the bloodstream within an hour, affecting the brain and impairing driving ability, but it takes 20 hours to be eliminated. So if you drink a lot in the evening, you might still be over the limit the following morning.

Any amount of alcohol will affect your judgement.

Nearly one in five of all deaths on the road are caused by drivers who have been drinking. One in three of the drivers killed in road accidents have levels of alcohol which are over the legal limit. The Sussex Police Road Accident Review shows that in 1992 alone a total of 111 accidents causing death or injury were due to drunk drivers. The risk of being involved in an accident increases in direct proportion to the amount consumed. You are not safe to drive, even if you are below the legal limit. Even one drink will have an effect on driving ability.

Drinking and driving has lasting consequences.

Legal : 5 years imprisonment for causing death by careless driving whilst under the influence of drink or drugs, Up to 6 months imprisonment, Fine of up to £2000, 12 month driving ban, Providing evidence of being medically fit to drive before your licence is restored, Possible referral to rehabilitation course.

Social : Criminal record, Loss of reputation, Effect on family life, Loss of driving licence, Loss of personal transport.

Conscience : Living with the knowledge that your irresponsibility has caused death, injury or severe distress to innocent people, Causing distress and shame to your family.

Financial : Fine, Possible loss of livelihood, Increased insurance cover, Legal expenses, Increased travel expenses.

Medical Consequences of Drinking Alcohol

Alcohol is a depressant; it affects your judgement, self-control and co-ordination, thus increasing your chances of having an accident. Excessive drinking can cause hangovers, dehydration, gastritis, ulcers, high blood pressure, vitamin deficiency, sexual dysfunction, brain damage, hepatitis, cirrhosis, cancer and obesity.

If you have an alcohol problem and you require help to control it, you, or your family or friends, can contact :-

Alcoholics Anonymous,
Head Office,
P.O. Box 1,
Stonebow House,
Stonebow,
York, YO1 2NJ.
Tel : (0904) 644026
London - Tel : (071) 3523001
Wales - Tel : (0222) 373939
Northern Ireland - Tel : (0232) 681084
Scotland - Tel : (041) 2219027

Alcohol Concern,
275 Grays Inn Road,
London, WC1X 8QF.
Tel : (071) 8333471
Wales - Tel : (0222) 488000

It is medically proven that drinking is bad for you, but you need never mix it with driving. Drinking and driving is dangerous and irresponsible, and you are endangering other people's lives as well as your own. How would you feel if your stupidity killed your best friend? Think about it!

The only safe course is not to drink and drive!

DRINKING AND DRIVING WRECKS LIVES.

annalise

Annalise are a rocking melodic hardcore band from Devon, they used to be Wordbug but have changed
their name and are going from strength to strength. There will be new releases soon, so check them out

BHP: So as usual, what's the line-up and who plays what?
ANNALISE: Adrian / Drums, Martyn / Vocals, John / Guitar and David / Bass.
BHP: How long have you been going?
ANNALISE: Seven Months.
BHP: I hear you used to be Wordbug - that hardcore outfit from Exeter, is this true? Why
the change?
ANNALISE: It's true. Wordbug's last show was in some bar in Europe. After the show, we sat
around with gallons of free beer and toasted the future. That was it; the end of
Wordbug. The whole thing was feeling tired so it was time to move on. We talked
through what we wanted to do and Seven months on, here we are.
BHP: Have there been any style / line-up changes since this vital juncture?
ANNALISE: Wordbug had 101 different line ups, the final line up of which became Annalise. Styl
wise, it's just taking what we've always done and always will do. Just playing the mos
honest and emotive music to us that we can. The words and music (infact everything
we do) are just how we want to do it. If others like it that's fine but it's very much ou
own thing.
BHP: Do you have any recording plans for the near future as I hear you are drawing up
schedules etc.?
ANNALISE: Our first EP 'Fettered' is out now on Out of order/Snuffy Smile. We'll be recording
again soon for a new release.
BHP: How do you come up with songs as a band? Is it one member? What's your secret?!
ANNALISE: Writing is real difficult. Basically we'll play over a new song for a few weeks, argue
constantly on what we should do with it, lose it, re-discover it on tape and then go with
the idea we had for it in the first place.
BHP: Tell us about your local Exeter scene, and your opinions on the UK scene in general!
ANNALISE: Punk and HC wise there isn't a scene here. There's a few punkers but mostly your
usual 'alternative' type crowd. There's us and a new band; Terminal Youth but there's
not an exclusively punk scene as such like there has been in the past. We always get
good crowd at our shows and we don't care what they're into. UK wise, I don't really
follow it that closely. If you went on the sheer number of bands mentioned in say,
'How we rock', you'd have to say things are healthy but for every Bob Tilton, there's 5
unoriginal, US wanabee emo clone bands. There's obviously some genuine, motivated
people out there with a real feel for what they perceive HC / Punk to be, which is cool
but like-wise, there's a lot of fakers around. I'm interested in what I like in the scene
without being into everything about it just because it's labelled 'Punk' or 'Hardcore' if
that makes any sense.
BHP: What do you all get from being in a band?
ANNALISE: Just the experience of it all. Things happen that don't, couldn't and wouldn't happen if
we weren't doing this.
BHP: Tell us a good fight story as we hear you're hard b'stards!
ANNALISE: My only fight stories come from being in bands. Our first show ended after 2 songs
when some guy jumped me. When I was in Mad at the sun, some guy went for me
with a lump of wood. I'm not into violence in the slightest but like I said earlier, it's al
part of the experience..... Then again, it might just be peoples way of telling us we're
crap!

BHP: Do a good bit of promotion and name some good fellow UK hardcore bands!!

ANNALISE: Tribute, Bob Tilton, Useful idiot, Understand.........

BHP: What do the band listen to? e.g.- birdsongs, each others farts??!

ANNALISE: Television, Hoover, Oasis, Jeff Buckley, Face to Face.

BHP: What do you guys reckon on the present 'Punk explosion' going on? e.g. Greenday, Offspring etc. Do you intend to get caught up in it?

ANNALISE: From experience, any half decent UK band could get 'caught up in it'. Labels, management etc. are all out there looking; people have been to see us numerous times now and advised us of what our 'next step' to a major should be. I've got nothing

against signing and I don't see it as 'Selling out'. To me, a couple of years of recording, touring; of just the experience of doing it is not something that's worth debating when the alternative is the 9 - 5, signing on or whatever. I've heard all the arguments about retaining control within the scene and creating our own network, well, that's fine. I truly admire the really genuine people I've met who believe in the D.I.Y side of thing but that just doesn't work for everyone. Would we go down the majors road? The D.I.Y side of things we enjoy and meeting the active people in the scene is one of the things we enjoy about being in the band. So I don't know. I know Adrian is dead against it 'cos one of the management companies said he should get his hair cut! It's unreal isn't it?

BHP: What was the first punk / HC record you heard / brought? Do you still like it!!??

ANNALISE: God Knows! The first one that actually moved me was 'Its alive' by the Romones, after that I was hooked!

BHP: Finish your interview with some nice / funny stories / comments!!

ANNALISE: It's.... I am....; I can't think! Thanks for the interview.

Annalise are on the Dag Nasty tribute CD out soon. Also featuring, Couch Potatoes, Hooton 3 Car, Horace pinker, etc, etc.

You can contact Annalise c/o 45 Baker Street, Heavitree, Exeter, EX2 5EA

Playing a gig

at a squat

in Germany

This is a excerpt from the shortly to be published **'BHP's Big Book Of Bullshit,'** a collection of urban myths revealed and real life stories. So keep them peeled in W.H.Smiths, OK.

For this instalment try to imagine everything herein with a German accent on it, kind of guttural, harsh, pidgeon English. Right. Oh, and swear a lot. And be very drunk.

So, you turn up eventually at the 'venue', which happens to be a huge disused factory, with not a single window, that is being squatted in. At first there is no one waiting near the entrance, and all you can see are a few rusting hulks, so you think you've stumbled onto the set of the new Mad Max film. Then, suddenly, this big hairy man, wearing only baggy combats and a ripped UK Subs T-shirt, (no shoes) lurches out of a doorway towards you with a shocked look on his face............

"No, I'm sorry, you cannot come in." *"WHAT! We're the band, we've travelled about 3000 miles to play here tonite."* "You are, err, how you say, driving a petrol powered vehicle. The use of which rapes mother earth. You cannot attend." *"What, well how else...."* "To gain admittance you must arrive on Rob Roskopp boards, performing tailslides and 360°s, and be followed by a pack of stray dogs." *"but"* "Also, you are wearing Vans skate shoes. You must only skate barefoot or in 18 hole surplus steel toe cap boots, or get in you will not." *"Look, you know, we're sorry about the truck, but we're here now, I mean, we may as well...."* "No, err, sorry, you are not wearing army fatigues. We, how you say, have a dress code." At this, what you presume is the promoter, produces a crumpled scrap of hemp paper and begins to read....... "Skin tight trousers, preferably combats. Black surplus jacket. No socks allowed ever, Rope belts or bullet belts only, Rolled up woolly hat (summer only), 1983 Discharge tour shirts with sleeves and sides cut off, boots or sandals, very dirty dreadlocks, body piercing and bad tattoos (preferably C.O.C.), petuli oil, home-made beads and necklaces of your own teeth......" He goes on and a crowd is starting to gather around you, looking you all up and down but not saying a word. Oddly enough, they all have correct dress, and smell.

A few more of your crew are now getting out of the van for a stretch, and the guy stops and screams, "NO. You have arrived with vaguely attractive females, they do not look like men! To be even remotely attractive is to be exploited by the Mass Kontrol State and, how you say, man is the bastard." *"But."* By now you're wondering if this is for real and worrying about being bitten, or shagged, by one of the numerous stray dogs. Will you ever get in? Another squat inhabitant runs towards you waving his arms and yelling excitedly. Luckily, a fire seems to have been started somewhere in the squat so they all run off to piss on it.

So you head towards the doorway and can't help but notice the graffiti and street art covering every inch of concrete with vivid depictions of family violence and disorder. There are posters for the show, printed on toilet paper with brown ink. "We mix a kind of inky paste, you know, out of our shit and piss. We use it for notices, letters and body-art." Says another local, "Do you play tonite?" *"Err, I think so."* "Then you are on the top floor, but the lift is broken, and the stairs are, how you say, very dangerous." *"Smashing."*

HAVE FIVE
CONDS.

Not being STUPID.
Matt backs AWAY.

GIVE ME --
A WHITE --

Three hours later you are sitting upstairs waiting for the show. You still do not know who the real promoter is, and you are waiting as the last support band practice. There is only a drummer and a guitarist who shouts, he has both your amps turned up to ten and obviously does not realise how close to death he is. The other supports have 4 bassists, 6 drummers, 2 guitarists, many dogs but, apparently no singers, although there may be a political activist speaking if you're really lucky. It all sounds like a banshee gargling glass and playing Napalm Death.

Of this whole eight storey factory only one small corner is regularly used, everywhere else is dripping with piss and has things scurrying over bodies, or else has a band practising in it that sounds like Discharge on speed. "Hey, we don't like melody, we like NOISE! - Extreme Noise Terror, Chaos UK, you know it is true." He plays air guitar. *"Moron."* You move, past the 'Gegen Everything' patches stall, to the bar, that only serves home-made cider and are offered some Vegetarian stew. *"Excellent."* But it has sausage in it, and probably rat too. "It makes it taste good. Yes." You haven't eaten all day. Your head and stomach ache. To add to this, the only toilet in the whole place has no lights, no lock, no flush and a pallet for a door, and the whole place is starting to fill with drunk punks, spitting, swearing and jumping on one another.

You're hanging out at the merchandise stall when this guy in a bright early 80's tracksuit comes over, "Hey, what is this vinyl. It rapes our mother earth of oil. We like tenth generation, poor quality ferric cassettes sent by pen pals only." *"What are you, an asshole?"* "No, I am guitarist." Some idiot who's been slamming to the support band tries to swap his mosh broken records for new ones, then some old guy, with mentally thick glasses comes over to tell you that if you give him a free record he'll get you a show at a 10,000 seat stadium nearby. You tell him that you have no interest in supporting The Spin Doctors in front of 10,000 tightly trousered hippies, so he can blow you.

It's nearly two in the morning so you go to play. Half asleep, blinded by smoke. Some people cheer, some people dance, one huge bloke in a cop killer T-shirt shouts 'Fuck off' after every song, but then tells you he loves you, and all the ugly girls try to get off with you. You're not even allowed to leave the stage until you've played many bad covers. It's getting desperate so it's time to find the promoter. You pick the most likely candidate and hassle him. "Hey, my friends, I am sorry, there is no money. It was an anti-fascist benefit for me and my komrades." *"But..."* "You can sleep here on cold floors, with beer, piss, dogs and Y-fronts." *"No, I really..."* "Or we can party all night and smash many things. We have one bottle of wine and many versions of 'SLFs Tin Soldiers' to dance to. Fun, I am thinking. No?" *"You sad asshole, give us some money."* It's looking bleak. Luckily, your driver has sneaked into this guys room and stolen all his money and records, and shat in his bed, so it's time to leave. You drive all nite to the next show, and it starts again............

"Tee-Hee!"
Cute and coy, Minnie can almost always get what she wants with a flutter of her long, feathery eyelashes.

"Yoo-Hoo! Mickey!"
The essence of femininity, Minnie likes to dress in ruffles and bows. Pink, of course, is her favorite color!

Minnie Mouse
Sometimes sweet, sometimes sassy, she's the "mouse next door" – and always Mickey's best gal!

Pennywise hail from Hermosa Beach, California, the home of Black Flag, Circle Jerks and Descendents to name a few. They have released three albums on Epitaph, 'Pennywise', 'Unknown Road' and the new 'About time' are all blasts of thrashy but melodic surfcore. BHP spoke to guitarist, Fletcher Dragee, to get an insight into what it's like being in a punk band becoming massive...........

BHP: So, Fletcher, you've been on Epitaph records, it seems, ever since the beginning. How did that all come into effect?

F.D: Well, we put out a single on Theologian and were getting radio airplay. When we went to do an interview we told the DJ we were looking for a label, he knew Brett Gurewitz (Epitaph boss-ed) and introduced us. We played him out tape and he just signed us. Epitaph was pretty small then, only Bad Religion and NO-FX, he signed us and Down By Law. It was all in one house, we watched it grow - Brett had faith.

BHP: Now that Epitaph's bands have become 'big business' what do you think of people who knock the labels credibility?

F.D: It's total bullshit. Most people don't know Brett, he is my friend. He believes in the music. At a major label the guy at the top doesn't give a shit whether it's punk or Country & Western, it's just a product. Brett is using the money to build Epitaph Europe. There's no sell out. He was offered $50 million for half the label, but said no way. He's even going to build his own pressing plant so he doesn't have to rely on anyone. Anybody who talks shit must be jealous.

BHP: OK, your new album 'About Time' continues to be fast and powerful but the lyrics seem to be getting more concerned and involved. With songs like 'Freebase' what are you trying to achieve?

F.D: Basically, a positive message. It's like 'Do what you want, don't listen to others or take loads of shit, don't waste your life. Do what makes you happy.' When you die you can say 'yeah, I did that.' As for 'Freebase', it's stuff we've been through. A friend of Jimmys (Vocalist-ed) is addicted to crack right now, this is like the last chance to help this guy. If we record something, it hits home hard. On our last album the track 'Vices' was about a heroin addict, he heard it and he got sober. If people can relate that's cool, if it helps, great, it's worth it. If ten people bought the album and we made no money that's fine.

BHP: This is going to be your first trip to the UK, this year your at Reading festival, etc. What are you expecting?

F.D: Well, i've heard it's really good. We didn't have the money before, because of low guarantees. It wasn't by choice, we couldn't afford to come over. I'd rather play in clubs. The ticket prices are too high at festivals and the merchandise prices get raised, the head bands charge $30 instead of $10. There will be people who hear us who wouldn't normally, they may buy the album in a few months.

BHP: Pennywise have a reputation for causing riots at shows, why do you cause them and do people get hurt?

F.D: It's just a bit of fun. The only time I start a riot is if the promoter treats us like shit. I've been arrested on stage by the police, handcuffed and thrown in jail. We're not into violence, but if someone trys to exploit us they pay the price.

BHP: Apparently, you guys like to snowboard. Is there any snow in California, and is it the same thrill as Skateboarding?

F.D: Yeah, there's snow in California. Mammoth Mountain is a big ski resort, only 5 hours from our house, or 2 hours from the beach house. We drive up to snowboard, rent a cabin and party, 25 days already this year. We've just got back from World Extreme in Alaska where we play every year. There are now no lifts so wehave to use a helicopter. This small town gets taken over for the gig. You may have seen 'King of the Hill' in Thrasher, that's a crazy show, everything got knocked down. We try to do cool things like that to keep our roots.

BHP: Is the US gripped in the same Quentin Tarantino fever as Europe?

F.D: It sure is - He ran a video store just up the street, I used to go in and talk to him, he knew everything about every movie ever made. I took a video back broken once, he kept phoning us and took back my dads card. Pulp Fiction is a great movie and has a great soundtrack.

BHP: Is California really so cool?

F.D: It's all too cool, everyone's on the edge. It's so fast you can never relax. Gangbangers, tough guys, homeless. There's so many new bands it's overkill. It's all about money.

BHP: And is Michael Jackson really a bad guy?

F.D: I think so, how can you say for sure? He could pay someone. He's never had a girlfriend - i'm not a big fan of M.J. He's changed again now, he looks Japanese. But it's like those expensive Mick Martin trials, Five years in Jail to be found innocent. It ruins lives.

BHP: I guess that's it Fletcher, anything to add?

F.D: Sorry we've not been to the UK before, were looking forward to coming to the home of the Sex Pistols. London and Los Angeles are legendary. Hopefully, no-one is gonna be standing around when we play. We'll have some fun.

QUENTIN TARANTINO'S SUCCESS STORY

To film buffs, Quentin Tarantino is the proof that, as he puts it, "If you love movies enough you can make them. You don't have to know a camera lens from a bag of sand." Tarantino loves movies so much that he borrowed bits of them for his own work. As he explained, some speeches in 'Reservoir Dogs' were based on scenes from Brian de Palma's 'Casualties of War'. He might have added that the names of the film's characters - Mr Brown, Mr Pink etc. - are reminiscent of the 1974 Train-Heist thriller 'The Taking of Pelham One Two Three.' Not that fans could care less about this. The fact that he refers to such cool sources just emphasises his good taste. Not only is Tarantino hip, he's deliciously naughty too. 'Reservoir Dogs' was banned from British Video release and it immediately became a permanent fixture of late-night Friday and Saturday cinema shows, thus ensuring its cult status. 'Natural Born Killers' was only released after months of agonising by the censors that guaranteed a tidal wave of publicity.

All that's left for Tarantino's triumph are the Oscars, which will be well deserved for a film like 'Pulp Fiction' which has a sensational script. But keen observers will note that Tarantino shares the nomination with another writer, Roger Avary, who only receives a 'story' credit on the film itself.

Certainly, Tarantino has made little effort to acknowledge Avary. When accepting a Golden Globe award in January for Best Screenplay, he made no mention of Avary, nor did advertisements proclaiming Pulp Fiction's many Oscar nominations reveal that Avary was a co-nominee. These oversights have come as little surprise to those who witnessed that much of Tarantino's best work was originally created with the collaboration of friends and colleagues, who's names have since been forgotten in the rush to make him a star.

One of those people is Cathryn James. She was Tarantino's manager for more that a decade. On the morning after the LA earthquake, he had his new business advisors call her to say that her services were no longer required. Those who knew both James and Tarantino were horrified. "She paid his rent, she supported him and she put up with all the rejection letters" Says Don Murphy, producer of 'Natural Born Killers'. "And the moment he gets some success, he fires her."

Tarantino's English is extremely shaky. He'd been held back a year and had quit before graduating. His scripts were packed with ideas thought up over group dinners & scribbled down on napkins. Craig Hamann, a close friend of Tarantino's would take the scraps away and turn them into a properly formulated scripts. Whenever Tarantino gets into trouble he calls Hamann, an example of this being a particular scene in 'Pulp Fiction' where Uma Thurman, playing a gangsters wife, snorts heroin, thinking it to be cocaine and overdoses. Tarantino asked Hamann to help make the scene work when the film was already in production. The result was one of the most memorable sections of a film packed with arresting images. But when 'Pulp Fiction' appeared, there was no mention of Hamann in the credits.

Tarantino first met Roger Avary, the 29 year old director of 'Killing Zoe' when he was a sales assistant at Video Archives. In 1987 Avary showed Tarantino a script he'd written called 'Open Road', which was 'True Romance' and 'Natural Born Killers' combined. He asked Avary if he could take it away and do some work on it. The result was hundreds of pages long but Avary suggested they concentrate on the story of two run-away lovers, Clarence and Alabama. This became 'True Romance'. Tarantino and Avary planned to direct and produce the movie themselves, but in the meantime they concentrated on polishing the scripts. Much of what emerged was entirely Tarantino's, but some of Avary's too, including two scenes that never made it to the final draft. In one, a man accidentally fires a gun inside a car, splattering another mans brains all over the back seat. In another, a gunman emerges from the bathroom where he's been hiding, fires off an entire magazine at his target at point-blank range, but misses with every shot. Both these scenes appear in 'Pulp Fiction'.

When 'True Romance' was premiered, Roger Avary sat watching, hearing many of his own lines and seeing his final scene. He didn't know whether to rejoice at seeing his work on screen, or weep at his lack of recognition, as all the plaudits went to Tarantino. For all his own work, Avary received nothing. For the ending which he totally created himself, he received less than $1.000. This was not the last time that he would have bitter regrets about his collaboration and friendship with Tarantino. Take, for example, the 'Top Gun' incident. Avary was having dinner with Eric Stoltz, who starred in 'Killing Zoe'. He was telling Stoltz a favourite theory of his, which was that the fighter pilot played by Tom Cruise in 'Top Gun' is really gay and the film is about him coming to terms with his sexuality. Stoltz covered his mouth in horror, and explained that Quentin had just 'Improvised' that exact speech while giving a cameo performance in a film Stoltz was making called 'Sleep with me'. The film was not a hit, but the speech received widespread publicity and was said to be typical of Tarantino's outrageous sense of humour. Avary told a friend, "I've realised I can't hang out with Quentin, if I talk with him, he sucks stuff from me."

This brings us to 'Pulp Fiction.' Avary wrote many scenes in this including the bizarre showdown in a pawnshop and the whole boxer story parts staring Bruce Willis. So why didn't he get a screen-writing credit? Well, originally he did. Tarantino's contract with Avary specified that the latter be fully credited, but the more time went by, the less Tarantino felt like sharing the glory. While Tarantino was staying with Avary & his wife Gretchen he managed to make sure his best friend wouldn't be in the 'Pulp Fiction' spotlight. Avary was editing 'Killing Zoe' and in serious need of cash. Tarantino still owed him $27.000, but didn't have to pay it until shooting began in six months time. Quentin offered to give him the money straight away if he would sign a paper, which he did. The new contract gave Avary a share in the films profits but absolutely no share in the glory.

Roger Avary now has one film under his belt and three more on the way. Under normal circumstances, a 'story' credit does not qualify one for an Oscar nomination for Best Screenplay. But thanks to the talents of his lawyers and the generosity of the 'Pulp Fiction' producers who put his name on their submission to the Academy, he may well be mounting the winners' podium with Tarantino on Oscar night. With his own career secure he is able to observe Tarantino's need to succeed and his carelessness about whom he steps on while he's doing it, and also to add: "I'm glad he's successful and I hope he doesn't fall on his face. But if he does, every single person he has hurt will be there for him."

In the words of Stanley Margolis (someone willing to finance 'True Romance'); "Quentin Tarantino is certainly a master film maker. No one says he has to be a nice guy as well."

The only devils in the world are those running in our own hearts. That is where the battles should be fought.

Mahatma Ghandi

DAWSON INTERVIEW

Dawson have always been a favourite of mine, ever since I heard them years back on John Peel. They have been around for a good six years now, I expect, playing a politically charged funky style of hardcore of hardcore reminiscent of Minutemen, Firehose, Victims family, the Ex or Glue. Their lyrics are intelligent, sometimes cryptic, their style eclectic but always interesting. Pop-Punk they ain't! And yes, they have appeared in MRR if that's your definition of 'Cred'. I'd like to thank Jer for responding to my questions at length, even though it took him a long time! Still, I knew he'd get back to me eventually - one can always rely on Dawson to come up with the goods. This interview is by Martyn.

BHP : Perhaps it's best to begin with names and roles in the band. Who's answering these questions?

JER : Because I'm so late in sending the answers, it'll just be me (Jer) answering to avoid lengthy organisation. Dawson is: Ali - bass, Craig - percussion, Jer - guitar, Robbie - drums. Everyone except Robbie does some shouting.

BHP : Can you describe your sound to those who have never heard you? Maybe name some influences....?

JER : Oh, I think you should do that. (Me?) I think our sound is still evolving so I don't really want to tie a lead weight of a description to its ankles! Influences? Musically? Emotionally? Politically? Personally? Spiritually? Mmm... for me...from Big Flame, and other noisy guitar tapes to (way back then) Crass, Big Black, Jean-Paul Sartre, John Peel, Billy Bragg (for all the wrong kinnock-loathing reasons), sheesh - lots of things saw with my own eyes, e.g. the first time I saw police beating up a 4'11" female friend of mine when I was 17. That was definitely a big influence. Being in court too. Music? Now? Less guitar stuff, loads of jazz, folk, weirdo, African, Asian, Middle Eastern, Aboriginal, nonsense, hip-hop, dub, ska, - even some techno and <u>still</u> the regular dosage of the Ex and Minutemen.

BHP : How did it come about that the latest LP 'Terminal Island' got put on the Hungarian label 'Trottel'?

JER : They offered. Mutual friends in Archbishop Kebab (a Scottish punk band too, folks) who had been released by them and so their business ethics were compatible with mine. We said yes.

BHP : Are there particular themes and ideas you're trying to address in your lyrics?

JER : Mmm, it's really hard (hey, I was talking about the lyrics - interviewer's lame double entendre).... it seems self-defeating to try and explain lyrics, I just think they should be heard or seen. Its like being asked for your opinions - without prompting - where do I start? I'll be cryptic and say my words tackle forms of oppression and ways of living I consider damaging. That vague enough for you?

BHP : Is 'Sappy Ambient' in any way an attack on ambient techno? Even if it's not, do you have any criticisms against electronic music at all?

JER : No, 'Sappy Ambient' is the usual 'tittle-from-meaningless-studio-babble' type situation. Well, Ali and Brycey listen to loads of techno, ambient, jungle, hip-hop, digi-dub and so love a lot of electronic music. like me, they hate a lot too - it seams silly to generalise. I'm sure if you'd asked me five years ago I would've prattled on about technology and synthetic music alienating people because of its predictability and soullessness - but that's just pseudo-journalistic rubbish. Question: If something is sampled does it change from being acoustic to electronic?

BHP: An unqualified electrician writes.... er, no, I don't think so. I think you might be in thewrong boat concerning your terms here, Jer. I think you're considering the change between analogue sounds (everyday noises like cars, birds, conversation) to digital sounds (the same noises except on CD). Tapes and records are still

transferring analogue sounds when we listen to them, that's why even top hi-fi buffs say they sound more 'natural' and 'raw' than CDs. CDs are digital, thus the sound created is rather artificial. So, if you take a sample and put it on a record, it doesn't really change, but put it on a CD, then it becomes digital, electronic and unnatural. Rumour has it that repeated listening to CDs can make you tired - the brain has to work overtime to transfer the digital sounds produced by the CD into analogue sounds - the only sound the brain comprehends. Ever listened to Black Flag 'The First Four Years' on CD? Sounds shite. But when I put on my warped scratchy record, it's like, wow, this still kicks butt. CDs are artificial, electronically created sound, however, the brain is so cleaver that you hardly notice the difference anyway, because all sounds are transferred into analogue signals we understand. Listening to CDs is hard work! Tapes and records are natural! <u>But</u>, and this is a big but, surely, In the studio, aren't things recorded onto DAT and that's digital ain't it? Shite! I'm confused. Cheers for asking Jer..!

BHP : Would you say there's anything that you're hoping to achieve by being in 'Dawson'? You've been playing together for a long time. What keeps you going? Is it down to the sheer enjoyment, or do you really believe you have something to say?

JER : Originally, I wanted to achieve everything with Dawson - I thought I could clear my eyes of everything I hated. Now I think I can be part of an alternative to how most people think music should be played, presented, enjoyed, i.e. I try hard to have "sound" "Business" ethics, not money-orientated rock star careerist bull ethics. The things I hope to achieve are mostly for me - to express myself, find catharsis for anger, to communicate with people, to be part of a culture that resists the mind-numbing deprivation of a world based on money. That is also why I do it - not just the love of music. I <u>know</u> I have something to say - in the same way that <u>everyone</u> has their own experience, observations that are their own. It's nice to try and share them....communicate.

BHP : You always put some great photos with the LPs, like the soldiers with gas-masks or the old ladies kneeling, or the totally bizarre old army General with no legs being saluted at. Are these all genuine pics? Who puts them together?

JER : Yeah, there all genuine. It's mostly me that has the books, but I confess, the General saluting was stolen from Tony from Badgewearer. (Another Scottish punk band too, folks).

BHP : I was pretty surprised at the second side of the 'How to follow...' LP, that is, no lyrics, just all rather dubby, tribally instrumentals. What inspired you to do that? It's good, certainty, but just a tad unusual - was there a good reason behind it, or did it just evolve that way?

JER : It just evolved. But, we had really cheap studio time so had a chance to play about with samplers and stuff. If we had the money to mess about in studios, things would be <u>FAR</u> more diverse. Hopefully, we will continue to expand anyway.

BHP : Would you consider yourself 'experimental' in any way?

JER : I don't know how to describe us. I suppose we're more experimental than Guns 'N' Roses and less experimental than Can or Faust. (Ask a stupid question.....)

BHP : What do you think about all this "Who's Punk?" shite we're reading about in MRR and plenty of Zines? What's your definition of 'Punk', because I don't have an all encompassing definite description?

JER : I've never considered myself a punk. (Did I ask you this?) In general, there are so many people with different ideas that the word is meaningless. I'm a bit perplexed why people would spend all their time discussing it.

BHP : A smart-arsed semantic philosopher replies: There can be no such thing as a meaningless word, for it would very much negate the possibility of its being a word in the first place. A word is a word in virtue of it explaining something - that's what language is all about! I don't think you answered the question here. I believe this to be a very relevant debate, and it would seem Dawson are probably one of the better principled, 'DIY', genuine 'Punk' bands about, especially if we take 'Punk' not in terms of image or music, but attitude.

BHP : 'Leaf Sweepers & Sandwich men' is a personal fave of mine. It's true that most jobs are completely soulless, and I guess in an ideal society we'd all be doing our own thing and enjoy producing for ourselves. But what immediate things do you think can be done in our present system to improve the lot of many people? Even under a fairer, more equal system, won't there still have to be leaf sweepers and sandwich men?

JER : I donno how I can personally "Improve the lot of many people" other than to try and create an alternative to a money-orientated world. I try and do that. I'm not a reformist - I think a "Fairer system" would mean the abolition of the system we have, which would mean no-one would have to do pointless (leafsweeping) or degrading (being a sandwich man) work in order to survive. It's the hierarchy and greed embedded in capitalism that means these jobs exist. For me, the song is also a question of the whole notion of work and what is considered worthwhile or useful, i.e. to counteract the idea that the unemployed are not contributing to society I'd ask: What are many who work contributing to other human beings? Work is often not analysed by people who hate their own work but still think it is the duty of the unemployed to work too. I refuse to do degrading work just because many others do.

BHP : What are you working on at present? Any news of new releases, tours etc? Perhaps you could list a kind of 'discography' and an address where people can get in touch....

JER : We're not doing much now. Ali is in Mexico and I've just moved 100 miles north of Glasgow. We've tentative plans to tour France and maybe some mainland countries in June and return to Iceland and the USA in September. I'm sure there'll be some recording too!

DAWSON DISCOGRAPHY

Romping Egos. 7" (1989); Barf Market: You're Ontae Plums. LP (1990): Lets Live. 7" - two songs on a compilation 7" (1990); How to follow so others will willingly lead.(Oh my Godley & Creme Cheese) LP (1991); Terminal Island. LP (1993); Split 7" with Ruins (from Japan) (1993); Small eared rank outsider. 7" (1994); CDs of the last two LPs (due 1995)

All Mail Is welcome : Gruff wit records. 41 Killermont Rd. Bearsden. Glasgow. G61 2JB. Scotland.

BHP : Any final comments?

Martyn : Thanks for being so patient. Here's a quote from 'In the Sprit of Crazy Horse', the book I'm reading just now about the treatment of American plains Indians by the FBI / Government in the 1970s and the false imprisonment of Leonard Peltier for supposedly killing two FBI agents. 'AIM' stands for American Indian Movement....

AIM leader Ted means: "It's hard to organise the people when the press are telling them that everything is okay. The government has done a hell of a good job colonising us. They give a guy a pick-up truck and a six-pack and he's satisfied. The Indians are satisfied to be miserably comfortable." (Pete Matthiessen, author) When I remarked that this wasn't true only of the Indians, that the whole population of the United States had been reduced from citizens to consumers, "We've been programmed to accept defeat," said Means, unsmiling, and Bob Rodidean (AIM activist) grinned briefly saying, "Some of us have been de-programmed." p423 'In the Spirit of Crazy Horse' by Peter Matthiessen.

SELF PUBLISHING

Many people dream of writing a book, an article, a poem or some form of work which they would like others to read and enjoy. Often though, the author may not have the resources, the contacts, the markets, or the know how to enable them to ever produce their work and make it widely available. Well, what do Beatrice Potter, Rudyard Kipling, Lord Byron, Mark Twain, D H Lawrence, Virginia Woolf and me all have in common? At some time in our careers we have all been involved in self publishing. You may have to consider this route into print if you are writing about a topic of limited interest, as national publishers will put profit first and hence rule out certain topics or unknown authors. You do not have their overheads, can edit your own work, typeset the manuscript yourself, and get a printer to run off a few copies. Self publishing also allows you to determine the timing of the production and release of your work, and enables you to retain total editorial control. The quality of self published work can be just as good as by any other route, as you will not risk your own money on anything of questionable value.

Once you know what you are going to write about, you start with research. Decide the book page size you like, select a size of typing, work out the average number of words per page, the number of pages your work will take, allow for any titles and illustrations, and round up to the next multiple of sixteen pages. You can now approach specialist book printers for several quotations on a number of books. This will tell you how much cash you will need and the average cost price per book. Knowing what the cost price is, you can come up with a sale price, remembering that if it is going to be made available through other outlets such as bookshops, they will expect a 33% discount. As a rough guide it needs to be at least three times the cost price. Self publishing can be a risk, as your own money is involved, so it helps to get advance orders and identify outlets first. Once you have committed yourself, issue a press release and make sure your address is included. A good press story brings enquiries in, and a lot of enquiries turn into orders. Don't be tempted to spend a lot on advertising as it is unlikely to produce a return of any size. Direct mail will produce orders if you can target people who are interested.

Once the orders are flowing, you will need to get your manuscript typeset on a computer, and printed with a laser printer. Ideally, for a book, you need an ISBN number, and you can get information on how to get an ISBN number by writing to : Standard Book Numbering Agency Ltd, 12 Dyott Street, London, WC1A 1DF. They can issue you with a number, and there is no charge for this.

You can now get the printing done, and get on with the distribution. You are required by law to give copies to a small number of libraries. Other legal matters to bear in mind are copyright and libel. Anything written is copyright. The copyright belongs to the writer during their lifetime and for 50 years after their death to their heirs. Libel can be defined as exposing a living person to hatred, contempt or ridicule by a defamatory statement. Avoid this, unless you enjoy courtroom dramas.

Publishing is said to be a pleasant way to lose money. While I would hope that you wouldn't lose too much, please don't expect to make a fortune. The best reason to publish anything is because you want other people to be able to see and enjoy your work. I wish you good luck and many re-prints!

If you're planning an A5 zine...
BHP can help you arrange cheap typesetting and printing
... so drop us a line!

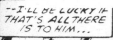

It is a real shame 'Take That' have split up, they have recently sent us a letter informing BHP there would be a joint release with Neanderthal, or Brainhandle soon. I've also received proof that Jabba the Hutt is on earth and Richard Stilgoe has moved to Crewkerne. The crew here at BHP are now all millionaires, certainly not thru the mag, but by being sent 500,000,000 in Slovenian currency – probably worth about ten pence.

This is a picture of Batman, for those of you that are blind or stupid, drawn for me by Will Simpson at the Glasgow Comic Convention. Cool, huh.

The Reviews section is not necessarily the editors view (but usually pretty accurate). We must stress it will always be an honest opinion, but everything sent in is worthy of your attention to support peoples effort. Anything missed out will be in the next issue, so send for it now.

RUTH RUTH - 'LAUGHING GALLERY'. The first track on this album is 'Uninvited'. The Stateside success single is a pretty catchy slice of power pop pie, a loser friendly ditty, but the whole record is original sounding and just commercial enough to become massive. Check them out while they're still cool. *American.*

NOFX - 'HEAVY PETTING ZOO'. Punk. Fun. What else can you say about this superb album. NOFX have a powerful yet melodic style all of their own, this sets them way above most of the crowd. Mike write hilarious but thought provoking lyrics, check out 'Hobophobic' and 'Hot dog in a hallway'. NOFX have had relatively little mainstream exposure but seem to be doing just fine. This, their sixth Epitaph album, will surely be a continuation of their success, allowing them to open more punk rock cafés no doubt. Recommended if you want to bounce off walls at parties. *Epitaph.*

Mystery Killer Attacks Hell's Kitchen

BAD RELIGION - 'ALL AGES'. This is the "best of ...." and although it's all very similar in style, despite some of it being ten years apart, there's some real classics on it. Everyone has their favourite Bad Religion songs and they're probably here. 22 songs including 'No control', 'We're only gonna die', 'Modern man' etc. *Epitaph*

TWO LINE FILLER - 'LISTENER'. Brilliant LP from this melodic hardcore band. Imagine Lanie from J.Church singing for early Samiam - amazing! Every song is soooo catchy, instantly singalongable and short. I recommend this to everyone, not just the pop-punkers, because it will make you happy. He's singing about your problems too, dude.... *N.R.A.*

LIFETIME - 'HELLO BASTARDS'. Best and shortest LP yet from New Jerseys 'Lifetime'. The sound has moved on from the previous 'Background' Lp, this time mixing hard, fast punk burnouts with bursts of Samiam style melody and beauty. Lyrically it's more of the same pessimism: "Next time a star shoots across the sky, I want to grab it and smash it under my feet - who the fuck wants to be happy?" Recommended. *Jade Tree*

DOWN BY LAW - 'ALL SCRATCHED UP'. Yet another great Lp from DBL. This is in the same vein as 'Punkrockacademy...' With lots of short punky songs, everyone of them is a classic. Dave Smalleys soulful, heartfelt vocals rule. If you're a fan so far, you won't be disappointed. One of the best bands on *Epitaph.*

SWINGING UTTERS - 'THE STREETS OF SAN-FRANCISCO'. More punkrock from S.F. This should appeal to Rancid Fans, it's even produced by Lars Frederikson from Rancid. It's pretty catchy but the music isn't very intricate (think Ramones). If you dig punk rock you could do a lot worse. *N.R.A.*

HOGANS HEROES - '101/3 FISTS AND A MOUTHFUL'. Aaaaarrggghhh! Full-on metal attack! I thought this lot were H/c but I guess I was very wrong..... you know it's H/c in places but I can't recommend it. Good solo's. *N.R.A.*

U.K. SUBS - 'BETRAYED' 7". U.K. Subs go emo shock!!!! Yes, it's true, I cannot believe that this is the same band that did 'Stranglehold' etc. 'Betrayed' is a really slow, laid back groove, kinda dreamy almost - you won't believe your ears! However, the B side is more like what we're used to! *New Red Archives.*

ASSERT - DEMO. Lemmy from Motorhead fronting Cryptic Slaughter. Good it is not. "Don't give up your right to feel", or your hard earned cash! "Give me the drug!" but don't give me this - turn it off Dave! "PSYCHEDELIC FRENZY....."etc.

DEAD BUT HAPPY - 'NOTHING IS TRUE'. Unfortunately we couldn't really hear this because the tape kept fucking up, but it must be good because there's a song called 'Razor blades ropes pills and bullets'. The sleeve has pictures of the Marx brothers - Harpo, Groucho, Chico and Karl?!..

THE CERVICAL SMEARS - 'ALL YOU NEED IS LIGHT, HEAT AND CHLOROPHYLL' DEMO. Oh jesus, these guys rule - they ought to be is charge of the country, everyone here at BHP, Potato Towers, pledges allegiance to them, and are prepared to sacrifice goats. I doubt that they're out of school yet, but the philosophy of their music belies their age. Indie punk with songs like Gingaaah, (chorus goes "Ginger - die"), Token lovesong, and metal mayhem (lyrics attached) will be the youths New Testament. I urge you to send for this masterpiece, from: A. Ford, 2 Parkside Place, East Horsley, Surrey, KT24 5BZ. My boys, the Smears! :- **'METAL MAYHEM'** - Welcome to hell.......Death, blood and destruction......Satan has come amongst us and he speaks through me......Semen dripping from a wound.....Scarred urban landscape of post-apocalyptic destruction and desolation...Disease, pestilence and death. Look at me with fear for I am Lucifer....I can see your sin and I know your evil....Die, all you sinners....Drum-fest...end. Superb or what!

THE MR.T EXPERIENCE - 'LOVE IS DEAD'. MTX have a lot to live up to, as one of Lookouts premier bands they will now have the worlds attention focused on them. This album does not kick off so well, kind of too throwaway pop, but as you get into it, it really improves. Some classic MTX stuff - 'The future ain't what is used to be', 'Dumb little band', 'Can I do the thing?' I think they're just too 'happy' to be massive though. *Lookout.*

URUSEI YATSURA - 'SIAMESE'. Glaswegion four piece debut single. Very abstract, one side sounds a little like Seam the other is choppy, alternative noise. It's pretty good in a weird sort of way. The name is Japanese for 'troublesome female'. *Ché.*

MR JOLLY - 'TWITCH'. This is really good, well produced, well packaged rock/pop hardcore from Norfolk. It reminds me of All and Dag Nasty in places, and there's no lyrics about combine harvesters in sight, so write to: Simon. 55 Colomb Road. Gorleston. Great Yarmouth. Norfolk. NR3I 8BU.

BOUNCING SOULS - 'MANIACAL LAUGHTER'. This is old school hardcore made modern. Bouncy guitars, powerful rhythms and anthemic lyrics. "People and money came and went, the only thing that stayed the same, were the feelings he felt when those records played." It's kind of like 7 Seconds meet OP IV and I love it. They hail from New Jersey and have toured all over, with Lifetime, Offspring and Rancid, and are now on *BYO.* Get it.

MUCKY PUP - 'FIVE GUYS IN A REALLY HOT GARAGE'. These guys have been around since 1985 and this is their seventh Lp, but they still know how to kick it, Skate rock style, ala Circle Jerks. Although this isn't quite as instant as the classic 'Boy in a mans world' you've got to love it. *SPV.*

YOU'RE NOT GOING TO *BELIEVE* THIS, BOY.

FUNBUG - 'SPUNKIER'. This is pop punk in a really Green Day, MTX, only know a few chords way. They're very good at it and obviously have fun but you've heard it all before. They also take too long to set up live and talk a lot about each others turds. *Golf.*

WAYNE KRAMER - 'DANGEROUS MADNESS'. STEPPENWOLF!! WayneCarr more like, *Epitaph* goes A.O.R.

SOULSTORM - LP. These guys are German, "you know it I am thinking." An awesome metal guitar workout and you should see the cover. For those of you who are unfamiliar with Germanys answer to Iron Maiden let me quote you some lyrics (not out of context) from the first song: "HEY! you need your fantasies! Don't oppress what your brain rend to you! - Hordes of demons from far away, Robots which want to rule the world....." etc. etc. (yawn). However, these guys do have an animal rights song, a bass player called Zong! and more guitar playing ability than a room full of Def Leppards ..... "Horror starts to rule your brain!......" etc.

MOREAU'S ISLAND - 'HAIRCUT' 7". Kinda slightly punky Indie music that has some very tuneful bits and not a 'Jangly' bit in sight! Very cool female vocals. According to the promo stuff Melody Maker seem very keen on them (if that sells it to you), and so am I! INFO: 12 Seafront road, West Ealing, London, W13 9HR.

CHINA WHITE - 'ADDICTION' CD. This band were very big in the early 80's, they took a 10 year break!? and reformed. They're good too - this sounds like Pennywise quite a lot of the time, Bad Religion, NOFX, etc., it has that Epitaph sound. Gets a little raw at times and reminds me of the Vandals. One foot on the monitor, smiling. *Lethal Records.*

-- ANY WAY SHE CAN --

LIFE....BUT HOW TO LIVE IT? - 'GREEN BURN'. Not very new but well worth checking out. Very intricate hardcore with excellent female vocals, lots of subtle changes and infectious tunes - okay? On *Fuck you all! records.*

BRUCIE BONUS - 'PASS THE TIME' EP. Melodic Hardcore from Leicester that reminds me of being happy at the best of times but Neds atomic shitepile at the worst. Send for it from: 29 Glen Way, Oadby, Leicester, LE2 5YF.

OI POLLOI - 'FIGHT BACK' LP. This is the stuff that's been released before buts its been unavailable for a while. Both sides were originally on split LPs, one with A.O.A. and one with Betrayed. Classic speed punk with slower bits, all very Ecco-friendly and anti-system - overall Very powerful and angry. 'Go green', 'You cough/they profit', 'Boot down the door' etc. If you think Rancid and Green Day are really 'punk' then think again..... *Campary.*

JUMPIN' LANDMINES - DEMO. We're sure this is very good but the tape must have been chewed up 'cause the sound kept coming and going....Punk.

60 FT DOLLS - 'STAY' PROMO. The guitarist is called Richard Parfitt. To his mates he's probably 'Rick'. C'mon Rick the games up! I bet Mike Cole is actually Francis Rossi eh? Trying to hide that familiar Quo groove behind some pseudo jam-style indie won't work either! The games up! Now, let's have a re-release of 'Rocking all over the world' please. "...and I like it - I like it - I la-la-la-like it - here we go-o...."etc.

MDM - SAMPLER. This kicks off with the best sample ever - worth getting for this alone! fans of old skool punk will love this, remember vice squad? Maybe a bit more 'Modern' sounding though. At times early Siouxie - style vocals mix with Life but how to live it. Sorry, i'm only making comparisons with female fronted punk/HC but that's what it is! Check it out. Mandy, 13 Lime Grove, Liverpool, L8 0SJ.

Riverdales

In 1994 Screeching Weasel recorded their fifth album, "How To Make Enemies And Irritate People" for Lookout Records. After completing the album, the second most successful band on the label (behind Green Day) broke up, leaving Ben Weasel, Dan Vapid and Danny Panic without a band and outdated punk surnames.

So, as Ben Foster, Dan Schafer, and Danny Sullivan, they formed the Riverdales (in punkland, there are already two bands called the Fosters and the Schafers) and came to the UK supporting Green Day. BHP went to meet them at a hotel in London to ask a few questions......

BHP: You once said that you'd never tour Europe. I think it was something about the money not being easy. Well now you're playing 5000 seaters. What brought about the change in heart and why?

BEN: That was when I was in another band. I was under the impression at the time that I'd never be in the kind of conditions I'm in now. We're sitting in a hotel, not a youth hostel, right. In the states for most of the Screeching Weasel tours we slept on the floors, on the last one we stayed in a couple of motels but you don't really have motels in Europe. We would never stay in the 'Holiday Inn' that would be too expensive.

BHP: How come you're staying here then?

BEN: Because the label said go to Europe and were prepared to lose a lot of money on it. I said I don't think it's a good idea, we've never taken a tour support before, but the other guys wanted to do it so I was out voted. At the very least we get to see some stuff and meet people.

BHP: Are you doing your own headline tour?

BEN: No - because then we'd have to play a long time, like more than 25 minutes. I have to stop between songs and rest my hand. We break a lot of gear too. No-one expects anything from the opening band. I don't like touring and playing. It's the same over and over. I like writing new music though.

BHP: What's the feedback been like from the LP?

BEN: I've only seen one review, in M.R.R. It made the indie charts in Rolling Stone, it's sold over 20,000 copies.

BHP: Why the musical regression to slower / simpler songs?

BEN: Because that's all I can play and it's more fun - you don't need to think about it. It's inspired by 50's music, Ramones, etc and there's a sexual undertone too. Go to a show, get sweaty and make out.

BHP: Will you be playing any Screeching Weasel songs on tour?

BEN: No, we did one because Jughead was there that night but not anymore.

BHP: What do you think of Straight Edge?

BEN: I think the movement is really silly, but I don't use drugs. I drink beer and wine at home but not when I go out. Generally speaking I think drug use is stupid and I wouldn't be in a band with anyone who smoked pot even. It's too much trouble.

BHP: Do you live off your music or do you have another job?

BEN: I sit on my ass and collect royalty cheques from Screeching Weasel. I haven't had a job since 1991, it was a library aid at a school I went to.

BHP: So, are you Lookouts number one priority?

BEN: Yeah, that's what they tell us, we're the cornerstone of the label, for now. But we're not gonna get as big as Rancid or Offspring. We have total freedom to do whatever we want. I'll do a solo album maybe - I'd like to work for lookout.

BHP: Do your songs take a long time to write?

BEN: No, I don't try - it's just boom, and the tunes done. I'm going to have my girlfriend name, Porsche, tattooed on my chest while I'm on tour - so I wrote a song about it in fifteen minutes. If you have to work on a tune, throw it away, it's no good.

BHP: What would you do without the band?

BEN: Watch movies, I love sitting in front of the TV watching Godfather, a Few Dollars More, Dawn of the Dead and I want to write. I'm writing about the summer I stayed in Jugheads basement, and short stories. I read Bukowski, Henry Miller, Stephen King, old crime novels.

BHP: Tell us something bizarre.

BEN: After a Screeching Weasel show, we were wearing leathers, this girl came up to me and Vapid and licked us. Nothing really bizarre happens to me, except playing shows.

BHP: When was the last time you kissed your mum?

BEN: Last time I saw her , we get on well.

BHP: And finally, and most importantly, what's your favourite food?

BEN: PIZZA! pizza, pizza, pizza.................... (goes off onto one, recipes, food stories, etc).

You can write to Ben and the Riverdales at: PO Box 66722, Chicago, Illinois 60666 - 0722, USA.

BIG MAC BECOMES RIVAL OF THE CROSS!

It has endured for almost 2,000 years as a so called symbol of faith and civilisation. But, in terms of public recognition, the Cross of Christianity has been overtaken by the logo of the McDonald's fast-food empire.

In a survey of 7000 people across Britain, Germany, the US, India, Japan and Australia, more were able to identify such symbols of capitalism as the Shell Oil logo, the Mercedes badge and the Mcdonalds 'golden arches' than the traditional image of Christianity.

Of the nine symbols used by Sponsorship Research International, the five-rings logo of the International Olympic Movement came out top with 92 per cent recognition rate, with the Cross trailing badly on 54 per cent. Joint second were McDonalds and Shell on 88 per cent, with Mercedes motoring in at 74 per cent, followed by the Red Cross/Red Crescent (47), last year's soccer World Cup in the US (36), the United Nations' globe-and-olive branches (also 36) and the World Wide Fund for Nature (28).

Although it was stressed that the result had been affected by the inclusion of non-Christian countries, church leaders admitted they were disappointed by the result

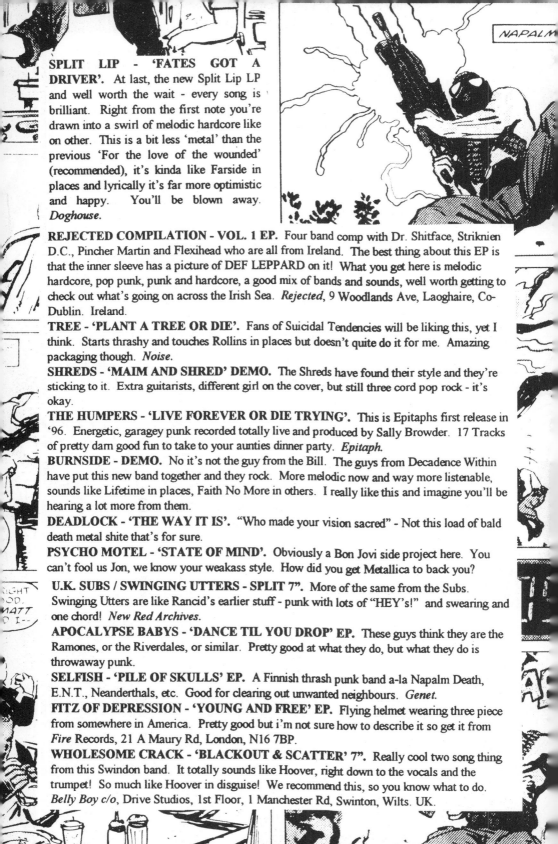

SPLIT LIP - 'FATES GOT A DRIVER'. At last, the new Split Lip LP and well worth the wait - every song is brilliant. Right from the first note you're drawn into a swirl of melodic hardcore like on other. This is a bit less 'metal' than the previous 'For the love of the wounded' (recommended), it's kinda like Farside in places and lyrically it's far more optimistic and happy. You'll be blown away. *Doghouse*.

REJECTED COMPILATION - VOL. 1 EP. Four band comp with Dr. Shitface, Striknien D.C., Pincher Martin and Flexihead who are all from Ireland. The best thing about this EP is that the inner sleeve has a picture of DEF LEPPARD on it! What you get here is melodic hardcore, pop punk, punk and hardcore, a good mix of bands and sounds, well worth getting to check out what's going on across the Irish Sea. *Rejected*, 9 Woodlands Ave, Laoghaire, Co-Dublin. Ireland.

TREE - 'PLANT A TREE OR DIE'. Fans of Suicidal Tendencies will be liking this, yet I think. Starts thrashy and touches Rollins in places but doesn't quite do it for me. Amazing packaging though. *Noise*.

SHREDS - 'MAIM AND SHRED' DEMO. The Shreds have found their style and they're sticking to it. Extra guitarists, different girl on the cover, but still three cord pop rock - it's okay.

THE HUMPERS - 'LIVE FOREVER OR DIE TRYING'. This is Epitaphs first release in '96. Energetic, garagey punk recorded totally live and produced by Sally Browder. 17 Tracks of pretty darn good fun to take to your aunties dinner party. *Epitaph*.

BURNSIDE - DEMO. No it's not the guy from the Bill. The guys from Decadence Within have put this new band together and they rock. More melodic now and way more listenable, sounds like Lifetime in places, Faith No More in others. I really like this and imagine you'll be hearing a lot more from them.

DEADLOCK - 'THE WAY IT IS'. "Who made your vision sacred" - Not this load of bald death metal shite that's for sure.

PSYCHO MOTEL - 'STATE OF MIND'. Obviously a Bon Jovi side project here. You can't fool us Jon, we know your weakass style. How did you get Metallica to back you?

U.K. SUBS / SWINGING UTTERS - SPLIT 7". More of the same from the Subs. Swinging Utters are like Rancid's earlier stuff - punk with lots of "HEY's!" and swearing and one chord! *New Red Archives*.

APOCALYPSE BABYS - 'DANCE TIL YOU DROP' EP. These guys think they are the Ramones, or the Riverdales, or similar. Pretty good at what they do, but what they do is throwaway punk.

SELFISH - 'PILE OF SKULLS' EP. A Finnish thrash punk band a-la Napalm Death, E.N.T., Neanderthals, etc. Good for clearing out unwanted neighbours. *Genet*.

FITZ OF DEPRESSION - 'YOUNG AND FREE' EP. Flying helmet wearing three piece from somewhere in America. Pretty good but i'm not sure how to describe it so get it from *Fire* Records, 21 A Maury Rd, London, N16 7BP.

WHOLESOME CRACK - 'BLACKOUT & SCATTER' 7". Really cool two song thing from this Swindon band. It totally sounds like Hoover, right down to the vocals and the trumpet! So much like Hoover in disguise! We recommend this, so you know what to do. *Belly Boy c/o*, Drive Studios, 1st Floor, 1 Manchester Rd, Swinton, Wilts. UK.

OFFSPRING - 'GOTTA GET AWAY' CD SINGLE. Their 'Smash' LP has sold over 7 Million copies now so here comes another single! I expect a lot of people already know this one - sounds like the others, Kinda like Nirvana in places. Go and see them at Glastonbury. *Epitaph / Out of Step.* Available in all record shops.

NO USE FOR A NAME - 'LECHE CON CARNE CD. I think this is the 4th LP from N.U.F.A.N. I Haven't heard this lot since their first EP back in 1990 ish - it's very different. Fans of NOFX will go crazy for this!! It rules - it has influences from the faster side of Green Day / Samiam / Pennywise etc. Really good. Check 'em out. *Fat Wreck chords.*

GUTTERMOUTH - 'FRIENDLY PEOPLE' CD. Unbelievable! Yet another band that has that 'Epitaph' sound. NOFX, Pennywise etc. But don't get me wrong - this is really cool. Some moments they sound like Dag Nasty or even Gorilla Biscuits. Honest - I can hear it! Worth your money for 'Jamies petting zoo' alone - check it out. *Nitro.*

BRAIN POLICE - 'FUEL'. At last - a band that doesn't sound like NOFX. This starts off very heavy (metal), it sounds like Torque. Then it really changes. All the other songs are semi-Acoustic weird-out. Then it gets heavy for a while again, then weird etc. etc. Does this sound like anyone, you wonder? Maybe Helmet during the heavy bits. Sorry. *BGR records* PO BOX 54, West PDO, Nottingham, NG7 6BW.

44 X ES - 'BANISH SILENCE'. This lot are the German version of Nine Inch Nails - very evil sounding industrial rock noise, ambient until the Slayer riffs kick in. Pretty good too except when they start to sound like the Sisters of Mercy and go a bit gothic in places. *When / Castle.*

CHANNEL ZERO - 'UNSAFE'. Starts off with a creepy sample about Vampires then starts to sound like the Soundgardens, the Metallicas, the Panteras etc. Meeeeetaaaaal!! Tasty Packaging. *Play it again Sam.*

STRONGARM - 'ATONEMENT'. Very, very heavy metallic hardcore with shitloads of energy, and melody. They seem to care, lyrics with lots of messages and they really go for it vocally too - crazy screams! They will be massive with the SXE crew although I don't know if they are SXE. Fans of Judge, Integrity, Earth Crisis, Slayer etc will also love it, amazing packaging. *Tooth and Nail.*

TILT - 'TIL IT KILLS'. Imagine Green Day with a female singer, but rocking out. This is their second album of high energy, melodic hardcore. 'Unravel' rocks like no other but they are all goodies. *Essential. Fat Wreck chords.* PS - I saw this on a listening post in Tower, can you believe that!?

D.F.L. - 'PROUD TO BE.....'. Long before Beastie Boys went rap, they were punk rock, and DFL carry on the Legacy. Raw punk riffs, meaty bass and poor singing. Very old school. 20 songs in 29 minutes and one of them last 7 minutes. *Epitaph.*

G//Z/R - 'PLASTIC PLANET'. Super group featuring Geezer Butler (Black Sabbath) Burton C. Bell (Fear Factory) Deen Castronovo (Ossy Osbourne) and another bloke. They sound like all your metal faves and make me want to sacrifice goats on a pentagram alter. *Raw Power.*

STANFORD PRISON EXPERIMENT / QUICKSAND - SPLIT 7". The track 'Your the Vulgarian' is also the opener on Stanford's new LP 'The Gato Hunch' and you can tell why. There's a killer powerful intro, and just as you start to think this is dragging on a bit your blown away with a nice heavy chuggy riff with a crafty rhythm. To me these guys always seem to mix a real classic early Quicksand type sound with your more new school effects but unlike Shellac, Sloy etc don't go that bit to far and therefore produce some nice hooks and the darker sorts of harmonies. The lyrics are sung meaningfully which is nice, and this ones got some mental guitar noise at the end if you like that sort of thing. These guys are even better live, and have a great debut as well. A fresh above average band. *World Domination, Island Red.*

OI POLLOI

FIGHT BACK!

RE-RELEASE OF TWO SPLIT LPS FROM THE SCOTTISH PUNKS
COMING SOON
NEW NAKED AGGRESSION 7"
NEW TERMINUS 7"
CAMPARY RECORDS
FRIEDRICHSTR.110
40217 DUSSELDORF
GERMANY
FAX (0)211-315748
DISTRIBUTORS ASK FOR WHOLESALE PRICES

HARVEYS RABBIT - 'WINDOW DRESSER'. These guys probably want to be Pulp but they sound like the Kinks on a bad day. I hope the good packaging doesn't fool you. *Rotator.*

THE SWEENEY - 'SHUT UP'. It starts off like Blur but before I had time to take a hammer to it, it went all poppy - get it for your dad because the B side is the Shadows. Daddio. *Rotator.*

RANCID - 'AND OUT COME THE WOLVES'. Now don't get me wrong - I love Rancid - but this seems a little week, maybe a regression. The first single 'Time Bomb' sounds like OP.I.V. meets the Clash and although it's another huge album the production is a little soft. The tracks are catchy though, maybe they're getting more poppy. 'Journey to the end of the east bay' and 'Old friend' are awesome. *Epitaph.*

RIVERDALES - 'THE RIVERDALES'. From Chicago, Illinois this is basically screeching Weasel playing Ramones songs. They're slightly better than that but not much and I can't get excited. Supported by Green Day here in the UK. *Lookout.*

LORDZ OF BROOKLYN - 'SATURDAY NITE FEVER' EP. Phat ass hip hop. "Come on it's Saturday night!" If ad rock was in New Kingdom you might get this. It's really bouncy and you will not be able to stand still. Get it for your next paartay. *American.*

GANG OF FOUR - 'SHRINKWRAPPED'. These guys were a 'Cutting Edge' band in the late seventies and were credited with influencing REM, Chilli Peppers, Nirvana, etc, etc. Odd that, considering how bald they sound. Reminds me of Joy Division, or even U2 at times. They'll probably be massive. Yawn. *When / Castle.*

ICEMEN - 'BURIED ALIVE' 7". This chugs along nicely in a New York sort of way until interrupted by a Gary Mooresque solo. Foot tapping happy songs. *Twilight.*

MTX / GOOBER PATROL - SPLIT EP. The Goobers I love, they remind me of muppets, Worzels, combine-harvesters - you know the sort of thing. They're improving too. Wahey. Typical fayre from Mr T - catchy pop punk, better than the average. Full marks for the cover too. On a new label, called *Punk as Duck* at 9 Christchurch Rd, Norwich, NR2 2AE.

ACTIVE MINDS - 'DIS IS GETTING PATHETIC......' EP. This 8 song, discharge style punk-o-rama was put out by no less than six labels! Comes with a hefty booklet that's very educating - did you know that under Islamic law you'd have your hands amputated for theft! *Looney Tunes* (among others).

ALICE DONUT - 'PURE ACID PARK'. This is their latest, and seventh, album and has a typically bizarre cover depicting new band members. It is their most accessible and radio friendly effort to date but wanders into really arty farty territory. On *Alternative Tentacles*.

SHEER TERROR - 'LOVE SONGS FOR THE UNLOVED'. Fans of New York hatecore, such as S.F.A. and Yuppicide (R.I.P.) will love this - I couldn't make out a word. Oi meets Thrash, but you'll probably know this lot by now as they've been going since 1985. *Blackout*.

STANFORD PRISON EXPERIMENT - 'THE GATO HUNCH'. This is the second album from these Californians. It sounds like Fugazi fronted by someone from Grange Hill. Produced by Ted Niceley. They are meant to rock live. *World Domination*.

GOD LIVES UNDERWATER - 'G.L.U.' Aaarghh. A more techno N.I.N. even more plastic than the doll on the cover. Produced by Mr Rick Rubin on *Onion*.

V/A - 'THE FALL AND RISE OF L.A.' A collection of fourteen unsigned punk/metal bands from L.A. with a reply card for the purchaser to vote for their fave. Most of them sound like Helmet apart from one Offspring clone and one that sounds like early Couch Potatoes. We voted for 'World of Pain'. *Noise*.

FIELD DAY - 'FRICTION'. These Canadians remind me of Dag Nasty, B.D.C, and Doughboys. Basically pop punk but kinda wimpy. *Modern Music / AGR*.

V/A - 'DIE NOW!' A great mixture of new bands and classic old ones, Stand Outs are Swing Utters, Outcrowd and Dead Guy. This is well worth checking out from *Engine / Blackout*.

THE VANDALS - 'LIVE FAST DIARRHEA'. Fast, Fun, Humourcore from these veteran punksters. "This is guaranteed to rock your Colon" and it does. Excellent tunes with classic lyrics. *Nitro*

HOOTON 3 CAR - 'DRONE'. An uptempo melodic HC band from Sunderland in the UK that really cook. The A-side is from their new album, 'Cramp like a fox', recorded at Frankie Stubbs studio, worth checking out, and the flip is a Dag Nasty cover. *Out of Step*.

Q SQUAD - 'PSYCHED........'. "Q Squad are a musical carpet which every H.C. and metal band freak will roll out with pleasure" says the release. However, four men with long hair who sound like Machinehead do not pump my nads. I'd have more fun rolling my own carpet. Look at them, just look at them. Ex members of Exhumer and features 'Big Fat mama' and 'Smells like a dead fish. *Noise*.

PENNYWISE - 'SAME OLD STORY' EP. The 'Wise are back and slammin' About Time album and this is the first single. Fast, rockin', sing along punk that'll have you so engrossed you'll be mowing dog turds on the lawn. *Epitaph / Out of Step*.

NOFX - 'LEAVE IT ALONE' EP. Possibly the best two tracks off the classic 'Punk in Drublic' album backed with two rarities worth checking out. It's great! A UK label licensing U.S. bands, how does he do it? *Out of Step*.

CHOCOLATE - 'BLUE STREAK' EP. Track one rocks, literally though, like Bryan Adams and track two and three obviously saw them with some excess studio time because they're better at hip hop than punk! I saw them live with Couch Potatoes and Goober Patrol but they sucked then too. *Out of Step*.

A BLACKPOOL - EP. A four band compilation featuring Shrink - a quite tuneful Indie band, Erase Today - talented and friendly but boring, K - think they're the Doors and Yellowfield - Blackpool's answer to the Beach Boys with Jean Michel Jarre on Keyboards. If you've nothing better to spend you're money on it's £2.00 from JSNTGM, 64 Sedbergh Ave, Blackpool, Lancs, FY4 4DQ.

Unilaterally.

"Oh, Mickey!"

Although she has an independent streak, it's no secret that Minnie's heart belongs to Mickey.

GET IT OFF ME-- (BEN-- STO

her head's on fire 🔥

HER HEAD'S ON FIRE

DAG NASTY TRIBUTE with

**Horace Pinker - Amazing Tails - Thirst!
Gomaz-io - Annalise - Tempo Zero -
Eversor - Hooton 3 Car - Loomis -
The Unknown - Couch Potatoes -
Wardance - Innerface - Serpico -
Alkaloid - Slug Bug - In Bloom.**

CD 400 BF / 9 £ / 14 $ ppd worldwide
cash (at own risk) or money order payable only to
DECONINCK STEFAAN or DE LEERSNIJDER WIM

FOOLSDAY

c/o DECONINCK STEFAAN
FONTEINESTRAAT 2
8700 TIELT

DE LEERSNIJDER WIM
KREKELSTRAAT 13
8770 INGELMUNSTER

BATTLE
RECORDS

BELGIUM

BIOGRAPHY

David Gamage began playing in bands in his teens and created BHP fanzine to share ideas and communicate with the hardcore punk rock music community.

His love and passion for the hardcore scene is clear to see in the pages of this zine and easy to hear when you listen to his music with bands Couch Potatoes, Joeyfat, Rydell and Come The Spring.

In fact, his passion and drive to help spread the music and the message to his peers went so far that he also promoted shows and started various record labels to get the music heard by a wider audience. That continues today with Engineer Records, that started back in 1999 and now has well over 250 releases under its belt.

David lives with his wife and two sons in an idyllic cottage in the East Sussex countryside. When he is not playing with his family and their six cats, his band, or at his publishing company, he continues travelling, creating music and writing.